Performance art and revolution

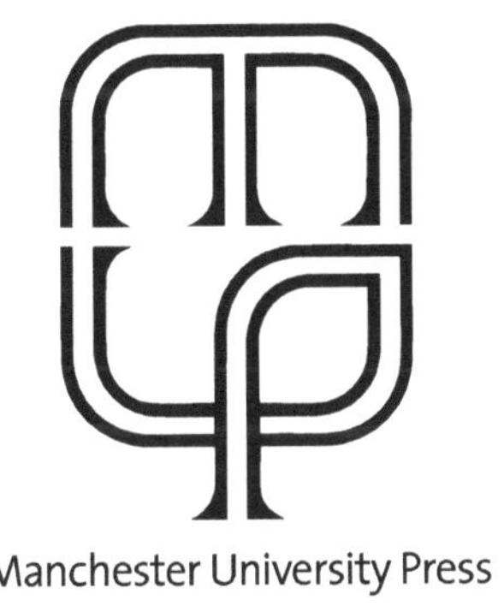

Manchester University Press

rethinking
art's histories

SERIES EDITORS
Amelia G. Jones, Marsha Meskimmon

Rethinking Art's Histories aims to open out art history from its most basic structures by foregrounding work that challenges the conventional periodisation and geographical subfields of traditional art history, and addressing a wide range of visual cultural forms from the early modern period to the present.

These books will acknowledge the impact of recent scholarship on our understanding of the complex temporalities and cartographies that have emerged through centuries of world-wide trade, political colonisation and the diasporic movement of people and ideas across national and continental borders.

To buy or to find out more about the books currently available in this series, please go to: https://manchesteruniversitypress.co.uk/series/rethinking-arts-histories/

Performance art and revolution

Stuart Brisley's cuts in time

Sanja Perovic

Manchester University Press

Published by Manchester University Press
Oxford Road, Manchester M13 9PL

www.manchesteruniversitypress.co.uk

British Library Cataloguing-in-Publication Data
A catalogue record for this book is available from the British Library

ISBN 978 1 5261 6766 8 hardback
ISBN 978 1 5261 9079 6 paperback

First published 2023
Paperback published 2025

The publisher has no responsibility for the persistence or accuracy of URLs for external or any third-party internet websites referred to in this book, and does not guarantee that any content on such websites is, or will remain, accurate or appropriate.

EU authorised representative for GPSR:
Easy Access System Europe – Mustamäe tee 50, 10621 Tallinn, Estonia
gpsr.requests@easproject.com

Typeset
by Cheshire Typesetting Ltd, Cuddington, Cheshire

Contents

Figures

Unless otherwise noted, all material relating to Stuart Brisley is courtesy of the artist and reproduced with permission.

Acknowledgements

The idea for this book first emerged out of a series of conversations with Stuart Brisley initiated by the writer Tony White when he was Creative Entrepreneur in Residence in the French Department at King's College London. I would like to thank Tony and CreativeWorks London for initiating this collaboration. I have also benefitted greatly from presenting aspects of this book on panels and talks at the 'Underground' Arts and Humanities Research Institute festival at King's College London, MAC Belfast, Modern Art Oxford, Camden Arts Centre, Cambridge Interdisciplinary Performance Network, Kunsthal Aarhus, Raven Row and resonance fm. I would like to thank the organisers of these events. I owe a special debt of gratitude to colleagues who generously commented on all or parts of the book: Jo Malt, who attended some of the performances with me, Jess Stacey, Nick Harrison, Ros Murray and, especially, Patrick ffrench, who read a whole draft at a very busy time. My almost daily conversations with Erica J. Mannucci and Rosa Mucignat about all things revolutionary have surely wound their way onto many pages of this book. I have also benefitted from many conversations with colleagues, in my department and elsewhere: Emma Bielecki, Martin Brady, Emily Butterworth, the late Simon Gaunt, Alice Hazard, Siobhan McIlvanney, Craig Moyes, Francisco Naishtat, Michael Newman, Karen Pratt, Charles Samuelson, Stefan Tanaka and James Wishart. Some of these discussions took place at the following venues: University College London French Research Seminar, King's College London French Department research seminar, History Genealogy Archaeology Workshop at Kingston University, the Political Imaginarium Research Seminar and the conferences for the Network of History and Theory. Here too I would like to thank the organisers of these events, in particular Berber Bevernage.

The two anonymous readers for Manchester University Press made some truly excellent suggestions for improving the manuscript. I also thank Lois Keidan of the Live Art Development Agency for a very useful discussion when I first began thinking about this book and Kathryn Woods for help at an early stage of editing. Parts of Chapter 1 were published in

Sanja Perovic, 'Dead History, Live Art: Encountering the Past with Stuart Brisley', *Rethinking History*, 21:2 (2017), 274–295. I thank Taylor and Francis for permission to reuse this material. King's College London kindly covered the cost of some of the illustrations. I am also grateful to Emma Brennan and Alun Richards of Manchester University Press for supporting this project and Judith Oppenheimer for excellent copy-editing. Any remaining errors are, of course, my own.

What these pages cannot convey is the friendship I have developed with Stuart Brisley and Maya Balcioglu over the years. Their hospitality will always remain with me. I want to especially thank Maya Balcioglu for ever stimulating conversation, support and for preparing the images for publication. My deepest thanks go to my family. To my mother, who read these pages so carefully, and Dimitris, who had lived alongside this project for many years. This book is dedicated with much love to my son Kimon, who was born when this collaboration started and has literally lived with it for as long as he can remember.

Introduction

This book explores the work of Stuart Brisley, the path-breaking English multi-media and performance artist. Hailed as the 'godfather of British performance art', Brisley became well-known in the 1960s and 1970s for a series of live actions that were feats of endurance as he subjected himself to hunger, extreme discomfort and exhaustion. His art is also known to be political and deals with a number of challenging social issues. Brisley's practice, developed over nearly seventy years, encompasses sculpture, installation, painting, photography, film, sound and writing. At its core lies a concept of performance art as a temporal process that resists the power of the permanent image, intimately tied to the image of sovereign power. This resistance is expressed through Brisley's commitment to keeping the revolution alive, as a past whose consequences remain undetermined. Yet, despite Brisley's seminal influence on British art, there is no major study that considers the body of his work, and his preoccupation with the practice and concept of revolution has scarcely been explored. Nor has there been any sustained consideration of the political context of his work, which presages the politically and socially engaged art practices of the twenty-first century.

This book considers Brisley's extensive engagement with the histories and imaginaries of revolution. In and through this engagement, it also asks whether and how performance can be used to think critically about the legacies of the revolutionary past. My aims are at once modest and ambitious. On the one hand, what I present in these passages is essentially an exercise in reframing. Elaborating Brisley's own allusions to the histories of revolution, rebellion and revolt as they appear in his works, I use the 'trope' of revolution to expand the range of references that can be used to understand and appreciate Brisley's artistic practices. On the other hand, this reframing also raises questions as to how these historical references should be treated. What happens to our understanding of revolutionary history when refracted through Brisley's performances? Can performance extend beyond its original context as an art activity to provide critical insight, even knowledge, about the past? And what is the role of historical reflection in establishing the meaning and value of performance?

These questions go to the heart of performance art, an opaque activity that continues to generate considerable debate over its meaning and value. Since its emergence during the 1960s, performance art has been closely associated with the presence of the artist's own body and its use to perform an action or series of actions. This conjunction of physical presence and presentness in time – something happening in the here and now – has distinguished performance art from other types of art as well as other time-based performances. Real skin is cut, real food consumed, real vomit spewed. Such liveness is frequently evoked as a guarantee of authenticity. It is what connects art to life, and cannot be choreographed in advance. Performance art, on this understanding, not only takes place in time but *unfolds through time*. Duration constitutes the frame and vehicle of its expression.

But performances also differ from everyday events in several important ways. They happen whenever an artist decides to intervene, break or otherwise suspend the ordinary experience of time and duration. Moreover, as it takes time for the consequences of any given action to unfold, a situation is created whose meaning is revealed in retrospect, by those who see it, talk about it, remember, record or register it in some way. For these reasons, performance has been frequently associated not just with the artist's presence and the time of the event, but also with the notions of absence, lack, repetition and trace.[1] This suggests, at a minimum, that performance is constituted out of not one but several layers of duration, each of which belongs to a different time frame. From the declaration of an artist's intention – always oriented towards the future – to the time of the event – always experienced as here and gone – to the situation created by the performance – whose meaning unfolds in retrospect – *performance reveals itself through what it is not*. This extends to the many afterlives through which any given performance is reconstructed and reworked, whether through the memories of eyewitnesses or, more likely, the traces that are left behind. These in turn reveal their meaning through yet another time frame: what we might call the distant past of historical reflection, inferred but never directly experienced.

From the outset, then, any writing on performance confronts the challenge of how to recover these multiple temporalities. Performance, after all, is an event that is difficult to locate. It is both dead and gone, yet kept alive so long as it is communicated and talked about. For all these reasons, since the 1990s, the discourse on – and practices of – performance art have shifted from emphasising the ephemerality and singularity of the event to focusing on how such events are captured by different media: photography, film, video and so forth.[2] But while much has been written about the different strategies of documentation used in performance art, less attention has been paid to the role of historical reflection in unfolding its meaning. This is even though all performances, even those that are personally witnessed, reveal their significance retrospectively, as events that have receded into the past. Subsequent events or the discovery of additional events may change our understanding of the performance, but not the event itself, which can be experienced only once.

This book proposes that historical modelling is a key component of any performance. It further suggests that the historical frameworks used to assess performances cannot be taken off the shelf or given in advance, because performances imply a certain participation in the event, whether we are direct witnesses or distant observers who remodel the traces left behind to create new meanings and interpretations of the event. Such a history must confront the role of real, physical time in altering our relation to the past. Although events may not change, our relationship to them does. Whatever framework we use, therefore, cannot be arbitrary but requires a decision to be made about what part of the past is still capable of generating meaning, and in relation to whose present and future.

These concerns are also central to Brisley's own understanding of his performance practice, intimately tied to an exploration of both individual and collective behaviours.[3] Brisley's performances stand out for their durational aspect, with some lasting weeks and even years. He is equally known for utilising the experience of lived, physical time to explore a number of political and historical conflicts: the Troubles in Northern Ireland, the First and Second World Wars, Britain's labour history, to name just a few. In each case, a past or ongoing conflict is probed for what it can tell us about present-day tensions and conflicts in the effort to imagine or enact a radically different future for the past. Brisley of course is not the only artist who began working in this vein in the 1960s; Chris Burden, Gina Pane, Marina Abramović and others were all experimenting with body art at the time. Nor is he alone in using a long time frame; Abramović, Burden, Tehching Hsieh and Linda Montano have all used long durations.[4] But Brisley's performances stand out for the steadfastness of their attempt to instigate a deep, potentially revolutionary, change. Revolutionary rupture is the red thread that connects his political concerns with equality, republicanism and dissent to his conception of performance as a temporal process that continually overturns entrenched hierarchies. It is also the subject of Brisley's ongoing confrontation with images of sovereignty, particularly those of the British monarchy, that feature in several performances as well as multi-media work.

Revolution also informs Brisley's work conceptually, insofar as every performance attempts to bring about a fundamental change of some kind, whose outcome cannot be known in advance. For Brisley, this essential incompleteness of performance makes it analogous to revolutionary events, which also seek to bring about a transformative change and whose meaning cannot be prescribed in advance. Like any revolution, his performances begin with a decision to act, a decision to make a cut in time. Once declared, this action needs to be carried out, regardless of the outcome. In addition to this time of intention, Brisley's performances emphasise how the meaning of any action unfolds over a much longer duration than the event itself. As with any revolution, the significance of a given performance lies not in its failure or success but in the way its consequences continue to reverberate and unfold, soliciting new kinds of commitment. By drawing attention to the duration over which an original event gains or loses meaning, Brisley's performances ask us to shift our critical vocabulary away from a narrative of events and towards an exploration of their many afterlives. Breadth and expansion become key terms, alongside a related terminology of dissolution, exhaustion and disappearance.

This last point is crucial. For if Brisley's performances enact a revolutionary cut in time, they also reflect on what happens when a revolution fails to take place, or when a rupture with the past is experienced only negatively, as an ongoing crisis or catastrophe. Given the collapse of the revolutionary paradigm worldwide, and, in Britain at least, the ongoing presence of the monarchy, Brisley's performances situate themselves firmly in the aftermath of a revolutionary history. They explore what happens when revolutions are treated as completed events that belong to a firmly historical past, rather than as events whose future remains undetermined. In other words, Brisley's performances ask us to think about whether and how the revolutionary desire for a deep, transformational rupture with the past can remain intelligible when hopes for a future revolution have been depleted. In a vital sense, then, Brisley's performances are made in – and are about – the wreckage of revolution. They pose the question of what is to be done with the remains of revolution, including the remains of his own previous attempts to bring about a transformative change of some kind. Is there a way to make sense of the effort to create a break in time in the face of historical failure?

Rarely, however, has the temporal form of Brisley's political commitments been assessed; much less used as a diagnostic tool through which to reconsider our own relation to the revolutionary past. This book sets out to develop the striking homologies between performance and the revolutionary process as suggested by Brisley's own artistic practice. It also goes further, to reflect on the impact of time and duration in how we receive and write the histories of both kinds of phenomena. I see Brisley's works, in their joint focus on duration and situatedness, as analogous to a revolutionary situation. Every performance – like every revolution – effectuates a cut in time. Through abstraction, performance re-enacts the dual aspect of revolutionary time as an event – a rupture with the past – and duration – the quest for permanent change. By bracketing time from the normal course of events, performance creates a space to reflect on the human capacity for change, that is to say, the ability of humans to liberate themselves from past habits, assumptions and reflexes to start anew. In its situatedness, however, performance also exposes the habits that the past transmits and which, inevitably, limit the scope for change.

There are, of course, important precedents for my attempt to link performance and revolution in this way. As Karl Marx famously argued, 'men make their own history, but they do not make it just as they please, they do not make it under circumstances chosen by themselves, but under circumstances directly found and given and transmitted by the past'.[5] For Marx, performance and performativity were central to the revolutionary experience. It is because the cut in time is so difficult to make that the French revolutionaries dressed up as ancient Greeks or presented the French Republic as ancient Rome incarnate. The cut in time requires a leap back in time that is also a way of springing forward into a future whose contours are yet unknown. At the same time, there is always the risk of parody, even self-deception, when a revolution repeats itself. For Marx, a true revolution is one that continually interrupts itself in the attempt to begin anew. What holds for revolution also holds, *mutatis mutandis*, for Brisley's performances, which can work only with what is already there, making cuts in time while remaining situated within time and history.

More recently, Alain Badiou has explored the ontology of revolution – in politics, art and love – in a manner that is morphologically similar to the approach of this book. Badiou emphasises real time as crucial for unfolding the intention as well as consequences of any revolution, which he defines as the attempt to create a cut in time.[6] For Badiou what distinguishes a revolution from other kinds of change is the effort to make it permanent. This requires a commitment on the part of the revolutionary or militant to remain faithful to the event regardless of the outcome, a commitment moreover that is clarified retrospectively by the situation that is created. He gives the example of 18 March 1871, the foundational event of the French Commune, when, for the first time in history, the workers constituted themselves as a political authority. Badiou argues that it was only subsequent events – including a fateful decision made on 10 May 'to save the revolution of March 18, which it had begun so well' – that transformed the events of 18 March from a relative beginning into an absolute one.[7] This was the moment when the revolutionaries declared themselves committed to the sequence of events that had been instigated by their actions. Revolutionaries, Badiou contends, are those who remain faithful to a 'certain organised control of time'.[8] This naming of the event and commitment to the ongoing experience of rupture – rather than its success or failure – enables a potentially endless and amorphous sequence of events to be seen as belonging to one and the same situation.

For Badiou, a similar relationship holds for artworks. The 'truth' of art is located 'neither in the work, nor the author, but rather the artistic configuration initiated by an eventual rupture'.[9] Art activity, in other words, is something recognised retroactively, whenever a creation is placed in a sequence of works that is publicly affirmed as the start of something new.[10] The break in time and the trace: these are Badiou's key terms. They are also central to the concerns of this book, which insists that the meaning of any performance is not found per se in the photos, films, videos or other kinds of documentation left behind by live actions but, rather, is something actively created – promoted even – through a retrospective reflection that unfolds the latent possibilities associated with the break in time, which always exceeds whatever historical trace it leaves behind.

To be sure, analogy and abstraction are usually considered anathema for any properly historical study of the past. Nevertheless, this book shows how the abstraction of performance *can* provide us with a type of knowledge about the historical pasts of revolution, precisely by refocusing attention on the multiple layers of time that condition any lived experience. Brisley's performances stretch out – sometimes over an almost intolerable duration – the revolutionary attempt to make a cut in time. In so doing they illuminate aspects of the revolutionary experience not normally visible from the historical record alone; namely, how a rupture may have been experienced in its own present, as a bodily action that solicits a range of reactions. This prolonged suspension of chronological time and sequence not only affects how the artist's own body is experienced and perceived but also extends to those reactions that influence the form and outcome of the action, regardless of whether they take place in the moment or long after the event has receded in time. These actions and reactions, I argue, shed new light on the ambiguous emotions that accompany any attempt to make a rupture with the past. This includes the dense, often subterranean connections that relate the experience of revolutionary revolt to feelings of revulsion; acts of destruction to the longing for conservation; or, indeed, the razing of symbols of vertical hierarchy to fear of the wasteland and the establishment of new monuments in their place – all subjects treated in this book.

An analogy is convincing, however, only if it changes our understanding of both terms under comparison. Conversely, therefore, I show how we can use what is known about historical revolutions to illuminate unnoticed, ignored or poorly understood elements of Brisley's performances. These range from Brisley's allusions to the history and legacy of revolutionary art, to formal considerations – such as the repeated use of the ten-day revolutionary calendar as a temporal frame – to his understanding of performance itself as a potential rupture in time that requires completion by others. Adopting this longer time frame of revolutionary history recontextualises not just the artist's physical actions but also the found objects, narrative texts, films, paintings, photos, even a virtual museum of ordure, all of which Brisley has manipulated in various ways in his efforts to instigate a revolutionary point of departure. As these references come equipped with their own histories and meanings, by expanding on their significance this book too aims to contribute to the artist's attempt to suspend chronological time and put the future into question. In this sense, what you will read in these pages is also a kind of performance, albeit one rooted in Brisley's practice and my own understanding of the history and imaginary of revolution.

As should be clear by now, this book is more than a monograph on a single artist. For I suggest that this interlacing of past and present is critical not just for writing a 'history' of Brisley's performances, but for all attempts to understand how the revolution was experienced in its own present, in a period of convulsive or even catastrophic change when the boundaries between past, present and future were incessantly redrawn. Reinhart Koselleck is one prominent theorist who has argued that historical narratives should integrate the perspective of the protagonists themselves, by focusing on how individuals come to express collectively shared experiences of time and duration.[11] Borrowing a structure from Fernand Braudel, Kosellek identified three different layers of temporality that make up historical time: that of events, which humans experience as singular; that of recursive structures that enable patterns to emerge and structures to be established against the linear flow of time; and the cyclical and repetitive time of nature and biology that do not belong to history, properly speaking, but condition historical self-understanding, intimately connected to our perception of the mortality and finality of human life.

I argue that this tripartite understanding of time as consisting of multiple durations is also essential for understanding Brisley's own work as a performance artist. First, there is the singularity of any performance as a one-time event which, as such, is unpredictable and open. Second, Brisley's performances tend to focus on simple tasks which themselves are embedded in recursive structures associated with social behaviour and expectations of what is to be done. Finally, in working with the limits of the human body and its capacity for self-expression, Brisley's performances draw attention to the possibilities but also constraints of natural, biological time which impede our capacity for radical change. Performance thus provides a unique space in which to address the more vexing issues that are thrown up whenever experiences of time and duration are addressed. How does an ontology, and maybe even anthropology of human time, as explored through Brisley's performances, relate to epistemological claims about historical events in the past? And if performance is conceptually productive in some way, for whom is this knowledge produced – the performer, the participants or both?

On this last point, the parallels with the revolutionary situation are illuminating in yet another way. Performance, after all, can mean any number of things to different people. There is no established framework for interpreting performance, for the same reason that there can be no 'school' for learning performance art. Any interpretation, therefore, is not produced sequentially, as something located in a linear time that goes forward from the work to its reception, but takes place simultaneously, as something produced by the performer and participant together in a time frame that consists of several overlapping layers of duration. Revolutionary ruptures reflect a similar orientation in time. They too are events for which the appropriate historical framework cannot be given in advance, for what is at stake is the emergence of something new, whose consequences cannot be foreseen. This lack of historical framework makes any intent to create a revolutionary rupture an extremely fragile, potentially ambiguous experience, continually open to fractures, revisions and retrospective judgements. For these reasons, revolutionaries and other partisans of historical ruptures have always had to *model* their own understanding of where they situate themselves in relation to a past, present and future that they are in the process of *actively constructing*. In a political situation, this modelling matters, because the bodily cost can be very high whenever revolutions fail. Hence why revolutionaries always have to publicly rationalise their historical model in some way, not only to obtain public support but also to keep it in the event of loss or failure. Although Brisley's performances are not political revolutions of this kind, they too require a historical model that needs to be publicly acknowledged in some way. Naming a process is a way to give it a value. It is what makes the effort to create a break in time something other than a completely subjective or voluntaristic intention.

It is far from obvious, however, that such a public exists for the reception of Brisley's performances. Even if it were to exist, this public affirmation is recoverable only intermittently via the artist's own anecdotes or the few eyewitness accounts that have come down to us through reviews, interviews and other publications. Apart from this dispersed, and often overlooked, discursive framework, Brisley's performances, like those of any other artist, are subject to evaluation by external measures and criteria, be they the historical chronologies of the art galleries and museums that collect his work, the art schools through which he has been associated or the students he has influenced, or, indeed, the commercial interests of an art market which increasingly treats even performance art as a vehicle for investment. Given this inherent instability – even weakness – of performance when faced with historical revisionism, the capacity of any performance to sustain its own historical models is doubtful at best.

But where an emphatic public is lacking, or perhaps never even existed, there is always conversation with others. Brisley's performances have long stood out for their conversational aspect. Often, he would break the frame of the performance to ask others about what they felt or thought was taking place, in the effort to destabilise any sense that there could be a final meaning or 'end' to the work. Indeed, most of the extant art-historical writing 'about Brisley', takes the form of conversations 'with Brisley'.[12] And while recorded or published conversations overlap with the interview and oral history – genres, as we shall see, that are also central to Brisley's artistic practice – they also differ from it insofar as conversations too are unique, unreproducible performances that require the participation of others for their completion.[13]

This attitude carries over to the structure of this book, which first emerged as a series of conversations with the artist about revolutionary time, a subject that I had previously written about in the context of the French Revolution.[14] Instigated by the novelist Tony White in 2013, these conversations initially concerned the prominent use of the ten-day week of the French revolutionary calendar in several of Brisley's performances. Since then, my ongoing conversation with Brisley over nearly a decade concentrated on the problem of how to recover and understand the revolutionary experience of time in his own performances and more generally. These discussions have taken a variety of forms, ranging from published and unpublished conversations, including with Brisley's partner and frequent collaborator Maya Balcioglu, public talks, correspondence as well as new performances created in response to these conversations. In a crucial sense, this problem of how to recover the role of real, physical time in constituting our relationship to the past is reflected in the overall shape of this book, which oscillates between a historically distant perspective on works that I have never encountered personally, but are still alive in Brisley's recollections, and those that I happened to personally witness or even have a hand in elaborating. What you will find in these pages, therefore, is not a standard art history based on a contextual or biographical study of the artist and his work. Rather, it is the outcome of a sustained collaboration between the artist and myself to identify what a revolutionary process of historical modelling entails and why it may be significant for the reception of performance art. For I too am interested in exploring whether it is possible to 'expand and stretch' the potential meaning of Brisley's performances to the point where they cease being art and become something else: a novel kind of activity for which prior references and knowledge no longer hold.

A key challenge of this book, therefore, is to reconstruct a history of Brisley's performances that takes seriously the artist's own commitments as well as attempts to model a revolutionary future for the past. At the same time, this book uses Brisley's performances to ask a more general question about where to situate the role of intention in constructing a legacy for a revolutionary past that for many people has become a relic of a historical process that is over and will never be repeated. It is well known, for instance, that revolutions challenge conventional habits of time and measure, drawing attention to the performative function of any historical frame. In its own time, for instance, the French Revolution cast itself variously as a regeneration, a restoration, a return to a golden age and the beginning of a new Year I of history. Viewed from the standpoint of how things turned out, these claims to be living in Year I of a new time can easily be dismissed as 'utopian', 'illusory', even 'fictional'; in short, as epiphenomena that have left the underlying trajectory of historical events largely untouched. Yet, to consider such events solely from the standpoint of historical outcomes, established with the benefit of hindsight and after the fact, fails to capture how the revolution was experienced in its own present, as an event still open to futures other than the one that came to pass. This raises the critical issue of whether such cataclysmic events should be judged externally, using conventional historical timelines, or whether they should be evaluated internally, according to measurements that are self-produced and reflect the subjective understanding of participants.[15]

I want to suggest that this problem of where to locate revolutionary intention – *and in what historical time frame* – also faces Brisley's performances and, by extension, all art activity that seeks to make a transformative change. How do we make sense of an activity that, should it succeed, would transform all prior understandings of the nature and limitations of art? What is the appropriate measure for an art activity that tries to cross the boundary into life? And when these efforts fail to make a break in time, how should we consider them in retrospect? As political gestures now empty of meaning? Or as traces of a commitment that may still be valid? In the case of Brisley in particular, it matters enormously whether the various radical social and political movements of the 1960s that inspired his first forays into performance are considered 'ironically', as events without consequence, that is to say, as 'illusions' that have left the underlying course of history more or less intact, or whether their intentions can still be considered valid, because their future is undetermined. These questions, in turn, are inseparable from the more general question as to whether and how far the politically motivated performance art of the 1960s can or should be reintegrated within a broader historical framework that goes back not just to the events of the 1960s but to an entire dimension opened up by the French Revolution of 1789, leading to the revolutions of 1848, the Commune of 1871 and the October revolution of 1917, as well as the various movements of anti-fascism, anti-colonialism, feminism and socialism whose future-oriented struggles for equality have so marked the history of the twentieth century and continue to influence contemporary discourses.

To be sure, this is a deeply unfashionable, not to say retrograde, way of thinking about history. We cannot deny that its coherence has been severely challenged by the far-reaching reappraisal of the meaning and function of historical time that has followed the collapse of Marxism and the various historical narratives that have been spun in its name. The definitive end of communism in Eastern Europe and Soviet Russia in 1989 seemed to vindicate the common sentiment that, with no more revolutions to look forward to, history would cease to function as a vector or locomotive of future change. The bicentenary celebrations of the French Revolution that took place the same year consolidated this vision. As the intellectual historian François Furet expressed it, the rational response to this 'shock of a closed future' was to accept that 'we are condemned to live in the world as it is'; that history would once again become a 'tunnel that we enter in darkness, not knowing where our actions will lead'.[16] In place of the 'mythology of beginnings and endings' that had characterised the revolutionary tradition, revolution would henceforth be just one story to tell in histories that could be constructed out of any number of ruptures and revisions.[17] For Furet and the generation that followed him, there is no such thing as absolute beginnings, only relative ones. Once this horizon of future promise is depleted, so too is the intelligibility of ruptures and breaks. As Bruno Latour remarks, 'Revolution is only one resource among others in histories that have nothing revolutionary; nothing irreversible about them.'[18]

These battles over how to conceptualise revolutionary historiography may appear a far cry from the concerns of most performance art, and as having little or nothing to do with how we write about it. But, as I show over the course of this book, this missing frame of revolutionary history forces us to rethink the ways in which we evaluate socially or politically committed art in the absence of a future revolution. Revolutionary history used to be oriented towards a utopian future that gave meaning to past struggles. Today this future has become part of the past. If it continues to live on, it does so as a memory, an after-image, or trace of a historical process that has now ended. Enzo Traverso has suggested that after the fall of communism in 1989, we have entered a new way of orienting ourselves to the past that is as decisive as 1789 was for the period ushered in by the French Revolution.[19] Faced with a new 'official' memory culture that implicitly or explicitly equates all revolution with totalitarianism, and for whom revolution itself is just one topic among others for professional historians to ponder, it is increasingly difficult to articulate the value of projects that put the revolutionary struggle for equality at the centre of their agenda. For Traverso, in the absence of a viable future, the task becomes one of maintaining a 'fidelity and awareness of the potentialities of the past'.[20] This commitment can take the form of a dissident memory and even a counter-history. For while historical narrative is subject to any number of revisions, memory traces are harder to manipulate and not so easy to efface.

This brings me to a more general question of why performance has become the focus of recent attention across the cultural field, and not just for histories of the Left. Indeed, part of my aim in this book is to connect Brisley's performances to this larger sea-change in which the meaning and significance of performance and performativity has greatly expanded our relationship to the past. In other words, instead of contextualising Brisley's performances as an art activity taking place within a narrowly conceived art world, I want to consider them more broadly as vital explorations of a cultural landscape in which the classical distinctions between memory and history no longer hold. The collapse of socialism's prognostic structure, coupled with the accelerating pace of technological change, has led a number of observers to describe the contemporary situation as a kind of 'suspended time', in which the past is still present because the future remains blocked. Hans Ulrich Gumbrecht has suggested that this unsettled feeling reflects a 'prolonged period of latency' that dates from the Second World War, in which even 1968 and 1989 – at the time hailed as milestones, moments of clarity about history's direction – have failed to serve adequately as turning points.[21] Latency expresses the feeling that there is something there – a historical trend, pattern or development – that resists interpretation even as it makes itself known through a kind of affective apprehension. It is expressed through mood, presence, immersion, feelings, repetitions and the uncanny, all terms familiar to the performance artist. Above all, latency expresses the idea that the past and the present both move in time. Even if the events and facts of the past do not change, our feelings about them can and do. Because the latent past is something that can be experienced as both event and repetition, it shares important characteristics with performance, an art activity whose prime material is duration and that too is constituted out of events and their repetition; that is to say, the way events are remembered, registered or otherwise repeated in the present. For all these reasons, performance has become an important resource, across the cultural field, for recovering what remains ignored, misunderstood, overlooked, neglected, forgotten or not fully repressed within the past.

Nowhere is this affective turn more evident than in the recent rapprochement between performance and historical studies. Numerous observers have noted the 'historical turn' in the art world, whether in the archival impulse since the 1990s,[22] the various exhibits and performances devoted to the intersection of art and history,[23] or indeed the attention paid to the phenomenon of re-enactment, either of previous performances or of other events from the past.[24] This historical turn within the art world has been accompanied by a 'performative turn' within the historical field, accentuated by the exponential growth of interactive museums, popular historical channels, re-enactment communities and preservation societies.[25] Historians increasingly emphasise 'affective' relations to the past or seek ways to provide a more authentic or spontaneous knowledge than the 'distant history' represented in textbooks.[26] Others have stressed the forensic value of performance as a means of recreating historical context, especially where the historical record is lacking.[27] The rise of this so-called 'forensic sensibility'[28] can be linked to the collapse of the historiographical categories used to filter and understand the past, inherited from the revolutionary nineteenth century, when the modern historical disciplines first emerged.[29]

As Rita Felski notes, there is a growing restiveness across the humanities with the complacencies of historicism which lock a given work or cultural production in its original context as if it were a 'kind of box or container' and assumes that history itself 'consists of a vertical pile of neatly stacked boxes – what we call periods'.[30] This vision of history as constituted out of sealed, non-communicative boxes, makes it difficult to consider not only why the past still matters but how it might continue to inform cultural production even today. It has also deeply influenced how we conceive the role of the artist. While it is commonly accepted that artistic works can and do resonate across time in non-linear ways, artists themselves are usually described in resolutely historicist terms. As counter-intuitive as it may sound, this way of contextualising artistic production contributes to the elevation of the artist as a genius or godhead. Artists are deified whenever they are presented as breaking through their narrow historical context, even if this breakthrough lasted only a short period or failed to be sustained.

Performance, on the other hand, is not an object that can be nailed down to a specific time and place. Erika Fischer-Lichte describes it as a self-generating event that creates its own conditions of reception, such that 'the aesthestics of production, work and reception as three heuristic categories seem questionable, if not obsolete'.[31] Since meaning is generated through interactions between the artist and participants, it can be located neither at the point of origin, say in the original intentions of the artist, nor at the point of reception, because there is no pre-existing 'work' for the audience to receive. Extrapolating from this observation, it is tempting to assume that performance, on account of its ephemeral nature, defiantly resists the grip of historicism that sometimes characterises writing on the arts. But this is not always the case. On the contrary, such an understanding often tacitly assumes that a work can still be fixed in its original moment of appearance. In other words, it assumes that, because a performance occurs only once, its 'original' meaning is roughly equivalent to its authentic 'historical' meaning. The resulting inclination is to contextualise works within a 'synchronic slice of time' rather than to consider how actions can operate across time, soliciting new audiences in new situations.[32] Any writing on performance that situates retrospective analysis exclusively at the end of a formerly alive, now dead, past, tends to imprison the original event in what Brisley calls the 'tyranny of its moment of revelation'.[33] More seriously, for a politically committed artist such as Brisley, this implicit historicisation also elevates the artist as the main subject of their work, as opposed to whatever subject matter their work deals with. The problem is compounded as performance has gone from being the 'runt of the litter of contemporary art'[34] to a major focus of institutional attention and acquisition. Not only is there a tendency for art writing to gravitate towards artists that are commissioned or collected by major art galleries, thereby increasing the value of these same collections; these institutions themselves promote their archives and, with it, a documentary style of writing about past performances.

This book attempts to forestall these historicising tendencies by self-consciously adopting two timescales: that of the recent past, as accessed through the artist's performances and his recollections, and the far longer historical time frame of revolutionary history, which serves to distance Brisley from his performances, preventing the all-too-easy conflation of Brisley's work with his biography and persona as an artist. It also extends a practice implicit in Brisley's own performances, which have often presented themselves as happenings in search of a frame, or at least as performances whose meanings are conditioned by the situation or context in which they take place. If a performance is entitled *Homage to the Commune*, it is because it took place in Milan, where the local government is called the Consiglio Comunale di Milano. If a concept such as *interregnum* is invoked, it is because the performance unfolded during a period of hung parliament when Britain's electoral system was literally held together by the Crown. If the artist's own relation to sovereign power is held up for scrutiny, it is over the course of a performance in the Royal Academy Life Room, founded by George III, a monarch who reigned in an age of Revolution. If a performance explores the absence of working-class history, it is in the context of an artist placement in the mining town of Peterlee. At the same time, the *Commune, interregnum, reign of George III* and *workers' memories* are all referents that recall a far longer history of struggles for equality and against the sovereign power. In these and other performances, the historical referent is never conflated with the time frame of the performance. Rather, it is treated as something akin to a found object: uncanny, fascinating, untimely, with the potential to reverberate in a shared, public memory as a catalyst for change.

A key challenge of writing about Brisley's performances, therefore, is to find a way to keep alive this historical *presence*, which incessantly refers to other histories and memories that go beyond the horizon of the art world. Of course, it goes without saying that any writing on performance can only restore such presence from a distance, through the work of historical reflection. In fact this book is doubly removed from the live event, both from Brisley's own performances which have receded into the past and from the revolutionary experience of rupture, whose traces we can only glean from the historical record. But where this book differs from academic history is in its acknowledgement that aesthetic forms also offer ways of thinking about the past that resist the 'conflation of the past with history'.[35] Despite all the recent attention to new ways of thinking about time and duration, academic history tends to assume that linear, chronological time is not simply a frame but a natural way of considering the past. My argument, in contrast, develops terms such as *frame, mise en abîme, situation, proposal, model* and *artist persona* as alternate ways of casting the relation of performance both to its own remains and that of the revolutionary past more broadly. I also rehabilitate the role of *analogy*, the *análogon*, in the Greek sense of proportion, correspondence or resemblance enabling reasoning on the basis of parallel cases. These terms are not chosen by author's fiat but are either suggested by Brisley or grounded in his practice, in particular his late works that seek to connect past performances to his own changing reflections and recollections of lived experience (including those of his past political commitments).

Contemporary art offers a precedent for this. In 1979 the Hungarian art critic László Beke provocatively defined the role of the critic as the person 'who tries his hand in *further creating the works of art* he tackles'.[36] Given the increasing tendency for contemporary artists to supply their own critical vocabularies, Beke argued that the only role left for the critic was to further eliminate the boundary between art and non-art by expanding the range of references that could be associated with any given work. I would like to offer this book as one such interpretative expansion. By expanding the temporal frame of Brisley's performances to also include references from a distant historical past of revolution, I show how performance can be used to identify those elements of revolution that may yet remain alive in the present, even if only in latent or not always obvious ways.

Such an approach differs from most publications on performance, which tend to assume either a short time frame of the recent past or adopt the accepted chronology which traces live art from its origins in the social art of the early twentieth-century avant-gardes to its re-emergence in the happenings of the 1950s and 1960s. Even in the case of studies that problematise the relation of performance art to history, the discussion tends to remain internal to the time frames generated by art history. As Claire Bishop has observed, this is regardless of whether the performance presents itself as an art activity or as a social activity that works outside the realm of art.[37] One exception to this general trend is Boris Groys, who has consistently pointed to the Russian and French revolutions in order to identify what is specific about contemporary art. As Groys has observed, what makes these contemporary art projects so different from anything that has preceded them is the attempt to make a difference in life by means of art alone.[38] However, contrary to the revolutionary avant-gardes, who mostly harboured such ambitions when they had the support of the revolutionary state behind them, contemporary art movements appear to want to go it alone. Although Groys is emphatic that contemporary art activism is a wholly new phenomenon, he nevertheless argues that it presupposes an understanding of revolution, if only because such art takes place in the aftermath of a history that began with the French Revolution.[39] In this sense, contemporary art is imbued with a post-revolutionary perspective that attempts to 'look at the historical period in which we live from the perspective of its end'.[40]

As Groys' own work has demonstrated, this longer time frame of revolutionary history has important implications for how we understand the so-called 'radicalism' of contemporary art. Performance art has frequently identified itself with the avant-garde principles of a sharp discontinuity with the past, captured most succinctly in the revolutionary myth of the *tabula rasa*. For this sense of radical rupture to be maintained, however, performance must resist becoming historical, which is to say that it must resist becoming like any other historical remnant, a fixed data point in the past that can be archived, collected and managed by institutions. Yet it is also fair to say that much of what counts as performance art today takes place in museums, places of collecting and linear chronology par excellence.[41] This increasingly comfortable relation between performance art and the museum raises a series of related questions. What is the relation between performance as a public art and public history, given that both are increasingly mediated by institutions? When museums exert their sovereign power to frame and reframe their own archives and collections, what remains of the ability of performance art to escape this frame? The French Revolution is a particularly appropriate context for these questions. For, in addition to its more radical promises of rupture, the Revolutionary period also founded the Louvre, one of the world's greatest art collections and the world's most visited museum.

Beyond the field of performance studies, then, this book contributes to a growing number of studies that have sought new ways to relate to the past as a lived experience, whether by adopting a 'history without chronology',[42] privileging temporal strata 'against periodization'[43] or by considering how artworks 'fold', 'collapse' or 'embed' different orders of orders of time in one another.[44] By bringing to bear the rich scholarship about the French Revolution onto the reception of contemporary performance art, this book also argues for a more dynamic, and historically informed, account of the relation between rupture and conservation, implicit in many performance practices. Last, but not least, I hope that scholars of historical revolutions may find in these pages something to reflect upon. For, as Gerard Raunig has shown for the nineteenth and twentieth centuries, art practices also have much to teach us about how revolution can be reconceptualised today as a 'constant overcoming of circumstances', an 'irresistible processual meaning' that is 'lost in the fixation on the image of a major rupture', itself drawn from a long history of attempting to take over a state power.[45]

My own attempt to develop a vocabulary of time and duration shared between performance and revolution is reflected in the double structure of each chapter. I use Brisley's performances to recover fragments of a 'lived' experience of revolutionary time as it might have been experienced subjectively, by protagonists of the event; conversely, I also make use of the historical record of revolution to identify trans-historical patterns of art and politics in Brisley's work, including his own attempts to evade the historicising tendencies of art history and, by extension, some of the conserving elements of the art world. Chapter 1 begins by contextualising Brisley's live performances within the artistic and political ferment of the 1960s, focusing on how his early performances were conceived as a type of *tabula rasa*, both artistically and politically. I then show how the ten-day week of the French Republican calendar – famous for having declared a new chronology beginning in Year I – has framed a number of Brisley's long-durational works from the 1970s to the 2010s. The French Republican calendar links together the themes of republicanism, atheism and equality that run through Brisley's oeuvre. It also raises the question of how to relate the linear, irreversible time of rupture to the cyclical structures of a shared, social experience of time.

Chapter 2 elaborates an additional aspect of the analogy between performance art and revolution, namely the struggle faced by both kinds of phenomena for a place in historical memory. I suggest that the various traces left behind from past performances – whether those of art or revolution – can be considered 'survivals'. This notion is closely related to the 'ghost dance', a term drawn from Native American rituals and applied by Brisley to explain the links between a cultural understanding of performance behaviours, and its use as a term of art. My focus is *Being and Doing* (1984), a film made by Brisley in collaboration with Ken McMullen, notable for its focus on East European performance artists, which I discuss alongside *Ghost Dance* (1983) and *Resistance* (1976), two films by McMullen in which Brisley played a role. I conclude by showing how performance behaviours can be used to recover not simply the past as it was but also the past that *was not*, including the unfulfilled pasts of revolution.

While it is common to associate events like revolution with bold declarations of rupture, Chapter 3 demonstrates how a new experience of time can emerge by intensifying the links a given place or situation may have with a pre-existing context. The focus is Brisley's pioneering *Peterlee Project – History Within Living Memory* (1976–77). Peterlee is a town that was built after the Second World War in the former mining region of the North East of England. As part of his placement with the Peterlee Development Corporation, Brisley helped the town's inhabitants to document their own collective history in the effort to create a platform for future political action. This chapter evaluates the project's successes and failures, to recover the point at which performance ceases to be a 'live proposal' and becomes instead a collectible or archivable object.

Chapter 4 looks at the *Cenotaph Project* (1987–88), Brisley's last public art project and one that addresses most explicitly the relation of performance to public history. A collaboration with the artist Maya Balcioglu, the *Cenotaph Project* involved exhibiting six models of the Whitehall Cenotaph, erected in London in 1919 to commemorate the end of the First World War, at six locations around the country. These six travelling cenotaphs, scaled down to match the height of a typical council flat, aimed to reconnect the monument with lived experience. Using these travelling installations as a springboard, I show how world revolution – and not just British imperial history – is an important discursive frame for examining the *Cenotaph Project* and, by extension, the Whitehall Cenotaph. I then adopt a wider trans-historical lens to consider how similar models were used during both the Russian and French revolutions to express emergent ideas of public art and history. I conclude by suggesting that the failure of revolutions to build lasting monuments provides a new perspective on revolution as an ongoing durational process, a permanent struggle against the imposition of vertical hierarchies.

Chapter 5 asks what happens in the aftermath of an incomplete or failed attempt at revolutionary rupture, when the past has been declared dead yet continues to survive, either as detritus to be disregarded or as remains to be collected and preserved. The *Georgiana Collection* and the *Museum of Ordure* are Brisley's longest durational works, the latter still ongoing. Both consist solely of detritus and waste. I show how Brisley's confrontation with this ambiguous treatment of the past as ordure sheds new light on the aftermath of the French Revolution. As Edouard Pommier has shown, this ambiguous status of waste is reflected in the 'Revolution's double language' of destruction and preservation.[46] For a cut in time does not just destroy an old past, it also creates a new one.

Chapter 6 considers Brisley's use of *mise en abîme*, increasingly prominent in his late works, which covers not just performances but also installations, photography, painting and film. By nesting references to prior works in new works, Brisley reactivates past performances, showing how they can persist and even act back on the present in some way. Expanding on the implications of this practice, I show how *mise en abîme* can be used to reveal a past excluded from officially sanctioned representations. Parallels are drawn between Brisley's late work and the use of *mise en abîme* in Velázquez' *Las Meninas* and Shakespeare's *Hamlet*. This chapter concludes by returning to the guiding questions of this book. Is there a way to re-experience the revolutionary past as an event with as yet undetermined outcomes, which is to say, as an event that still has the capacity to act back on us? Second and conversely, if revolutionary intentions remain, in many aspects, unfulfilled, what can performance art tell us about the debris left behind in the absence of collective transformation?

Notes

1 Although performance art began as the discovery of the body, since the 1990s, particularly under the influence of French theory and psychoanalysis, the terms have shifted to emphasise the body's absence. As Peggy Phelan notes, 'Without a copy, live performance plunges into visibility – in a maniacally charged present – and disappears into memory, into the realm of invisibility and the unconscious where it eludes regulation and control.' See: Peggy Phelan, *Unmarked: The Politics of Performance* (Abingdon: Routledge, 1993), p. 148.

2 See, inter alia, in Nick Kaye, *Multi-Media: Video – Installation – Performance* (Abingdon: Routledge, 2007); Amelia Jones and Adrian Heathfield (eds), *Perform, Repeat, Record: Live Art in History* (Bristol; Chicago: Intellect, 2012); Philip Auslander, *Liveness: Performance in a Mediatized Culture* (London: Routledge, 1999); Philip Auslander, *Reactivations: Essays on Performance and Its Documentation* (Ann Arbor, MI: University of Michigan Press, 2018); Gabriella Giannachi and Jonah Westerman (eds), *Histories of Performance Documentation: Museum, Artistic, and Scholarly Practices* (Abingdon: Routledge, 2017).

3 I use the term 'performance' when discussing Brisley's art for two reasons. First, it is his preferred term, predating 'live art', a designation which emerged in the mid-1980s. Second, 'performance' also references collective forms of behaviour that are central to Brisley's practice. For a definition of liveness in relation to both theatre and visual arts, see Paul Allain and Jen Harvie, *The Routledge Companion to Theatre and Performance* (London: Routledge, 2006), pp. 168–169.

4 For the rise of so-called endurance art, and these artists in particular, see Lara Shalson, *Performing Endurance Art and Politics since 1960* (Cambridge: Cambridge University Press, 2018).

5 Karl Marx, 'The 18th Brumaire of Louis Bonaparte', in Jon Elster (ed.), *Karl Max: A Reader* (New York, NY: Cambridge University Press, 1986), p. 277.

6 'What counts here is not only the exceptional intensity of sudden appearing of singularities (i.e. the fact that it is a matter of a violent and creative episode in the domain of appearing) but also what of uncertain and glorious consequences an evanescent emergence makes available to lived time.' Alain Badiou, Steve Corcoran and Bruno Bosteels, 'Logic of the Site', *Diacritics*, 33:3/4 (2003), 141–150, p. 147.

7 Badiou cites the Central Committee. Ibid., p. 144.

8 Alain Badiou, *Being and Event*, trans. Oliver Feltham (London and New York City: Continuum, 2005), p. 211.

9 Alain Badiou, *Handbook of Inaesthetics*, trans. Alberto Toscano (Stanford, CA: Stanford University Press, 2004), p. 12.

10 'The public is part of what completes the idea'. Ibid., p. 74.

11 See Reinhart Koselleck, *Sediments of Time: On Possible Histories*, trans. Sean Franzel and Stefan-Ludwig Hoffman (Stanford, CA: Stanford University Press, 2018), in particular 'Histories in the Plural and the Theory of History: An Interview with Carsten Dutt', pp. 250–265.

12 Most recently, Stuart Brisley, *The Stuart Brisley Interviews: Performance and Its Afterlives*, ed. Gilane Tawadros (London: Book Works and DACS, 2020); Stuart Brisley, Jem Finer, Maya Balcioglu and Francesca Hughes, in V. Honoré and M. Ribadaneira (eds), *Drawing Room Confessions: Stuart Brisley* (London: Mousse Publishing, 2017); see also the extensive interview in Nick Kaye, 'Stuart Brisley', in *Art Into Theatre*, 1st edn (Abingdon: Routledge, 1996), pp. 73–88.

13 For Brisley's oral history, see Stuart Brisley, National Life Stories: Artists' Lives. Interview by Melanie Roberts (1996), The British Library. For oral history as a method for documenting performance, see Heike Roms and Rebecca Edwards, 'Oral History as Site-Specific Practice: Locating the History of Performance Art in Wales', in Shelley Trower (ed.) *Place, Writing, and Voice in Oral History*, Palgrave Studies in Oral History (New York: Palgrave Macmillan, 2011), pp. 171–192.

14 See Sanja Perovic, *The Calendar in Revolutionary France: Perceptions of Time in Literature, Culture, Politics* (Cambridge: Cambridge University Press, 2012).

15 I discuss this problem in Sanja Perovic, 'No Future or Still in Year One? Revisionist versus Lyricist Approaches to the French Revolution', *Poetics Today*, 37:2 (2016), 249–268.

16 François Furet, *Interpreting the French Revolution*, trans. Elborg Forster (Cambridge: Cambridge University Press, 1981), pp. 9–11; *The Passing of an Illusion: The Idea of Communism in the Twentieth Century*, trans. Deborah Furet (Chicago, IL: University of Chicago Press, 2000), p. 502.

17 See the interview with Furet, *Le Nouvel Observateur*, 28 February to 6 March, 1986; cited in Christophe Prochasson, *Francois Furet: Les chemins de la mélancolie* (Paris: Stock, 2013), p. 130.

18 Bruno Latour, *We Have Never Been Modern*, trans. Catherine Porter (New York: Harvester Wheatsheaf, 1993), p. 48.

19 Enzo Traverso, *Left-Wing Melancholia: Marxism, History, and Memory* (New York City, NY: Columbia University Press, 2016), pp. 2, 57.

20 Ibid., p. 52.

21 Hans Ulrich Gumbrecht, 'How (If at All) Can We Encounter What Remains Latent in Texts?', *Partial Answers: Journal of Literature and the History of Ideas*, 7:1 (2009), 87–96, p. 94. DOI: 10.1353/pan.0.0134. See also Hans Ulrich Gumbrecht, *After 1945: Latency as Origin of the Present* (Stanford, CA: Stanford University Press, 2013).

22 Notably, Hal Foster, 'An Archival Impulse', *October*, 110 (2004), 3–22; Okwui Enwezor, *Archive Fever: Uses of the Document in Contemporary Art* (Göttingen: Steidl, 2009).

23 For a consideration of these trends see Jane Blocker, *Becoming Past: History in Contemporary Art* (Minneapolis, MIN: University of Minnesota Press, 2015); for a related discussion in the field of performing arts, see Charlotte Canning

and Thomas Postlewait (eds), *Representing the Past: Essays in Performance Historiography* (Iowa City, IA: University of Iowa Press, 2010).

24 See, notably, Rebecca Schneider, *Performing Remains: Art and War in Times of Theatrical Reenactment* (Abingdon: Routledge, 2011) who links the 'practice of re-playing or re-doing a precedent event, artwork or act … in performance-based art to the 'burgeoning of historical re-enactment and "living history" in various history museums', p. 2. See also Shalson, *Endurance Art*, pp. 146–182.

25 For an overview see Jerome De Groot, *Consuming History: Historians and Heritage in Contemporary Popular Culture* (Abingdon: Routledge, 2008).

26 On this re-orientation, see Mark Salber Phillips, *On Historical Distance* (New Haven, CT: Yale University Press, 2013); Vanessa Agnew and Jonathan Lamb (eds), *Extreme and Sentimental History*, Special Issue, *Criticism*, 46:3 (2004).

27 See Gabriella Giannachi, Nick Kaye and Michael Shanks (eds), *Archeologies of Presence: Art, Performance and the Persistence of Being* (Abingdon: Routledge, 2012). For performance as a field of practical intervention, see Forensic Architecture Research Agency, based at Goldsmiths University.

28 Lynn Hershman and Michael Shanks, 'Here and Now', in Gabriella Giannachi, Nick Kaye and Michael Shanks (eds), *Archeologies of Presence: Art, Performance and the Persistence of Being* (Abingdon: Routledge, 2012), pp. 225–234, p. 255.

29 On this point see Chris Lorenz and Marek Tamm, 'Who Knows Where the Time Goes?', *Rethinking History: The Journal of Theory and Practice*, 18:4 (2014), 499–521; Hans Ulrich Gumbrecht, *Our Broad Present: Time and Contemporary Culture* (New York, NY: Columbia University Press, 2014); François Hartog, *Regimes of Historicity: Presentism and Experiences of Time*, trans. Saskia Brown (New York, NY: Columbia University Press, 2015). For a representative sample of essays on the topic by historians, see Chris Lorenz and Berber Bevernage (eds), *Breaking Up Time: Negotiating the Borders Between Present, Past and Future* (Göttingen: Vandenhoeck & Ruprecht, 2013).

30 Rita Felski, 'Context Stinks', *New Literary History*, 42:4 (2011), 573–91, p. 577.

31 Erika Fischer-Lichte, *The Transformative Power of Performance: A New Aesthertics*, trans. Saskya Iris Jain (London and New York: Routledge, 2008). p. 18.

32 See Wai Chee Dimock, 'A Theory of Resonance', *PMLA*, 112: 5 (1997), 1060–1071, p. 1061. doi.org/10.2307/463483; Felski, 'Context Stinks', p. 578.

33 Stuart Brisley, 'The Photographer and the Performer', in Alice Maude-Roxby (ed.), *Live Art on Camera: Performance and Photography* (Southampton: John Hansard Gallery, 2007), pp. 83–88, p. 88.

34 Phelan's expression: *Unmarked: The Politics of Performance* (Abingdon: Routledge, 1993), p. 148.

35 On this point see Alun Munslow, 'On "Presence" and Conversing with the Past: Do Historians Communicate with the Past?', *Rethinking History: The Journal of Theory and Practice*, 18:4 (2014), 569–74, p. 574.

36 László Beke, 'Towards a Voluntaristic Art Criticism', *Art Monthly*, 3:26 (1979), 2–5, p. 3.

37 Claire Bishop, *Artificial Hells: Participatory Art and the Politics of Spectatorship* (London: Verso, 2012), pp. 19, 174.

38 Boris Groys, *Art Power* (Cambridge, MA: The MIT Press, 2008); Boris Groys, 'On Art Activism', *E-Flux Journal*, 56 (June 2014), 1–14, p. 1.

39 'The French Revolution turned the design of the Old Regime into what we today call art, i.e. objects not of use but of pure contemplation. This violent, revolutionary act of aestheticising the Old Regime created art as we know it today. Before the French Revolution, there was no art only design. After the French Revolution, art emerged – as the death of design.' Groys, 'On Art Activism', p. 6.

40 Ibid., p. 10.

41 On this point see also Catherine M. Soussloff, 'Art History's Dilemma: Theories for Time in Contemporary Performance/Media Exhibitions', *Performance Research, A Journal of the Performing Art*, 19:3 (2014), 93–100.

42 See Stefan Tanaka, *History without Chronology* (Amherst: Lever Press, 2019); for an earlier path-breaking example see Hans Ulrich Gumbrecht, *In 1926: Living on the Edge of Time* (Cambridge, MA: Harvard University Press, 1998).

43 On the debate within history on this move see Helge Jordheim, 'Against Periodization: On Koselleck's Theory of Multiple Temporalities', *History and Theory: Studies in the Philosophy of History*, 51:2 (2012), 151–171.

44 Most notably, Alexander Nagel and Christopher S. Wood, *Anachronic Renaissance* (New York: Zone Books, 2010).

45 Gerald Raunig, *Art and Revolution: Transversal Activism in The Long Twentieth Century*, trans. Aileen Derieg (Los Angeles, CA: Semiotext(e), 2007), p. 27.

46 Edouard Pommier, *L'Art de la liberté: Doctrines et débats de la Révolution française* (Paris: Gallimard, 1991), p. 108.

In 1984, Peter Gorsen described the performance movement that had emerged in the 1960s as a kind of existentialism. Art was once more 'overstepping the mark in its attempt to relate … to the cohesion of life'.[1] Yet Gorsen detected an agnostic attitude on the part of most artists, who worked in full awareness that all prior attempts to relate art to life had failed. Stuart Brisley's artistic practices reflect a similar agnosticism about the ability of art to create social or political change. Much like the revolutionary avant-gardes of the early twentieth century, he has persistently attempted to push artistic forms – be they sculpture, painting or happenings – to the point where they dissolve into everyday life or become something else.[2] Unlike them, however, Brisley explores the revolutionary potential of art from a position of cultural defeat, or at least an awareness that the long tail of revolutionary art endures in the absence of a politically viable concept of rupture. If, then, Brisley's practices can still be considered revolutionary, it is not in the avant-garde tradition of wanting to level all differences between art and life. Nor are they political in any overt sense. Rather, as I shall show in this chapter, his performances are revolutionary by analogy only.

Brisley's performances are known to last days, weeks and even years. They begin with a decision to act, a decision that effectuates a cut in time. Normal habits of time and duration are suspended, allowing for an action or a set of actions to be perceived as if they had their own integrity. At the same time, such performances test the artist's own commitment to maintaining this suspended time for long enough so that fundamental changes can happen. Brisley has described such performances as attempts to enter 'an originary day one … almost like an entry into day one of the revolutionary period'.[3] Like any revolution, they need to be carried out, regardless of their eventual success or failure.[4] How long this effort takes and how far it diverges from an initial intention becomes an integral part of the experience itself. Such endeavours cannot be evaluated by the usual criteria of success or failure because what is at stake is not reform, the use of art to ameliorate life, but a transformational change of some kind.

But how do we measure performances that unfold over days, weeks, months or even years? The broad time span, so characteristic of Brisley's performance practice, is not easily mapped onto a chronological time of measure. For chronological time cannot tell us anything about how an event or sequence of events comes to be experienced, shared or understood, all modes of apprehension that presuppose a perceiving subject. In contrast to *chronos*, the time of measure, performance events refer to qualitative experiences of time, what the ancient Greeks called *kairos*, the right time, the time of opportunity, when an action or decision needs to be made. It requires us to pay attention to how events are experienced internally, by agents who have no prior knowledge of the outcome of their actions.

This chapter argues that Brisley's performances can be considered 'revolutionary' not because they aim for a total fusion of art and life but, rather, in their attempt to model new relations between past, present and future within a situation that itself is experienced as ongoing, without a clearly discernible end of some kind. As the Introduction already notes, to write this kind of 'internal history' of performance art, we need to take seriously the historical models that Brisley provides for thinking about his own practice, intimately tied to the histories and imaginaries of revolution. At the same time, Brisley's understanding of performance as a process whose initial terms are revealed at the end implies a new role for the writer or critic – in this case myself – who is called upon to complete the meaning of the works in question. As the associations made by any participant or observer are potentially endless, this too is another way of relating performance to life or what lies outside the frame of art.

It is not enough, however, for an artist to merely declare an analogy between performance and revolution. To be meaningful, any analogy needs to be expanded and developed in a manner that adds something new to our understanding of both terms being compared. My procedure in this chapter is, accordingly, two-fold. First, I establish the links between Brisley's repeated references to a revolutionary day one and his more general understanding of performance as an incomplete process that develops over a broad time span. Second, I use the 'trope' of the French revolutionary calendar, whose ten-day week has structured a number of Brisley's performances, in order to investigate how revolution itself can be understood as an ongoing, temporal process. I conclude by examining *Before the Mast* (2013), a ten-day performance that I personally witnessed and also discussed with the artist in a series of conversations that took place before and after the performance. As I show, Brisley's attempt to re-enact revolutionary rupture also exposes the mechanisms of reaction latent in any revolutionary situation. In so doing, it provides new insights into how the revolutionary attempt to create a new Year I might have been experienced in its own present, when the future outcome was not yet known.

The turn towards performance: some personal experiences of rupture

Given that duration is something both individually experienced and collectively constituted, all performance is autobiographical in some way. Brisley's own turn towards performance is the culmination of several personal, artistic and political experiences of rupture that are inextricable from his development as an artist. If I begin, therefore, with a few biographical remarks, it is not simply to situate the artist and his work but also to highlight the recurrent themes and experiences that, over the course of seven decades, have continually pushed Brisley's artistic practices into new directions.

Like other artists of his generation, Brisley first articulated his performance practices out of a frustration with the limits of painting. Born in 1933, Brisley primarily trained in representational painting: first at the Guildford School of Art (1949–54), then at the Royal College of Art (1956–59). While still a student, Brisley abandoned realism for materialism, or what is commonly called abstraction.[5] Under the influence of continental European artists such as Burri, Tàpies, Wagemaker and Cruixart, Brisley developed a highly gestural technique that worked with the material and substance of painting, treating painting itself as a 'kind of skin' that could be subjected to violent acts (burning, scraping, cutting, hammering).[6] In this search for an artistic form 'which actually showed the history of its own making',[7] Brisley began to explore a paradox central to a number of his best-known performances, namely that the destruction of a work could also function as a kind of completion.

After graduating from the Royal College of Art in 1959, Brisley continued his exploration of materialism during a year-long residency at the Akademie der Bildenden Künste München. In a notable personal gesture of rupture with inherited forms of art-making, before leaving for Germany, Brisley destroyed all the artwork he had made while a student, chucking it out of the window because he 'didn't see a future'.[8] During this same year and in search of a fresh start, Brisley made contact with a number of artists travelling and working across the Munich–Zurich–Milan triangle. These included notable practitioners of concrete art as well as future members of the Groupe de recherche audio-visuel, who used activity-based art to challenge ordinary conventions of time and perception.[9]

Brisley's turn towards performance can be situated in this general expansion of the visual arts towards time-based and process art that took place during the 1950s and early 1960s.[10] But he never abandoned representational painting. As Michael Newman has observed,[11] a continuity with painting remains apparent in many of Brisley's actions. His performances have used images (created by himself or others) as well as paint, chalk and other media associated with painting. On multiple occasions, he has even used his own body to make markings, in a manner that recalls the Viennese actionists, such as Günter Brus (who covered his body with paint) or Otto Mühl (whose films made little distinction between human material such as flesh, blood, vomit, semen and other kinds of material, such as water and paper). The highly introspective performances of Brisley's late career, have reinforced this connection between performance and the visual arts. Brisley has used performance to create new paintings, photography, film and installations which have, in turn, reframed his own perception and public reception of past performances.

Brisley's training was remarkably Continental for an English artist of his generation. It was also marked by personal and collective experiences of rupture that reached beyond the realm of art, notably those occasioned by the Second World War and its aftermath. Brisley's own childhood had been marked by the war.[12] His earliest awareness of the atrocities of Nazi Germany were filtered through radio broadcast and film. For instance, as a schoolboy, shortly after the war, he was taken to see films documenting the British liberation of the camp at Bergen-Belsen, a formative experience for his own later reflections on how media registers human catastrophe. In fact, Brisley's first direct encounter with Germany had taken place during his National Service with the British army when he was posted to Langeleben, a few kilometres from the border with East Germany. Arriving in 1955 just as the Warsaw Pact was declared and the Allied occupation of Western Germany ceased, it was there that he experienced what he would later describe as the brutalising effects of senseless military discipline and the British class system.[13] During his military service, Brisley also undertook what, in retrospect, can be considered his first performance, when, to stave off the boredom of confinement, he dug a hole big enough to stand in. A kind of trench without a purpose, this hole reflected Brisley's feelings about his own role in the postwar British army.[14] A similar act was reprised in subsequent performances in which he used his body to create, mark or otherwise dig a hole.[15] It was while stationed in Germany that Brisley also met members of the Mixed Services Organisation, made up of displaced persons left behind in Western sectors of occupied Germany who chose to work for the British army rather than go home. Many years later, Brisley created his alter ego and artist persona in the image of one such person: Rosse Yael Sirb, a curator of a *Museum of Ordure*, a displaced person drawn to misplaced things.

Brisley's return to Germany as an art student in 1959 allowed him to witness, at first hand, how a defeated country came to grips with its difficult past. At this time, documentary films about the camps were broadcast in cinemas around the country. Brisley would later recall the stench of sweat that emanated from the audience, as if a physiological process of learning were taking place. The young German artists whom he met were fiercely antimilitaristic and grappled extensively with the problem of how to contextualise cultural activity after their country's political and moral defeat. This so-called

'German problem' became Brisley's own challenge when he began making his first live actions. This is evidenced not only in those performances that directly addressed the memory of atrocity but also in his conviction, increasingly pronounced in later works, that performance is an activity that lacks a frame because it is based on experiences which, like death and destruction, cannot be recuperated.

As Brisley's early experiences attest, the language of abstract art in this period remained broadly international, deeply marked by the experience of the two world wars and their aftermath. However, the declaration of the Warsaw Pact in 1955, followed by the construction of the Berlin Wall in 1961, splintered whatever remained of this shared language. Like other socially committed artists of his generation, Brisley was intensely interested in crossing this political divide. A subsequent residency in Berlin in 1974 brought him into contact with the main practitioners of performance-based art (including Joseph Beuys, Günter Brus and Marcel Broedthaers). During this same year, he travelled to Warsaw to meet the performance and theatre artist Józef Szajna, whose work he had first encountered at the Edinburgh Festival of 1972.[16] Szajna's practice of combining visual images, found objects and narrative to dramatise, among other things, his experience as a concentration camp survivor, strongly influenced the development of Brisley's own performance art. This can be seen in Brisley's pronounced attention to spaces of confinement as well as the use of his body to reconstitute the experience of catastrophic destruction and its aftermath.

But before looking east, Brisley had in fact moved west, with a prolonged stay in America, first at Florida State University in 1960–62, where he completed an MA dissertation on British constructivist art, followed by a stint as an assistant professor at Cornell, where he was put in charge of running the Architectural League programme in New York City.[17] By this time Brisley's habit of incorporating found objects, discarded furniture and other detritus into artworks had expanded to include types of open-ended installations that could be put together in several different ways. Living in New York City in the heady years of 1962–64, Brisley met many artists associated with Kaprow's happenings and witnessed several early performance works. Even so, it was only after his involuntary return to Britain in 1964, expulsed from the United States on account of an overstayed visa, that Brisley produced his first performances.

Brisley has described his return to Britain as painful, noting that the experience of 'being cut down to size' was particularly traumatic.[18] His forced departure from the highly active New York scene of the early 1960s precipitated once more the sense of having come to a stop as an artist, or at least, as an artist who makes objects. This second rupture with established ways of thinking about and making art soon coincided with a third rupture, both artistic and political. It was instigated by the sit-in of May 1968 at Hornsey Art School, where Brisley had been employed since 1965.

In a year of student disturbances at universities across the UK, Hornsey achieved notoriety for the scale and ambition of the student occupation.[19] Brisley played an important role in the seven-week-long protest movement that eventually led to the closure of the college and the dismissal of numerous staff members. In fact, it was partly on the strength of his involvement on behalf of the students at Hornsey that he was subsequently appointed student advisor at the Slade School of Fine Art, eventually becoming Professor of Media Studies, with the distinction of being the only professor directly appointed by the student body.

The conflict at Hornsey was as much educational as political. Hornsey's massive expansion in the 1960s had been accompanied by a new experimental curriculum that called for more direct links between practising artists and art education. Although the details of this complex event need not detain us here, it suffices to note that the Coldstream-Summerson report of 1962 had called for a complete restructuring of art education, incorporating a new stream called 'Visual Research' as a required part of the new curriculum. Brisley, who had been appointed as part-time lecturer for this stream, later recalled that this field had been left entirely open and was developed by students and teachers together in a 'lateral, communicative process'.[20] By 1968, 'Visual Research' had come to challenge the traditional fine art categories in the school through its explorations of film, performance, installation and other proto-conceptual art.[21] In his own statement to the college during the sit-in, given on behalf of the Student Action Committee as an anonymous 'Visual Research Lecturer', Brisley inveighed against a specialist art education that reproduced a 'mole-like blindness of the specialist to everything but his own "hole"'.[22]

In many ways, the Hornsey occupation can be seen as the culmination of a more general expansion throughout the 1960s of theories and practices of communication. By this time, terms such as 'communication', 'education' and 'democracy' had become almost interchangeable in higher education establishments across the liberal West and elsewhere.[23] I note this because the notion of art as a communicative process is fundamental to Brisley's own understanding of performance as a potentially transformative social activity, or at least an activity in which the distinction between art and social life is not always sustained. Brisley's efforts to establish an artists' union in 1971 were motivated by the same concerns as his support for a National Union of Students, namely that the arts could be integrated in a wider social reform that, as he put it, would make 'materialism a common value rather than a common currency'.[24] If Brisley's involvement with the artists' union was ultimately short lived, this was due in part to his abiding concern with finding new meanings and functions for art rather than with ameliorating the living conditions of the artist.[25] Revolution, not reform, was the goal as well as the basis for his early forays into art activism.

Significantly, this revolutionary understanding of art as a potential medium for transformative social change was closely linked to an aesthetics of both realism and incompletion. Brisley would later hypothesise that the development of performance art in Britain could be linked not just to Coldstream's educational reforms, but further back to the Euston Road School that developed around Coldstream and others in the late 1930s.[26] This British realist group stressed the importance of creating socially relevant art, even as it reacted against the avant-garde and neo-avant-garde movements prominent in other countries, notably America, where important strands of performance art had also emerged. Out of this effort to capture the social and historical conditions of lived experience came a heightened awareness of the provisional nature of all aesthetic representation. This stance was emphatically expressed by Frank Auerbach, who rarely finished a painting, preferring instead to begin again the next day. A similar aesthetics of incompletion remains central to Brisley's own artistic practice. As I will show, it too can be considered 'realist' insofar as it insistently points to a concrete referent that remains outside the frame of action and is never wholly subsumed within it. By the same token, Brisley's performances draw attention to the provisional nature of all artistic 'frames', that is to say, the way these external referents also express other histories, other contexts that, in turn, are capable of reframing any attempt at representation.

I will expand on this important point below. For now, it suffices to note that this was a context in which direct action could be either political or artistic, with little to distinguish between the two. A case in point is Brisley's associate Gustav Metzger, a prominent anti-nuclear war activist whose 1966 Destruction of Art Symposium brought together many of the foremost practitioners of the 1960s avant-garde in London to 'relate the element of destruction in Happenings and other forms of art' to 'destruction in society'.[27] Brisley's first performances took place shortly after the symposium and can be seen as the culmination of his previous attempts to create a *tabula rasa* of sorts. According to his own admission, they reflected a personal need to start again, not from the position of an artist who stands outside the world, but as someone who is resolutely located within it, especially when it comes to matters of survival.

Tabula rasa: a first analogy between live art and revolution

Brisley's first performance, *White Meal* (1966), took place during the Middle Earth festival in Covent Garden (figure 1.1). It focused on the simple act of eating. Brisley shared a three-course meal with his wife. The clothing, furniture and faces of the performers were painted white, they wore white gloves and the food they ate was white, to better draw attention to the habits of this basic, daily activity. As the performers were blind, completing the task also required communication with, and help from, those who were present. The meal ended with Brisley smoking a cigarette and accidentally setting fire to the table. Brisley would later recall that such actions were liberating because they took place without any preconception of what art could or might be. Akin to the found objects privileged by Dadaists and Surrealists, these actions were free from intellectually imposed categories, yet expressive of social context.[28] Although they took place in time, their time frame was not predetermined. Rather, duration was measured internally, by the time it took for any given act to be accomplished. Even in Brisley's early, and from a certain perspective rather rudimentary, performance pieces, duration was used to explore social conditioning. What happens to the habits and rituals of everyday life under conditions of survival, when everything is abstracted or stripped back?

Two works from 1970 directly confronted the recursive time of everyday habits and the institutional structures that are either grafted upon or embedded within them. *Celebration of Institutional Consumption*, which took place at the Brighton Festival, staged an annual dinner of an imaginary institution, with performers given a few instructions and a role to play in advance but no script.[29] At the beginning of the fourth course, a speech was given by one of the performers that began by arguing that law and order were a prerequisite for social stability, before veering into fascist references as it became increasingly incoherent. While the dinner was unfolding, a figure in a cage suspended above the dinner table was disembowelled in intervals until all its insides were hanging over the table to demonstrate the 'active destructive forces at work' (figure 1.2).[30] Brisley's aim, as expressed in his proposal, was to demonstrate the necessity of questioning 'institutional behaviour', especially when 'institutions repel pressures for change/evolution on the basis of the proven worth of their procedures, rather than the basis of principles upon which they were built'.[31]

A similar divergence between foundational principles and institutional practices was expressed in *Celebration of Due Process*, an action that took place at the Royal Court Theatre during the festival 'Come Together'. Rather than create a new work for the theatre, Brisley focused on the rituals surrounding the space itself, notably the national anthem, which at the time was played before every theatre performance. Brisley and ten other performers stood in front of the audience and played 'God Save the Queen'. The audience stood up. Once they sat back down, 'God Save the Queen' was played again. The audience stood up, confused. This was repeated several times to increasingly loud objections from the audience. The anthem was then played backwards, and the performers stood on their heads and did other things. As the ensuing disorder increased, Brisley interrogated the audience about whether they believed that God would save the queen, going through the sabre-rattling anthem line by line. While this was going on, a few performers built a cage at the top of which they fastened an office chair. At the end of the performance, Brisley climbed into the cage, sat in the chair and vomited to the anthem.

Extensively reviewed in the press, this action did much to consolidate Brisley's reputation as an *enfant terrible* of the art world.[32] In it, we can trace the elements that would characterise many of Brisley's iconic performances of the 1970s: the focus on the ritual function of everyday behaviour, the use of the artist's own body as a site of confrontation (the real vomit spewed in response to institutionalised expressions of monarchy) and the effort to converse with the audience through an almost Brechtian breaking of the framework of art. Performances such as these differed significantly from the theatrical arts. For Brisley, the long-established history of theatre as an institution meant that the public was always treated as an 'audience' of some kind, even if this was challenged in one way or another. By contrast, performance as developed in the field of visual arts invoked the more primary definition of performance which, for Brisley, referred to the action or process of accomplishing a task.[33] This understanding of performance as the fulfilment of an action foregrounds both its intentional aspect – the directing of energy to get something done – and the unintended consequences that arise whenever a task is pursued in public over a period of time.

This understanding of performance as an 'anti-performance' was made explicit in *Homage to the Commune*, an action performed in Milan in 1976 as part of an overview dedicated to British art. The action took place in the Galleria Vittorio Emmanuele II, the historical arcade at the commercial heart of Milan, where Brisley undertook to construct a wooden rose, a representation of the Commune, Milan's local government, around which he performed ritualised actions such as shredding his clothes to convey individual freedom and expression (figures 1.3 and 1.4). The rose was a public symbol, anchored in both the individual and collective understanding of the people, and the action attracted a great number of onlookers. One man who came each day on a bicycle used song to explain Brisley's action to the onlookers; another became aggressive until Brisley handed him the knife he was using, at which point the aggression stopped. In the case of both the song and the transfer of the knife one could say a direct action had taken place.[34] According to Brisley, at this point an initial concept, based on Brisley's intervention as an individual artist, had 'been overcome, was transformed by others with a collective concern, through a public process'.[35] Performances, in other words, express an inaugural force when authority is not 'governed' but shared.

As this last example makes clear, Brisley's performances were never just about the body. As Michael Newman observes, Brisley has used his body to understand how power works, in particular with respect to labour relations

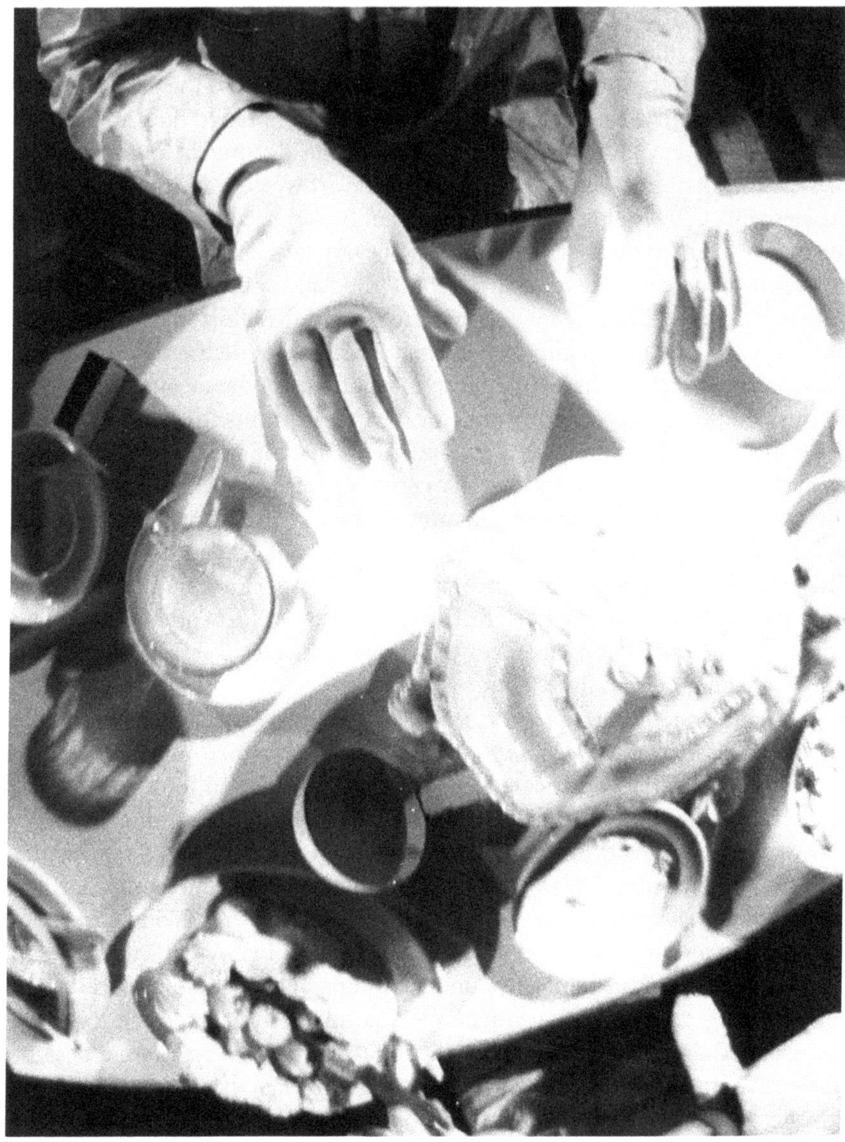

1.1   *White Meal*, Middle Earth/WHSHT Event, London, 1966

and class struggle; an endeavour that shares important affinities with feminist performance artists such as Ulrike Rosenbach or Valie Export, who also used their bodies to explore the gendered nature of social conditioning.[36] Brisley's own analogy for understanding how the body can be used to gain tactical knowledge of social systems and their strategies is the *Procrustean Bed* the

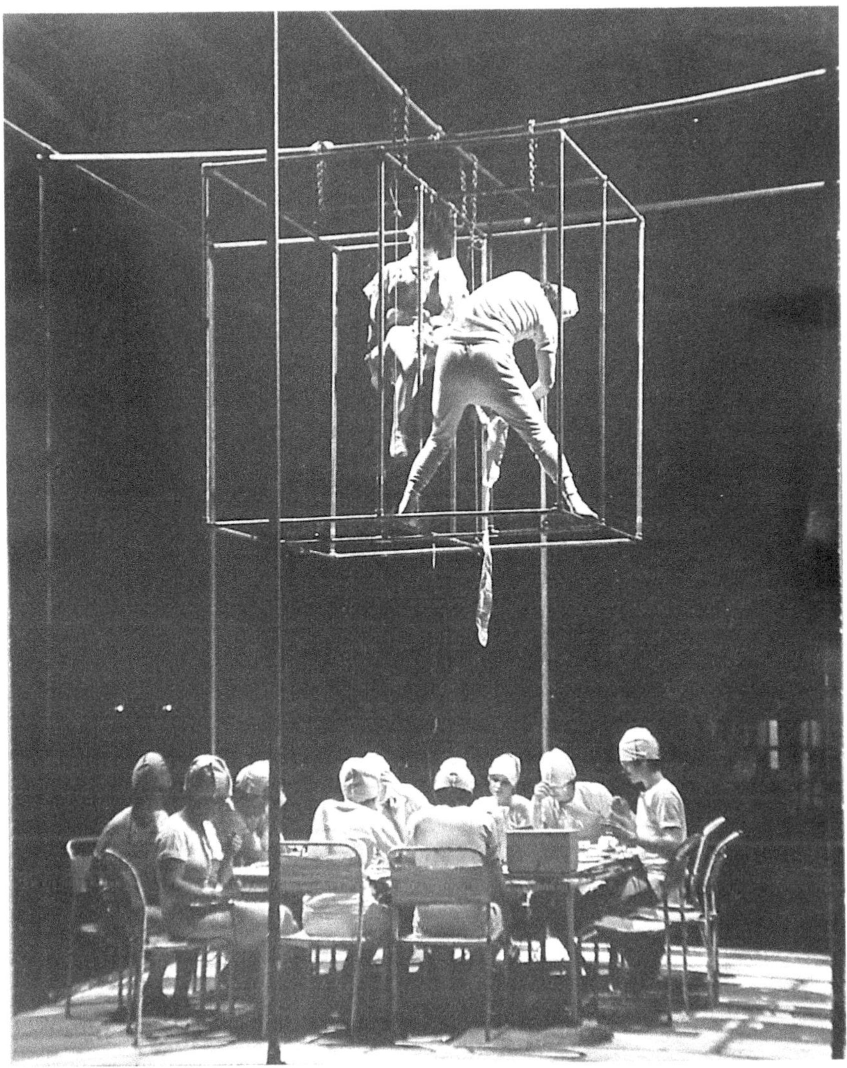

Celebration for Institutional Consumption, Brighton Festival, 1970   **1.2**

subtitle of a 1973 performance, which used the body to explore how systems enforce authority. In Greek mythology, Procrustes was the name of a robber from Attica who compelled his victims to fit the size of an iron bed, either by stretching them or cutting off their legs. All of his victims died, and he was eventually killed by Theseus in the same manner. 'Procrustean bed' has since become proverbial for cruelly forcing someone or something to fit an arbitrary length.

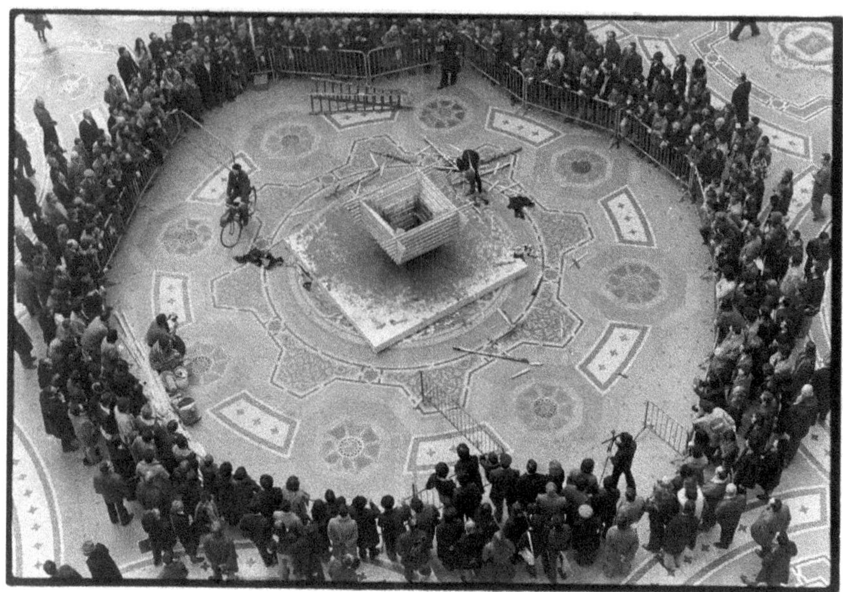

1.3   *Homage to the Commune*, Milan, 1976

This Procrustean conceit can be applied to many of Brisley's live actions, which expose how imposed parameters of *Measurement and Division* (the title of a 1977 work) wield their authority by co-opting natural or embodied processes, such as eating, sleeping, standing, breathing. In the latter performance, this thwarted human potential was expressed by Brisley's act of suspending himself upside down in an elaborate grid-like scaffolding that he built on the roof of the Hayward Gallery in London over the course of about two days. A related distinction between the body as a source of freedom and a locus of social conditioning is thematised in *12 Days* (Rottweil, 1975), a performance during which Brisley built a prison to the dimensions of his own body, in private, which he then proceeded to break out of in public, in front of viewers who included school children.[37]

In Brisley's performances, the same body is both the subject *of* an action and subject *to* an action. The same body, in other words, is used to explore the difference between a creative or *constituent power* (the ability of the body to create a cut in time, a new situation that potentially could serve as the basis for novel forms of collective behaviour) and an established or *constituting power* (the way in which all bodies are subject to existing norms and constraints, especially those engrained in habits of being and perceiving). My allusion to the terms 'constituent' and 'constituting power' is, of course, deliberate. Although the concept of a constituent power has a long historical lineage, it gained an important new meaning during the revolutionary eighteenth

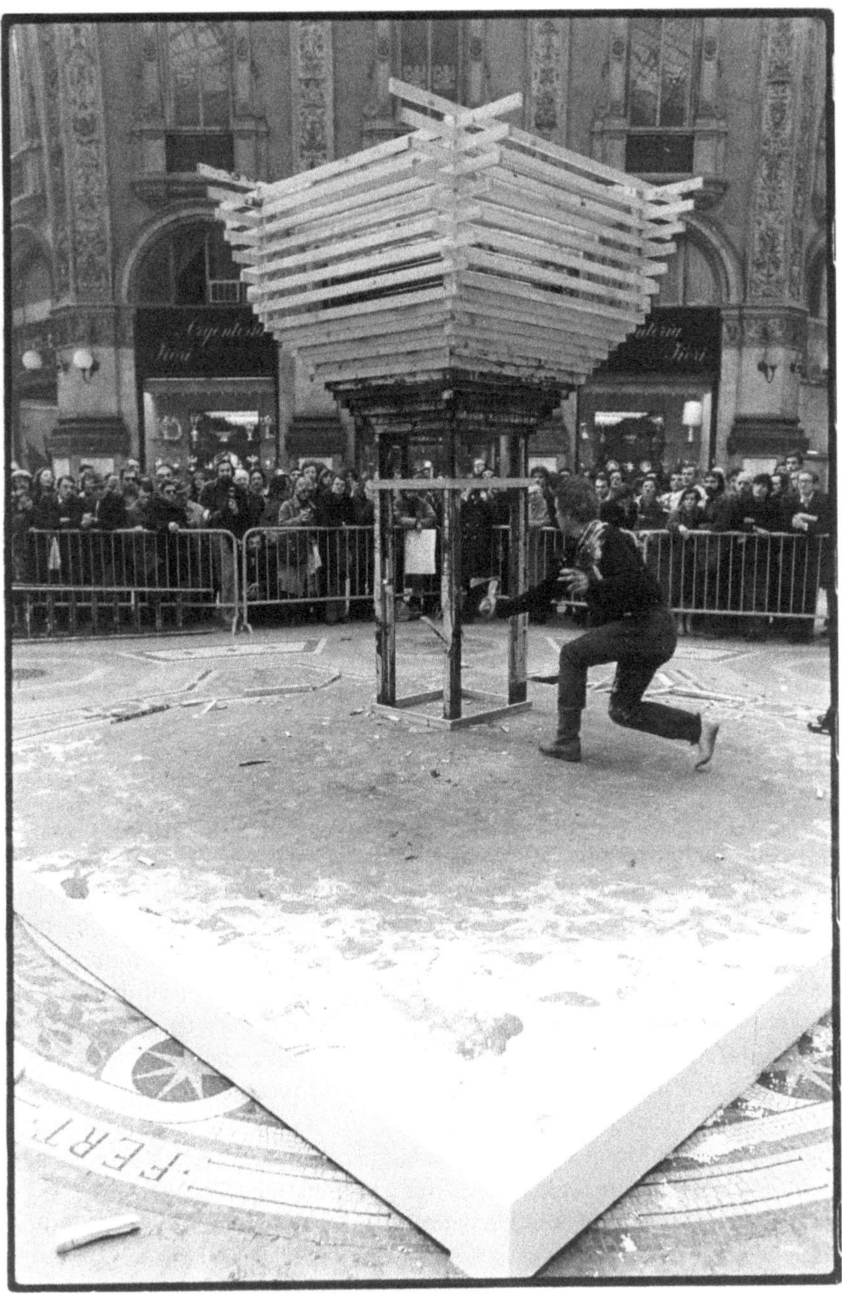

Homage to the Commune, Milan, 1976

century, when it became associated with popular sovereignty, as the work of Andreas Kalyvas has shown.[38] A constituent power belongs to the time of foundation. It expresses actions of making, doing, founding and communicating, all vital components of any action that seeks to institute a new order whose outcome and final form remain unknown. It emerges whenever people come together without knowing the outcome of their actions. A constituting power, by contrast, belongs to a lexicon of command and control and can be personified by an individual. As Kalyvas observes, the question that emerged during the Revolution and that has remained urgent ever since is 'whether popular sovereignty, that is democracy, can exist only as a form, a regime, and a constitution or, rather, must retain its informal, disobedient, eruptive and revolutionary powers'.[39]

But what, if anything, can the experience of duration itself reveal about this revolutionary situation? In the performances discussed above, Brisley has used his own body not just to create a cut in time but also to prolong this effort at rupture over a broad – and often increasingly uncomfortable – time span. As I will show, this broad time span makes possible a reflection on the types of behaviours that can emerge whenever our habits and rituals are dissolved or the normal flow of chronological time is suspended. It reveals, in other words, what can happen in the absence of form, or at least in a situation whose final form or outcome is not yet known.

Revolution as subject and duration

Brisley began his long-durational performances out of an interest in everyday tasks, including simple biological actions, such as eating and sleeping. The choice of 10, 12 or 14 days for an action was, in this sense, pragmatic. For instance, two weeks is the approximate time it takes for food to rot. In his performance *And for today … nothing*, one of three Life Situations commissioned for Gallery House in London in 1972, Brisley immersed himself in a bath of blackened water for approximately two hours a day over two weeks while a pile of offal rotted beside him (figure 1.5). The action stands out for its shock value. It is also notable for how it referenced Jacques-Louis David's famous painting *Marat à son dernier soupir* (figure 1.6). As David's title indicates, his aim was to depict Marat as he drew his last breath, killed in the bath where he spent most of his time seeking relief for a debilitating skin disease. Brisley's performance re-enacted key elements of both the title and the painting, implicitly contrasting his own barely breathing body, submerged in the bath, with the expiring breath of Marat. This juxtaposition was further contrasted with the time it took for animal flesh to decay. The layering of several, contrastive situations of life and death highlighted the tension between two opposing aspects of the human experience of duration: as continuity – the way any given identity persists over time – and as ceaseless change – the way any given form also unravels over time.

But how do we represent the threshold in which change takes place? Both David's painting and Brisley's performance allude to the moment of death: when one identity or substance changes into another. In David's painting, Marat's dying body is still recognisable as the living Marat. Change is represented in the form of an ongoing continuity with a previous identity. Contrast this with Brisley's act of lying submerged up to his nose in a bath full of water. This action required him to endure both the discomfort of cold water and the stench of rotting flesh. Brisley's action approached the limit of life and death, not by collapsing the time in which breathing and rotting take place but by holding apart for as long as possible the moment of change when life becomes death.

These attempts to re-enact elements of David's painting in real time invite a reflection on the multiple time frames that make up any given revolutionary situation. David's painting, after all, responds to this situation in several ways. First, as T. J. Clark observes, David's painting stands out for the way it avoids all reference to Marat's actual dead body.[40] This is in sharp contrast to the other objects in the painting which, as Clark notes, appear all too real. Second, the painting demarcates a new, political role for the artist. It does this not only by means of its highly conspicuous dedication but also by strongly differentiating the time of the event represented *within* the painting from the time frame in which the painting was undertaken and completed. Within the painting, Marat's death is marked by the conventional date of 13 July 1793, boldly scripted on the letter held out in Marat's dying hand. This letter was the subterfuge used by Marat's assassin, Charlotte Corday, to gain access to him. The dedication itself, however, is prominently dated Year II of the new revolutionary calendar. In other words, Marat's death is reframed as part of a new timeline, a new temporal framework instituted to mark the end of all kingship and the beginning of a new republic. David's prominent use of the Republican calendar was thus a stark warning to other would-be assassins and counterrevolutionaries that the king was dead, the past was past and there was no turning back. This reframing is even more significant because the painting was undertaken during the summer and fall of 1793, when the form of the new calendar was still being debated (it was officially backdated to 1792) and the young republic still lacked a working constitution. In this sense, David framed his work by referring to a *missing* calendar – a Year I that had been declared but was not yet in place because the conflict between the past and present was still ongoing, as Marat's own assassination made clear.

David resolved this problem of missing revolutionary beginnings – what we might call an unlocalisable Year I – by monumentalising Marat as a martyr to the Revolution, made not of decaying flesh but of some other, more durable substance, expressed through the classicising pose and the smooth marmoreal skin devoid of Marat's well-known skin disease. As Clark observes, this monumentalised body is set against a seemingly unfinished background. This background scumbling not only makes the painting appear unfinished, abstract, as if made of pure painterly matter; it also references the speed with which the painting was executed, expressing the convulsive events of the Revolution. Brisley's action, by contrast, is all about the body and what it can endure. Furthermore, by drawing attention to the passage of physical time, it foregrounds matter itself, the way form is constituted, or dissolved, through varying lengths of duration. Brisley's action foregrounds not the heroic accomplishment of revolutionary rupture, but a sense of stasis, even inexorable decay, a mood also captured by the prominent ellipses of the title *And for today … nothing*.[41] The action implies that even this heroic declaration of Republican time suppresses the finite, embodied nature of human time, the joint source of birth and decay. It suggests, in other words, that the revolutionary problem of how to replace the executed king with a new sovereign body of the people remains unresolved, so long as a transcendental political substance – whether represented by the eternal, undying body of the king or a perpetually dying Marat – trumps a *mortal*, finite, democratic substance.

Because it unfolds in real time, Brisley's action also draws attention to what remains unspoken in David's painting, namely that part of David's original intention had been to pose the very real, embalmed body of Marat in a *tableau mort*. This was supposed to resemble the painting he had done of another revolutionary martyr, Le Pelletier, which hung in the Convention, and whose funeral he had also organised. But the task proved almost immediately impossible, given the manner of the death, Marat's skin disease and the rapidly decaying body. Marat's putrefying body also disrupted the funeral cortège that David had choreographed in his capacity as the Revolution's 'official artist'. This disruption was political as well as aesthetic. As the historian Jacques Guilhaumou has shown, Marat's funeral, and subsequent efforts made by people to commemorate him, triggered an unprecedented popular participation in the political process far greater than the revolutionary government had either envisioned or intended. This was seen during the seven-hour parade of Marat's dead body throughout the streets of Paris, when the mourners – many of whom were women – improvised ritual gestures to hide the stinking body which was turning the funeral shroud green.[42] It continued afterwards, in the numerous cults that sprang up, both officially and informally, to commemorate a 'Friend of the People'. The historical details of this struggle over representation need not detain us here, except to note that the continual *presence* of the dead Marat expressed a much more ambiguous experience of a suspended time than David's painting suggests. Guilhaumou reminds us that, on the one hand, these cults to Marat were encouraged by the revolutionary administration because they shored up a government that still lacked a proper constitution; on the other hand, the prolongation of these popular – yet unsanctioned – rituals also provoked a backlash.[43] When the new constitution was finally declared, it was immediately suspended, precipitating what retrospectively became known as the Reign of Terror.

What we see in the painting, however, are not these new collective forms of behaviour but a new role for the artist, who represents the sovereign people only by highlighting their absence. David's painting privileges an individual body of a singular person. It represents a transcendent Marat that displaces both the living Marat, the 'Friend of the People', and the collective expressions that converged around the dead Marat.[44] To recall Kalyvas' terms, we can say that Marat's dead body expressed a state of exception that oscillated between an emergent constituent power (that of a people communicating its will in unprecedented and unauthorised ways) and an equally emergent, but opposing, constituting power (that of the new revolutionary government, which struggled to impose a constitution and a legal regime).

I have dwelt on this problem of revolutionary beginnings because this question of how to experience a revolutionary day one expresses a key element of Brisley's artistic practice. Even more so given that the challenge Brisley posed to David's painting can also be directed to the photographic record of his own action. The odourless black and white photographs that remain from this action today only frame a few moments out of an extended period that lasted nearly two weeks. They do not capture the action itself, much less how it activated the reviled elements of both animal waste and dead, yet unburied, flesh. Much like David's own painting occludes the *presence* of Marat's dead body, these photos neither reproduce nor record Brisley's performance but function in a different time frame, one that contains only traces of its original form.

This raises the question not only of how to 'frame' any attempt to make a break in time but also how to reframe it once the attempt is over, when images and representations circulate in the absence of the body. Again, the contrast with David's painting is revealing. Whereas David framed Marat's death as if it belonged to an already accomplished rupture with the past, Brisley's performance emphasised an *unaccomplished* rupture, in which every day for two weeks there was 'nothing'. Whereas David sought to create a permanent image that would *complete* the revolution, Brisley remodelled the traces left behind by his ordeal to make the difficult and destabilising film *Arbeit Macht Frei* (1973). Although this film was emphatically a new work, in a different medium, it too focalised on the act of drawing one's breath and reworked some of the same materials, notably Perspex, the plastic sheet and water. The film begins with a long sequence of Brisley vomiting, seated on an object that resembles a sarcophagus. It then cuts to graphic imagery of a head that repeatedly breaks and disappears from a surface, as it is submerged in black water, pressed against glass, swathed in clingfilm. The film ends with a sequence of an open mouth and a soundless scream, an almost abstract black and white image.

What, then, connects the incomplete rupture of *And for today … nothing*, with a film depicting an artist subjecting his body to vomiting and simulating an airless scream in response to a human catastrophe? The film's title refers to the slogan erected over the gates of some Nazi concentration camps. This slogan has become synonymous in the collective imagination with the Holocaust, in which six million Jews, and between 200,000 and 1,500,000 Roma, so-called politically or sexually 'deviant' prisoners and others were killed. According to Brisley, the vomiting represents his reaction to the slogan – the body rejecting what the mind cannot digest.[45] But if this phrase constitutes the title of the performance and attributes some meaning, it is also a historical reference that exists outside the frame of art. It is both a reference to events that took place *and* a linguistic fragment that circulates as part of a public culture, testifying to a collective awareness of the event even if it is not entirely representable. The performance is not 'about' the slogan, nor does the slogan 'represent' the performance; rather, the two are contingently related, each existing in their own time frame. The cruelty of *Arbeit Macht Frei* is not simulated; it is linguistically present as a set of command terms that may provoke different reactions in different people, depending on their proximity to or distance from the historical event of the camps. The performance, on the other hand, produces its own duration. Brisley really did vomit for a very long time. But the film also slows it down, distending the time it takes for this and the film's other actions to unfold, giving the viewer the opportunity, so to speak, both to stand inside the event, as it unfolds in real time, and to observe it distantly, from the outside.

Michael Newman has suggested that across Brisley's works, the '*becoming-trace* of the presentation … points in two directions: towards the memory of revolution and towards the memory of atrocity'.[46] Both revolution and catastrophe can be characterised as cataclysmic events, impossible to memorialise yet present in the traces they leave behind. Such events lack a frame yet require some sort of frame, no matter how provisional, if they are to be figured at all. We have already noted how Brisley's first experiences of Nazi atrocities were mediated through film and radio and how, while living in Germany in the 1950s, he was able to observe the physiological reactions that people had when watching documentary footage from the camps. In both these instances, a kind of radical education took place, communicating through bodily reactions what cannot be rationalised through language. In this sense, *Arbeit Macht Frei* can be seen as a riposte to Theodor Adorno's famous proclamation that after Auschwitz to write poetry is barbaric because culture itself had become barbaric.[47] Brisley's film suggests that this dichotomy between culture and 'barbarism' (a shifting term that denotes whatever lies outside a given value system) may be a false one. If Auschwitz circulates as a name or even a slogan that produces physiological reactions, then it has already been internalised as part of the public imagination. Anything part of the public imagination is, *ipso facto*, available for art.

In a rather astonishing observation, Brisley has noted that in all the reviews and commentaries on this work, 'hardly anyone takes notice of the title' and that he wishes 'somebody will write about *Arbeit Macht Frei* in terms of what it is'.[48] Yet the use of titles that repeat or otherwise reference linguistic slogans or historical fragments that circulate publicly recurs throughout Brisley's practice. They function both as internal references within a work *and* as frames that demarcate the work from what lies outside it.

This double-sided function of the title as both inside and outside the work is evident in *ZL656395C*, another Life Situation that Brisley undertook for Gallery House in 1972 (figure 1.7). In addition to serving as a title, *ZL656395C* referred to Brisley's actual social security number, which he changed by deed poll to be his proper name for the seventeen days he was resident at Gallery House. The challenge was to occupy a closed room, formerly an office, for the duration of the action and to do as little as possible. The letterbox in the wall at standing height served as a slot through which the artist was seen. Brisley spent most of his time in a wheelchair. Immobile, depersonalised, with even his hands and face painted grey, Brisley's body was both the subject of the action and subject to the gaze of others that he himself could not see.[49] If Brisley's position in this room resembled that of a prisoner in a cell, what was it that the viewer saw? A prisoner? An artist? A 'general human being' classified by a national insurance number or even, as Michael Newman suggests, 'prisoners of Auschwitz ... reduced to the lowest ebb, to nothing but survival close to the end'?[50]

As Brisley has subsequently observed, the very elongation of a work, frequently taking the artist to the point of exhaustion, is a way of approaching the 'edge' when 'one changes psychologically' to 'find a connection with what is not human'.[51] It is important in this regard that the ordeal of *ZL656395C* really took place. Brisley really did change his actual name by deed poll and he really did occupy the room for seventeen days, trying to be as passive as possible. Through these actions an exceptional situation became a kind of self-imposed rule or even norm of behaviour, at least for the duration of the action. This is what it means to create a cut in time, to lift one sequence of events over and against engrained habits and perceptions. Moreover, by adopting what Brisley calls a 'broad frame of a period of time' these long durational works allow the perception of any given action to 'shift and change'.[52] Since the outcome of any declared action is impossible to choreograph over such a length of time, this frees it from any notion of a purpose or goal. It also exposes the artist to maximum risk – whether that of failure, or of damage to the artist's body or health during extreme feats of endurance.

Here, the analogy between performance and revolution becomes most apparent. For revolutions too are events that grow in retrospect, all the more so when the failure to achieve an intended liberation provokes a reflection that deepens and widens the significance of the act itself. This prompts the question of the meaning of failure, whether in a revolutionary situation or indeed in any action that aims to cross the boundary separating the imagination from life. For instance, *ZL656395C* was stopped fifty-five minutes before its allotted time with the artist declaring the attempt a failure. But a failure of what? What does it mean to fail at a self-imposed task? Such pre-emptive declarations of failure feature in many of Brisley's works. He has described them as Brechtian attempts to break the frame of an action in order to encourage those present to consider the 'inadequacy of the terms success or failure in art activity'.[53]

By blocking the sense of an ending, Brisley's declarations of failure force us to recognise just how much we identify the 'meaning' or 'subject matter' of a work of art with the idea of completion. Whenever a work is presented as complete or a performance is perceived to have taken place in a fulfilled time, there is a tendency to identify the work's form with its content. By contrast, Brisley's declarations of failure enable a sustained focus on the present, the way in which any given present is open to future outcomes, other than the ones that obtained in actuality. As paradoxical as it may sound, both the declaration of the artist's commitment to transformational change and his acknowledged failure to achieve it serve to move the focus away from the artist and his intention. Instead of focusing on a pre-existing subject (for example, the artist himself as a subject to whom the effects of performance can be attributed), we are encouraged to think forwards toward a *future* subject, the one created by virtue of participation in the event. It is in this sense, then, that Brisley identifies his durational works 'like an entry into day one of the revolutionary period, at least by implication'.[54]

The remainder of the chapter links this idea of a *revolutionary day one* to the ten-day week of the revolutionary calendar, the durational frame Brisley has used for numerous performances over a period of nearly fifty years. This calendar runs like a 'red thread' connecting the ensemble of Brisley's performances to the themes of republicanism, atheism and equality. It is also key to understanding how a broad time frame can be analogous to a revolution, at least insofar as it transforms ordinary actions and tasks into states of exception, which may or may not be revolutionary in themselves. At the same time, the French revolutionary calendar, as I have already suggested, encapsulates a paradox endemic to all actions that seek to effectuate radical social and political change, namely that it is a projected time frame for a revolutionary Year I that

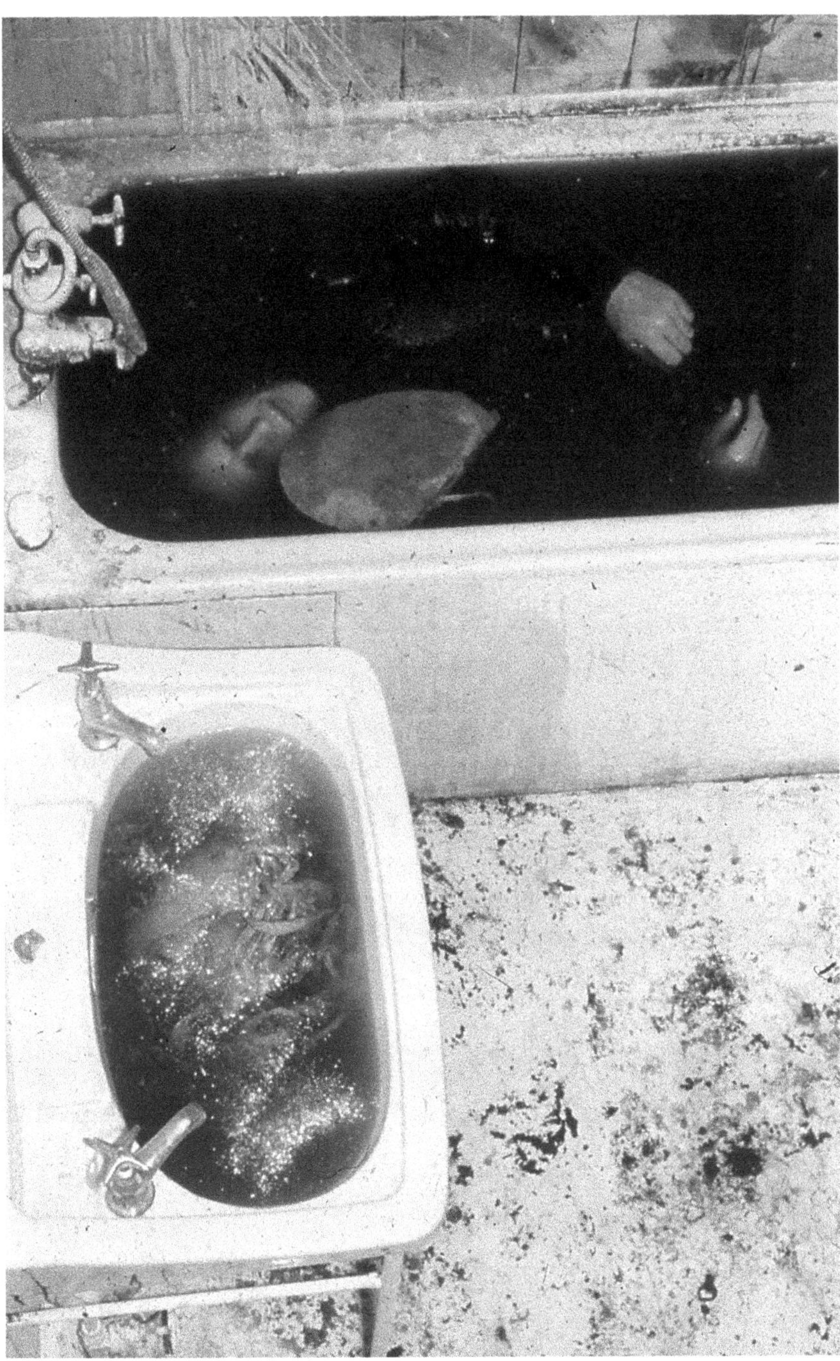

And for today … nothing, Gallery House, London, 1972   **1.5**

was never successfully implemented, partly because foundational events are usually consecrated many years after the fact, when an entire public has come to see the significance of the event.[55] Declarable, performable but radically undatable, Year I is made present by its absence from all established timelines and chronologies.[56] Like all performances, it is a unique first time that appears as such only retrospectively, as a repetition or trace of a missing event.

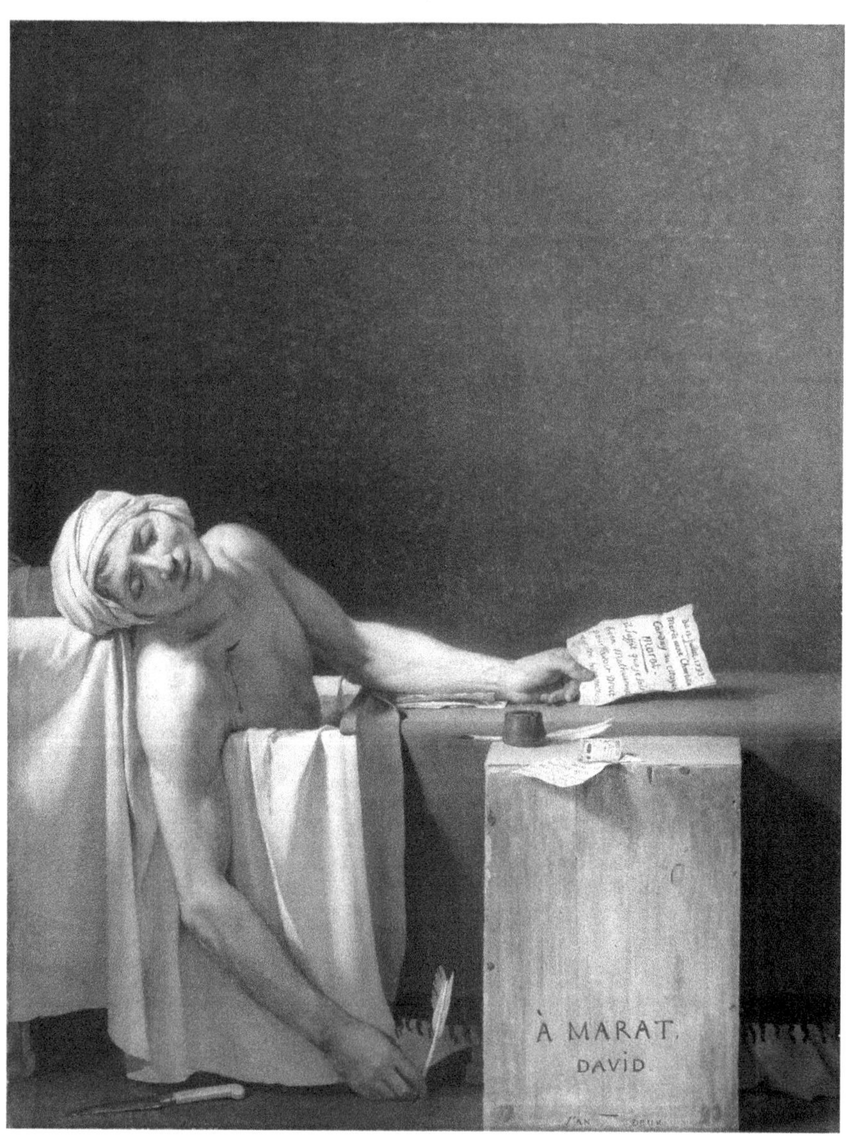

1.6 Jacques-Louis David, *Marat à son dernier soupir*, 1793

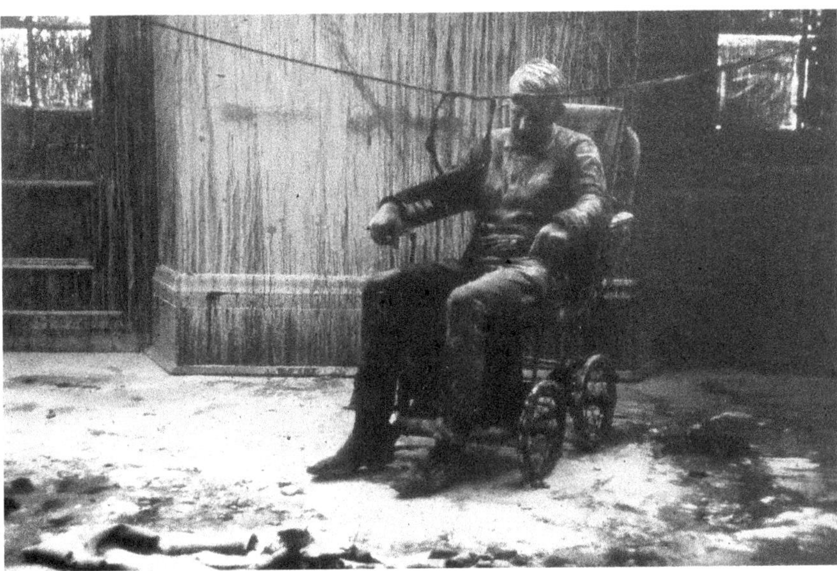

ZL656395C, Gallery House, London, 1972   **1.7**

Ten days *or* the missing frame

In any calendar, authority is wielded by appropriating natural referents (the seasons, the sun, the moon) in the service of non-natural or socially constructed units of time. Members of a given social group partake in rituals that coalesce around certain peaks of time, traditionally marked by the turning of the seasons and the different phases of the agricultural year. But days of work and days of rest are never equally distributed, nor given to everyone. The same rituals that synchronise and provide a shared experience of time also reinforce social divisions. This is why, throughout human history, unsanctioned civic or ritual calendars have been used to defy, repel or otherwise subvert the vertical hierarchies that establish themselves in time's image. With the advent of the Industrial Revolution, with its mechanised, standardised units of time, this long history of resistance through calendar time has mostly been forgotten.

Brisley's long-durational performances revive this history of resistance by self-consciously referencing the ten-day week of a defunct French Republican calendar. This short-lived calendar actively sought to level social hierarchies by making time equal for everyone, but, due to its failure, ended up as a 'missing frame', projecting a timeline for a permanent revolution that never was. On the one hand, as we have already seen with David's painting of Marat, this calendar expresses a high point of revolutionary culture, a moment of *élan* in which revolutionaries tried to create a new future for the past. The Republican calendar, after all, did not just attempt to begin history anew; it also altered every aspect of people's relationship to time – religious, social and political. Months were renamed after the seasons and the seven-day Judeo-Christian week was replaced by a new ten-day week called the *décade*. Gone was the memory of the Sabbath, when God himself took a rest. Instead, human time and its agents became the material through which a break with the religious and political structures of the past was to be accomplished. On the other hand, especially when considered in retrospect, the revolutionary calendar stands for everything that fails when a revolution oversteps the mark. Referencing it is thus a way of recalling both the revolutionary intention to make a transformative change and the failure to achieve this ambition. In this sense, Brisley's repeated use of the ten-day week reinforces an analogy with revolution at the same time as it disrupts it, prompting a closer look at the ambiguous legacy of any attempt to make a cut in time.

In *10 Days* (Berlin, 1973), Brisley spent the Christmas period from 21 to 31 December sitting at a long table. Three meals a day were served for ten days, but Brisley ate nothing, either serving the untouched meals to passers-by or leaving them uneaten (figure 1.8). Every day the leftovers piled up, rotting. And every day a new seating was placed, as if for a banquet. On 31 December, Brisley took off his clothes and crawled through the rotting food, as if to mark the ritual purging associated with the dying of the old year and the birth of the new. The ten days of fasting in the presence of abundant food thus opposed one sanctioned state of exception (the conspicuous consumption of the Christmas season that was especially marked in West Berlin in the 1970s) with a state of exception that was voluntarily assumed.

Throughout the 10 Days, there was no reference to the 12 Days of Christmas. Instead, the self-imposed task of fasting produced its own division of time, a closed, alternate world regulated solely by the task at hand. Demarcating a new boundary between inside and out, the action presented itself as a kind of negative version of the immemorial link between feasting and the marking of time. In its regressive aspect, Brisley's action was also confrontational. The food left to rot stood as a stark remainder, a material leftover that was not taken up by the conspicuous consumption that symbolised the Christmas period. It resembled very much what Georges Bataille calls the *informe*, a formlessness that often appears as a kind of material excess that displaces or 'declassifies' all forms even as it conditions them.[57]

Although one could say that the action terminated on New Year's Eve, its concept did not stop there. When Brisley visited a doctor to complain about the pains that had resulted from this ordeal, which had taken place in an unheated room, the doctor recalled similar symptoms in his own patients who were once hunger-artists, displaying their craft (starvation) in circuses and travelling fairs in Germany during the interwar years.[58] This ordeal was famously captured in Kafka's eponymous story about the hunger-artist who, in defiance of the new values that were making him obsolete, starves himself to death to prove his worth. Brisley, by his own admission, did not know of this story beforehand. The uncanny parallels between his performance and those of the hunger-artists emerged only retrospectively, as the doctor's memories, and Kafka's story, added another lens through which to view the performance.

10 Days is one of the few performances that Brisley has re-enacted. When it was performed at the Acme Gallery in London in 1978, Brisley's implied rejection of the sanctioned display of excess during the West Berlin Christmas season was redirected towards the upstairs/downstairs divisions of the British class system. As the Acme Gallery occupied three floors, on the top floor three meals a day were prepared and cooked by Manfred Blob who also acted as a waiter. On the middle floor, Brisley was seated at the end of a long table as each day the meal would be refused and either offered to someone else, if they were present, or left uneaten on the table (figure 1.9). On the ground floor, after each meal, a place was set for a banquet. At the end of ten days, there were thirty places and the last day ended with a meal celebration. Whereas the Berlin *10 Days* had been sparsely attended, the London *10 Days* was widely publicised. Many visitors came to the gallery and all lunches and dinners were eaten.[59] Brisley recalled waiters on annual leave arriving from other restaurants in London. On Christmas Eve, homeless people had begun to show up. On Boxing Day some people even called up to see if they could make a 'reservation'.

Compared to the Berlin *10 Days*, the Acme action provoked more interaction between people from different walks of life, including professionals from the food trade. It also revealed a different side to the festive calendar – as a time of suspension and leisure in which the conventions associated with ritual behaviours could be shifted. Waiters were served, homeless people ate and discussions ensued around the difficulty of eating or not eating while being watched or watching others eat. But whereas the Berlin event ended in a festive atmosphere, in London the banquet had a different effect. According to Brisley, the 'slow unfolding formality of the ritual bore like a burden to emphasise the deadliness of the class system in Britain'.[60] Additionally, as this time Brisley had sought medical advice about how to fast appropriately, he could observe the subtle variations by which his fasting (now medically controlled) body became more vital and healthy as the days went by. This was in sharp contrast to many of the participants, who suffered from hangovers and the usual side-effects of overconsumption during the festive season. One could even say that the artist's body had become a carnivalesque body of sorts. It recalled those etchings, in the folkloric tradition, that depict the old year as an aged, grotesquely starving body and the new year as a fat, glossy body, harbinger of the material abundance to come.

Pitting ten days of fasting against the festive, social calendar, both these actions created states of exception that made visible the normally tacit rules of social behaviour. In both cases, too, the 'hunger-artist' appeared as a kind of Diogenes figure, someone who used concrete actions to explore the limits of civilised behaviour, where nature and convention begin to diverge.[61] Diogenes was the ancient cynic known for rejecting all social and material conventions, allegedly choosing to live in a barrel with nothing but a staff, cloak and lamp. He became famous for ostentatiously performing his rejection of society in public, through such basic actions as urinating or masturbating or talking back to authorities. This includes his possibly apocryphal rejoinder to Alexander the Great to move away and stop blocking the sun. Peter Sloterdijk observes that if Diogenes later became associated with such Enlightenment figures as Rousseau or Diderot, it is because of the way he exercised his freedom of speech and action *in public* and not away from society, as generations of sages and philosophers had done before.[62] Detaching himself from society, while remaining firmly in the centre of it, he used concrete actions to shine a light on the limits of reason itself.

This notion of performance as a public intervention through concrete action was made explicit in *Bourgeois Manners: Brute Force and Bloody Ignorance* (London, 1988). Brisley worked for ten days using waste products dug up from a private garden in London, sheeps' skulls from a local butcher, as well as air, water and fire. The task was to underscore the wastage of resources, natural and human, within a class system consolidated by small property-owners. Some of the elemental forces, like fire, the artist could barely control, placing the performance 'on the edge of legality' (the performance was commissioned for the festival Edge 88, which asked artists to produce works 'on the edge'). These elements were contrasted with more discreet sources of structural violence, including those exerted on performance art when appropriated by a higher or elite culture. On the last day the space was 'absolutely packed out' and Brisley became angry at the talking.[63] Confronting the public, he told them 'they were only prepared to engage in a nice Saturday afternoon's entertainment'.[64] He then moved to an adjacent room for the remainder of the allotted time.

The implication was that the artist had patently failed to take the public over the edge in his various activities with elemental forces over the course of the ten days. Or perhaps this was something only individuals could do for themselves. Whatever the interpretation, the reference to the ten-day week of a failed revolutionary calendar made clear that the performance had attempted to oppose a bourgeois calendar in which all actions, no matter how 'edgy', fell 'in line with other activities which have been packaged into commodity form, eg. holidays'.[65] Brisley's failure implied that, so long as the overall context in which art activity was experienced remained untouched, it was not possible for art to cross the boundary into life. In other words, no matter how long Brisley manipulated the full attributes of an elemental matter that belonged to everyone – 'fire, smoke, water and material and the changing qualities of natural light' – the outcome was a reversion to the status quo.[66]

Brisley's self-assessment suggests that even explosive, uncontrollable and potentially destructive forces, what we might call the power of art or metamorphosis at its most primordial, can be repackaged as just one event among others on a cultural calendar. This ultimately reversible time of performance, in which risky acts are co-opted by an 'elastic bourgeois ideology',[67] has also been the subject of a number of introspective works of Brisley's late career. *Drawn* (London, 2016) was a four-day performance that reflected on the multiple connotations of the term: as an art activity, the act of following a path, the stretching of an action over a period of time (figure 1.10). 'Drawn' also suggested Procrustean notions of being stretched or fitted to an arbitrary standard, whether in space or by mechanised units of time, and recalled Brisley's earlier performances on similar themes. For six hours each day, Brisley undertook actions that explored all of these meanings. On several occasions throughout this action, which I happened to witness, clingfilm was stretched across the length and width of a very long room, creating intricate patterns of gossamer ribbons that reflected the surrounding light. The material reached its most taut and formalised expression at the maximal point of tension. This was the point when an inert plastic surface appeared as if it had changed state, becoming almost liquid with light. It was also the point when resistance failed and the stretched clingfilm sprang back again to its starting point, emphasising the short, almost imperceptible, interval that separates a creative power of resistance from a reactive force that snaps, breaks or tears through an existing form or organisation of space. This action, like several others in the performance, made visible the boundary between what is drawn and drawn-out in the artistic sense (forms that are always incomplete and ongoing) and what is drawn and stretched in the Procrustean sense, fitted to an arbitrary length to the point of breaking down.

Next Door (the missing subject) (2010) is another ten-day work that foregrounds a similar time of suspension. The performance took place immediately after the UK elections in 2010, which had resulted in a hung parliament after over a decade of Labour government. Over the same period, Brisley occupied a bankrupt shop adjacent to the Peer gallery in London, whose premises the gallery had recently acquired. There he assumed the persona of his alter ego, R.Y. Sirb, the curator of an imaginary *Museum of Ordure*, and spent ten days – the equivalent of one week on the French Revolutionary calendar – rearranging the detritus left behind by the previous failed businesses that had occupied the council-owned property, as onlookers observed either from the street window or via a hole that had been cut in the gallery wall (figure 1.11). Alongside the rubbish, he placed his own paintings of the Queen and Prince Charles (entitled *Monarch at Bay* and *Seeing Red*, respectively). Inspired by media photos, these artistic misappropriations of the images of monarchy alluded to the discussions about electoral form that were taking place at the time but excluded all mention of the British monarchy. Propped up alongside the detritus, the royals were made to witness, as it were, all that lay outside the frame of discussion. This included just not their own role in the electoral system, but also the entropic trail of capitalism, indicated by the detritus of failed businesses that Brisley manipulated into ever more precarious configurations until it became almost impossible to move without the whole structure tumbling down.

In this work, the ten-day revolutionary calendar was explicitly set against a constituting power, in this case quite literally Britain's suspended democracy, which, in this period of hung parliament, was held together by the remnants of outmoded monarchy that, according to Brisley, obstructed any real possibility of political change. The significance of Britain's political stasis was further elaborated in a diary, titled *Next Door (the missing text)*, in which Brisley, in his persona as a curator of ordure, expressed his own understanding of the various actions that took place over the course of the performance.[68] The idea of 'stasis' is expressed repeatedly in the diary, either directly, through references to a political 'stalemate', or indirectly, through colloquial expressions (such as the 'elephant in the room'). As the diary explains, 'the missing text (subject) is in effect a number of subjects': it refers to the 'fact that there is a non-democratic stratum at the apogee of society' that contributes 'to the rumbling dissatisfaction with what parliament stands for and who it serves'; but it also refers to the mute heap', 'unstable heap', 'potentially dangerous, even lethal' heap. Commenting on Brisley's performance, Nasser Mufti suggests that 'all these missing subjects', 'ultimately point to a situation of "stasis"'.[69] Stasis is an interesting choice of terms, for, as the classicist Nicole Loraux has observed, it was synonymous with the ancient Greek term for civil war.[70] Stasis connotes a stopping of time that arises whenever there is an uprising, rebellion, or two opposing sides stand up against each other. Such a situation is characterised by simultaneous 'agitation and motionlessness', when a structure may be weakened by internal contradictions but still manages to impede change.[71]

This reference to a state of arrested development is reinforced by the three revolutionary paintings also referenced in Sirb's diary that provide yet another frame for understanding the action. These are Delacroix's *Liberty Leading the People* (1830), Géricault's *Raft of the Medusa* (1819) and Caspar David Friedrich's *Eismeer* or *Arctic Shipwreck* (1824). Each painting reflects a commitment to a revolution of some kind. Each also depicts a scene of destruction and, in the case of Géricault and Friedrich, quite literally a catastrophe. And each painting captures various states of arrested movement by adopting a foreshortened perspective in which the movement appears to spill over the frame, preventing the viewer from obtaining sufficient distance to the action.

After the ten-day action in the shop came to an end, Brisley continued to work with the traces left behind by the event, making a film and a triptych of paintings based on photographs taken by his frequent collaborator Maya Balcioglu at various points of the action. Titled *The Missing Text, Interregnum*, each of Brisley's large canvases depicts the heap as a kind of arrested movement. This heap can be set in motion at any time, whether through a gesture of freedom, like in Delacroix's painting, or as a release from an unimaginable catastrophe, like in Géricault's painting.

But it is Caspar David Friedrich's *Arctic Shipwreck* (1824), also known for many years under the evocative title *Wreck of Hope*, that is the pivotal reference, both for the live performance and for the triptych of paintings created in retrospect (figure 1.12). In Friedrich's painting, the ice floes themselves are the main focal point, jutting diagonally and horizontally as if still capable of creating new scenes of destruction. The actual shipwreck is barely visible, captured as if in a frozen or permanent state of the aftermath. No victims are visible, much less survivors or witnesses of any kind. Like with many of his landscapes, Friedrich's painting was a composite image, constructed in his studio and based in part on ice floating in the river Elbe. It captures a catastrophe without witnesses that nevertheless appears as if filtered by memory and historical distance. Hans-Christian Oeser has observed that this painting communicated Friedrich's own wrecked hopes for a republican, democratic future for Germany. Just as the ship is frozen in ice, Friedrich perceived Germany's future as similarly frozen in the aftermath of the Congress of Vienna, which reimposed the monarchical order across Europe.[72] Oeser suggests that if Friedrich was rediscovered over the course of the 1970s, it was partly thanks to artists and writers associated with the Left, especially in Germany. These artists and writers drew parallels between Friedrich's desolate landscapes and their own feelings of stagnation after the political failures of the 1960s, which they also depicted through recurring images of ice and glacial freezing.

Friedrich's iconic painting, then, provides yet another context for considering Brisley's own triptych of paintings, also painted in the artist's studio after the event. Brisley's 'frozen' images of political stagnation suggest the wreckage of capitalism is too tumultuous for any individual to witness; that it too needs to be filtered by distance before it is graspable as an image. Intriguingly, the third painting in the series offers a glimpse through a window to a world outside the shop. One could describe this as Brisley's attempt to gesture towards an opening, if not quite the moment of hope captured so evocatively by Delacroix and Géricault. But, unlike the great

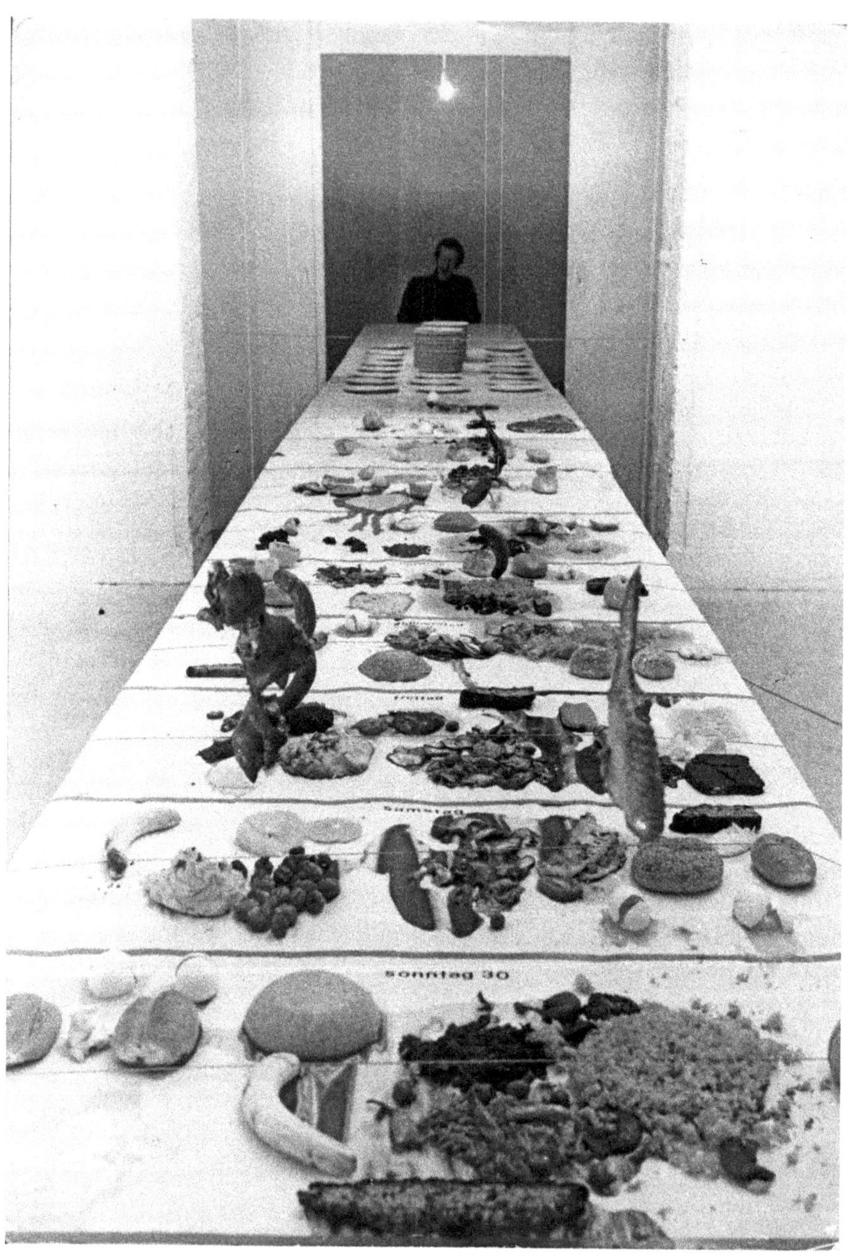

1.8   *10 Days,* Editions Paramedia, Berlin, 1973

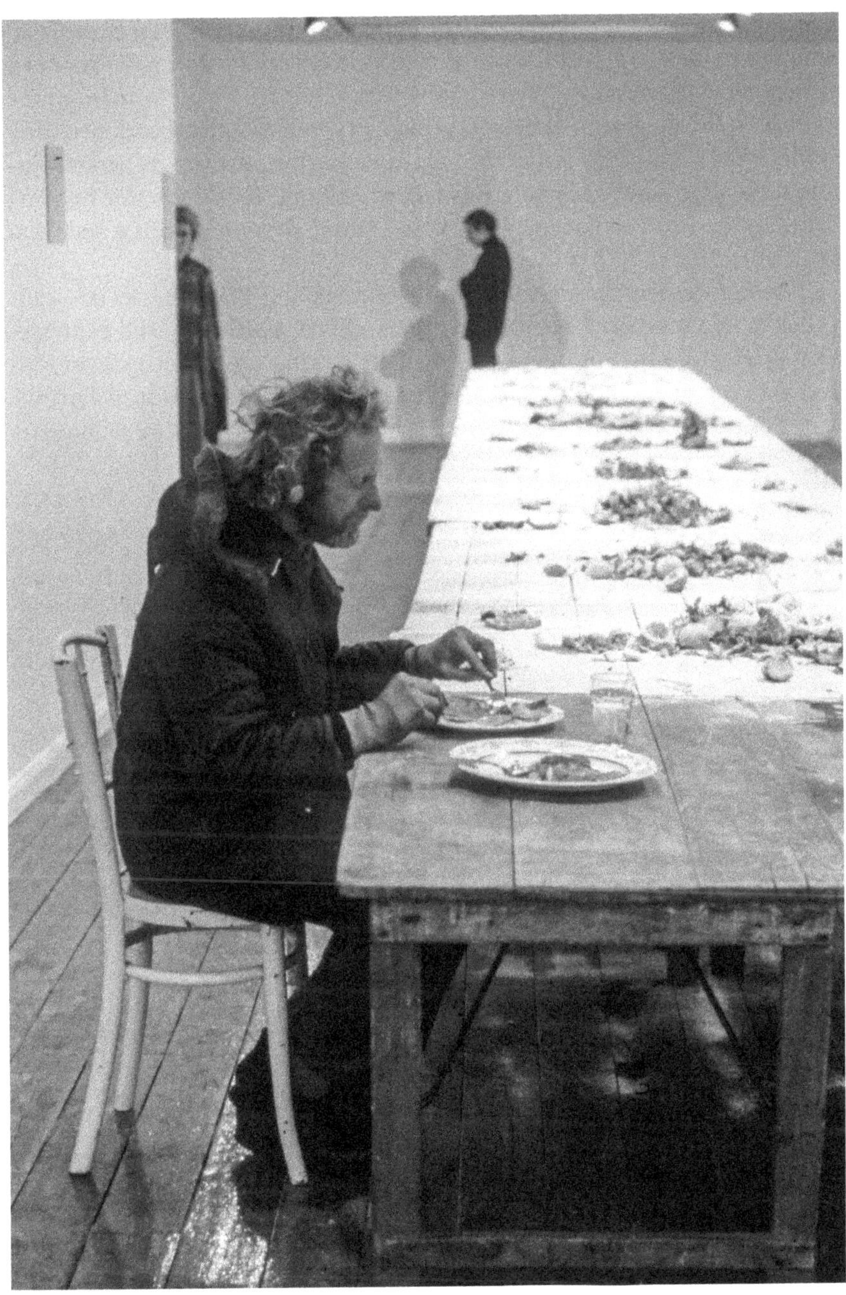

10 Days, Acme Gallery, London, 1978

1.9

Romantic artists of the revolutionary nineteenth century – who rearranged reality to fit their compositions – the objects in Brisley's paintings appear just as they were captured by photographs taken during the performance. The window is not allegorical. It depicts the actual window of the abandoned shop in which the action took place. Through it, we see the car that was parked outside at the time when the photo was taken. Tellingly, for Brisley, the opening is also the point of contact between what is framed by the painting and what exists outside it.

Taken together, the performance, paintings and diary entries are thus linked to two images of destruction. The first is revolutionary and expresses what Brisley calls the entropic forces that infringe the 'unspoken codes of conduct between rulers and subjects'[73] assimilable to the aforementioned dynamic of action and reaction. The second is catastrophic. Unlike revolutionary

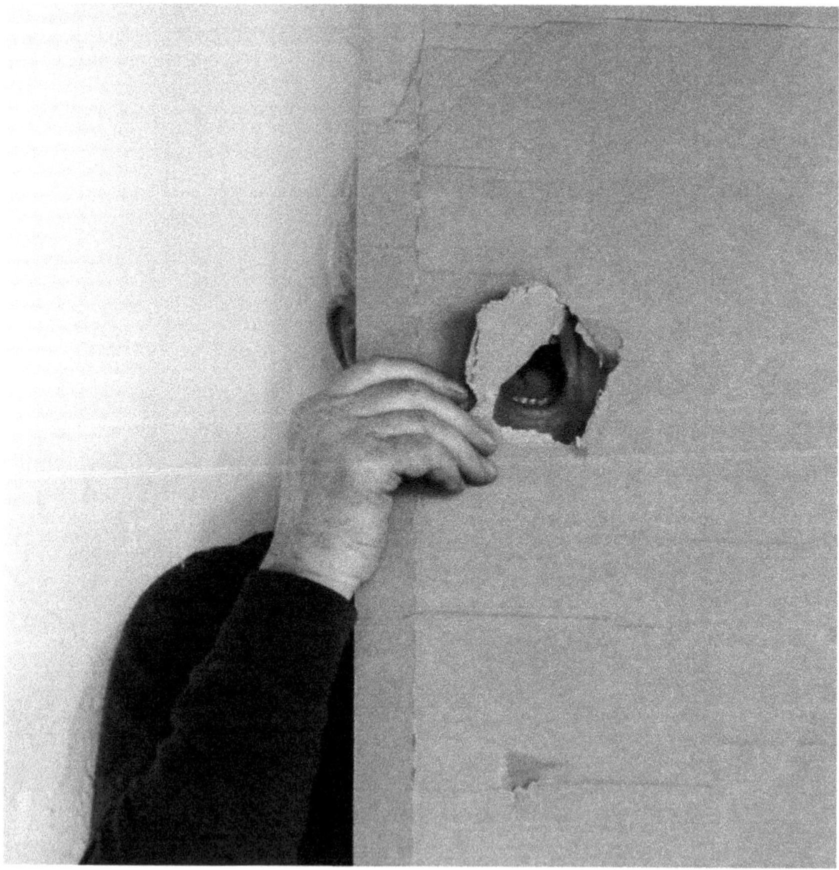

1.10   *Drawn*, The David Roberts Art Foundation, London, 2016

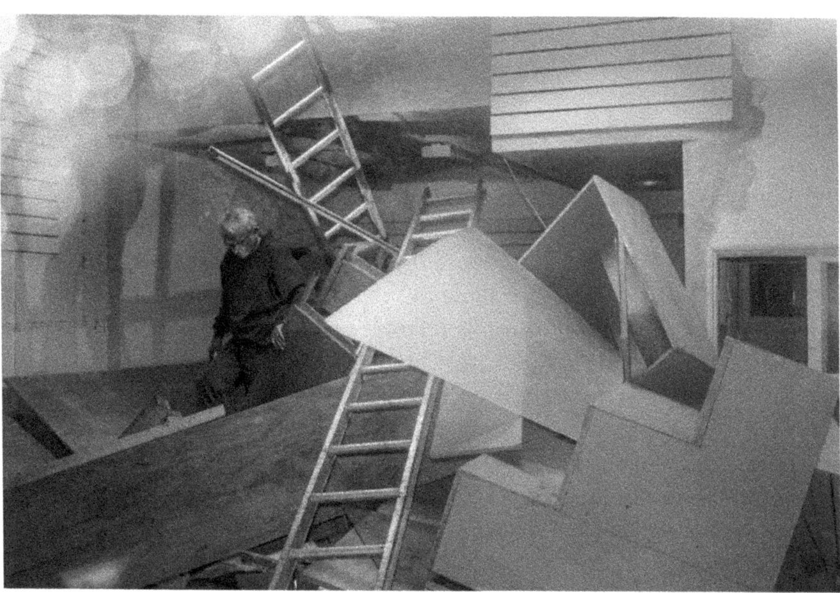

Next Door (the missing subject), Peer, London, 2010 **1.11**

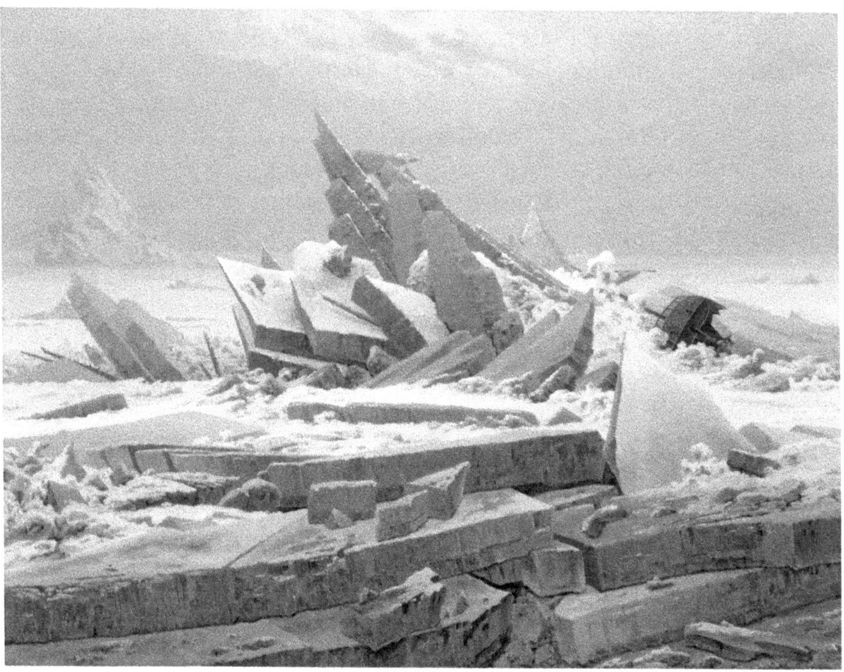

Caspar David Friedrich, *Das Eismeer*, 1824 **1.12**

crises, which contain a sense of direction – or at least the feeling that power can be reversed – catastrophes are directionless. They spill out in ways that no one can control and imply different strategies of survival. These two related, but very different, experiences of destruction are the subject of *Before the Mast* (2013), a ten-day work that makes multiple, explicit references to the revolutionary calendar.

As this was a performance that I happened to witness and to which I contributed some objects and ideas that reinforced the overall revolutionary 'frame', I would like to conclude by considering in more detail how this performance elaborates the various references to revolutionary time that we have been tracking throughout this chapter. Along the way I also reflect on my own role in 'completing this action', whether as a member of the viewing public or as a collaborator who engaged in a series of conversations with the artist that took place before and after the event. Can performance be used forensically to reveal critical insight into how a revolutionary situation may have been experienced in its own historical present, even if only by analogy and through abstraction?

Before the Mast

This performance unfolded over one revolutionary hour (approximately two and a half hours) for one revolutionary week. It began at 14:00 hours on 21 November (the month of Frimaire on the Republican calendar) and started half an hour later each day. It took place in an eighteenth-century Georgian town house on John Street, near Gray's Inn, in London, in a room that was being stripped down by the gallery owner. Before entering the room, visitors were greeted by a reprinted poster from Year II which celebrated the Festival of Reason in the Commune of Ris, just outside Paris, whose inhabitants had replaced their patron saint with Brutus. According to the poster, the festival was to culminate in a bonfire, destroying all the symbols associated with the religious and feudal past. In addition, thus, to the revolutionary calendar which scheduled the performance, the public was also confronted with a second frame: a poster announcing a popular, carnivalesque celebration of Year II, which pointed outside the frame of the action, to a festive time of the street that occurred in a different country, over two hundred years ago. Contrasting this 'revolution from below', the performance took place in a dedicated gallery space, reminiscent of an eighteenth-century salon. All aspects of this space became part of the action: the newspapers stripped from the walls were crumpled and torn, the dado climbed, the fireplace scribbled upon. Additional objects used by the artist included several chairs, a trestle table, a rubbish bin, string, a measuring stick and a mirror, which was first propped up on the fireplace and later became an active component of the action.

The public viewed the performance via a gap between out-swinging double doors which led into the room and were held open by a taut string. Only a handful of people could fit at any given time, as if to acknowledge that in any long-durational work people moved in and out at arbitrary junctions. We became aware that our viewpoint too resulted from occupying a position in space. The overall effect was that of multiple frames and several perspectives. Combined with the features of this elegant, geometrical eighteenth-century reception room, the result was almost Rococo. Our reliance on the mirror to see aspects of the room that remained outside of our line of vision drew attention to the embedded or 'framed' nature of all perception. As in the Rococo manner, the performance foregrounded the changing situations of both the viewer and the viewed, and the variable intensity that this interaction assumed over time.

The artist himself was inconspicuously dressed. At times, he wore a sweatshirt with Commoner written on it. On some occasions, this became an ominous prop when he covered his head and made gagging noises. Other times, he wore whitewashed glasses and made choking and wheezing sounds, sometimes with the mirror held to his throat as if it were a decapitation device or guillotine. At all times, however, he wore a distinctive prosthetic nose (figure 1.13). Brisley notes that it was mostly worn to establish 'distance from his own body' – to emphasise the difference between having a body and being a body, so to speak. The exaggerated nose also provided a focal point, alternatively communicating a comic or melancholy mood, much like the nose of a clown. In fact, there were several prosthetic noses which, at one point were perched, almost like small birds on a telephone wire, on the string dividing the audience from the performance space.

At least one of these noses was modelled on the rather prominent proboscis of the French revolutionary militant Sylvain Maréchal, who first devised the idea for a revolutionary calendar in 1788, a year before the transformative events of the Revolution took place. Maréchal was also notorious for being an outspoken regicide, atheist and one of the first anarchists. He subsequently participated in the Conspiracy of the Equals with Babeuf, the first revolution against the revolutionary state, whose aims were expressed in his 1796 *Manifesto of the Equals*, which called for the conjoined abolition of private property and the destruction of all the arts to achieve a 'real equality'.[74]

The revolutionary hour, the ten days, the nose referencing the calendar's inventor and the poster signalling the festivals of reason, all set the parameters for the action itself. As Michael Newman notes, they also inevitably raised questions about those very parameters.[75] Which revolutionary time was being referenced? The festive time of the street, of a world turned upside down celebrated by the aforementioned poster? Or the rational time of the calendar, of decimal measure and division, which was instituted partly to stamp out

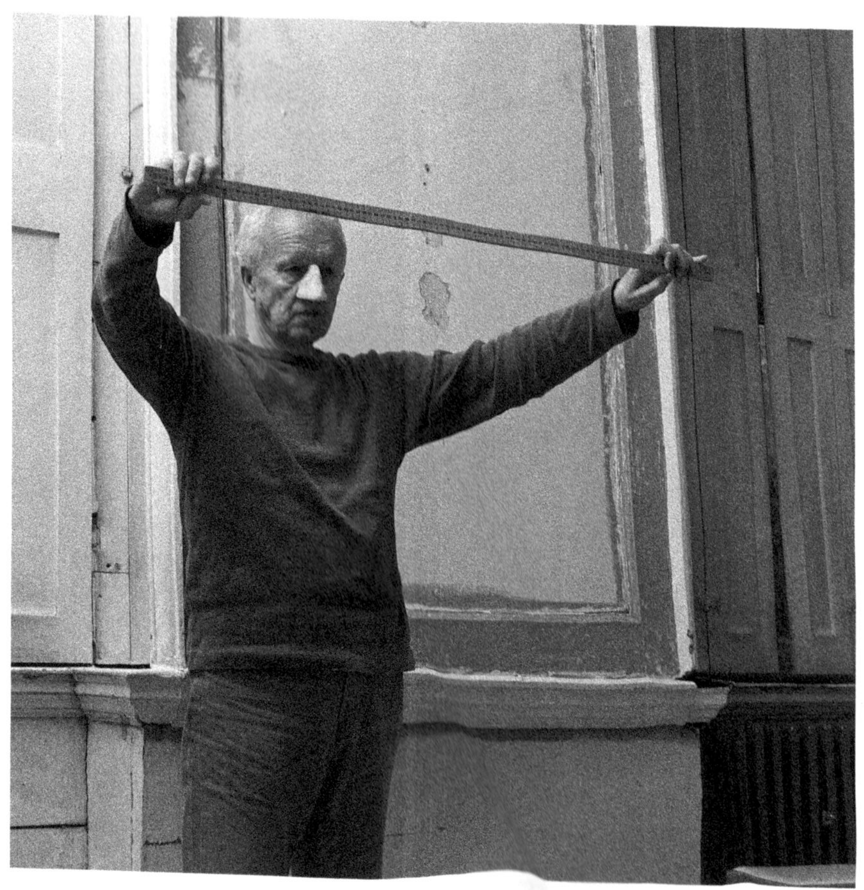

1.13   *Before the Mast*, domobaal, London, 2013

such populist exuberance? And which Maréchal was referenced? The utopian young poet who invented a revolutionary calendar to reflect his egalitarian commitment? Or the revolutionary turned dissident, one of the first to criticise the contradictions of the revolutionary state? As the deliberately tendentious title makes clear, the action was conceived neither as a literal nor a figural re-enactment of the Revolution but as an exploration of a more general situation of inequality and revolt. 'Before the mast' is a colloquial expression that refers to the living quarters of the crew, traditionally situated in the ship's prow: 'The crew being the largest number of men with the least status where mutineers might be found' and 'seeds of rebellion sown out of the intolerance of the imposition of inhuman disciplines meted out'.[76] It is also the title of Richard Dana's *Two Years Before the Mast*, a memoir originally published in 1840 and which chronicled the author's experience of living among common sailors in the front of the ship, formative for his later role as a prominent anti-slavery activist.

As this proliferation of quite distinct historical references makes clear, the action referred to the reality of revolution by analogy only. Here, the attempt was to create a situation resembling a totalising, encompassing cataclysm (the defining features of revolution, according to Brisley) using the 'full attributes of the human body'. In other words, the action served as a model through which to analyse the limitations of the revolutionary situation – in this instance the desire to begin anew and institute a durable experience of equality – through the limits of the human body. A model can be tested and, as Brisley notes, also repeated. It has an iterative structure that, at least in principle, can be extended beyond the frame of the performance itself.

The first limitation that Brisley set was to work only with what already existed in the room, or what was contributed by those watching the performance. This restriction reflects the limiting aspect of all revolutions which, despite their claims to radical change, are constrained by working with what is already there, the habits and reflexes of the 'collective mind', as it were. The performance started by exploring key notions associated with the original meaning of the term 'revolution': as regeneration, a joint return to the balance and order associated with the Classical past, as well as a natural time governed by the cyclical and astronomical rotations of the planets. The idea of balance and order was expressed vertically: the chairs, table and rubbish bin were suspended in various configurations which invariably collapsed. As the chairs and table legs broke and the rubbish bin cracked, the opportunity for balance and order progressively eroded. The public became aware of a loss of form. With the tools for representation (the table, chairs, bins) dismantled, the capacity for purposeful activity was reduced. The artist too became increasingly lateral, crawling on his hands and knees, even rolling on the floor as there was less and less to construct with.

In a post-performance conversation, Brisley identified the paradox of revolutionary time as 'a continual breaking-down and fracturing that goes on', a 'falling into a state of rubbish' even as 'the actions actually imply something else'.[77] As time passed, a number of actions took place. The newspaper was read or torn up; the walls were tapped for their resonance; the volume of the room was measured. Sometimes the movements assumed the form of a *tableau vivant* – perhaps of an orator speaking, a figure giving benediction, a body separated from its head by a guillotine. Crucially, the idea of an original day one was also explored through sound. Actions were sometimes accompanied by humming, gurgling, retching or a deep grumbling that began in the belly and struggled to reach the throat. Brisley explained that these sounds articulated 'a sort of prior condition to the use of language', a language of communication that is 'not a language of articulating ideas'.[78]

Here we approach what is arguably the most radical aspect of Brisley's relation to the historical past. Kalle Pihlainen notes that the metaphor of the past as a foreign language or country is proverbial among historians. He argues that it is particularly misleading, as the past does not use language and does not speak, indeed does not constitute a coherent entity.[79] Brisley's use of sound suggests a similar incapacity to grasp what is unthinkable, uncontrollable – one is tempted to say 'volcanic' – in our relation to the past. Sound bleeds across any attempt at framing. Travelling beyond the circumscribed space, Brisley's noises disturbed other unsuspecting visitors to the gallery, presumably even the neighbours downstairs. As he joked, it was tempting to see how far the desire for levelling hierarchy could go, seeping through the floorboards, disturbing the flat below, flattening out further in a bottomless pit … The result, as Brisley observes, was as if 'the end of the work is the starting point of the revolutionary intention'.[80] As time went on, the inability to create form without introducing something new in the situation meant that both artist and the viewing spectators arrived at the 'absolute nadir of emptiness'.[81]

To my mind, this increasing disintegration of form over time reveals four aspects of the revolutionary experience which can enhance our understanding of the challenges faced by any attempt to enact a total rupture with the past. First, it reinforces the recognition that the French Revolution – contrary perhaps to popular opinion – did not begin with the idea of a *tabula rasa* or zero hour. As already mentioned, Year I was not instituted in the form of a new calendar until 1793, four years after the transformative events of the French Revolution began. Maréchal's *Manifesto of the Equals*, arguably the most radical demand for a total rupture with the past, was not written until 1796, when the Revolution's radical phase was supposed to be over. So, the first insight is that the call for radical beginnings comes not at the historical origin of the process but at its end. It is as much a declaration as a reaction to an ongoing situation, namely, as we see here, the difficulty of sustaining the radical impulse for moral and political regeneration.

The second insight is a heightened awareness of the radical disjunction between rupture and creation. Perhaps because we are so used to avant-garde associations of the *tabula rasa* with the creation of new forms and attitudes, we tend to assume that the impulse to rupture is inherently creative. Brisley's performance, however, suggests that rupture and creation are processes that rarely coincide in the revolutionary situation. First, it is difficult to create new forms without drawing on something from the past, thereby invalidating the postulate of a radical rupture. Second, for new forms to gain traction, to appear 'as something', they typically have to belong to – or function as – new institutions. Any re-institutionalisation inevitably reproduces authoritative structures of some kind, leading away from the radical impulse to absolute equality.

The third insight is not conceptual but emotional. As Brisley and several spectators noted, the situation became more toxic as it wore on. This suggests interesting parallels with Brisley's earlier *And for today … nothing*, which also explored the tipping point between form and formlessness. In the earlier performance, Brisley's attempt to endure the toxic situation associated with death and the loss of form offered a fresh perspective on the historical experience of the death of Marat, who quickly tipped from being a hero, immortalised in statues which were to replace the statues of saints throughout France, to an abomination, a name to be uttered with disgust and preferably forgotten. Taken together, both performances underscore the toxic nature of any revolutionary situation that goes on for too long and reveals itself to be not a new beginning but an increasingly ambiguous 'interregnum'.

The fourth insight concerns the challenge of this formlessness to our customary understanding of artistic endeavour. On several days, Brisley stopped his performance before the allotted time to declare it a failure. But a failure of what? On one level, the several declarations of failure that punctuated *Before the Mast* can be read allegorically: that the revolutionary hour can never be reached. On another level, allowing the action to end 'successfully' would suggest that final statements are possible. Failure thus also refers to the difficulty of sustaining formlessness. To what extent can one endure the radical impulse towards a total rupture with the past? As Brisley added after one of his declarations of failure, 'even in destruction there is always conservation'.[82]

This impulse was already apparent during the French Revolution, when the revolutionaries rushed to conserve the various markers of the past even as they destroyed them. As we shall see in more detail in Chapter 5, the Louvre was instituted as a state museum partly as a reaction against the speed of rupture. Through conservation, objects that, although officially 'dead' from the point of view of revolutionary rupture but were considered by many to still be 'alive', were repurposed as art.[83] Brisley's performance, in contrast, invites us to consider the difficulty of carrying through any declaration of thoroughgoing rupture. True rupture, as Kazimir Malevich famously argued – and indeed Sylvain Maréchal before him – would require the courage to destroy for good all existing artworks, knowing that new forms and works would eventually be created.[84] This goes against the logic of the modern museum which, as Boris Groys observed, consolidates the opposition 'dead past, living present' as one internal to the museum. Dead artworks are scrupulously preserved, while 'living artworks' are those that signal a break with tradition, until they too are collected by the museum.

To counter both this impulse to conservation and the way it consolidates an 'avant-garde' interpretation of art that may be reactionary in its outcome, Brisley has emphasised incompletion as a way of reviving what remains still living in the revolutionary past. Since its performance, elements developed in *Before the Mast* have been included in new works, including a film, series of photographs and other performances. The soundwork *Workers of the World Unite*, also performed in the persona of the curator R. Sirb, took place on 19 February 2014, at Kunsthal Aarhus. It accompanied the launch of a new book presenting over a hundred covers of the *Communist Manifesto* in multiple languages published by the *Museum of Ordure*. Dressed in black and wearing the same prosthetic nose, Brisley held a measuring stick to his throat, producing gagging and choking sounds until he finally gasped out the slogan 'workers of the world unite, unite!' Here, too, the performance invites us to reflect on the futures of the revolutionary past by reframing a real, nowadays mostly dismissed, historical referent. The numerous translations of the *Communist Manifesto* are presented not as a historical curiosity but as a historical *presence*. This presence reframes the question of revolution-ary ends as one of beginnings. What would it mean to enter a day one of the revolutionary period, and when would it begin?

Expanding the referent; completing the rupture

This chapter has reconstructed Brisley's decades-long engagement with the problem of how to instigate a truly transformational social and political change, one capable of rupturing with the past's habits and social structures once and for all. Along the way, I have tried to make explicit the analogies between Brisley's performances and the revolutionary situation, both of which operate by effectuating a cut in time. This cut suspends the normal progress of time and duration to allow an action, or series of actions, to be perceived as belonging to a new time, and a new situation. I have further suggested that this analogy between performance and revolution allows us to see how Brisley's performance can also function heuristically, by recovering what one might call the 'anthropological limits' of any situation that qualifies as 'revolutionary' or belonging to a putative Year I. In contrast to history, which reconstructs the past after the fact, from a point exterior to the events themselves, Brisley's actions offer a perspective from 'inside' the revolution-ary situation, allowing it to be analysed and experienced in a lived time, that is to say, a time in which the future is still open.

Within this time frame, the *presence* of the historical referent disrupts what Alun Munslow terms the 'conflation of the past with history' by revealing other unrealised presents of this past.[85] In so doing, Brisley's perfor-mances ask all those who engage with them to at least minimally acknowledge the truth-value of the referent: not in the sense that one can never 'know' what went on in the minds of long-dead people, but in the sense of acknowledging a reality outside the frame of the performance. For those of us who approach these performances many years after the event, these references exhort us to complete their meaning by expanding on their latent or undeveloped potential. This implies that authenticity is found not in the 'originary' event, but on the side of declaration and commitment, whether to the 'unfinished futures' of revolutionary history or, in the case of catastrophe, to the memories, whether individual or collective, that keep this past alive even in the absence of witnesses. Anything else would reproduce the false dichotomy between the 'temporary' and the 'permanent' which, for Brisley, remains fundamentally undemocratic.

Notes

1 Peter Gorsen, 'The Return of Existentialism in Performance Art', in Gregory Battcock and Robert Nickas (eds), *The Art of Performance: A Critical Anthology* (New York: E. P. Dutton, 1984), pp. 76–79, p. 76.
2 On the re-evaluation of the revolutionary avant-garde in the context of the 1960s, see the important exhibition 'Transform the World! Poetry Must Be Made by All', Moderna Museet Stockholm, 15 November–21 December 1969. As the curator Ronald Hunt notes: 'Freed of form it [artistic imagination] might be revealed as a common property to all men. Such freedom is a vital process to the process of revolution *and* to a post-revolutionary situation (new society).' Exhibition catalogue no. 84, p. 6. I thank Brisley for this reference.
3 Stuart Brisley, Sanja Perovic and Tony White, *Before the Mast: Into Day One of the Revolutionary Period: A Conversation* (London: Domobaal/Mummery +Schnelle, 2013), p. 12.
4 Stuart Brisley, Sanja Perovic and Tony White, Unpublished conversation (2013).
5 Conversation with Brisley, 26 August 2020, Lydd-on-Sea.
6 Brisley, National Life Stories, C466/43/04 F5276B, p. 96.
7 Brisley, National Life Stories, C466/43/07 F5279A, p. 144.
8 Brisley, National Life Stories, C466/43/05 F5277A, p. 103.
9 Brisley cites the Brazilian artist Almir Mavignier, who taught at Ulm, and Von Graevenitz as influences, observing that Munich was on an axis that connected the New Bauhaus based in Zurich with a vibrant art scene in Milan. Brisley, National Life Stories, C466/43/05 F5277B, p. 115.
10 Allan Kaprow, for instance, famously posited that the logical next step of 'Pollock's near destruction of this tradition [of painting] may well be a return to the point where art was more actively involved in ritual, magic and life'. Allan Kaprow, 'The Legacy of Jackson Pollock (1958)', in *Essays on the Blurring of Art and Life*, ed. Jeff Kelley (Berkeley, CA: University of California Press, 2003), pp. 6–7.
11 Michael Newman, *Stuart Brisley: Performing the Political Body and Eating Shit* (Belfast: MAC Belfast, 2015), pp. 5, 14.
12 The Polish Free Army had bases near his parental home in Haslemere. And he grew up with various evacuee children who stayed with his family. Some distant cousins later perished in a bombing raid near Gravesend. At the Guildford, Brisley encountered numerous refugees, and also students from Egypt and other

countries, who had come to study photography there. See Brisley, National Life Stories, C466/43/01 F5273A, pp. 2–3.

13 Brisley arrived in Germany on 3 May 1955, a few days before the end of the British occupation of Germany. He was then sent to Langeleben, near Braunschweig on the East German border, to listen to foreign Morse code transmissions. While there he was promoted to corporal, in charge of food and perishable stores. See: Stuart Brisley, National Life Stories, C466/43/03 F5275B, pp. 72–74.

14 Brisley, National Life Stories, C466/43/03 F5275B, p. 76.

15 Including *Survival under Alien Circumstances* (1977) performed with Christoph Gericke, 1977 at Documenta 6, discussed in Chapter 5.

16 *Replique*, directed by Szajna, was presented as part of Atelier'72 showcasing Polish art, in collaboration with the Łódź Museum of Art. This was the year that Richard Demarco had invited key members of the Polish avant-garde to the Edinburgh Festival, including Tadeusz Kantor, Ryszard Stanislawski, director of the Muzeum Sztuki in Łódź, and Wieslaw Borowski, director of the Foksal Gallery in Warsaw. See Demarco digital archive collection: www.demarco-archive.ac.uk/assets/2972-p1972_jozef_szajna_replique_atelier_03972_edinburghp (accessed 21 October 2019). At the festival the previous year, Brisley had presented *Car Showroom Event*, for which he was given a car showroom filled with old cars that he and his assistants crashed and took apart as they wished. See Brendan Flynn, 'Stuart Brisley as a Performance Artist'. MA dissertation, 1974, Tate Gallery Archive (TGA) 201114/3/5/10.

17 The dissertation, on the English constructivist Victor Pasmore, was completed under Karl Zerbe, a German émigré and associate of Max Beckmann, whose works had been singled out for being 'degenerate' during the Nazi regime. Pasmore strongly influenced the shape and outcome of Brisley's ground-breaking *Peterlee Project* discussed in Chapter 3.

18 'I'd lived in the States for about five years, and I came back to England and it was a very depressing event … when I came back it was like everything shrinking. Like England is so full of small and intimate, you know, rather limiting features. Coming back was like that, and my work literally came to a stop, and in a sense I was thinking of things that couldn't be made.' Brisley, Perovic and White, *Before the Mast*, p. 12.

19 Lisa Tickner notes that 'by the end of 1968 there had been protests at seventeen universities and six local-authority colleges in the UK'. See: Lisa Tickner, *Hornsey 1968: The Art School Revolution* (London: Frances Lincoln, 2008) p. 152, note 50.

20 Stuart Brisley and Gilane Tawadros, *The Stuart Brisley Interviews: The Art of Performance and Its After-Lives* (London: DACS/Book Works, 2020), p. 14.

21 Speakers invited during the sit-in included 'Buckminster Fuller, Joan Littlewood, Sir John Summerson, Professor Nikolaus Pevsner, Sir Robin Darwin (Rector of the Royal College of Art), Professor Richard Wollheim, and the radical psychiatrist R. D. Laing'. They also organised seminars with 'Reg Butler, John Latham, Bernard Cohen, Bryan Kneale and Richard Hamilton'. See Tickner, *Hornsey 1968*, pp. 37–38.

22 'Hornsey College of Art Student Committee, Statement by Visual Research Lecturer', 1968, www.stuartbrisley.com/pages/39/60s/Text/Hornsey_College_of_Art_Student_Action_Committee______Statement_by_Visual_Research_Lecturer/page:7 (accessed 6 February 2021).

23 This can be observed in a series of publications from the early 1960s, including Raymond Williams, *Existing Alternatives in Communication* and *Communications*, both 1962; Marshall McLuhan, *The Gutenberg Galaxy* (1962) and *Understanding Media: The Extensions of Man* (1964) and Jürgen Habermas, *The Structural Transformation of the Bourgeois Public Sphere* (1964). See Staffan Ericson, 'The Lecture Room (1962) – on Dark Rooms, Antennas and Synchronization of Education', oral presentation www.diva-portal.org/smash/get/diva2:1307041/FULLTEXT01.pdf (accessed 6 February 2021); for McLuhan's influence in particular see Catherine Spencer, *Beyond the Happening: Performance Art and the Politics of Communication* (Manchester: Manchester University Press, 2020), pp. 18–19, note 12.

24 The National Union of Students was to be the first step in a 'national campaign at all levels of society to present the case for direct action in social structures; i.e. to become a real educational force'. Brisley, Unpublished remarks on the National Union of Students Conference in 1969, TGA 20042/2/2/4. This conference famously pitted Jack Straw's demand for wider political involvement of the union against Trevor Fisk who wished to retain a core focus on education.

25 'I was not interested in issues of "security" (basic income and so on) but with the search for new "opportunities" to make art.' Conversation with the author, 26 August 2020, Lydd-on-Sea.

26 Conversation with the author, 20 December 2016, London.

27 This symposium is credited with stimulating an encounter with members of Fluxus and the Viennese actionists. Participants included Al Hansen, Wolf Vostell, Yoko Ono, Günter Brus, Otto Mühl and Hermann Nitsch. Metzger's own auto-destructive art reflected his participation in the campaign for nuclear disarmament, including in the Direct Action Committee Against Nuclear War (DAC). See Andrew Wilson, 'Papa what did you do when the Nazis built the concentration camps? My dear, they never told us anything', in Gustav Metzger and Andrew Wilson, *Damaged Nature, Auto Destructive Art* (London: Coracle Press, 1996).

28 For a related definition of the surrealist term 'found objects' see Ian Chilvers and John Glaves-Smith, *Dictionary of Modern and Contemporary Art* (Oxford: Oxford University Press, 2009), p. 521.

29 As the proposal noted, 'Celebration for Constitutional Consumption is an investigation into relationships among people. It is not a play. There is no script, the participants are not actors, nor are they expected to act. There is no stage. There are no props. There is no direction. There will have been no rehearsal. It cannot take place in theatre.' See Stuart Brisley, 'Celebration for Institutional Consumption' (1970), TGA 201114/3/3/1.

30 Stuart Brisley, 'Proposal for Celebration for Institutional Consumption', www.stuartbrisley.com/pages/29/70s/Text/Proposal_for__Celebration_for_Institutional_Consumption_/page:3 (accessed 5 June 2022).

31 Stuart Brisley, 'Celebration for Constitutional Consumption' (1970), TGA 201114/3/3/2.

32 This includes reviews in *Punch, Time Out, The Observer, The Listener, The Guardian* (Caroline Tinsdall on 2 November 1970), *The Spectator* (Nicolas de Jongh on 16 November 1970), *The Evening Standard* (Milton Shulman on 20 October 1970), and *The Sunday Times* (Philip Norman on 1 November 1970).

33 '[P]erformance has a more appropriate definition in relation to visual art – to carry out duly: To act in fulfilment of to carry into effect'. E. M. Melizabeth Kirkpatrick, *Chambers 20th Century Dictionary* (Cambridge University Press, 1987); it is this aspect which brings the term into focus in relation to art'. Stuart Brisley, 'Anti Performance Art', in *Arte Inglese Oggi, 1960–76: Milano, Palazzo Reale, Febbraio–Maggio 1976*, 2 vols (Milan: Electa, 1976); pp. 416–417. Cited by Wayne Enstice, 'Performance Art's Coming of Age', in *The Art of Performance: A Critical Anthology* (New York: E. P. Dutton, 1984), pp. 80–87, p. 84.

34 Tim Brennan recalls Brisley discussing this performance at the Slade School with his students as a moment when authority is shared. Brennan, 'Of Commune and Community', in Stuart Brisley, *Stuart Brisley, The Peterlee Project 1976–1977* (Aarhus, DK: Aarhus: Antipyrine with The Museum of Ordure, 2014), pp. 131–136, p. 131.

35 Brisley, *Homage to the Commune* (1976) (London: domobaal/Mummery +Schnelle, 2013). Originally published in the catalogue *Inglese Arte Oggi (1960–1976)*.

36 Newman, *Stuart Brisley*, p. 48.

37 Brisley described this performance as 'an everyday thought with subjective implications: make your own prison (I built a box the size of the limits of my own body)'. Stuart Brisley, *12 Days* (London: domobaal/Mummery +Schnelle, 2013).

38 Andreas Kalyvas, 'Constitutent Power', in J. M. Bernstein (ed.), *Political Concepts* (New York, NY: Fordham University Press, 2018), pp. 87–117.

39 Ibid., p. 103; see also Raunig's discussion of the constituent republic, in relation to creative and instrumental powers in *Art and Revolution*, pp. 56–64.

40 As T. J. Clark notes : 'In David's painting Marat's body is maneuvered into a state of insubstantiality … This is partly because so much of the body in David is kept in shadow, and one which in David's treatment of it seems to make Marat much the same substance – the same material – as the empty space above him. The wound is as abstract as the flesh' (p. 39). As Clark goes on to observe 'the body is not there in the Marat in the same way as the main objects which David has gone to such pains to make real' (p. 40). See: Timothy James Clark, 'Painting in the Year Two', *Representations*, 47 (Summer 1994), 13–63.

41 Newman suggests, 'Performance art could be understood as having the potential to reverse the sublimating trajectory that David secularised and left in suspense', *Stuart Brisley*, p. 14.

42 For Guilhamou, the participation of so many women, especially during the first two ceremonies honouring Marat, is evidence of this extension. Jacques Guilhamou, *La Mort de Marat, 1793* (Brussels: Editions Complexe, 1989), p. 90.

43 Ibid., p. 44.

44 Clark suggests that 'from the point of view of those trying to represent it … the body of the people was always sick. It needed some radical purging. And ultimately there was only one way to do this. It had to be killed in order to be represented or represented in order to be killed. Either formulation will do. Marat is the figure of both.' Clark, 'Painting in the Year Two', p. 50.

45 See the interview with Catherine Wood: Stuart Brisley, 'Stuart Brisley: Arbeit Macht Frei in Conversation with Catherine Wood', curator, Tate Audio, 7 October 2011, www.tate.org.uk/context-comment/audio/stuart-brisley-arbeit-macht-frei (accessed 10 December 2015).

46 Newman, *Stuart Brisley*, p. 8.

47 'Even the most extreme consciousness of doom threatens to degenerate into idle chatter. Cultural criticism finds itself faced with the final stage of the dialectic of culture and barbarism. To write poetry after Auschwitz is barbaric. And this corrodes even the knowledge of why it has become impossible to write poetry today.' Theodor Adorno, *Prisms*, trans. Samuel and Shierry Weber (Cambridge, MA: MIT Press, [1967] 1981), pp. 17–34, p. 34. On this oft-misquoted statement see James Schmidt, who notes: 'The barbarity of continuing to write poetry after Auschwitz requires a discussion of what counts as barbarism – which would force us to ask uncomfortable questions about how we go about distinguishing barbarism from culture.' Schmidt, 'Poetry After Auschwitz – What Adorno Didn't Say', *Persistent Enlightenment*, 2013, https://persistentenlightenment.com/2013/05/21/poetry-after-auschwitz – What Adorno did not say/ (accessed 23 August 2020).

48 Brisley and Tawadros, *The Stuart Brisley Interviews*, p. 23.

49 The objectifying power of the gaze was also the subject of *Artist as Whore*, the third Gallery House performance made that same year, discussed in Chapter 6.

50 For Newman, 'the replacement of the name by a number cannot but recall the concentration camps'. Newman, *Stuart Brisley*, p. 18.

51 Brisley and Tawadros, *The Stuart Brisley Interviews*, pp. 3, 5.

52 Brisley, Perovic and White, *Before the Mast*, p. 2.

53 E-mail communication, 4 February 2014.

54 See Brisley, Perovic and White, *Before the Mast*, p. 3.

55 On this point see, Perovic, *The Calendar in Revolutionary France*, pp. 12–13.

56 Charles Péguy called it the uncountable 'Year Zero'. Charles Péguy, *Clio: Dialogue de l'histoire et de l'âme paaïenne* (Paris: [1909–12] 1931), p. 115.

57 Georges Bataille, 'Informe', in *Oeuvres complètes de Georges Bataille I, Premiers écrits* (1922–1940) (Paris: Gallimard, 1970), p. 217.

58 Personal conversation, 15 June 2015, London.

59 Breakfasts were mostly uneaten and one meal had to be divided in two because there were two visitors. Telephone conversation with Brisley, 14 May 2022.

60 E-mail communication, 7 January 2016.

61 For this association of Diogenes with performance artists in general and Brisley in particular, see Ian Cutler, *Cynicism from Diogenes to Dilbert* (London: McFarland & Co, 2005), pp. 121 and 143.

62 Peter Sloterdijk, *Critique of Cynical Reason*, trans. Michael Eldred (University of Minnesota Press, 1988) p. 160–164. Both Rousseau and Diderot in fact were among

the first to formulate theories and practices of performance outside the theatre arts, and, in the case of Rousseau, *against* the theatre arts (notably in his *Lettre à d'Alembert sur les spectacles*).

63 Telephone conversation with Maya Balcioglu, 14 May 2022.

64 Stuart Brisley, 'An Account of Stuart Brisley's Work "Bourgeois Manners – Brute Force and Bloody Ignorance"', 1988, TGA 201114/3/14/7.

65 See the annotated draft by Maya Balcioglu and Stuart Brisley, 'Against Cultural Bacchanal', 1989, www.tate.org.uk>items>201114-3-14-2 (accessed 17 December 2017).

66 Brisley, 'Stuart Brisley's Work "Bourgeois Manners"'.

67 Ibid.

68 Stuart Brisley, *Next Door (the missing text)* (London: domobaal/Mummery +Schnelle, 2013), p. 12.

69 See Nasser Mufti, 'Seeing Stasis', www.stuartbrisley.com/media/1124779795887a78bafc1b0.58460666.pdf (accessed 12 July 2018). Also: Mufti, *Civilizing War: Imperial Politics and the Poetics of National Rupture* (Evanston, IL: Northwestern University Press, 2017).

70 See Nicole Loraux, *The Divided City: On Memory and Forgetting in Ancient Athens*, trans. Corinne Pache and Jeff Fort (New York, NY: Zone Books, 2002), p. 64. For stasis as a gegensinn and its use, in ancient Greek, as a term for both actual and latent civil war, see pp. 104–108. See also Giorgio Agamben, *Stasis: Civil War as a Political Paradigm*, trans. Nicholas Heron (Stanford, CA: Stanford University Press, 1998), discussed in Chapter 4.

71 See Mufti, 'Seeing Stasis'. Also: Mufti, *Civilizing War*.

72 Hans-Christian Oeser, 'Ice as a Metaphor for Political Stagnation: Some Cultural Parallels between Germany after 1815 and West Germany after 1971', *The Maynooth Review/Revieu Mha Nuad*, 11 (1984), 60–75.

73 Brisley sees his own 'misappropriation of images of monarchy' as this kind of action, as noted in the diary entry for 21 May 2010. Brisley, *Next Door (the missing text)*, p. 12.

74 As we shall see in Chapter 6, this *Manifesto* was used to frame the ending of *Breath* (2014), a 2014 performance by Brisley that also incorporated elements of *Before the Mast*.

75 Newman, *Stuart Brisley*, p. 29.

76 E-mail communication, 4 February 2014.

77 Brisley, Perovic and White, Unpublished conversation.

78 Ibid.

79 Kalle Pilhlainen 'There is Just no Talking with the Past', *Rethinking History*, 18:4 (2014), 575–582, p. 577.

80 Brisley, Perovic and White, Unpublished conversation.

81 Ibid.

82 Said to the author after the end of the performance on Day 6.

83 See Andrew McClellan, 'Musée du Louvre, Paris: Palace of the People, Art for All', in Carole S. Paul (ed.), *The First Modern Museums of Art: The Birth of an Institution in 18th- and Early-19th Century Europe* (Los Angeles, US: Getty trust

Publications, 2012), pp. 213–237. As McClellan notes, 'blatantly royalist images were kept in storage or destroyed, but a strict arrangement by school and chronology neutralized the spiritual content of religious icons by re-identifying them as masterpieces of art history', pp. 225–226.

84 Boris Groys, *Art Power* (Cambridge, MA: MIT Press 2013), p. 26.

85 Munslow, 'On "Presence" and Conversing with the Past', p. 574.

2 Ghost dances in history and performance

Performance art differs from other art forms in its evanescence. A one-time event, it is no sooner there than gone. Any interpretations, therefore, are essentially created in retrospect, filtered by the photos, films, videos, recordings and documents it leaves behind or the memories of those who witness or talk about it in some way. Yet memories are fragile; documents partial; and images capture only a few moments out of an extended duration. None of these traces 'records' the live performance, but each functions in a different time frame to offer a 'distant window' into the past.

This chapter considers the form and function of this 'distant window' and how it may be used to create a context for performance art that goes beyond art and its histories. As performance has entered mainstream art and theatre history, documentation has been frequently used as a blanket term to cover all kinds of traces: from original proposals, sketches or plans made by artists, to photos, films, videos or other artistic works that are made from the event, to testimonials, artist interviews and life stories. This has encouraged thinking about performance in terms of a 'contradictory, mirroring practice of documentation and disappearance'.[1] But, if much ink has been spilled on the question of how to document and historicise performance art, less attention has been paid to how our reconstructions of performance events are conditioned by what is forgotten, dispersed or remains unknown about the original event – by far the greatest part of any past.

The question thus arises of how the images, videos, films and testimonies through which we access past performances are conditioned not just by absence or lack but also by what is overlooked or remains latent in these remnants from the past. Should they be understood as belonging to a past action whose meaning has been fulfilled? Or are they better understood as remnants of a past performance that, although dead and gone, may still be capable of communicating a potential future in some way? More generally, how do we unlock this experience of the past itself as something potentially alive and ongoing? These are critical issues not just for performance art but for all forms of embodied interactions that strive to communicate and survive in the absence of reminding objects.[2] It is also a central concern for the thesis of this book. As I show in this chapter, if there is a revolutionary potential of performance art, it lies in its kinship with other kinds of embodied yet evanescent behaviours, including collective ones, that exist outside the world of art and too are forged through the experience of loss, dispersal and forgetting.

Following Georges Didi-Huberman, this chapter adapts Aby Warburg's notion of the 'surviving image' to interpret the afterlives of performance art. Warburg speculated that the iconic images found in Western art expressed a far longer history of performance behaviours, such as those found in festivals, rituals, dances and other collective experiences of time and movement.[3] Although these performances were by nature evanescent, they also reappeared in the form of sedimented gestures that repeat across time: be it in the form of proverbs, legends, mannerisms or other gestural patterns, shared by a culture or a group. As Didi-Huberman observes, these surviving images do not belong to the past of recorded history. Nor do they express sanctioned traditions. Rather, they are best understood as evidence of a break in transmission, of what gets retained when all other elements of a once-living present (with its own sense of past and future) have been effaced.[4] Expanding on this notion in his own work, Didi-Huberman has shown how images themselves can carry a memory of these ruptures and breaks because they bear the imprint of what takes place outside the frame.[5]

Adapting this notion, this chapter argues that the afterlives of performance art are survivals in a double sense. On the one hand, they are traces of a movement and action otherwise lost to time. On the other hand, these traces can be associated with other images, sequences, narratives and testimonials to reveal a far longer history of collective behaviours. For Brisley and other performance artists who conceive of performance as a way of communicating with a public through a shared imagination, the challenge is to recover this 'anthropological' past of shared gestures, mannerisms and attitudes.

As in Chapter 1, my point of departure is Brisley's own performances and reflections on the moving image. I begin with *Being and Doing* (1984), a film written by Brisley and directed by Ken McMullen. This film, which is constructed entirely out of fragments of past performances, explores performance as a 'ghost dance', referencing the term also used to describe the new rituals that emerged among Native American communities at the end of the nineteenth century as they faced the imminent collapse of their way of life. These rituals shared visions of an incipient end-time that would destroy the White man's culture as a prelude to renewal. In his film, Brisley extrapolates this notion of the 'ghost dance' to explore the links between performance understood as an intervention undertaken by an individual and performance as it relates to ritual or collective social behaviours that arise in moments of crisis or catastrophe, when social groups are faced with the death of their own culture or values. The role of ritual in expressing this time of crisis is also explored in two films directed by Ken McMullen, *Ghost Dance* (1983) and *Resistance* (1976), both of which feature performances by Brisley. Expanding the range of references associated with the ghost dance in all three films, this chapter develops Brisley's efforts to find a context for performance that goes beyond art history.

It goes without saying that this chapter's focus on film is not entirely accidental.[6] For film is a medium that confounds the usual dichotomies between the recorded and the performed past. Like photography, film records. Unlike photography, however, film records real duration. It enables past durations to be temporally re-experienced in the viewer's own present, even as it collates and assembles visual and auditory sequences at will. Film is thus simultaneously a powerful tool of revisionism and a means to reactivate images and sequences from past performances that might otherwise pass unnoticed or are forgotten or repressed. This double-sided nature of film is reflected by the questions posed by all three films: What is resistance? How is it documented and communicated? Can these survivals resist being recuperated and revised in terms of dominant cultures?

Being and Doing

Being and Doing seeks to demonstrate the following propositions:

>All behaviour is performance
>Performance behaviour is a condition for art
>Performance behaviour refuses to recognise the death of community in society
>Performance behaviours are ghost-dances in a dying culture.[7]

These propositions elaborate a viewpoint already expressed by Brisley in 1974: that the appropriate context for understanding performance is not theatre or any of the theatre-related arts, but any collective behaviour that expresses the 'public imaginative life of groups'.[8] This includes ritual behaviour which, like the ghost dance itself, belongs not just to recursive social time but can be revived in times of crisis when inherited values no longer seem adequate. To be sure, Brisley is hardly the first artist to pit ritual time against theatre. Erika Fischer-Lichte has observed that, from Nietzsche onwards, the ritual structure of performance has been repeatedly invoked against canonised art forms, in an effort to establish a wider, more collective origin of both art and culture.[9] This happened in the 1870s, most emphatically with Nietzsche's *Birth of Tragedy*, a publication that drew attention to the ritual function of myth. It happened again with the first avant-garde movements of the twentieth century, which privileged the direct communication of ritual in their attempts to cross the boundary separating art from life. More recently, the 'performance turn' of the 1960s has brought renewed attention to the ritual structures of everyday life, not just in theatre and the arts, but also as they are elaborated in philosophy, anthropology, sociology and other cognate disciplines.

Brisley's propositions, however, suggest a far longer trans-historical origin for performance art than some of the modernist art movements described above. This is because, for Brisley, performance expresses a fundamentally antagonistic relation with society. As Brisley notes, performance art proceeds from a place of alienation. It refuses to recognise what has already taken place, namely the death of community in society.[10] Brisley uses the term 'ghost-dance' to describe the condition of being an artist in a society in which 'social consciousness is becoming a fiction, a cultural memory'.[11]

As I have already indicated, ghost dances first came to prominence in the 1890s, when they were performed by a number of Native American communities as they came under extraordinary pressure to change their way of life. It is important to note that some of these rituals were also highly mediated cultural expressions, attracting public attention just as early film technology was developing. Philippe-Alain Michaud has observed that some of the earliest ghost dances were recorded by the kinetograph, a device which creates the illusion of movement by using a strip of sequential images.[12] This was the case with the *Indian War Council* and the *Sioux Ghost Dance*, captured by Dickson's kinetograph in 1894 as part of the Buffalo Bill travelling show. Other ghost dances were registered, for documentary reasons, by researchers in the process of collating the first ethno-archaeological collections that also emerged around this time. Whatever the destination, these recordings were ghostly in two ways. First, they did not preserve the actual duration of the dance but used technology to recreate the *illusion* of movement (they were spectral in this way). Second, many of these dances were recorded and/or staged, for commercial reasons, a few years after the crushing defeat at Wounded Knee in 1890, which marked the end of Native American autonomy. These recordings, in other words, did not just create the spectre of the moving dance but captured the 'reality of the disappearance' of the dancers in question.[13]

Michaud has suggested that these early recordings of ghost dances are best understood as 'survivals' in Aby Warburg's sense, not least because the rituals witnessed by Warburg in Arizona and New Mexico partly inspired his concept of the 'survival'.[14] Some of these rituals were already on the way to becoming folkloric spectacles. The Antelope Dance of the Pueblo people, for instance, was performed 'more than three generations after the disappearance of the antelope herds'.[15] Deprived of their practical aims, these rituals were survivals in a double sense. They were ghost-like in their transience, and because this transience was no longer embedded in a pragmatic situation – a practical past – that was continually lived forward. This last point is key:

survivals are those transient performances that mark or repeat the break in transmission. Unlike rituals that remain embedded in a practical life, they express memories that have, partially at least, lost their social function. Yet these shared memories not only persist; they also *resist* the ascendant or dominant cultural frameworks that have replaced them.

This idea that collective memories of cultural defeat can serve as sites of resistance was elaborated by the American anthropologist Weston La Barre in his book, *The Ghost Dance: The Origins of Religion.*[16] Published in 1970, and influenced by psychoanalysis, La Barre's study expands the term 'ghost dance' to show how cultures all over the world and across time have created new rituals to express the experience of living in a kind of end-time, when old forms are no longer valid and new cultural expressions have yet to emerge. Whatever reservations one may have about La Barre's psychologising approach, it is relevant to our discussion of performance art for two reasons. First, La Barre insists on the important role played by anachronism in cultural innovation. Dissent from an ascendant or dominant culture frequently assumes a regression to prior or more basic forms. These forms are always present in society as latent resources that, when activated, enable ongoing resistance and new forms of counter-cultural survival. Second, and relatedly, he shows how cultural innovation is triggered when conflicted and conflictual individuals find themselves permanently exposed to the competition between different, ultimately incompatible, worlds. La Barre insists that this crisis of identity needs to be understood as something experienced *concretely*, by traumatised individuals or groups of individuals rather than as an impersonal cultural force.[17] He uses the term 'shaman' to describe this type of 'pathological individual' who nonetheless manages to convince others to share his visions of an apocalyptic future.[18]

La Barre's study was published at the same time as performance art was emerging as an alternative form of artistic activity that aimed to bypass both the art object and the notion of the artist as creator of a work. In fact, this idea of a 'ghost dance' was taken up by several filmmakers, performance artists and philosophers throughout the 1970s and 1980s to describe a perceived loss of social function for art. Joseph Beuys is the artist most readily associated with the figure of the shaman. But this notion of the conflicted individual can be equally applied to other artists and even revolutionaries, all those seeking a radical break with their own present in the absence of any knowledge about what the future will bring. For Brisley in particular, the term 'ghost dance' implied a shift of focus away from aesthetic innovation or 'newness', values typically associated with modernism and the historical avant-garde. Ghost dances, after all, are characterised by their appeal to a common fund of cultural memory. No matter how regressive and, from the perspective of a dominant culture, 'irrational' they may be, by giving voice to expectations that remain unfulfilled, these ghost dances also challenge authoritative structures. Moreover, like with the Native American ghost dances that gave birth to the term, these unfulfilled expectations demand public acknowledgement. For Brisley and other like-minded artists, the notion of the 'ghost dance' articulates an ethical demand for art to be transformative and non-metaphorical in some way. This implies a new role for the performance artist as someone capable of expressing resistance to the world order by placing themselves *in* it, opposing thereby the traditional claim that art can provoke and change the world because of its distance and autonomy *from* it.

This effort to delineate a new context for performance art is the subject of the film *Being and Doing*. In addition to positing a 'collective' origin for performance art in shared social rituals, the film shifts the focus away from those art-historical narratives that privilege an American neo-avant-garde origin. This rejection of the political categories of East and West is reflected in the film's form, which is presented as a montage of photographic and filmic documentation of performances, mostly by artists from Eastern Europe including Tibor Hajas, Raša Todosijević, Zbigniew Warpechowski, Natalia LL, Milan Knížak, Ewa Partum, Jan Lococh and Jerzy Bereś. These performances are further juxtaposed with footage from two of Brisley's performances, *Between* (1979) and *Approaches to Learning* (1980), both with Iain Robertson, as well as footage of social rituals that have nothing to do with art. As the Polish artist Natalia LL observes in the film, artists in Eastern Europe occupy a double position. They oppose the governments and institutions that have stripped away the meaning of a socialist art. But they are also critical of the capitalist art system whose processes 'only serve the West'. This conviction that performance was a mode of dissent against both socialist and capitalist (or perhaps even all) systems is expressed by several artists featured in the film.[19] As many of these artists were little known in the West at the time, the film thus aimed to communicate to an English-speaking audience the significant performances undertaken by artists in Eastern Europe, many of whom faced various kinds of restrictions, including on travel itself.[20]

Brisley's film, however, makes the wider, more radical proposition that there is in fact no established context or frame for understanding performance art. If performance is an activity that changes meaning depending on the context (political, aesthetic, religious, cultural etc.), then the validity and purpose of any retrospective 'framing' becomes paramount. What sort of 'frame' will help us to reconstitute an action whose original intent, in part, was to go beyond the limits of the art object and seek new ways of communicating with people? Second and relatedly, how do we resist those historical frames which seek to limit performance art to already established art histories? In other words, how do we resist not only those histories that privilege the permanent object and the art collection but also the idea of the artist himself as the author of the work, the one who brings it to completion?

The film opens with the sound of military drums and the clicking of a camera shutter, recorded over photos depicting the imposition of martial law in Poland in 1981 and still images of a performance by Tibor Hajas.[21] These photos set the stage for the film, which explores the links between performance and dissidence. The soundscape is overlaid with the voice of the Serbian (then Yugoslav) artist Raša Todosijević shouting the question 'Was ist Kunst?', an action he repeatedly performed in front of a seated woman in the period 1976–81. We are then shown footage of the action itself. The artist is off screen so that we only hear his voice aggressively, mechanically, almost insanely repeating this abstract question to the passive woman on-screen, whose black and white image slowly changes to full colour. Brisley's voice-over tells us that this performance expresses the profound alienation of the artist, unable to overcome the division between active subject and passive object. This alienation, he also tells us, contrasts sharply with the time of ritual, which the film defines as a 'collective behaviour without observers'.

Brisley's own reply to Todosijević's unanswerable question appears in the next sequence. The viewer is presented with a montage of documentary footage from the Haxey Hood, a ritual with pre-industrial agrarian origins that continues to be celebrated every 6 January in Lincolnshire, England. As Brisley's voice-over relates, its origins are uncertain, its form simple. A blood-coloured two-foot tube is thrown in the middle of a field and locals vie with one another to push it towards one of two pubs. The film segment begins with close-up shots of participants singing an old ploughman's song in a pub. One of them confesses that he 'would like to believe' that the ritual dates from the thirteenth century, injecting a note of self-awareness, even performativity, into the proceedings.[22] Folklorists have suggested a more recent origin in conflicts over land that emerged in the early modern period as private landowners seized land, either overtly or by 'improving' it. In Haxey, this happened in 1632, when Charles I sold some land to a Dutch speculator to drain. According to some interpretations, the tube represents a drain-pipe, a reminder of the protracted struggle over land rights that took place as rough pasture gave way to intensive farming, and other Dutch settlers arrived, displacing the local population.[23]

Whatever its origins, this ritual is regressive, occupying an uncertain space between ritual and disorder, an aspect reflected in the film footage. The camera adopts a low angle, panning out once dusk closes in until all we see are fragments, the liminal space between light and dark. Brisley's voice-over describes the ritual as breaking the 'boundaries of property and the law'. 'Farmers hate it', he says, and 'smear their fields with chicken shit to prevent it from happening'. Ambulance and police remain on standby. Still, the ritual persists, a 'ghost from the pre-industrial past', whose 'key to meaning', the film tells us, 'lies in the imaginary space created by those who are seen and those who are seeing'.

In one of the film's final sequences, the viewer is presented with another equally atavistic ritual: the yearly celebration of the Padstow Hobbyhorse (or 'Obby Oss') in Cornwall. The ritual takes place on May Day every year and involves a man dressed up in a horse's mask and a wooden hoop covered in sailcloth who is incited to dance by a 'teaser'. According to one popular tradition, any young woman found under the horse's skirts would become pregnant within the year. Here too the origins of the ritual are uncertain. There is some evidence that it was already present in the eighteenth century.[24] Since the nineteenth century, there have been two horses that confront each other: the traditional red horse, which comes out of the pub, and the blue horse, which represents the Church and, Brisley suggests, was brought in during the nineteenth century to 'clean the ritual up'.[25] Although today the festival is a major tourist attraction, in the early 1980s it was still susceptible to public derision. Knowing they would never be allowed to film the event, Brisley and McMullen reconstructed it instead from existing photos and documentary footage. They also filmed it from an airplane, the aerial perspective emphasising the ritual's marginal and shifting status – on the edge of civilised life, as land turns into sea. The Hobbyhorse, as Brisley observes in the film, can be found throughout Europe and parts of Asia. A demon, a symbol of male fertility, it was long feared and despised by Church authorities. Even as late as the 1980s, people in Bulgaria were able to recall priests' warnings that if men died while wearing the costume, they would not be buried on consecrated ground.

The film suggests that rituals belong to a time without spectators, when participants and observers remain, at least hypothetically, indistinguishable. Contemporary performance art, in contrast, requires not just an individual to make the attempted cut in time but also witnesses to give this attempt a social and historical reality: to observe it and narrate to others what was seen and felt after the fact, without which the action would be forgotten. This intrusion of (temporal and spatial) distance makes any performance both a ghost dance of a disappearing event and a way of orienting oneself towards a future that may or may not materialise.

Another sequence of the film recounts the reactions of an unnamed witness to a performance of *The Hand and the Nail* by the Polish artist Zbigniew Warpechowski, which culminated in the artist driving a nail through his hand. Brisley recalls one commentator describing it as a gesture of ultimate commitment to the task of 'taking things sufficiently earnestly', which few artists ever do.[26] Another witness describes his own sweat and fear once he realised what the artist was about to undertake.[27] This fear was so strong that he had to leave the premises shortly afterwards. His shock subsequently interfered with his memory of the event. All he could recall was the 'dominance of that physical act' and little else. A live performance, it appears, is just as hard to retain in its integrity when it is highly memorable as when it is not.

But while this action is narrated through voice-over, the film presents the viewer with footage from an unrelated performance: Brisley's *Approaches to Learning*, an action performed with Iain Robertson that begins with one man getting out of a lift and approaching another man (figure 2.1). They both pace in circles until one hits the other, who falls and then gets back up to continue pacing in a circle. This fragment is followed by footage of Warpechowski's preparation and performance of *The Short Electrical Love Story* (Poland, 1979), an action in which he wrapped himself in light bulbs and used movement to create lines and circles of light on the wall and ceiling of a darkened room. At the end there is one light bulb hanging from the ceiling, creating a shadow which, according to Warpechowski, looked like that of a hanged man. While this action is shown, Brisley reads out a published text by Warpechowski in which the artist recalls the 'excitement', 'euphoria' before a live action, the sense that there is no turning back. These words are overlaid by a highly evocative soundtrack of electronic music. The original documentary footage is thus expanded beyond its two-dimensional screen surface, to include new formations in both time (personal memories and soundscape) and space (the almost spectral, fragmented collage that strings together moments from the live action). This wholly new and densely atmospheric re-mediation supplants both the original performance and any documentation that may have survived from its making.

Another unnamed witness describes a performance by the Polish artist Jerzy Bereś which took place in 1981 in Miastko, a village about 140 kilometres from Gdansk, three weeks after Solidarnosc and shortly before the imposition of martial law, in front of members of both the artist's union and the communist party. According to this oral testimony, a naked Bereś painted his feet and walked over a canvas with the words 'Political Mess' written on it. He then painted his knees and crawled over the canvas, before giving the spectators a brush and paint. The action ended when the canvas was burnt. In the action that is being recollected here, the presence of political representatives was key to the work's reception. As Brisley notes, the brush was given not just to anyone but to the person whose role was to inform the authorities of what had taken place and whose identity was an open secret.[28] But this pointed action is not what we see in the film. Instead, we see footage from a different event, a re-enactment, done by Bereś in private and away from political tensions. In the footage shown in the film, we see Bereś painting the word 'Ghost' in English, on his chest, before proceeding to cross it out.

The film juxtaposes this re-enactment with another action by Bereś: *Romantic Manifestation*, which took place in the city square in Krakow in late November 1981. Here too the only evidence we are shown is a filmed re-enactment by the naked artist, accompanied by the narrative voice of a witness. This sequence begins with grainy images of a public square. Brisley informs us that this is where people queued for food at all hours of the day. A woman's voice in Polish then narrates Bereś' action, which consisted of a series of simple gestures. A wooden handcart was wheeled into the middle of the square carrying five bundles of kindling, each labelled with a word. Bereś then wrote the word 'freedom' on the ground and lit the fires. As he proceeded, hundreds of people gathered around the five fires. What they experienced only they know. But the witness tells us this was the 'last manifestation of spirit' before the 'manifestation of power' took place three weeks later in Krakow and elsewhere in Poland, when martial law was imposed. This play on Bereś' choice of words referenced nineteenth-century Polish romanticism, when Poland's struggle for independence from neighbouring empires had to be expressed 'spiritually' because it had failed politically. But even in this supposed eyewitness testimony, retrospective analysis has expanded the meaning of the original action. The imposition of martial law, occurring three weeks after the event, becomes a new frame that reveals the latent meaning of the action. By the time Brisley's film was made in 1984, even this military administration had collapsed, once again changing the relation between the past and future of the original action. Our apprehension of the performance, it would seem, is as shifting and malleable as memory itself.

Testimony, of course, can be treacherous and brings with it its own frames of reference. *Being and Doing* cites the case of Milan Knížak, the Czech artist sentenced to imprisonment in 1971, the end of the so-called era of normalisation after the Prague Spring, because his performances allegedly discredited the image of Czechoslovakia abroad. Photographs were key to the conviction. As the film's voice-over indicates, they enabled a live action with a presumably public intent to be reclassified as an 'internal question of pornography against the state'. As this example makes clear, performance behaviour can be a criminal activity or an art activity, depending on how it is framed. Who has power controls the definition, and no image, document or memory is sufficient for adjudicating between the two. In the case of Knížak, the same photographs that were the pretext for his arrest were also the basis for obtaining his release. They made possible an international campaign that reframed his alleged 'crime against the state' as a state crime against individual freedom and artistic expression, a crime that really did discredit Czechoslovakia's image abroad.[29]

It is precisely because the ultimate context of an action cannot be decided in advance that any performance remains vulnerable to revision and reinterpretation. This indifference towards context foregrounds how public revelation of an action becomes the only way to locate it in time and history.

Sometimes this confrontation with a dominant reality takes the form of a physical protest. In many of the examples in the film, we see how an artist interposes their body in real time in a manner that suspends the patterns and rules of acceptable behaviour. But acts of confrontation can also be staged in mediated ways. This is the case of Ewa Partum's *Self-Identification* (1980), in which the artist superimposed her naked silhouette on several photos depicting urban scenes, including the famous photograph in which a naked Partum is face to face with a female militia officer directing traffic. The actions depicted in Partum's photos never took place. Yet they changed perceptions of public space, at least for the small number of people who first saw them. When this photograph reappears in *Being and Doing*, its meaning has been reframed. A single work, belonging to a specific place and time, becomes part of a sequence of images that recontextualises it as part of a longer history of dissident behaviour.

It is therefore ironic that a 1985 review of *Being and Doing* chastises the film for failing to 'deal with the question of what (in terms of meaning) and how (as a medium) performance art actually communicates to its observers'.[30] It also criticises the film for proffering no 'criteria by which one might recognise any qualitative difference between contemporary shamanism and panhandling charlatanism'. In a way, the reviewer has put their finger on the very point, namely the underdetermined character of any performance. The appropriate criteria for determining the authenticity of the performance, if such a thing is even possible, may well be restricted to those witnessing, experiencing and remembering the action, a circle that naturally diminishes over time.

Brisley reflects on the connections between memory and lived experience in the voice-over that accompanies footage from *Between* (1979), also undertaken with Iain Robertson. The younger man was in his prime, while Brisley was double his age, about to enter what Carl Jung has called the final stage of life, characterised by 'maturity, old age, and anticipation of death'.[31] To dramatise this age-related power differential between them, the two men attempted to ascend a steep ramp over a period of several days, wearing nothing but a few bandages to protect themselves, while preventing the other from gaining stability (figures 2.2 and 2.3). A witness to the action described the steepness of the ramp 'as an area of unpredictability' forcing both artists to be 'constantly in a state, or anticipated state of imbalance'.[32] But what happens after the slope is disassembled and the action is no more? What the viewer hears in the film is Brisley's voice recalling the impression that his partner and nemesis had changed, becoming more 'primitive', while he had stayed the 'same as I've always been'. This suggests not only a certain limit to understanding what had taken place, but also the way memory of the event remains continuous even as it changes. Significantly, *Approaches to Learning* and *Between* were Brisley's last openly confrontational actions. Increasingly difficult to undertake physically as he grew older, they also obscured other ways of understanding the subject matter of a performance. Bereft of an appropriate context, they had also become predictable, in danger of being seen as an artist's trademark. As Brisley observes in the film, it is no longer possible to express conflict, or dissent, within a social context in which 'disasters' and 'catastrophes' can no longer be openly acknowledged.

As should be clear by now, *Being and Doing* adopts the methods of expanded cinema to address the reception of performance art in a post-revolutionary context that extended across the iron curtain. Expanded cinema refers to how film was used by artists in the 1950s and 1960s to disassemble simulated realities of commercial film, in which sound, image and action all appear to coincide. Valie Export, for instance, has defined it as 'an analysis carried out in order to discover and realise new forms of communication and deconstruction of a dominant reality'.[33] *Being and Doing* operates a similar process of deconstruction and recreation in the effort to heighten perceptual awareness of past performances. What the various voices in the film reference or recall only occasionally coincides with what is shown on screen, which is given its own space and time to unfold. This sequential layering of different narrative points of view with non-corresponding images and an atmospheric soundtrack all serve to draw the viewer's attention to different structures of communication, thereby expanding the temporal and spatial coordinates associated with documentation. This expansion, moreover, is crucial for demonstrating a key premise of the film, namely that these 'survivals' from past performances gain new meanings, and unfold new possibilities, when they are put in motion. In this sense, they are best understood not in relation to the world that preceded them (their original or historical context) but in terms of what they make possible.

Being and Doing thus foregrounds how performance art survives through the memories it leaves behind and the new works that it makes possible, be they photography, video, film, paintings or any other kind of form. This complex memory culture exceeds any purely 'documentary' relation because it relates in a highly mediated way to what we might call a 'collective' or public memory. There is no space here to develop the complex topic of collective memory, which covers several distinct functions.[34] I would like to note, however, one aspect that seems germane to performance art, namely the important distinction between communicative and cultural memory that Jan and Aleida Assmann have demonstrated in their influential works on the theme. As Jan Assmann explains, communicative memory is inherently embodied.[35] It is shared between an individual and their contemporaries through physical interactions. It is also limited in time to around eighty years, the duration over which three generations interact, and is at best only loosely supported by material objects or institutions. Cultural memory, in contrast, is 'embedded' and not just 'embodied'. It is based on fixed points in the past that are formalised through traditional rituals, symbols, narratives, calendars, objects and landscapes that have been designed to retain it. Formal and institutional, cultural memory is preserved not collectively, but by custodians of the past. Such curators care for the past (the original meaning of the term 'curator') by assuming the role of cultural specialists, be they shamans, bards, priests, archivists, librarians or, indeed, artists.[36]

Keeping this distinction in mind, one could say that performances survive in time thanks in part to an informal, communicative memory. In contrast to institutionalised rituals, monuments and other durable objects – all of which express permanence and are preserved thanks to the intercession of specialists – performances happen only once. This essential evanescence situates performance outside the hierarchy of value that privileges the permanent object over transient forms of communication. At the same time, and as we have already seen with the ghost dance, this awareness of transience can serve as a latent form of resistance against the cultural establishment. Whenever performances appear to suspend the normal ways of being and doing, they express what Jan Assmann, following Aby Warburg, has called 'mnemonic energy', even if only for a certain, limited duration.[37] This capacity to resist the linear flow of time, moreover, is what gives certain live actions their utopian edge. Perhaps, then, it is more accurate to describe performance art as an interrupting action, one that defers or otherwise resists the passage from communicative to cultural memory; from what is collectively experienced but perishable, to what is culturally embedded but no longer collectively experienced, or at least not without specialist mediation.

I mention this because, nowadays, museums and art galleries have become the privileged repositories for performance art, whether by commissioning new live art or by reclassifying the images and documents created through live performances as objects worth collecting and archiving. This process converts tenuous traces of past performances into 'works' to be collected or 'documents' to be archived. It also, *mutatis mutandis*, creates a more durable cultural memory out of transient performance behaviours. Such a reframing makes it difficult to see how performances may relate to forms of collective expressions that are otherwise forgotten or partially repressed, or even how transience itself might serve as an important vehicle of dissent.

It also makes it difficult to see how performance might be considered 'revolutionary'. Yet both performance and revolution are events for which the appropriate context of reception cannot be decided in advance and must rely on public revelation to give them meaning. One could say that

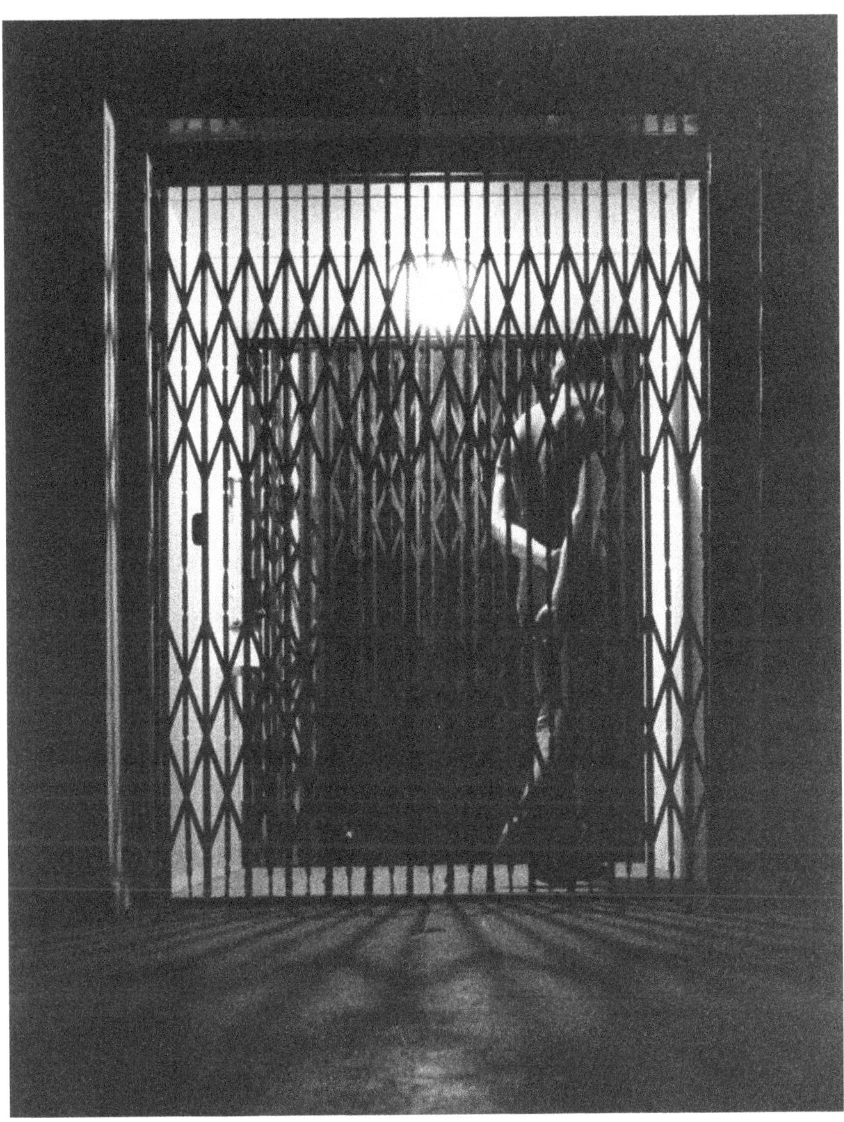

Approaches to Learning, Ikon, Birmingham, 1980   **2.1**

live actions, such as those performed by Bereś or Knížak, are analogous to revolutions whenever they are publicly perceived to have created a breach, discontinuity or gap within the 'normal' sense of historical progress, even if the artist in question is not a revolutionary in the narrower political sense of the term. This last point is crucial. As Marc Augé has observed, a society ruled entirely by governance has no future.[38] In such a society, revolutions have no

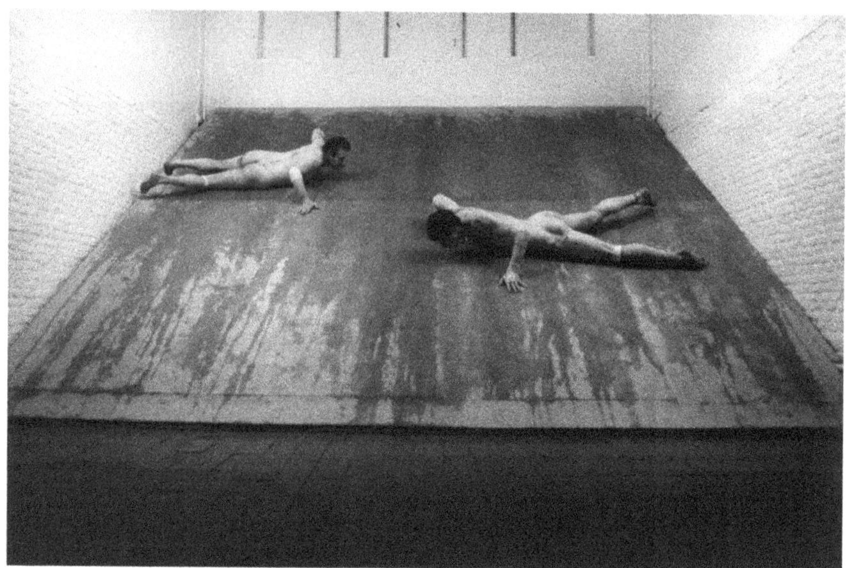

2.2 *Between*, de Appel, Amsterdam, 1979

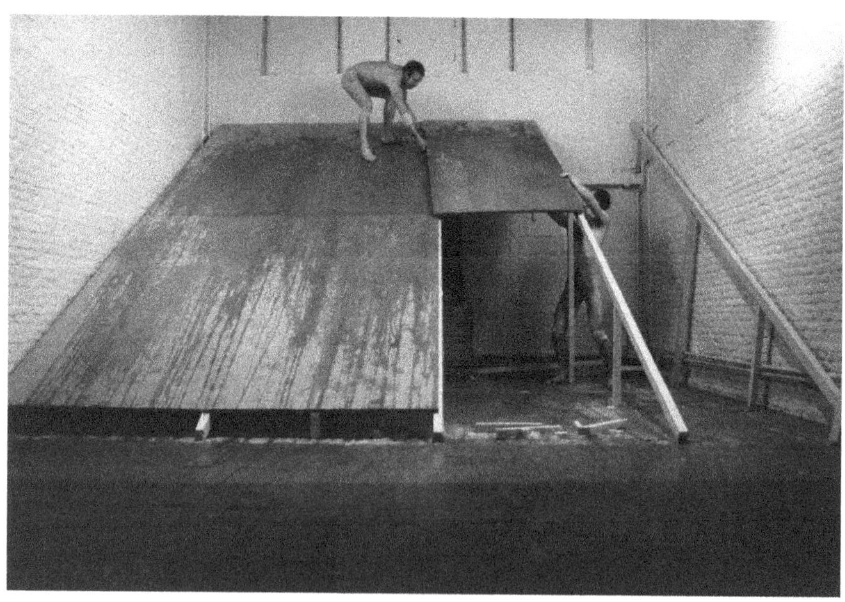

2.3 *Between*, de Appel, Amsterdam, 1979

place for the same reason that rituals no longer exist. For rituals too 'aim to create the feeling of a beginning'.[39] Like revolutions, they express the cut in time that changes you, the way rituals around birth, naming or death allow the individual to pass from one state to another.

So far, we have considered how Brisley models his own understanding of performance as expressing a set of dissident behaviours that, for him, are trans-historical. In what follows I propose to expand this idea by further elaborating the analogy between performance and the ghost dance established in *Being and Doing*. I take my examples from two films by Ken McMullen which feature performances by Brisley. My aim is not to discuss the films per se, which merit their own separate treatment elsewhere, but, rather, to elaborate their historical references to revolution and resistance. In so doing I hope to enlarge the cultural and historical framework through which the surviving images and traces of Brisley's own performances can also be interpreted and understood.

Ghost Dance and *Resistance*

McMullen's film *Ghost Dance* explicitly takes up the role of the artist as shaman, someone who gives voice to expectations that remain unfulfilled. It explores how a world thoroughly mediated by electronic technology leads to a revival of an anachronistic belief in ghosts. The film's fragmented aesthetic, and constant reworking of its initial premises, conveys the impression of a society that is rapidly disintegrating. In such a society any new myths appear, at best, only as ghost dances: regressive, irrational, even frankly comical expressions of a profound sense of alienation.

In the film, Jacques Derrida, who has a cameo role, elaborates on the significance of the title. He observes that ghosts arise whenever the usual processes of mourning are interrupted for some reason; when the dead, instead of being assimilated by the living, continue to exist alongside them as a malingering presence that disrupts the ordinary experiences of time as linear and irreversible. Derrida claims that such ghosts are not confined to the past. In a world in which desire and our relation to reality is increasingly mediated by images, even 'the future belongs to ghosts'.

The centrality of remediation to modern myth becomes especially obvious in situations of historical defeat. In a particularly interesting set of sequences, the film returns several times to the downfall of the French Commune, a pivotal event in both the history and memory of revolution. It obsessively reconstructs traces left behind by the event, notably the well-known photo of the executed Communards, stacked in rows in their coffins. The film manipulates this recorded image repeatedly: dipping it in seawater (like so much photographic fluid), burying it in mud, using it as a wall poster, even juxtaposing the dead Communards to black and white photos of the film's actors. In one notable sequence, the camera films its characters filming or photographing the Wall in the Père Lachaise cemetery, the place where 147 Communards, including women and children, were executed in 1871, after a last, desperate battle with the troops of the French government stationed in Versailles.

These remediations capture an important aspect of the historical event, namely that this Wall is not a burial mound in a traditional sense. At the time, the executed bodies were thrown into an open trench and families were refused burial markers. It was not until 1909, almost forty years after the event, that a plaque was installed and a monument erected, not at the Wall but elsewhere in the cemetery, commemorating all the victims of the conflict without distinction.[40] In fact, the Wall had first become a *lieu de mémoire* informally, by virtue of the annual pilgrimages by the workers' movements that began in the 1880s as a way to keep memories of the Commune alive in a city that even today bears almost no trace of the almost 10,000 (possibly more) estimated victims killed, and many more imprisoned or deported by the French government to penal colonies. In a 2004 interview with McMullen, the philosopher Oscar Guardiola Rivera claims that when the film premiered in Bogota in 1984, several hundred people showed up to attend the screening. All were apparently riveted by the scenes that took place at the Wall, a placeholder for all those ghosts that exist 'outside history' and fail to be politically acknowledged, a situation with obvious parallels to the Latin American context of the 1970s and 1980s, where bodies of leftists were still missing or unaccounted for.[41]

The manner in which the Communards were commemorated suggests that when it comes to situations of historical defeat, the passage from an informal memory culture, created by participants, eyewitnesses and immediate descendants of those involved in the event, to canonised representation, occurs via various kinds of performance behaviours, including those mediated by photography and film. It also poses a more difficult question of how to create a collective memory for revolutionary movements that have politically failed and can no longer transform their defeat into the hope of an imminent future revolution. Enzo Traverso observes the close affinity between film as a medium and contemporary representations of the revolutionary Left tradition. He notes that this history of defeat cannot be communicated through the conventional markers of cultural memory (monuments, rituals, remembrance ceremonies etc.) because these invariably belong to the victors and not to the vanquished. By contrast, film's visual imaginary captures how the dream of communism might live on as a 'realm of memory'; that is to say, not as a 'reliquary form' of a defeated past but as a 'lived past' that expresses a future, even if this future is no longer transmissible.[42]

Indeed, as Derrida reminds us, both in the film and in his book *Specters of Marx,* a spectre exists as an event (it visits the person or place it haunts) and as a repetition (a spectre 'returns' from the dead, and perhaps not just once).[43] As repetitions that are potentially without origin, spectres force us to rethink the relations between past and present from a position outside the modern historical worldview. Since the ideological and historical defeat of communism, this worldview has assumed that the revolutionary past is over and that no future sequence of events can reactivate its memory. As François Furet expressed it, with no more revolutionary change to anticipate, revolutions should henceforth be studied dispassionately, as a distant, dead past to be reconstructed using the usual methods of the historical profession.[44] Derrida, however, points out that this revolutionary historiography – that used to circulate under the label of Marxism – continues to haunt the liberal West after both its historical defeat *and* its defeat as a once viable memory culture; that is to say, as a way of connecting the past to the future. If anything, all the diverse ways in which Marxism has been written out of history throw into sharper relief the tenacity of its survival. Unhinged from any authoritative framework, Marxism appears as a ghost from outside history, interrupting and disrupting the liberal consensus about progress with recurring visions of unfulfilled promises.

The status of this unassimilated past – and how it relates to victorious ideologies – is also thematised in McMullen's earlier film, *Resistance* (1976), about French fighters who fought against the Occupation during the Second World War. Its pretext was the discovery, by the British historian Rodney Kedward, of the transcript of a group therapy session undertaken by five French ex-resistance heroes who, in 1948, found themselves in various stages of mental breakdown. Some had committed crimes that ill-fitted their status as heroes; others were haunted by their memories of wartime betrayal. All of this was at odds with the national mythology of 'resistance' that had been constructed after the war. McMullen asked the actors, who included the performance artists Stuart Brisley and Marc Chaimowicz, to improvise, over a continuous period of twenty-four hours, a situation based on the script, in front of a practising psychoanalyst. The traumas of the historical actors were thus re-enacted through the conscious and unconscious desires of the film's participants, in the effort to create not a historical fiction but a 'historically-based fiction'. As the narrative voice-over remarks, 'improvisation tends to throw up realities amongst its fictions; the participant's own realities come through, resisting the stories imposed on them'. This double investigation of resistance – of the original historical protagonists in 1948 and of the filmed participants in 1975 – was in turn juxtaposed with photographic and filmed documentation, not only from the war itself but also from various historical revolutions and scenes of social unrest, including from the torrid decade of the 1930s that led up to the war.

But the main action concerns the characters themselves and the evolution of their relationship over time. Shut up in a Devon farmhouse, tensions escalated over the course of the twenty hours of isolation, as each performer developed their historical character. Brisley played Sam, who had been a communist before he was excommunicated by the party in the 1930s. He based his performance partly on recollections of his father, who had been a union organiser and had participated in the General Strike of 1926. Over the course of twenty hours, we see how Sam/Brisley develops a visceral rivalry with Marc Chaimowicz, himself born in post-war Paris and whose Polish father was Jewish. Chaimowicz plays an eponymous character called Marc, a petty crook who ended up glorified by the war and whom the British psychoanalyst accuses of pushing 'the past away, ridiculing it, resisting it, hiding his own problems'. This contrasts with Sam/Brisley who is keen to explore the past, even as he admits its disintegrating qualities. As time goes on, Sam/Brisley appears to increasingly lose any sense of historical distance from his character. The film culminates in what appears to be the attempted suicide of the character but was also the very real act of Brisley falling into a frozen pond on the grounds of the estate. This act could be interpreted as Sam's inability to sustain his position when faced with the denials and aggressions of Marc. But it also expresses Brisley's inability to understand his character. In the film, Sam/Brisley identifies this point of no-turning-back with the revolutionary situation, in which too 'there is no choice just a necessary act, and all other choices don't exist anymore'. One of the last clear words we hear in the film comes from the real, not fictional, psychoanalyst, chastising the actors for 'taking it too far'.

This non-metaphorical act of falling into a pond contains an element of risk, or at least a point of not turning back. Brisley's action – and the reaction of the other witnesses to it – breaks the narrative frame of the film. It thus serves to underline the key difference between film and performance. Film is created in stages and actions. Editing is always possible. Things can be added in or cut out to create a selective memory. Performance, on the other hand, is a continuous process whose outcome can never be controlled in advance. In this sense, it is more akin to actual memory, which also continually moves in and out of definition.

Given this kinship with memory, performance provides us with ways to access the past that can be historically revealing in their own way. This becomes evident if we consider in more detail Kedward's ground-breaking studies of the French resistance that provided the pretext for the film. By collecting individual, highly localised memories of resistance, Kedward was able to counter public memory as it had been constituted after the war through 'official' representations or in media-conscious commemorations. Significantly, these memories expressed themselves in part through a visual language of images. As he observes:

The dream image is one of the most constant in the recollections of the period. Resisters often remember 1940–41 as a kind of waking dream; they talk of searching blindly in the night, of outstretched fingertips groping for constant, and dreamlike visions of adventurous operations, which far outrun the sober calculations of their rational selves. The most basic accounts of early resistance show an amazing number of grand designs projected by individuals unconnected with each other, and such designs contained the seeds of almost all future resistance, theory and practice alike.[45]

These memories may be isolated and individual, specific to time and place, but in their aggregate they are 'cultural in origin and expression' and, in this sense, generic.[46] These images may include fragments of a publicly shared memory (Kedward cites a 'barricade' tradition that circulated as folklore or the 'long tradition of pride in patriotism in revolt' that stems from the French Revolution[47]). What they communicate, however, is not tradition but a largely inchoate desire for a rupture with the past. Kedward describes this desire as a 'grand design', a model for a history that the protagonists do not yet know how to make. In the absence of prognostic knowledge, the body and its gestures play a vital role. Kedward observes how, in his interviews with old Maquisards in rural France, a kind of scenario would repeat in which drinks would be served and a female member of the household – a wife, sister, daughter – would stand in the doorway, correcting or adding to the old man's recollections. He began to notice that this same 'woman in the doorway' would frequently appear in various archival records from the time of the Occupation, 'prolonging police enquiries, misleading their search, feigning ignorance, covering tracks'.[48] According to Kedward, this communicative memory reveals something about the anthropology of resistance that is distinct from the kind of public or 'cultural memory' of resistance as constructed by political parties and the government after the fact.[49]

I want to suggest that the filmic memories of performance discussed in this chapter express something similar. They showcase neither history understood as a verifiable record of events nor a public memory as it is officially constructed. Rather, they access the dreams and hopes of the past, which are always future oriented. Didi-Huberman has used the image of the firefly to express this capacity of images to resist oblivion and the destruction of experience. His essay *Survival of the Fireflies* takes as its starting point the eerie glow of night-time fireflies evoked by Pasolini in his reminiscences on his own youth and involvement in the Italian resistance.[50] In Italian, the term *lucciole* has multiple connotations. Beyond denoting actual fireflies, it is slang for prostitutes and used colloquially to refer to the lights that illuminate a film set as well as the flashlight of the usherette who guides you to your seat.

More euphemistically, *lucciole* referred to the signals sent out by Italian resistance fighters during the war. In his essay, Pasolini contrasted the intermittent light of these 'fireflies' – with their intertwined connotations of resistance, desire and love of cinema – to the quasi-permanent lights of a film industry obsessed with the power of images, that he likened to the searchlights of the fascist government during the Second World War. Expanding on this notion, Didi-Huberman suggests that: 'Firefly-images, on the brink of disappearance' resist the power of the permanent image, which is also an image of power.[51] They offer a 'glimmer of a counterforce', an ongoing work of resistance that is incomplete because it takes place in the absence of any salvation or belief in future utopia.

By way of concluding, I would like to suggest that, if anything, the ghost-like images of revolt and revolution discussed in this chapter may well be more present today than during the 1970s and early 1980s, when the failure of revolution was so keenly felt by those on the Left. Indeed, as we move further away from the triumphant 1990s with its proclaimed end of history, it is striking just how persistent these memories of past struggles for equality have proved to be. This prolonged afterlife of a past that is supposed to be dead and gone underscores how the passage of time continually reframes our relationship to the past, bringing us at times closer to and not further away from events in the past. So too with the images of performance art, which continue to circulate and emit a weak presence in the public sphere even when any personal memory of the event has long since disintegrated. It remains to be seen whether these images will communicate in a way that goes beyond the individual artist or work in question. Or whether they too will finally stand still, immobilised by a cultural memory – and industry – for which the permanence of the image – and the market value of the individual artist – is key. But, as I have tried to show in this chapter, when associated with other images, they can be used to reconstruct an alternative history of collective behaviours that goes beyond the individual person or artist in question. How this alternative history is expressed in Brisley's public art projects is the subject of the following two chapters.

Notes

1 Matthew Reason, *Documentation, Disappearance and the Representation of Live Performance* (London, UK: Palgrave Macmillan, 2006), p. 8. This turn towards documentation emerged in the 1990s as scholars grappled with the difficulties of interpreting an art form witnessed by a small and vanishing number of people. See notably Amelia Jones, *Body Art/Performing the Subject* (Minneapolis, MN: University of Minnesota Press, 1998); '"Presence" in Absentia: Experiencing Performance as Documentation', *Art Journal*, 56/4 (1997), 11–18. Observing the ubiquity of recording practices, Philip Auslander has disputed the very distinction between 'live' and 'recorded' performances, arguing that documentation is what

'frames' an event as performance and allows it to circulate as such. See *Reactivations: Essays on Performance and Its Documentation* (Ann Arbor, MI: University of Michigan Press, 2018); 'The Performativity of Performance Documentation', *PAJ: A Journal of Performance and Art,* 28:3 (2006), 1–10. Rebecca Schneider argues that to consider performance as 'disappearance' is to limit ourselves 'to an understanding of performance predetermined by our cultural habituation to the logic of the archive', *Performing Remains,* p. 98. For the evolution of this debate see Heike Roms, 'Eventful Evidence: Historicizing Performance Art', in Barbara Büscher and Franz Anton Cramer (eds), *Fluid Access: Archiving Performance-Based Art* (Hildesheim: Georg Olms Verlag, 2017), pp. 93–101, available online www.per fomap.de/map2/geschichte/romsengl/eventful-evidence (accessed 13 July 2021).

2 A concern also shared by popular histories that are recalled through performance and re-enactment, as Schneider demonstrates in *Performing Remains.*

3 For 'performance' in relation to visual arts see especially 'The Theatrical Costumes for the Intermedi of 1589', in Aby Warburg, *The Renewal of Pagan Antiquity,* trans. David Britt (Los Angeles, CA: Getty Publication, 1999), pp. 349–401, extensively discussed by Philippe-Alain Michaud, *Aby Warburg and the Image in Motion,* trans. Sophie Hawkes (New York: Zone Books, 2004), pp. 149–170.

4 Georges Didi-Huberman, *The Surviving Image: Phantoms of Time and Time of Phantoms: Aby Warburg's History of Art,* trans. Harvey Mendelsohn (State College, PA: Penn State University, 2018), pp. 25, 27, 161.

5 Notably, his discussion of the Sonderkommando images of the concentration camps in *Images in Spite of All: Four Photographs from Auschwitz,* trans. Shane B. Lillis (Chicago, IL: University of Chicago Press, 2012).

6 Barber notes: 'performance artists have often distrusted the sequential form of film' (p. 21), which can 'edit, overhaul or overrule performances' duration (p. 26). Stephen Barber, *Performance Projections: Film and the Body in Action* (London: Reaktion Books, 2014).

7 Stuart Brisley, Action Forms Thought, TGA 20114/3/10/6.

8 See Brisley, Statement for the London Performance Centre Steering Committee, 11 November 1974, TGA 20114/3/5/11/1/7, p. 1.

9 Fisher-Lichte, *The Transformative Power of Performance,* pp. 33–35.

10 'Central to these rituals – and similar ones across Europe – is that the "acting out" or performance of feelings and perceptions is necessary to re-assert the spirit of collective experience. Performance Art springs from related impulses, but self-consciously draws on the artist's sense of alienation and isolation within society.' Brisley, Being and Doing Leaflet, TGA 201114/3/11/7.

11 Ibid.

12 Michaud, *Aby Warburg and the Image in Motion,* pp. 59–66.

13 Ibid., p. 66.

14 Ibid., pp. 149–150. See also Kurt W. Forster, 'Aby Warburg: His Study of Ritual and Art on Two Continents', trans. David Britt, *October,* 77 (1996), 5–24. https://doi.org/10.2307/778958 (accessed 28 June 2022).

15 Ibid., p. 186.

16 I thank Maya Balcioglu for this reference.

17 Weston La Barre, *The Ghost Dance: The Origins of Religion* (New York, NY: Doubleday, 1970), p. 277.

18 Ibid.

19 It was also shared by other artists acting in the 1970s and 1980s, including Joseph Beuys, Jaros Kozlowski and Andrzej Kostołowski, Zoran Popović and others. This disarticulation of Western from Eastern European art history has been addressed by Piotr Piotrowski, *In the Shadow of Yalta: Art and the Avant-garde in Eastern Europe 1945–1989*, trans. Anna Brzyski (London: Reaktion Books, 2009); and in initiatives such as the Contemporary and Modern Art Perspectives at MOMA, whose stated mission is to examine 'artistic modernism beyond the frameworks provided by Western European and North American avant-gardes'. See also Amy Bryzgel, *Performance Art in Eastern Europe since 1960* (Manchester: Manchester University Press, 2017); Klara Kemp-Welch, *Networking the Bloc: Experimental Art in Eastern Europe 1965–1981* (Cambridge, MA: Massachusetts Institute of Technology Press, 2019).

20 As Brisley observes 'no one was interested at the time'. Telephone conversation, 28 June 2022.

21 Photos of the military takeover in Poland were by Iain Robertson. Telephone conversation with Brisley 28 June 2022. This political regime lasted from 13 December 1981 to 22 July 1983, so was contemporary with the making of this film.

22 Perhaps a reference to the Lady de Mowbray legend: her hat, having blown off as she was passing by Haxey Hill, was chased down by two peasants, whom she rewarded for their gallantry by promising every man on Haxey Hill a measure of land if they re-enacted this episode each Twelfth Night.

23 See Venetia Newall, 'Throwing the Hood at Haxey: A Lincolnshire Twelfth-Night Custom', *Folk Life*, 18:1 (1980), 7–23. For an excellent discussion of the ritual's past and present incarnations see Catriona M. Parrat, 'Of Place and Men and Women: Gender and Topophilia in the "Haxey Hood"', *Journal of Sport History*, 27:2 (2000), 229–245.

24 According to one account, the Oss, alongside red-cloaked women, had scared off a French ship that in February 1797 landed at Fishguard to stir up the Welsh into a revolution. See B. C. Spooner, 'The Padstow Obby Oss', *Folklore*, 69:1 (2012), 34–38.

25 The blue-ribboned Oss was introduced by the Methodist Temperance society in the nineteenth century. See Helen Cornish, 'Not All Singing and Dancing: Padstow, Folk Festivals and Belonging', *Journal of Anthropology*, 81:4 (2016), 631–647. Brisley suggests that this basic conflict stems from the nineteenth century, when folklore was sanitised. Telephone conversation 28 June 2022.

26 Conversation with Brisley, 10 September 2022.

27 The witness was in fact Brisley's accountant at the time. Conversation with Brisley, December 2016, London.

28 Telephone conversation with Brisley, 28 June 2022.

29 For this international campaign, see Kemp-Welch, *Networking the Bloc*, p. 61.

30 Paul Taylor, 'Being and Doing', *Monthly Film Bulletin*, 52:612 (1985), 16–17.

31 A Proposal De Appel Robertson/Brisley, TGA 201114/3/7/1/.

32 John Roberts, 'Between: Stuart Brisley and Iain Robertson Friends, Enemies and Rivals', *The Performance Magazine*, 5 (April 1980), pp. 20–21, TGA 201114/3/7/3/.

33 Valie Export, 'Expanded Cinema, Expanded Reality', in *Expanded Cinema: Art, Performance, Film*, ed. A. L. Rees et al. (London: Tate Publishing, 2011), pp. 288–298, p. 289.

34 Halbwachs, who coined the term, observes that collective memory is always a memory of social groups which prevent other memories from forming and developing in their midst. See Maurice Halbwachs, *On Collective Memory*, ed. and trans. Lewis A. Coser (Chicago, IL: University of Chicago Press, 1992), pp. 38, 53, 93, 189. See also Aleida Assmann, *Cultural Memory and Western Civilization: Functions, Media, Archives* (Cambridge, MA: Cambridge University Press, 2011); Jan Assmann, 'Collective Memory and Cultural Identity', trans. John Czaplicka, *New German Critique*, 65 (1995), 125–133. On forgetting as a condition for remembering see Paul Ricoeur, *Memory, History, Forgetting*, trans. Kathleen Blamey and David Pellauer (Chicago, IL: University of Chicago Press, 2006).

35 Jan Assmann, 'Collective Memory and Cultural Identity', pp. 126–129.

36 Reflecting on the growing surplus of documentation, especially in the digital age, Aleida Assmann has even identified a third type of memory, a disembodied, non-biological 'storage memory' which contains 'what is unusable, obsolete or dated' with 'no vital ties to the present and no bearing on identity formation'. Assmann, *Cultural Memory and Western Civilization*, p. 124.

37 Jan Assmann, 'Collective Memory and Cultural Identity' p. 129.

38 Marc Augé, *The Future*, trans. John Howe (London, UK: Verso Books, 2014), p. 51.

39 Ibid., p. 21.

40 The controversies around the commemoration of the Commune continued as late as 2000. Janice Best observes that the first monument, *Victimes des Révolutions*, although intended as a symbol of reconciliation, contained subversive elements such as chunks of the actual Wall which were integrated as part of the relief. See 'Une Statue monumentale de la République', *Nineteenth-Century French Studies*, 34:3/4 (2006), 303–322, p. 316.

41 This interview, along with several others, accompanied the 2004 DVD release of the film.

42 Enzo Traverso, *Left-Wing Melancholia: Marxism, History, and Memory* (New York City: Columbia University Press, 2016), p. 97.

43 Jacques Derrida, *Specters of Marx: The State of the Debt, the Work of Mourning, and the New International*, trans. Peggy Kamuf (Abingdon: Routledge, 1994), pp. 123–126.

44 Furet, *The Passing of an Illusion*, p. 502.

45 Roderick Kedward, *Occupied France: Collaboration and Resistance 1940–1944* (Oxford: Wiley-Blackwell, 1991), p. 47.

46 Roderick Kedward, 'Resiting French Resistance', *Transactions of the Royal Historical Society*, 9 (1999), 271–282, p. 272.

47 Kedward, *Occupied France*, p. 50.

48 Kedward, 'Resiting French Resistance', p. 276.

49 Kedward suggests that this anthropology can serve as the basis for a comparative history of resistance: 'the decades of East European resistance to the pathology of Stalinism … or the long histories of resistance to apartheid in Southern Africa,

allow models of clandestine activity to emerge, which fit closely with paradigms of resistance in Nazi-occupied Europe', 'Resiting French Resistance', p. 272.

50 Georges Didi-Huberman, *The Survival of the Fireflies*, trans. Lia Swope Mitchell (Minneapolis, MN: University of Minnesota Press, 2018). Pier Paolo Pasolini's first article appeared in the *Corriere della Serra* on 1 February 1975. It was republished as 'L'articolo delle lucciole', in Pier Paolo Pasolini, *Scritti corsari* (Milan: Garzanti, 1975), pp. 160–168.

51 Didi-Huberman, *Survival of the Fireflies*, p. 82. Didi-Huberman cites Laura Waddington's film *Border* (2004) as an example of a firefly image.

Performance art and revolutions are analogous activities insofar as both are events that seek to inaugurate their own histories. As such, they cannot be explained solely by reference to the historical contexts that preceded them but need to be understood from the perspective of the future that they make possible: the new subjects and new identities they produce in their wake.[1] But Brisley's performances are also unlike revolutions insofar as they take place in a time of the aftermath, when ruptures such as those associated with revolutions no longer seem possible. Reflecting on this difficulty, Brisley's long-durational works demonstrate that a new experience of time can also emerge by intensifying the links a given situation may have with a pre-existing context, in a manner that also activates the latent possibilities associated with this past.

This was the challenge of Brisley's *Peterlee Project*. Frequently hailed as a pioneering archival arts project, Brisley has always insisted that this was neither an archival project nor an arts project but, rather, an attempt to use performance itself to bring about a deep-seated social and political transformation. The project began when Brisley was employed as a Town Artist in Peterlee, one of the original twelve New Towns erected in Britain after the Second World War to alleviate the scarcity of housing. Peterlee is located in England's North East, an area rich in mining life and its traditions. Yet, upon arriving there in 1976, Brisley was struck by how little this mining history seemed present in Peterlee, which appeared to be 'without history', dominated in all aspects by the paternalistic Development Corporation that had built it and still controlled many aspects of the town's life.[2]

Subtitling his project 'History Within Living Memory', Brisley set out to help the town's inhabitants recover their collective past, anchored by a shared history of mining, by collating their personal photos, documents and oral interviews (figures 3.1 and 3.2). According to Brisley, the intention was 'to stretch performance into a continuous engagement with the everyday', until it 'dissolves into the social environment as an agent'.[3] As the town's oldest inhabitants had moved to the region as children, when the first pits were sunk in the North Sea, Brisley saw an opportunity to reactivate a still living 'communicative memory' that spanned three generations, correlating to the roughly eighty or so years over which such informal memories are communicated and retained by living people. Significantly, this communicative memory spanned the mining history of the region, the very history that appeared to be missing in Peterlee. The *Peterlee Project*, in other words, aimed to use these collective memories as a means of raising the historical consciousness of the town's people about their own past, present and future. Through Brisley's intervention, a past that was embodied in the town's inhabitants as an affective feeling and focus for collective identification, but had never become explicit, was to serve as a potent resource that could potentially even challenge the role of the Development Corporation in people's lives.

But, for this engagement with the everyday to remain continuous, the performance had to remain open, capable of generating new subjects and actions that could resist being reabsorbed into the very historical context that the performance sought to illuminate and, in the last instance, challenge. For reasons that I explain below, this did not happen in Peterlee. Yet, while the project failed to create a continually useable resource, it succeeded in achieving a certain archival *presence*. The 2,000 photographs, 1,000 slides and 50 taped interviews became the basis of the most significant archive of local and mining history in the North East of England, today dispersed between the Durham County Archive, the Tate Gallery and the original mining villages to which some elements have since been returned.[4] It also served, briefly, as the impetus for the building of a future museum of local history, as well as becoming an important reference in the art world. A project, thus, that set out to animate a still living past, produced instead an archival past and an art object mediated and supported by institutions.

The *Peterlee Project* thus takes us to the heart of performance art and how it models its relation to time and history. This includes the relation of performance to what the philosopher Michael Oakeshott has termed the 'practical past': that collection of riddles, sayings, songs, traditions, rituals, exempla, mythologies, shared stories, reference points and recollections that make up a people's own understanding of the 'way it used to be'.[5] Emerging out of a practical engagement with the world, this past is intersubjective, embodied in individual and social identities, and – crucially – future oriented, invoked as a way of dealing with a present situation that always involves an intended or hoped-for future. Given its overwhelmingly pragmatic and future-oriented dimension, Oakeshott argues that this practical past cannot be grasped by conventional historical methods. Even when elements of this past are registered or recorded in some way, they reappear in the present only as 'traces' or 'survivals', fragments from ways of living and being otherwise lost to the present. Oakeshott contrasts this living, embodied past with the historical past which, he argues, was experienced by no one, being an inferential construct made up by historians and other professionals engaged in reconstructing a past from the traces that the practical past has left behind.[6]

A similar understanding of the practical past lies at the heart of the *Peterlee Project*, which too orients itself towards the future. As Hayden White has observed, whether he intended to or not, 'Oakeshott provided a basis for shifting the burden of constituting a useable past from the guild of professional historians to the members of the community as a whole.'[7] In contrast to the historical past, which expresses how things *were* and therefore cannot serve as a guide to the future, the practical past expresses how things *are* and, more importantly, what *they could be*. For White, a heightened awareness of the practical past – especially as expressed through literature, poetry and other works of the imagination – can serve as a model or guide to the future, especially in situations where other kinds of social or political utopias appear to be markedly absent. In fact, White argues that the practical past can be revived as a kind of utopian action itself, exemplified, for instance, in the ancient ideal of history as 'propaedeutic to life in the public sphere'; or, to use a more modern example, the pragmatic orientation towards the past summed up by Lenin's well-known phrase 'What is to be done?'[8]

Keeping this distinction between the practical and historical past in mind, I propose to evaluate the successes and failures of the *Peterlee Project* by highlighting how a practical past becomes a historical past and the role that institutions play in that process. In so doing, I hope to map out the potential, as well as limitations, that attend public art projects, as the practice has developed since the 1960s. Can performance art – as it often claims to do – challenge our attitudes to the past and, with it, our predetermined futures? Or does it merely end up reinforcing the status quo? And in cases when a performance does appear to provide a kind of knowledge about a collectively shared past, where does the knowledge lie – on the side of the performer, the participant or both?

The context: Peterlee

Situated in County Durham, Peterlee New Town was developed primarily to relieve the overcrowding in the nearby mining villages which, by the end of the war, was so severe that some families were reduced to living in the limestone caves along the coast.[9] As early as 1944, the local council had mooted the idea of building a new town on a single site that would overcome the legacy of the original mining villages. Cheaply built and constructed in full view of the slag heap, these villages served as a constant reminder of the dirty, uncertain, dangerous and low-paid nature of the work itself. Moreover, as the housing was owned by the colliery companies, the miners were effectively tenants and could be evicted at any time for any reason. As the council's first report expressed it, 'there was no escape from it; it was coal all the time'.[10] The control of the mining companies even extended to leisure time and entertainment, which the colliery companies had been obliged to provide since the Mining Industry Act of 1920. This economic stranglehold, and absence of any alternative industry, was imprinted in the family structures and ways of life of the miners themselves. Prior to the post-war nationalisation of the mining industry, boys had been typically sent to the pit at the age of fourteen; girls of the same age either assisted at home or entered domestic service in urban centres to relieve the burden on their parents.

Peterlee New Town, in contrast, was to exemplify social progress, rationalised urban planning and the push towards a more diversified economic base which had become increasingly urgent after the war. 'Farewell Squalor' was the title of the council's idealistic report, and it expressed nothing less than the desire to liberate people's eyes, hearts and minds from the omnipresent headgear: so oppressive yet so fundamental to a community in which the common good – and shared suffering – meant everything (figure 3.3). As town surveyor and engineer C. W. Clarke observed, not without emotion: 'Where else is shown the same sympathy in bereavement, assistance in necessity or rejoicing in good fortune between members of a community? Any attempt to plan for an area must seek to preserve this spirit.'[11] In fact, Peterlee was the only New Town built at the request of the miners themselves.

These utopian ambitions were also evident in the original town plan, designed by Berthold Lubetkin, who had pioneered modernist architecture in Britain.[12] Although his plans were eventually rejected, this modernist impulse remains visible in the small number of flat-roofed houses designed by the constructivist artist Victor Pasmore in the 1950s. In fact, when Pasmore returned to Peterlee in 1970 as Peterlee's first Town Artist, he designed the Apollo Pavilion, the town's most famous landmark (figure 3.4). Neither a sculpture nor an enclosed building, this 'inhabited structure' aimed to give 'dignity, focus and impact' to the built environment.[13] Initially reviled by the town's inhabitants, the Apollo Pavilion is today widely regarded as the first large-scale public structure in Britain. It also attracted the attention of Brisley, who, as we have already seen in Chapter 1, had a long-standing interest in English constructivism, in particular, its attempt to integrate art and architecture into the original concept and design of a building.[14] As contemporary observers noted, Brisley's own project can be considered a continuation of Pasmore's attempt to created inhabited public spaces.[15] But, unlike Pasmore, who built something new that remained empty and unloved, Brisley used memory and lived experience in the effort to stretch and extend performance into the gaps or spaces of the existing architectural order, in order to liberate its emancipatory potential.

To a certain extent, time was the most obvious and, in many ways, the only material available for such a project. As Oscar Negt and Alexander Kluge have observed in their own investigation of the emancipatory potential of the industrial context, first published in 1972, the abstract time of capitalism acknowledges only the logic of the working day. Even free time is subsumed under the quantifiable categories of overtime and leisure time. Within such a context, time is structured as cyclical, repetitive and directionless, in which anything 'historical would be a residue'.[16] Against this abstract understanding of time, remembrance and shared memory serve as vital resources of self-expression, even resistance against a life context otherwise thoroughly delimited by the demands of labour. Given this industrial context, as applicable to factory employment as to life in the mines, the challenge of the *Peterlee Project* was two-fold. To what extent could the working-class citizens of Peterlee regain control and truly inhabit their town as a public space as the original architects and designers had intended? And how could a life context that was mostly experienced as a private and highly fragmented affair become something public and shared?

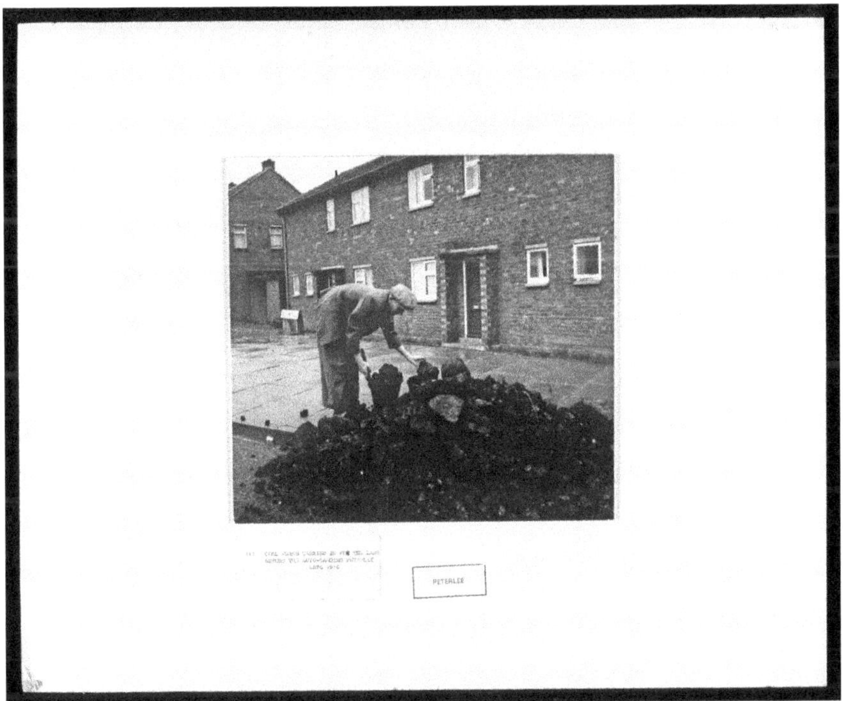

'Coal being Carried in for the last before the autobagging', late 1950, *Peterlee Project – History Within Living Memory*, 1976–77   **3.1**

But neither the town's avant-garde origins nor its mining history were much in evidence when Brisley first visited Peterlee. From the perspective of Brisley, who had been brought up to believe that miners were the 'avant-garde of the working-class',[17] there was not much to register the symbolic figure of the miner as the vanguard of the proletariat, the one who did the riskiest work, under the most perilous conditions. Instead, Brisley noticed three things. First, as already noted, although the area was rich in mining history, the inhabitants did not connect to this history, despite almost all being descendants of the original mining families. Second, the Peterlee Development Corporation (PDC), directly appointed by the government to build the town, was the dominant authority, yet unaccountable to the elected local council. As Brisley noted: 'Its influence *seems* evident in every sphere of life in Peterlee, yet the general public is remarkably ignorant of what it does.'[18] Third, his placement as a Town Artist working on behalf of the PDC coincided with a moment of liberalisation, when the PDC wanted to shed its authoritarian image and devolve power to local authorities.[19] Like in the case of the other New Towns, this was a public agency, directly appointed by the

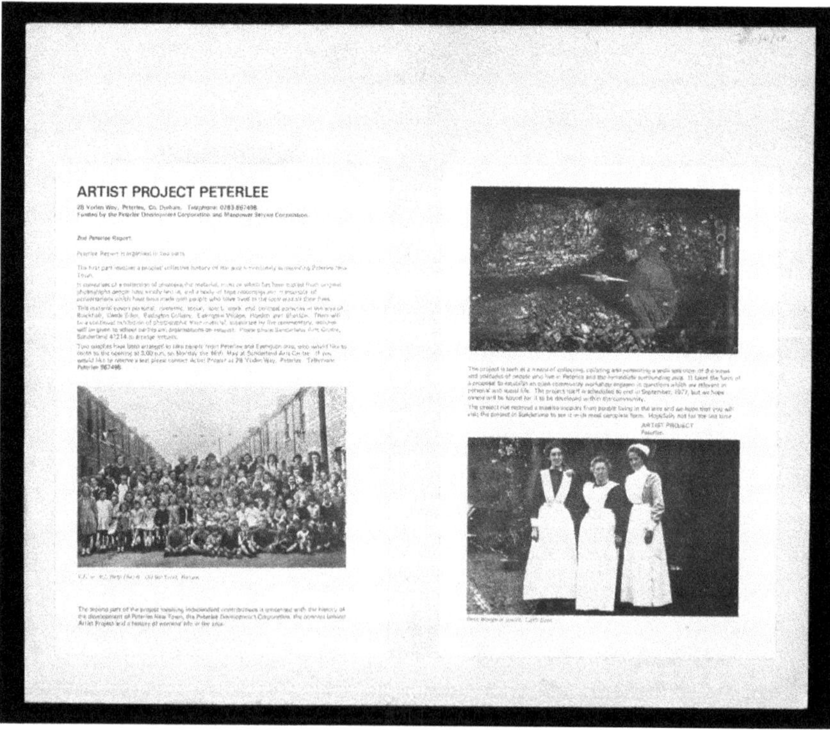

3.2   *Artist Project Peterlee, 1976–77*

government and answerable only to it. It was also a major landlord, owning most of the land, houses and a substantial proportion of industrial and commercial property. From the town's inception, there had been little or no attempt to involve the local people, with the PDC deciding even such minutiae as the colours people were permitted to paint their front doors. More egregiously, the Corporation continued what earlier detractors had called a 'history of indifference'; 'of the Corporation imposing and expropriating', and 'devaluing the significance of local people and their communities, their values, their problems and their aspirations'.[20]

Reflecting these three observations, Brisley's intervention as a Town Artist operated across two modes: first, by creating documentation to form a living history of Peterlee, second, by attempting to transform this heightened awareness of a shared life context into a platform for debate and political action.[21] Key elements of this second mode included commissioning studies that historically analysed the role of the PDC, not known for its transparency, and instigating workshops whereby the town's residents could connect this newfound historical consciousness to their present and future concerns. Together these two modes were intended to liberate the utopian, experimental spirit in

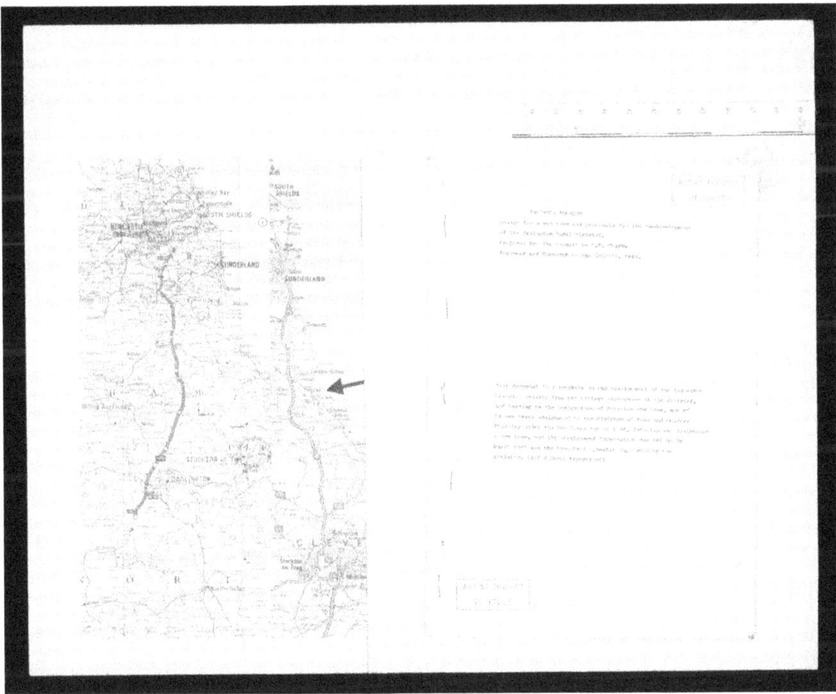

Artist Project Peterlee, 1976–77   **3.3**

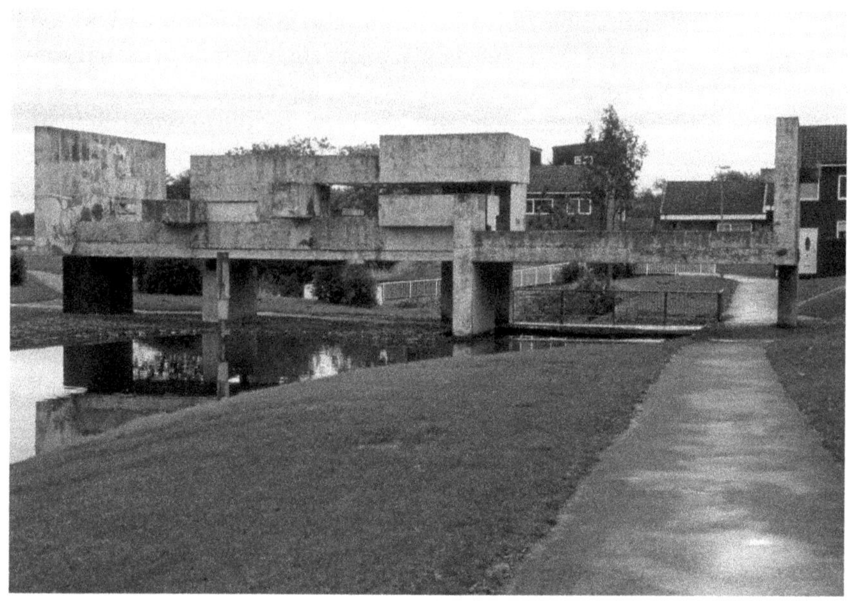

3.4 Apollo Pavilion, *Peterlee Project – History Within Living Memory*, 1976–77

which Peterlee New Town was originally conceived. The *Peterlee Project* was thus imagined as an action that would force open new channels for 'communication *and* participation' that would be 'effective and not token'.[22] As in Brisley's previous performances, the aim was to create a new context – 'a vast resource of contextual imagery and audio interviews' – in which authority could be resisted or shared.[23] In the last instance, the aim was to restore 'a measure of self-government for the people of Peterlee',[24] 'in keeping with the original intention of New Towns as experimental communities, conceived in the spirit of idealism'.[25]

The *Peterlee Project*: public history and participatory art

So far I have discussed the social context of Peterlee and the mining culture that inspired Brisley's involvement. But what was the context for the *Peterlee Project* itself? And how do we make sense of a performance in which the only material for action is this admittedly nebulous notion of 'social context'? In an important sense, the *Peterlee Project* embodies a shift towards a more contextualised understanding of social change that was widely shared by historians and theorists, especially on the Left, throughout the 1960s and 1970s. In fact, the *Peterlee Project* itself can be situated at the confluence of two movements: the boom in public history and the rise of the participatory arts movement.

Both emerged around the same time as part of a 'temporal turn' that took place across many domains, with the basic premise that duration over time was more revelatory for understanding how social structures endured and changed than permanence in space. Both movements also, it must be said, emerged when the *loss* of social context was keenly felt in advanced capitalist countries as they transitioned into the post-industrial age. This sense of an accelerated rate of change, combined with the disappearance of traditional historical referents, focused attention on the remnants of what then was experienced as a still living past; whether in the form of a soon-to-be-obsolete industrial landscape or in the echoes of a rapidly disappearing popular culture that, at least for some thinkers and activists on the Left, had long been considered a vital resource for collective identity and resistance.[26]

More specifically, the 1970s witnessed numerous public history projects in Britain and elsewhere that either gave shape to the *Peterlee Project* or influenced its immediate reception. Within Britain, these included the History Workshop, established by Raphael Samuel in 1976 as a collaborative effort to write social history 'from below'; the Hackney Writers Group, which consisted of non-professional writers who probed East London history through individual life stories; and the Popular Memory Group, established at the University of Birmingham in 1979–80 to explore oral and popular memories as 'additional' or 'alternative ways' of writing working-class, feminist and other histories that challenged dominant narratives. Earlier, the Mass Observation Unit of 1937 had asked ordinary people to document their lives. Although it had shifted towards market research after the Second World War, it was revived again in 1981 as a public resource and has been in continuous use ever since.[27] These projects all shared the belief that an awareness of history as 'living memory' was the crucial first step towards making history 'common property, capable of shaping people's understanding of themselves, and the society in which they live'.[28] This was especially urgent for historians of the Left as they sought new ways to connect local struggles to a larger context, whose contours were no longer self-evident with the increasingly apparent collapse of Marxism and other grand narratives of history.

Many of these home-grown movements were themselves inspired by post-structuralist theories of social change that had emerged in France and elsewhere in continental Europe at the time. This orientation away from an event-based historiography can be seen, for instance, in Foucault's attempt to write a history without subjects or agents, Castoriadis' call to recognise the 'multiple species of time[29] and Althusser's insistence on the 'different historical temporalities living the same historical time'.[30] Earlier in the century, the Annales school in France had already pitted a *longue durée* against the 'capriciousness' of the event.[31] Post-structuralist thinkers further developed this overall orientation away from event-based history by emphasising the event-structure of duration itself.[32] Duration was no longer conceived as static but as something constituted out of actions. As the same action could be both repetition and event, duration enabled continuity and change to be conceptualised together. In these new theories of historical change, anachronism and asynchronicity (the persistence of old habits under new structures) were rehabilitated as important new concepts, motors of history, even. No longer negatively conceived as retrograde holdovers in a historical time configured as resolutely linear and progressive, they were recast as latent forces, capable of igniting rupture and, potentially, even revolution. This emphasis on the multiple durations of historical time was not confined to thinkers on the Left. A similar point was expressed from the opposite end of the political spectrum, notably in the work of the conservative German historian Reinhart Koselleck, for whom the focus on duration, as captured by the dictum *semper idem, semper aliter* (always the same, always different), implied a plurality of identities and positions whose conflicts were not up to the historian to resolve.[33]

Yet even advocates of public history were quick to notice the discrepancy between its strong political intentions and the 'fairly meagre' political effects.[34] This failure to produce the desired social change renewed scrutiny of the differences between the practical and historical past. Remarking on the explosion of study circles within the Scandinavian working-class movements, Jorma Kalela observes how this 'history from below' challenged the historical profession in at least two ways.[35] First, by posing the question of *who* was addressed by any so-called 'historical study' of the past; second, by linking this question of *who* was being addressed to new understandings of *what* was relevant in the understanding of this past. Recounting his own involvement in a workers' history group at a Finnish paper mill, Kalela recalls how participants were relatively uninterested in the history of the unions or their own class struggle. Cultural or 'ethnographical' interests in the everyday predominated, while the classic notion of history as the recovery and study of past conflict was either submerged or disregarded. As the Birmingham Popular Memory Group observed, in most cases, it was the 'author' or 'historian' who gained historical consciousness on behalf of their sources, who mostly remained 'untouched' by the transaction. This was admittedly a rather fatal flaw for any popular or socially oriented historiography for which local awareness of the larger context of collective struggles was an essential element in the struggle for a better world.

This difficult question of how to translate an understanding of social context into social and political agency was also apparent in the participatory arts projects that emerged in the 1970s. As Boris Groys observes, the phenomenon of art activism is central to our time because it is a new phenomenon. Unlike the critical art movements of recent decades, its key characteristic is that it attempts to work 'not inside the art system, but outside it, in reality'.[36]

Groys notes that never before had artists imagined such a thing was possible; even the Russian avant-gardists attempted to use art to change social reality only when they briefly had the entire state apparatus behind them.

In Britain, the Artist Placement Group (APG), which had negotiated Brisley's residency with the PDC, played a key role in this reorientation towards social context.[37] Founded in 1965 by John Latham and Barbara Steveni, it sought to place artists in various industrial and institutional contexts. These included the petroleum company Esso, the British Steel Corporation, ICI (Imperial Chemical Industries), as well as various government offices. As Brisley understood it, APG's central concept was the 'recognition that the event is more permanent than the object; or that "Time" extendedness is of greater structural relevance than space';[38] in other words, that duration itself had a structuring quality that enabled as well as constrained the ability of individuals to engage with their environment. This same emphasis on duration was central to the strategy of the 'open brief' that was negotiated by APG on behalf of its artists. The artist was recast as an 'incidental person' (APG's term), free to produce anything, including nothing, so long as they did not 'knowingly do anything to prejudice the company's interests'.[39] The corporation, in turn, paid for the placement, in the hopes that it would derive benefit from the artist's external perspective.

The negotiated nature of the 'open brief' led to important disagreements, however. These were voiced by several artists – including Brisley – who objected that the very concept of an artist residency 'ultimately gravitates to the source of power'.[40] According to Brisley, what was missing from APG's time-based concept of art was an understanding of labour relations as conflictual; that the interests of the shop floor and management did not always converge. In other words, and despite the laudable reorientation towards social context, the APG's promotion of 'art for art's sake' perpetuated the separation of art from industry.[41] This dynamic is evident, for instance, in Ian Breakwell's well-known placement at the Department of Health and Social Security in 1976.[42] Breakwell was recruited in the role of professional observer on the strength of his work documenting so-called 'normal life' in his *Continuous Diary* (1964–85). His final report, summarising his experience at Broadmoor psychiatric hospital, was co-written by architects who utilised his placement to lobby for the redesign of clinical space along less authoritarian lines. The report, however, was not favourably received and was eventually restricted under the Official Secrets Act.

As Claire Bishop has remarked, in hindsight, APG's main innovation was to focus attention on the social impact of art, including the all-important 'question of evaluation and over what period of time such judgments should be made'.[43] What began as an innovative attempt to move away from the primacy of the concrete art object – by this time fatally compromised by a growing art market – also instigated a new approach to determining art's value in terms of 'demonstrable outcomes'.[44] Bishop argues that in Britain this time-based understanding of art as process also gave rise to the so-called 'creative and cultural industries' that continue to privilege an individualist, entrepreneurial model of art even when it comes to so-called social or community action.[45]

Conflicts between artists and management also emerged in APG's other placements, including Stuart Brisley's fellowship at the Hille Furniture Factory in 1970 in Haverhill, Suffolk, which proved formative for his later experience at Peterlee. Brisley's initial intention, as formulated in the feasibility study he drew up, was not to create any sort of artwork but, rather, to 'formulate methods to extend communication between the various aspects of shop floor working' and, in the last instance, 'between the shop-floor and management'.[46] Recalling Negt and Kluge's analysis of the factory context discussed above, one could say that the Hille Fellowship aimed to transform the factory floor into a kind of public sphere, or at least to provide the factory worker with an overview of the whole process of production and not just their compartmentalised function; in other words to enlarge a truncated perspective that prevented a worker's ability to make sense of the factory context.[47]

Brisley's choice of site was the machine polishing room, where the hardest and dirtiest labour took place. When he had first arrived, he observed how the men in the polishing room referred contemptuously to the windows, which had been placed high enough to provide light but not low enough for them to see through and get distracted from their work. Brisley considered this to be symptomatic of an 'undeclared conflict'.[48] He consequently decided to undertake three actions: to paint the machinery in various football team colours as a way of gaining the workers' trust; to engage the workers in the construction of a free-standing sculpture in the effort to shift the context of what could be considered meaningful work; to instigate the use of noticeboards for the workers to use. The second action resulted in the Poly wheel, a free-standing structure resembling the shape of a Ferris wheel made of 212 Robin chairs (figures 3.5 and 3.6). Although designed to represent the idea of factory work as a treadmill, this abstract, elegant structure was in fact favourably received by both workers and managers. It eventually assumed pride of place as a permanent installation at the entrance of the factory. The third action was less successful from Brisley's perspective. It was eventually taken over by management as a useful means of top-down communication, scuppering Brisley's attempt to increase opportunities for lateral consultation and exchange across the factory floor.

The experience at Hille solidified Brisley's conviction that a radical artistic position had less to do with content – for instance, the expression of intolerable human conditions – than with a far-reaching extension of the methods and purpose of art itself. This change was 'revolutionary' insofar as it involved a complete revaluation of values. Brisley imagined that if art could be pursued as a 'human value' rather than a 'material value' (whether this material related to objects or even the artist himself as a 'specialist' or craftsman), this would provide a new, utopian, basis for human interaction, one that could eventually overcome the traditional barriers separating art from industry, science from art and so forth.[49] Although we seem far removed from the physical exertions of Brisley's other performances, this attempt to leverage performance into a type of social action nonetheless continued the strategy of his previous attempts to make a cut in time. In fact, it made explicit what had remained implicit in many of Brisley's actions: that resistance to hierarchy, and rupture with past habits, need not assume the 'event-time' of certain kinds of protest art but could potentially operate through communication and temporal extension alone.

Yet is there not something quixotic in this attempt to extend a public language of art into an industrial space that was by definition private? And even if the labour itself rested on cooperation, how was this cooperative basis to be communicated in a factory context that constituted, as Negt and Kluge point out, 'an arcane realm', 'protected by factory-security', law-enforcement measures and 'legal institutions'?[50] And yet, if this context of living, so central for working-class identity, could not be made public, emancipation could not take place. Making something public, however, requires a public language. This is difficult to achieve in non-bourgeois contexts, where manual work experience and industrial work habits do not readily translate into a language of the public sphere, which is universalisable precisely because it is abstract.[51]

The presence or absence of such a language is especially evident whenever authorities seek to delegate their power through some notion of a 'public interest'. It is striking in this regard that the greatest resistance to Brisley's interventions in Peterlee arose over who had control over the communication process. While Brisley's relationship with the management in the Hille factory remained cordial, in Peterlee the breakdown in communication was complete. It began in early 1977 when the PDC blocked Brisley's attempts to create ongoing workshops. When positions became vacant to work on the project, the artist was not consulted. When the material was transferred to local authority control, as the artist had intended, all the materials pertaining to research on its own organisation were removed.[52] 'The Project', as Brisley put it, 'remains unrealised, having become an awful parody of itself.'[53] And yet, it also succeeded, rather spectacularly, in achieving what it did not set out to do. In addition to the aforementioned archive and heritage museum, which was proposed but ultimately never built, it also featured in a number of national and international exhibitions, including the Northern Arts Gallery,

Newcastle upon Tyne (1976), and various exhibitions showcasing the APG at Acme Gallery and Whitechapel Gallery, London (1977), the 1977 Documenta in Kassel, Germany, and in a 'series of podium exchanges' with the German government in Bonn.[54]

The project's ambiguous success thus raises questions about the analytical potential of any performance that presents itself as a type of social action. For, as Claire Bishop has observed, socially conscious projects are always judged by the criteria of art even when they 'were perceived to be worthwhile precisely because they were non-artistic'.[55] The question rarely arises of whether the action itself succeeded in achieving its stated aims. In so doing such art opens itself to objections from both sides: that it privileges social or political imperatives at the expensive of making something that looks like art; conversely, that because it is classified as art, it fails to make any social or political impact. As Groys observes, the former objection can be dealt with easily enough. At least since the French Revolution, there is no such thing as a universally agreed criterion of good taste. Art is whatever others choose to call art. The second objection, however, is more serious because it suggests that whenever artists try to intervene in the world, far from challenging it, they only end up aestheticising it. This aestheticisation, in turn, becomes part of the problem.

In light of these criticisms, Brisley's repeated characterisation of the *Peterlee Project* as *neither* an art project *nor* an archival project, much less a heritage project, is revealing. This can be clarified by means of two contrasting examples of art projects that also used performance to assess England's industrial heritage. The first is Christian Boltanski's 1994 *The Lost Workers: The Work People of Halifax 1877–1982*, which occupied a former industrial site – the Dean Clough Carpet Mill – in which former employees and their families were invited to deposit memorabilia in the boxes set up in the exhibition space so as to create their own archives. In this installation, collective memory was used to regenerate a sense of working-life context around an otherwise abandoned site. But although Boltanski's 'archive' was kept open for a period after the exhibition closed, it remained part of the exhibition space, subordinated to the overall aesthetic design and impact of the installation as intended by the artist and thus constrained by the conventional time frames of an art world organised around the short-term event.

The second contrasting example is Jeremy Deller's *Battle of Orgreave* (2001). This action focused on a commonly perceived 'watershed' moment in British labour relations: the violent clash between miners and police which took during the miners' strike at Orgreave, Rotherham, South Yorkshire on 18 June 1984, widely accepted to have been instigated and planned by the police. Its aim was a kind of recollection through re-enactment, in which the staged or scripted nature of the original event would be thoroughly exposed.

The large-scale re-enactment featured around 800 people, including some 280 local residents, and was filmed by the BBC.[56] It is commonly understood to have overturned whatever remained of the official version of events in the public imagination. And yet, although this re-enactment involved local people and took place under public conditions, it arguably still produced an abstract understanding of history. The emphasis on a 'milestone moment' meant that the outcome was known in advance. And even if some of the original participants took part and a small number even switched their historical roles, the two sides remained identified with their respective professions (either that of a miner or a police officer). The end result may have been therapy for some, provocation for others; in either case, a dominant *narrative* account of history prevailed in which there is only one path from the past to the present.

Brisley's project differs from both of these art-driven interventions in its insistence on a continuous engagement with the everyday, performed over a long, potentially unending duration. The relative formlessness of Brisley's intervention, which delegated the work of collating, collecting and recording to the participants, was part of the effort to establish a sense of history that was internal to the town's inhabitants, using focal points generated by the act of collecting itself. It is interesting to note that in his own research on the General Strike of 1926, partly based on interviewing residents in Peterlee, Brisley observed how people mostly remembered the demand for greater freedom rather than that of higher pay.[57] This freedom was also asserted in the decision not to work and, for instance, to go swimming during that hot summer. The strike, in other words, was remembered as a flight of freedom from one organised experience of time – of work, schedules, the extractive economy – into another, less controlled experience of time. Seen in this light, the *Peterlee Project* was concerned less with *conserving* a memory relating to the past than it was about redirecting the *pleasures of recollection* towards liberating people and their lived experiences from the abstract time of labour. In this sense, the *Peterlee Project* aimed to recreate the conditions for experiencing a pleasure and fullness of time, through a wasting of time that also resists the dominant order.

As for Brisley himself, his own experiences at Peterlee subsequently informed several performances that he undertook personally, in his capacity as an artist. Among them is *Beneath Dignity* (1977), an action on the Procrustean theme that took place once a day over three days on a quayside in Bregenz, Austria (figure 3.7). It was inspired by hearing an account of how miners moved their bodies in extremely circumscribed spaces when following a new seam. To enact an analogous experience of constriction, Brisley constructed five wooden frames to the size of his own body with arms outstretched, a nod towards da Vinci's famous drawings of the

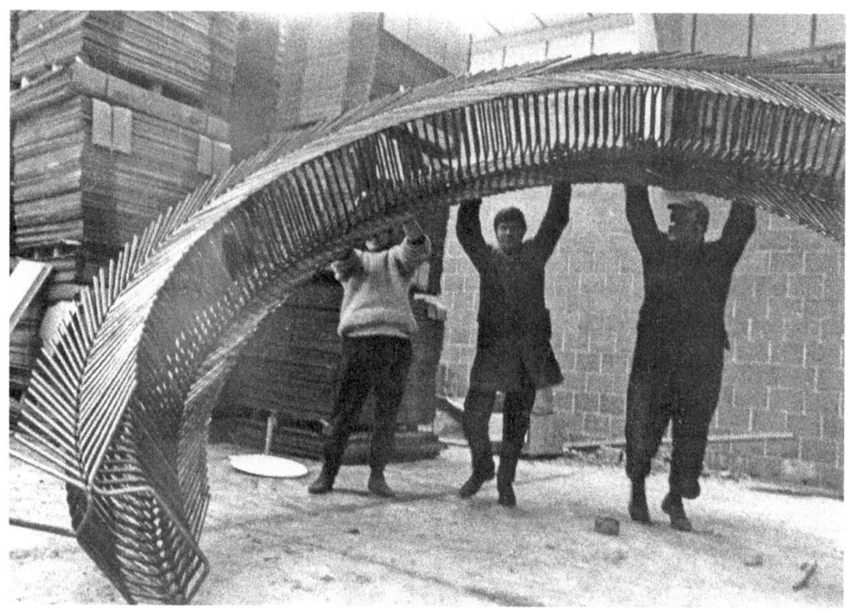

3.5   Hille Fellowship, Haverhill, 1970

'Vitruvian Man' whose ideal proportions could be measured by superimposing a circle and a square. A black nylon cord in the form of a cross was stretched over each of the frames, which were then placed one beside the other on the quay. Brisley crawled under the cord. With his now severely restricted bodily movements, he marked out a trace in each frame. In the first he simply made movements; in the second he used water to leave behind a trace; in the third, chalk; in the fourth, white paint; and in the fifth, black paint. At the end, he emerged from the last frame and jumped into the lake, leaving behind only traces – so many imprints of a body that was no longer recognisably human. But even in this highly personal, and deeply physical, attempt to enact the condition of being a miner using nothing but his own body and the language of art, there is a public dimension. Brisley recalls how a member of the public, out of his own volition, undertook to organise the crowds that gathered on the quay, each day more numerous. On the third day, Brisley arranged for a boat to carry him away from the quay so he would not have to walk back through the crowd, drenched with water and dirtied with paint. Against the background of his recent experiences at Peterlee, one is tempted to read this final evasion as an attempt by the artist to escape the gravitational pull that always tends towards a management structure of some kind, even if only by identifying an action as a completed work, undertaken by an individual artist.

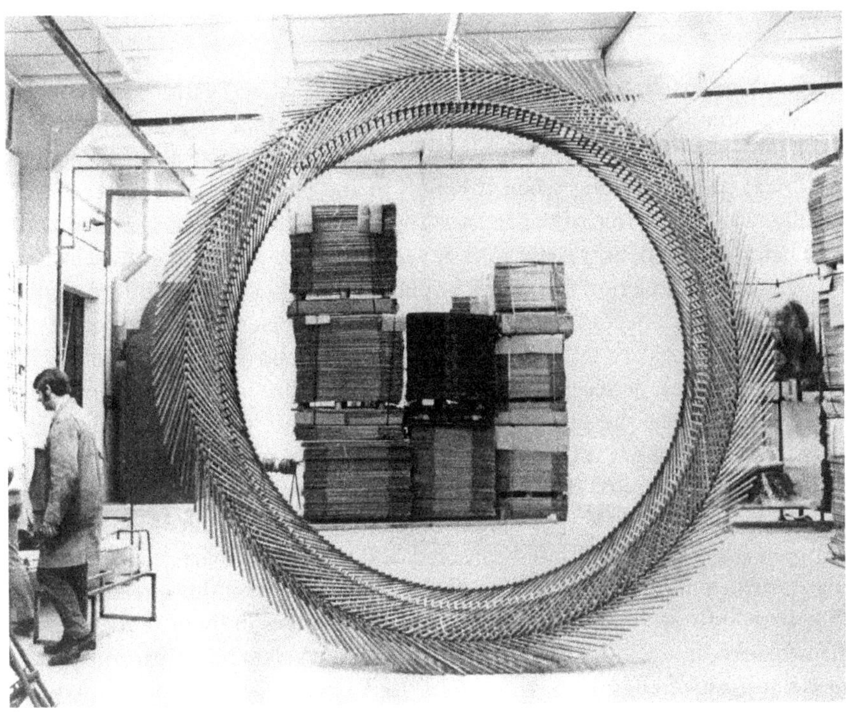

Hille Fellowship, Haverhill, 1970   **3.6**

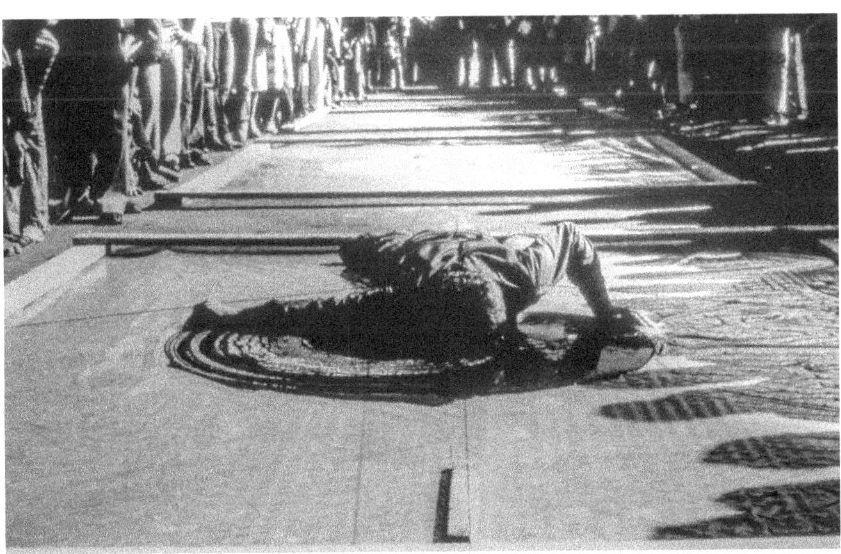

Beneath Dignity, Bregenz, 1977   **3.7**

A productive failure?

The ambiguous status of the *Peterlee Project* as a 'successful failure' thus raises a number of questions: how does performance relate to historical consciousness? What is the difference between the practical past and the historical past, including when it comes to the pasts of performance itself? Finally, what is the role of the artist as the agent who brings the performance into being but who, as we saw with *Beneath Dignity*, wishes to evade closure, the way any completion of a work implicitly, or explicitly, elevates the artist as the ultimate subject of the action? In the case of Peterlee, it is important to note that the project's failure was instigated from above as well as below. By disabling the link between past memories and future political demands, the PDC ensured that the project's 'analytic component remained fallow'. The *Peterlee Project*, as we recall, was intended as a theoretical model that could, in principle, be applied elsewhere. More generally, by denying the project's formal concept, the PDC also denied its participants the ability to distinguish between what Hayden White has called 'the radical, primary and determining transformations' that make up the social context and those relationships that were 'only secondary, superficial or local changes in them'.[58] As we have already seen, it is not the practical past per se that raises historical consciousness but the awareness of how it can be used as a model. A model, by nature, repeats and, in its repetition, reveals the difference between what is stable or structural and what is epiphenomenal in any given situation.

The project was also blocked from below, by certain participants who did not accept its critical goals and 'continually attempted to order the project in terms of their own work experience', which included reproducing workplace hierarchies from their own past experience and, above all, not offending their employer.[59] Brisley, after all, was employed by the PDC and, by extension, so too were the six local people that he hired and trained to do the interviews. As Brisley subsequently observed, the people of Peterlee who most clearly understood, and supported, the political goals of the project were the local leaders, that is to say, local intellectuals who were capable of translating this particular life context into a more universalisable and recognisable language.[60]

This raises once more the crucial question of how performance communicates within a public sphere. Hayden White, as we have already seen, has suggested that increased attention to the practical past might revive the ancient understanding of history as a 'propaedeutic to public life'.[61] But Brisley's experience in Peterlee suggests otherwise; that there cannot be an emphatic understanding of a so-called *public* history so long as the problem of language is not addressed. Even in instances when this life context does succeed in galvanising a certain kind of energy, as in Peterlee, it risks being disrupted by other competing interests; in this case, an authority that sought to protect itself by reasserting control over the communication process. Can there be a public discourse that expresses a context of living that comes from below? Or is this context of living something that can be reconstituted only negatively, through a discursive analysis of its ultimate failure to be expressed?

We are thus faced not only with the problem of 'whose history?' but also of how to account for the role of the artist or activist as mediator. We could say that Brisley's role in the *Peterlee Project* was to address the community and, in so doing, bring it into being in some way. When the project was exhibited at the Sunderland Art Centre, Brisley enlarged the photographs and designed the accompanying text, providing visibility, and therefore a kind of added value, to what otherwise would appear as a merely informal collection, or, as Brisley put it, a kind of 'self-generating heap'.[62] To be informal is to be without time-resistance and therefore to be, in a certain way, formless. In this instance, Brisley's act of *framing* conferred value and status on the collection even if, as Marc Crinson notes, it had 'an alien sense of order and aesthetic',[63] also evident in the photos taken by Brisley himself of Peterlee (figure 3.8).[64] In this sense, one could say that Brisley's role was to provide communicative memory with the kind of status normally reserved for objects of cultural

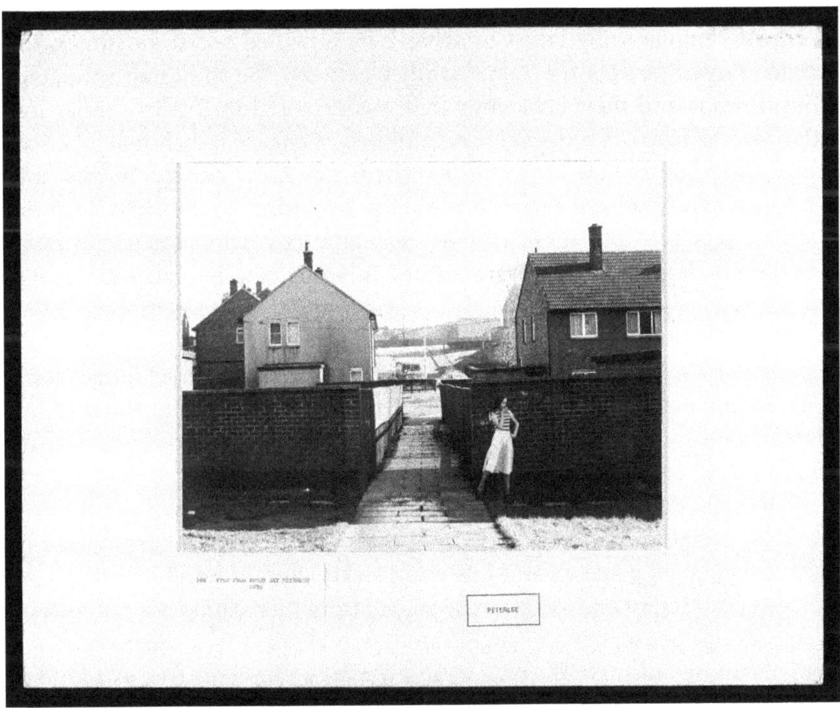

'View from Yoden Way', 1976, *Artist Project Peterlee*, 1976–77   **3.8**

memory. By creating a bordered time outside time, this living past was stretched and extended by the force of attention. It was granted a certain mnemonic pulse that enabled a receding past to last a bit longer and be that much more useful. Indeed Brisley notes that the oral history component of the project continued all the way to the miners' strikes in the early 1980s after the PDC had turned over the truncated collection to Easington District Council.[65]

At the same time, the failure of the project to pass into the hands of a 'collective responsibility' indicates the necessity of ongoing external intervention – an impossible and undesirable task. Some parts wound up in the district council archives, although not all the material was archival; other parts of the project ended up at the Tate archive, although the collection was intended to serve as common property and never presented itself as the property of the artist. Since 2004, Brisley, along with the artist Tim Brennan, has sought to return elements of the collection to local users, with some success. However, even though a continuation of the project would have enabled participants to gain a new perspective on events that have occurred since, this potential was never realised. On the contrary, the gradual loss of a sense of community whose shared reference points were grounded in lived experience appears to have further eroded the project's potential to serve as an iterable model.

Having emphatically failed to achieve its intended social outcomes, the *Peterlee Project* reveals the same conflict between the founding principles of institutions and their behaviour that was explored in Brisley's other live actions in the 1970s. A bureaucracy continued to engage in habitual practices even if these contradicted the reasons why it came into being – in this case, to create a new town and a new community. According to the artist, even the so-called 'positive outcomes', such as Easington District Council's proposal to build a heritage museum, were framed in terms of a 'bureaucratic image' and not as a people's project.[66] Such a memory might be useful for promoting kinship ties and notions of community based on identity, but it is no longer a resource for a new, or different, future. In other words, it can no longer serve as an emancipating function, which as Martin Jay notes in a different but related context, involves freeing 'the self from its subjection to the past, from being a mere "subject" with its connotation of subjection'.[67]

One might counter that, however minimally, the irritation of the authorities proved that the model could work; that some kind of confrontation or rupture had taken place, even if this was quickly suppressed. But perhaps the more precise kind of knowledge to be gained from such a model is not historical knowledge per se, but an insight into how a people's past can be used as a form of counter-history. The project as a whole can be conceived as a kind of counter-extension. By intensifying people's relation to their local context, the project enabled private memories to spread into the public, saturating spaces that had heretofore been wholly organised around economic imperatives. And while it failed as a self-generating process – a continuous archive or an archive 'without origins' – it did succeed in illuminating an important aspect of the contemporary relation to the past. History is no longer the purview of the historian. Rather, a new person has taken his place – he who administers the past. Inadvertently perhaps, but significantly, the *Peterlee Project* created a conflict between two ways of understanding the role of the 'activist administrator', the one who mediates between institutional demands and what is often called 'communities of interest'. On the one hand, Brisley's intervention enacted the *persona* of the artist as a *civic individual* who institutes a collection but is blocked from exercising any 'constituent power'. On the other hand, his paid position at the PDC enabled him to adopt the *persona* of an *administrator* who acts on behalf of the institution, and who seeks public approval as a necessary precondition of this legitimacy but ultimately only as it accords with the institution's bureaucratic self-image. In the *Peterlee Project*, the civic individual failed and the administrator succeeded. Bureaucracy ended up determining the sociological, as well as artistic, outcomes of the project.

In subsequent projects, Brisley would pursue this understanding of performance as a counter-extension that operates over a long duration to throw a spotlight on the role of institutions in mediating a living process that is inherently fragile and subject to revision. Chapter 4 discusses the *Cenotaph Project*, Brisley's last public art project and one that most explicitly engages the artist as a civic individual. Chapter 5 considers Brisley's longest durational works, lasting several years, in which he undertakes the personas of both the civic individual and the administrator, in the attempt to create institutions whose parameters and public manifestations he could control.

Notes

1 Drawing on the work of the French phenomenologist Claude Romano, Martin Jay argues that events which 'radically upend their contexts' need to be 'understood less from the world that precedes them than from the posterity to which they give rise'. Birth, from the viewpoint of the person born, is one such event; revolution may be another. See: Martin Jay, 'Historical Explanation and the Event: Reflections on the Limits of Contextualization', *New Literary History*, 42 (2011), 557–71, p. 564.

2 'And if you went to the mining villages there was a tremendous sense of tradition and history which was, however short, intense, but in Peterlee itself you had no sense of it at all', Brisley, National Life Stories, C466/43/11 F5283A. p. 218.

3 Stuart Brisley, *Stuart Brisley, The Peterlee Project 1976–1977* (Aarhus, DK: Antipyrine & Museum of Ordure, 2014), p. 5.

4 The archive can be found at Durham County Archives, www.durham.gov.uk/arti cle/2075/People-Past-and-Present-Archive (accessed 5 March 2020); the Tate Gallery

www.tate.org.uk/art/archive/tga-201114–4/brisley-artist-project-peterlee (accessed 15 May 2015; relocated from the APG archive upon Brisley's request); it was revived by the artist Tim Brennan, in collaboration with Brisley, in 2004. See 'Town Art Project Completed 28 Years after Its Launch', *Northern Echo*, 1 March 2004.

5 Michael Oakeshott, *On History and Other Essays* (Oxford: Blackwell, 1983), p. 13, pp. 16–17.

6 Ibid., p. 33.

7 Hayden White, *The Practical Past* (Evanston, IL: Northwestern University Press, 2014), p. 98; see also Jonas Ahlskog, 'Michael Oakeshott and Hayden White on the Practical and the Historical Past', *Rethinking History: The Journal of Theory and Practice*, 20:3 (2016), 375–394.

8 White, *The Practical Past*, pp. 8–9. White argues that although history is a realist discipline, in describing how this and not another past informs the present, it also produces utopian thinking as its other. See Hayden White, 'The Future of Utopia in History', *Historein* 7:12 (2007), 12–19.

9 Brennan, 'Of Commune and Community', p. 134.

10 See the report by C. W. Clarke, architect-surveyor to Easington Rural District Council, 'Farewell Squalor', 1946, TGA 201114/4/19.

11 Clarke, 'Farewell Squalor'.

12 See John Allan, 'Lubetkin and Peterlee', in Thomas Deckker (ed.), *Modern City Revisited* (London: Taylor & Francis, 2000), pp. 103–124.

13 Victor Pasmore, letter to Gary Philipson, General Manager of the Peterlee Development Corporation, 30 May 1976. For this letter and more documents, including correspondence and press-cuttings from 1976 to 1984, see https://apol lopavillion.info (accessed 31 May 2016).

14 Brisley had in fact worked in the College of Architecture while employed at Cornell University between 1962 and 1963. He also had completed an MA dissertation on Constructivism in England while at Florida State University in 1960–62. As he recalled: 'I thought that the architecture and the art should be integrated at a much earlier state in the concept of what a building is for, you know, like how, what its purpose is, what its function is, and then how an artist could work in relation to the way that would evolve, you know. So, it was claiming a rather important role for the artist, other than as a decorator or someone who, you know, like, is employed to stick the badge on at the end.' Brisley, National Life Stories, C466/43/06 F5278B. p. 136.

15 Notably Caroline Tisdall, who favourably compared Brisley's aim to give people social tools to Pasmore's 'imposed aesthetic'. Caroline Tisdall, 'Caroline Tisdall Describes How the People of Peterlee, a 30-Year-Old "New Town" Are Creating Their Own Archive', *The Guardian*, 10 June 1977.

16 Negt and Kluge derive their analysis from Adorno's account of how time is reconfigured according to the logic of commodity production. See Oscar Negt and Alexander Kluge, *Public Sphere and Experience: Toward an Analysis of the Bourgeois and Proletarian Public Sphere*, foreword by Miriam Hansen, trans. Peter Labanyi, Jamie Owen Daniel and Assenka Oksiloff (London: Verso Books, [1993] 2016), p. 19.

17 Cited in Bishop, *Artificial Hells*, p. 336. Brisley recalls that his father had been a strong union worker for the railways, and was involved in the National Strike of 1926.

18 Stuart Brisley, 'Peterlee Project', TGA 201114/4/12, p. 5.

19 'One also gains the impression of some liberalisation of the Development Corporation and an attempt – very gradual and overcautious – to communicate with and discover the people of Peterlee'. Stuart Brisley, Peterlee Development Corporation, TGA 201114/4/14, p. 7. The Chairman of the PDC at the time of Brisley's appointment was Dennis Stevenson, then 25 years old. Sir Dennis would later go on to chair the Board of Trustees at the Tate as well as serve as Chancellor of the University of the Arts London. He was also chairman of the bank HBOS during the 2008 financial crisis when it collapsed and required a government bailout.

20 According to Brisley's report, these statements came from two officers who resigned from the Development Corporation, 'having concluded that the Corporation was socially destructive and hence should be completely dissolved'. See Brisley, Peterlee Development Corporation, TGA 201114/4/14, p. 8. 'The conflict between the locality and the Development Corporation broke out almost immediately, due to the fact that, unlike most New Towns, Peterlee began as a partly local initiative, with local roots', TGA 201114/4/10. Also reproduced in *Stuart Brisley, The Peterlee Project 1976–1977.*

21 See *Artist Project Peterlee, Second Report*, TGA 201114/4/17.

22 Brisley, TGA 201114/4/16, p. 10.

23 As Tim Brennan, who revisited the project in 2004, describes it. See Brennan, 'Of Commune and Community', p. 136.

24 Brisley, TGA 201114/4/15, p. 9.

25 Brisley, TGA 201114/4/16, p. 10.

26 See Andreas Huyssen, *Twilight Memories: Making Time in a Culture of Amnesia* (Abingdon: Routledge, 1994). For the relation between museumisation and the waning industrial landscape see pp. 14, 30.

27 Initiated by the anthropologist Tom Harrisson, the painter/film-maker Humphrey Jennings and the poet Charles Madge, this project straddled the line dividing sociology from advertising and social control.

28 Raphael Samuel, 'History Workshop Journal', *History Workshop*, 1 (1976), 1–3.

29 Cornelius Castoriadis, 'Time and Creation', in John B. Bender and David E. Wellbery (eds), *Chronotypes: The Construction of Time* (Stanford, CA: Stanford University Press), pp. 38–64.

30 See Louis Althusser et al., *Reading Capital*, trans. Brewster Ben and David Fernbach (London: FerVerso, 1970); first published in French (Paris: Maspero François, 1965).

31 Fernand Braudel observed that short-run time corresponds to the 'most capricious and deceptive of durations', whereas slow-moving, long-lived structures reflect the perception we all have of the 'mass' and 'force' of historical change. Fernand Braudel, 'History and the Social Sciences: The Long Duration', *Political Research, Organization and Design*, 3:6 (1960), 3–13, p. 5.

32 On the history of the longue durée see Jo Guldi and David Armitage, *The History Manifesto* (Cambridge, UK: Cambridge University Press, 2014), pp. 14–37.

33 Reinhart Koselleck, 'Histories in the Plural and the Theory of History: An Interview with Carsten Dutt', in *Sediments of Time*, p. 255.

34 As noted by the Birmingham Popular Memory Group. See CCCS Popular Memory Group, 'What Do We Mean by Popular Memory?', trans. Faculty of Commerce and Social Sciences. Vol. 67. Stencilled Occasional Paper. University of Birmingham, January 1982.

35 Jorma Kalela, *Making History: The Historian and the Uses of the Past* (New York City, NY: Springer, 2011), pp. 104–106.

36 Groys, 'On Art Activism', p. 1.

37 For an excellent discussion of the APG, see Bishop, *Artificial Hells*, pp. 163–177; for Brisley's two placements with the APG see pp. 167–168 and pp. 173–174.

38 Stuart Brisley, *First Peterlee Report 1976*, p. 2.

39 Cited in Stuart Brisley, 'No, It Is Not On', *Studio International*, 183:942 (March 1972), p. 96, TGA 20042/2/2/5/2.

40 Ibid. See also Gustav Metzger, 'A Critical Look at Artist Placement Group', *Studio International*, 182:940 (January 1972), pp. 4–5. This problem was debated at the Sunderland Arts Centre, with representatives from the PDC. In a letter to Steveni dated 17 June 1977, Dave Brown observes: 'If the artist refuses to compromise, then his activity will eventually be regarded as subversive to the aims of the department or firm; otherwise, the artist will have to compromise by offering to help the firm or department with its aims.' Brown concludes that the Artist Project Peterlee 'will also become subversive to the Corporation's aims and hence unwelcome and unsupportable.' TGA 20042/1/3/46/14, pp. 1–3.

41 These criticisms were voiced on several occasions. In a letter to APG dated 30 June 1971, Brisley observed that 'competition is inherent in the industrial context between management and workers' and that 'the artist' raising the 'level of attention' in this field, while at the same time accepting the conditions which create the polarity, merely enforces the status quo.' TGA 20042/1/1/2.

42 See Bishop, *Artificial Hells*, p. 172.

43 Ibid., p. 174.

44 Ibid.

45 Congruent with the analysis by Luc Boltanski and Eve Chiapello, *The New Spirit of Capitalism*, trans. Gregory Elliott (London, UK: Verso Books, 2007).

46 Bishop, *Artificial Hells*, p. 166.

47 'For the overwhelming majority of workers, the place where they spend the greater part of their waking hours is marked by strictly delineated and limited room for movement. They are not capable of perceiving the compartmentalised space within the factory as a totality. Whereas other groups, such as foremen, clerical workers, to say nothing of members of the board or security personnel, are virtually obliged to gain an overview, the productive activity of the worker is harnessed to individual components of the factory's overall machinery. This constitutes one blocking element, which in and of itself prevents the experiencing of the external factory setting as a whole.' Negt and Kluge, *Public Sphere and Experience*, p. 16.

48 Brisley, National Life Stories, C466/43/08 F5280B, p. 166.

49 This position is expressed in an unattributed typed manuscript by Stuart Brisley, in 1971. See www.stuartbrisley.com/pages/29/70s/text (accessed 17 April 2018).

50 Negt and Kluge, *Public Sphere and Experience*, p. 50.

51 Negt and Kluge argue that the working-class experience is doubly removed from representation: from the actual power structure of the ruling classes and from a public sphere saturated by a mass media that represents vested interests and an entrenched social hierarchy.

52 This included, inter alia, a project entitled 'Comparative studies in New Town Planning' by Gary Armen and a 'history of women in the area' by Pat Gallagher, both commissioned by the project in 1977. At the time, Brisley believed that these had been destroyed. Years later, Brisley discovered that they had in fact been retained by APG, now part of the Tate Archive.

53 Stuart Brisley, Personal View of Some Aspects of the Peterlee Project (1 January, 1976–August 31 1977), TGA 20042/1/3/45/7, p. 3.

54 The APG exhibitions are listed in a letter to Dennis Stevenson from Barbara Steveni dated 16 January 1978, TGA 20042/1/3/45/10. See also www.tate.org.uk/artistplacementgroup/chronology.htm (accessed 13 October 2022).

55 Bishop, *Artificial Hells*, pp. 19 and 174.

56 'Domesday Project Recorded Miners' Strike and Pit Closure', www.bbc.co.uk/domesday (accessed 3 May 2014).

57 'The strongest sense about the 1926 strike was the weather … because all these people had been down the mines, you know, and there they were on strike. It was the summer, and it was a beautiful summer so they all went swimming … and it made me realise that strikes are often about demanding your freedom, not about asking for more money', in Brisley, National Life Stories, C466/43/11 F5283A, p. 220.

58 White, *The Practical Past*, p. 51.

59 Stuart Brisley, Artist Project Peterlee January 1976–1977 Observations, TGA 20042/2/2/5/1–7. 'They continually attempted to order the project in terms of their own working experience. What appeared to be acceptable was behaviour which conformed closely to notion of work as experienced in industrial conditions Regular established work periods were favoured (necessarily in relation to other rigidly ordered patterns of living, eg. meal-times). The appearance of order and hygiene was required. Above all a sense of hierarchy was needed […]. Since there was no easily detected hierarchy in the project, there were continual attempts to set up rigid bureaucratic procedures which were antipathetic to the proposed openly structured workshop.' On this point about workplace hierarchies see also Neylan Bagcioglu, 'Delegating (Community) Action: Stuart Brisley's Peterlee Project', *Stedelijk Studies*, 3 (2016), 1–14. Bagcioglu considers this project a 'failed success' in which Brisley succeeded in sharing authority and overcame the idea of the artist as producer of a work.

60 Brisley observes that even within the group of local people employed to work on the project there were clear divisions between those who 'had experienced higher education, expressed themselves differently … [and] had a far stronger grasp

of the full implications of the project'. Brisley, Artist Project Peterlee January 1976–1977 Observations, TGA 20042/2/2/5/1–7, p. 7. On this question of language, the sound recordings are also a resource for Pitmatic, a regional dialect closely related to mining work that is hardly spoken anymore. I thank Maya Balcioglu for this observation.

61 White, *The Practical Past*, p. 8.

62 Brisley, National Life Stories, C466/43/11 F5283A, p. 219.

63 Ibid., p. 220.

64 Reviewing the 2004 exhibition at Vardy Gallery, Sunderland, Marc Crinson observes: 'The photographs of the area, collected by local people and re-photographed at the time, appear in the display all as the same size, mounted, and grouped by local village. So, while they lose the specific contexts of their highly localised social uses as photographic objects, they gain representative value as standing for an organic locality, the village as anthropological place.' Crinson, 'The Incidental Collection: Stuart Brisley's Peterlee Project', *Mute*, 1:28 (2004), www.metamute.org/editorial/articles/incidental-collection-stuart-brisleys-peterlee-project (accessed 3 April 2018).

65 Brisley, conversation with the author December 2016, London.

66 'In place of a notion of a community action workshop, the Easington District Council proposed to build a second heritage museum thereby finally contradicting the notion of the project as a people's project.' Stuart Brisley, Personal View of Some Aspects of the Peterlee Project, TGA 20042/1/3/45/7, p. 3.

67 Jay, 'Historical Explanation and the Event', p. 566.

The monument and revolutionary time: 4
the *Cenotaph Project*

The *Cenotaph Project* (1987–91) was Brisley's last major public art project.[1] Created in collaboration with Maya Balcioglu, this public art installation engaged the radical, even revolutionary, potential of performance art to directly confront the role of monuments in creating, as well as denying, a shared sense of history. In so doing, it posed questions that are also central to this book: what is public art? What is public history? How can performance, with its emphasis on the presence of the human body, be used forensically to recover experiences of time and duration otherwise denied by official representations of both art and history?

A cenotaph is literally an empty tomb (from the Greek *kenos*, empty, and *taphos*, tomb). It both conceals remains that are elsewhere or unable to be buried and serves as a powerful signifier of state and military power. It thus raises important questions about what is 'above ground', state-sanctioned and revealed and what remains underground, buried and concealed. The *Cenotaph Project* involved exhibiting six models of the Whitehall Cenotaph, erected in London in 1919 to commemorate the end of the First World War, at six locations across the UK (figures 4.1 and 4.2). The model cenotaphs were scaled-down to 7 feet, 6 inches – the height of a typical council flat ceiling. By reducing the monumental aspect of the Whitehall Cenotaph to the dimensions of a domestic object, the *Cenotaph Project* invited the public to consider the official monument not as an unalterable monolith, but as part of a useable past, something that might even be placed inside an ordinary home, to become part of people's everyday life. 'Project', as the artists note, is a term that captures both the idea of a proposal, scheme or design (*OED*'s first definition) as well as a throwing or casting forward, a reference to the power of the imagination that transports and projects us continually into the future.

Although performance art is not commonly associated with stone sculptures, the challenge of this project was to ascertain whether a past that had been treated monumentally was still capable of coming alive again and, in this sense, also express a future. The Whitehall Cenotaph is a mute signifier of official history, commemorating events whose memory must be defended.

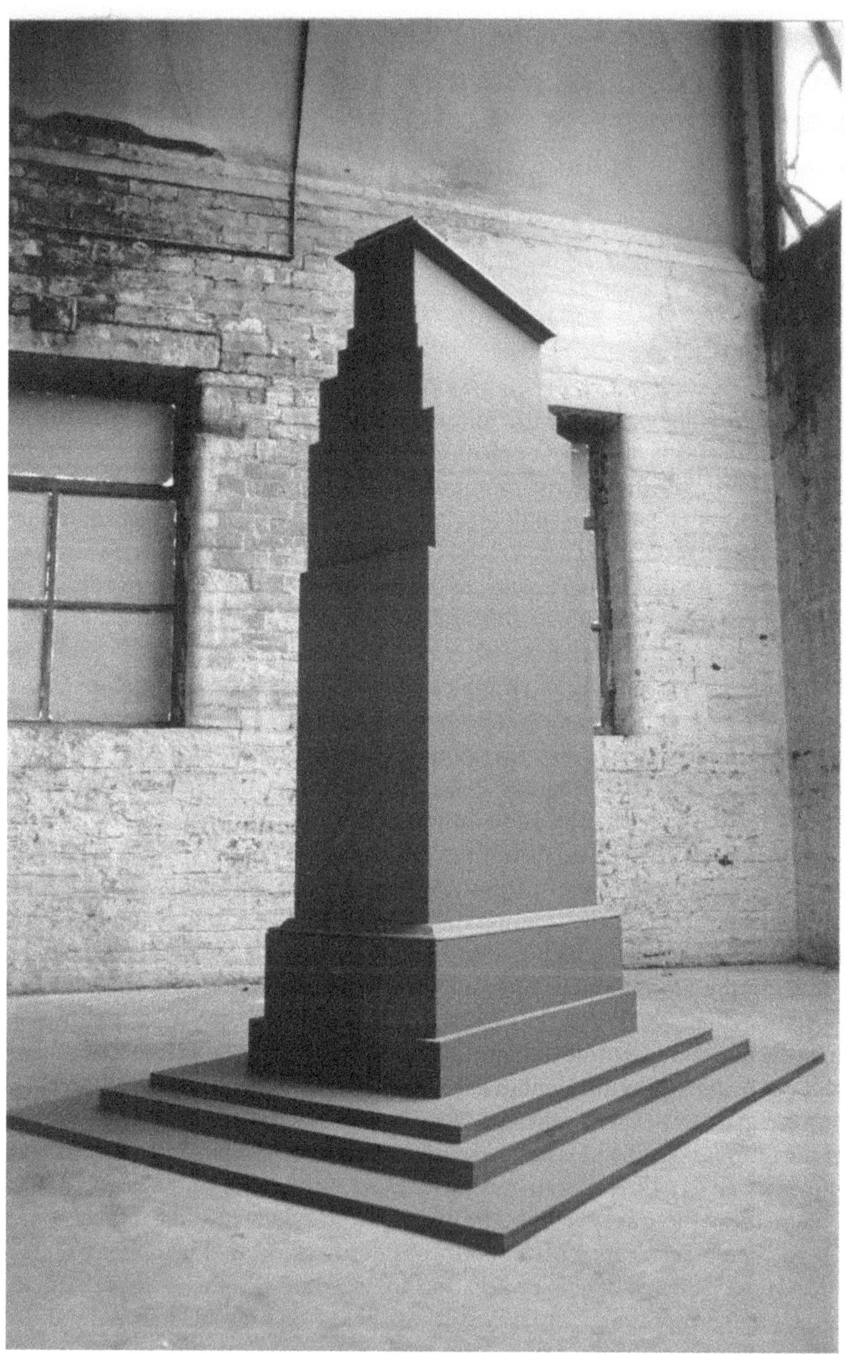

4.1   *The Cenotaph Project,* 1987–91

For the six smaller cenotaphs, in contrast, public space was not a territory that must be secured but a sphere to be multiplied through public conversation. As Brisley and Balcioglu's cenotaphs travelled around the country, local communities and civic associations were invited to discuss their own personal and collective memories of the monument. Whereas the anonymity and simplicity of the original Cenotaph aimed to avoid offending any group or class of society, the very mobility of the small-scale models encouraged local communities to reframe their relation to the national past on their own terms, in the effort to recover what elements from this past were still ongoing, or unfinished.

The *Cenotaph Project* thus used the presence of the model in the effort to provoke new kinds of individual and collective behaviours, including those expressing dissent from official history. In so doing, the artists also drew attention to an important element of the Whitehall Cenotaph's own past: namely that it too had originated as a hastily erected, temporary object. In what follows, I want to expand this insight further by considering what the *Cenotaph Project* might tell us about how a monument functions as a site of both collective action and reaction. Following the artists' own lead, I will first use the *Cenotaph Project* to analyse a latent, and often overlooked, history of the Whitehall monument itself, namely its role not only as a war monument but also a bulwark against the momentous experience of social upheaval which, in 1919, also included the very real threat of a Bolshevik revolution in

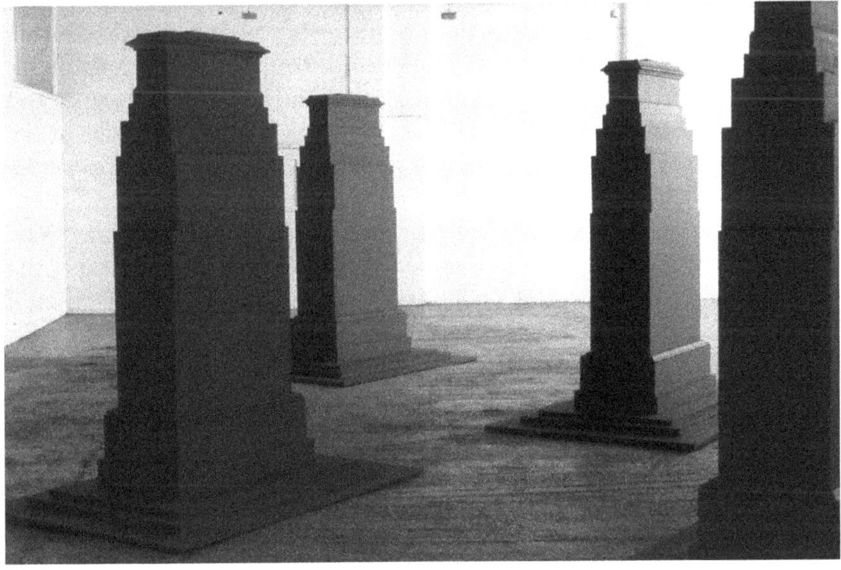

The Cenotaph Project, 1987–91   **4.2**

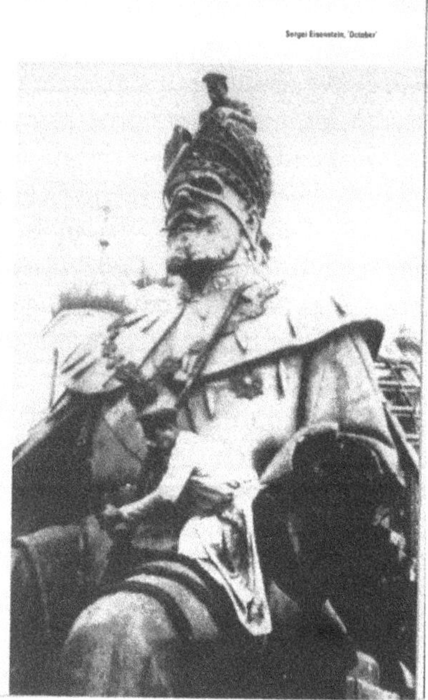

The first Cenotaph was conceived as a temporary icon, focus of the Victory Parade which took place on the 19 July 1919. It was situated in Whitehall. There was a massive public response to it, being immediately accepted as the focus for the site for public mourning, evidenced by the masses of flowers which were laid around it in the days following the parade. The government declared that in view of the response the memorial would be made permanent. Although it was decided to move it elsewhere to avoid traffic problems likely to be caused by its position in the middle of the road, public pressure against its removal ensured that the permanent version was built on the original site. The Cenotaph also became the agent of remembrance of those who were killed in the Second World War. After that its terms of reference as a memorial to subsequent wars is unclear. For example, the undeclared war in Ireland engages the armed forces in what are described as policing in the preservation of peace, limited engagement, while the opposing forces are described as terrorists, guerrillas or freedom fighters, depending upon the ideological context. Overriding this summary of the simplistic plot of the game we are given lies in the assertion of the Union, a United Kingdom. The very fact of continuous disunity and all that it implies, challenges the arching of monarchic rule over the Islands. Consequently there can be no critical discussion concerning the resolution of the Anglo-British military occupation in Ireland which does not bring into public discourse the condition and future of monarchy, constitution and parliament, the emancipation of the Irish, the Scots, the Welsh and the English.

The monument stands mute.

4.3   Stuart Brisley and Maya Balcioglu, *The Cenotaph Project*, 1987–91

the West. I will then situate the Cenotaph within a wider history of both war and revolution, a history in which the presence or absence of monuments can be used to recover collective reactions to historical rupture and cataclysmic social change. I will conclude with a brief consideration of the 'paper architecture' of the revolutionary eighteenth century, the first time that artists and architects were faced with the challenge of creating a public language of art. My question is a simple one, although perhaps not so simple to answer: is there an aesthetic form that enables the revolutionary experience to break through the vertical hierarchies of representation? To put it another way, is there a way of giving form to a shared public experience that escapes the monumental order to express the human body as it is – perishable, mortal and in time's power?

The monument as model

The Whitehall Cenotaph consists of an empty tomb erected on top of a rectangular pylon. It was originally established to commemorate the nearly 1.1 million soldiers who died fighting for the British Empire, of whom 499,161 were recorded missing and 173,213 had been found but not identified, and buried as 'unknown'.[2] After 1945, its meaning was extended to include the dead of the Second World War, as was customary with many war memorials across Europe. Today it is the focal point of the annual Armistice Day celebrations, the basis of the official calendar of commemoration across the UK. Its placement directly in Whitehall, the seat of British government, confers a sense of unity to the state which, in turn, sees itself reflected in the monument's stability and permanence. It also serves to remind the government of the sacrifices that have been made.

But this was not always the case. As is well known, the Cenotaph originated as a temporary structure designed by Sir Edwin Lutyens for the Peace Parade of 1919.[3] In fact, the idea for Brisley and Balcioglu's *Cenotaph Project* first emerged when Brisley encountered Lutyens' original model during a residency at the Imperial War Museum in 1985. Less than one metre tall, the model made visible an aspect of the Cenotaph not always apparent to those who encounter only its permanent manifestation, namely the lack of foundation. Most public monuments are designed with a specific location in mind. This is the case with Lutyens' other war memorials, which, as Brisley has observed, demonstrate a 'highly dramatic placement in landscape'.[4] Lutyens' model cenotaph, however, displayed a complete absence of regard for a suitable approach. Designed to be lightweight and portable, its shallow, liquid-seeming base made clear that it was destined to be a temporary structure among others.

This sense of the provisional is also reflected in its numerous iterations. Fifty-five cenotaphs were erected in the UK alone, and many others across the former British Empire, in different scales and variations. From its very inception, then, this indifference to site and capacity for multiplication served to distinguish Lutyens' model from traditional monuments, whose commemorative function is strongly tied to place. A second distinguishing feature lies in its name. Most monuments are named after the thing, deed or event they commemorate. The Cenotaph, however, names itself. As Sergiusz Michalski has observed, the structure takes its '*technicus terminis*' as its proper name and references nothing else.[5] Considering that the specific, technical meaning of the term 'cenotaph' would have been lost on most people, it is striking how quickly and universally it was adopted by the general public. This suggests a certain self-evidence – even power – of the form. As a contemporary witness reported in 1920, the monument's success was due to a design 'that looks like what it is … [and] says simply and precisely what it has to say'.[6]

The Cenotaph's origin as a self-referential, provisional structure lies at the heart of the *Cenotaph Project*, which can be described as an attempt to reactivate the architect's model against the permanent monument. As Brisley would later recall, by the time he had encountered the model, living memories of the war had all but faded. Even the Imperial War Museum resembled an enormous 'rubbish heap', its curators overwhelmed by the task of categorising and archiving material objects that no longer had a place in everyday life.[7] Against this formless, undifferentiated detritus of the past, Lutyens' model stood out as an aesthetic presence that had outlived its original social, political and practical function. Freed from its pre-established associations, and akin to the found objects of surrealism, it was as if the passage of time itself had released the model's latent power as a free-floating form.

Working solely with the model's formal properties, the *Cenotaph Project* challenged the official monument in several ways. First, Brisley's cenotaphs are smaller and more abstract than the official monument but larger than Lutyens' original model. Second, as already noted, they are not scaled arbitrarily but to the height of a modest council flat, the minimum legal height deemed acceptable for human habitation. Third, and relatedly, Brisley's cenotaphs are temporary installations. Models, as Horst Bredekamp observes, have been used by architects for millennia to foresee the feel or outcome of a design. While in their diminutive, scaled-down function, they are 'deficient' with respect to reality, models also add something to it, what Bredekamp calls a 'psychological surplus'.[8] Throwing us back on our own powers of perception, they make visible our own contribution to any given reality, present or future, which is always partial and incomplete. By reactivating the model's relation to an embodied imagination, the *Cenotaph Project* thus sets itself against all that is fixed by the official monument and, by extension, a state-sanctioned vision of the past. This includes the way the official monument occupies both a static space and a routinised time, anchored by the annual calendar of civic remembrance.

The small-scale 'model' cenotaphs also drew attention to the official Cenotaph's formal language as an abstract structure, built around an empty space. A cenotaph, after all, is a very specific form; a negative version of the traditional burial site, always tied to place and particular bodies. As an empty structure, it lends itself particularly well to diminution, abstraction and multiplication – all familiar terms in the lexicon of contemporary sculpture and installation art.[9] This underscores the provisional nature of all cenotaphs, bound to nothing and containing nothing. By placing the official structure '*en abîme*' as it were, the *Cenotaph Project* transforms it into what Koselleck calls a 'negative monument', that is to say, a structure that 'demands meaning and no longer establishes meaning'.[10]

Through minimal alteration and relying solely on the aesthetic parameters offered by the original historical model, the *Cenotaph Project* accomplishes a reversal of perspective that also reveals the extraordinary mutation in the experience of war that had begun with the First World War and was fully accomplished by the Second. As Reinhart Koselleck has observed, the concentration camps, air raids and atomic bomb annihilated not just the living bodies of combatants but also the physical remains of both soldiers and civilians.[11] And yet, as the artists point out, this profound transformation of warfare over the course of the twentieth century has had little or no impact on the language and rituals of commemoration used throughout Britain, all of which were first established in the wake of the First World War. By drawing attention to the Cenotaph's form, structured around the absence of physical remains, the *Cenotaph Project* suggests another way of reading the history of twentieth-century warfare: as a series of ongoing ruptures with the consensus established after the First World War. In particular, where the Whitehall Cenotaph erected a barrier between 'foreign war' and 'British peace', the *Cenotaph Project* encouraged open discussion of past and present conflict, including what the artists describe as the 'potentiality of war to spill out over everyone', thereby raising the 'questions of what war is, could or might be' (figure 4.3).[12]

By freeing the Whitehall Cenotaph from the formulaic language of commemoration, the model cenotaphs instigated a new relation to the public monument. As they travelled from Gateshead to Cambridge, Halifax, Govan, Derry, Cardiff and Portsmouth, the cenotaphs became the pretext for a public discussion about the legacies of all twentieth-century wars. Formerly associated with the military and industrial centre of British Empire, many of these places now occupied the domestic fringes of the British Isles. Bringing a cenotaph to these localities could not help but raise the question of how 'local' local history truly was, but also how these local histories might relate to a state history that continually remakes the relation between centre and periphery in its image.

The Quakers attending the Kettle's Yard event in Cambridge recalled the Pacifist movement, whose followers had been branded as traitors during the First World War. They also spoke of the peace marches of the 1920s and 1930s which attempted to rebaptise the Cenotaph as a 'peace' rather than 'war' monument. The installation in Govan was attended by Scottish communists who discussed the waves of national strikes that followed the war. In Halifax, veterans' groups spoke out against attempts made by the local council to move their own war monument. In Portsmouth, debates centred on the control exerted by the local authority. In Derry, the project was met with silence. If the *Cenotaph Project* can be credited with reviving local memories, it also met with resistance. The artists did not receive sufficient funding for the project to take place in Stornaway or Coventry. The site at Newport was cancelled. They were not invited to exhibit at the Piers Art Centre in Stromness.

In each place, then, the *Cenotaph Project* galvanised the language of art as a means to probe the ongoing existence of a 'history within living memory' (to recall the subtitle of the *Peterlee Project* discussed in Chapter 3). But its ambitions went further; for the artists also sought to recover a history of the collective behaviours that the monument had provoked. To this end, they commissioned the art historian Penelope Curtis to write a 'performance history' of the Whitehall Cenotaph, detailing its evolution from a temporary structure to permanent monolith.[13] In what follows, I propose to extend Curtis' pioneering 'performance study' to consider the more general question of what happens to the culture of public monuments after the experience of great destruction. How did the Whitehall Cenotaph as a model of ritual, stasis and order impose itself in the aftermath of a historical experience of destruction that had otherwise demolished much of the authoritative basis of the old culture, including the role of the artist in that culture? Conversely, is there an aesthetic form that allows this latent context of both war and revolution to break through the vertical hierarchies of representation, and if so, how?

The Whitehall Cenotaph

As already mentioned, the Whitehall Cenotaph stands out for its double origin as both an intentional and unintentional monument. Its first function was processual. It came to public attention as the object saluted by the Generals Foch and Pershing, Field Marshall Haig and Admiral Beatty and the allied troops as part of the celebrations of the Paris Peace Accord. The idea for such a monument was inspired by French plans for a catafalque to be saluted by the troops during their own celebrations of the conclusion of the Treaty of Versailles. Prime Minister David Lloyd George insisted on a similar tribute to the dead, one that would be 'sufficiently high to be impressive' but secular enough to reflect the different nationalities of the war dead. Although the catafalque was rejected as being too French and too Catholic, the idea of a secular monument, taking the form of a 'simple pylon' but 'sufficiently impressive', eventually prevailed.[14] When Lutyens proposed a cenotaph or an empty tomb, erected on top of a rectangular pylon, the simplicity of his design was immediately seized by the governing authorities as an adequate representation, not just of the allied war dead, but also of the imperial troops.[15] The Foreign Minister, Lord Curzon, explicitly praised it as an 'imperial monument', while General Haig described it as a 'symbol of the empire's unity'.[16]

Official intentions aside, the public reaction to the monument was by all accounts unexpected. The very simplicity of the design served to focalise the grief of a public who had been deprived of the opportunity to bury their war dead. The initial structure had been intended to last for a week, but already on 21 July 1919 *The Times* noted that the dignity of the cenotaph was such that it 'appears to be of more lasting material than the other decorative efforts'; and that 'Sir Edwin Lutyens's design is so grave, severe and beautiful that one might well wish it were indeed of stone and permanent'.[17] On 23 July, Sir Alfred Mond suggested to the War Cabinet that the erection of a war memorial 'on these lines' and in this 'historic spot' would 'solve the difficult question of a

War memorial which is bound to become the subject of public interest'.[18] On 30 July 1919, the Cabinet decided that the cenotaph would be re-erected in permanent form on the same spot on the grounds that 'the cenotaph in its present position had memories which could not be uprooted'.[19] Even as late as November and December, the newspapers reported that crowds continued to 'gather in absorption round the monument's base', oblivious to the 'two streams of traffic in Whitehall'[20] and the 'mud which splashed from passing vehicles' on wet days'.[21] Lutyens would later recall that 'Time passed and the plain fact emerged by the hour that the Cenotaph was what the people wanted [...] It was a mass-feeling ... the human sentiment of millions.'[22]

This site-specific aspect of the Cenotaph did not preclude it from being erected elsewhere. Numerous cenotaphs were set up in different London neighbourhoods and around the country. These were the focus of various ceremonies, which sometimes featured several cenotaphs, such as two in Woolwich in 1919, with one transported by van.[23] Even Lutyens' temporary cenotaph continued to be used. After the cenotaph itself was dismantled, its sarcophagus continued to be honoured in the yearly commemorations that took place at the Imperial War Museum: first at Crystal Palace, then at the museum's new home at the Imperial Institute in South Kensington.[24] Meanwhile, the wood that made up the rest of the structure was turned into souvenir models by wounded ex-servicemen to raise funds for blinded soldiers and sailors. A model that coexisted alongside the final work and continued to inform numerous copies and versions of the original suggested an unconventional and altogether novel way of conceiving public sculpture: as an act, rather than an object, as a performance that could happen at multiple sites at the same time because the audience was an active agent in the activity. As Alex King has suggested, the Cenotaph drew much of its energy from the way it appeared to formalise a largely improvised set of mourning practices that had sprung up in the early years of the war, when informal war shrines had been set up in the neighbourhoods and communities of the fallen soldiers.[25]

This raises the question of how a sculptural form imposed from above – and consolidated through a state calendar of ritual and order – might relate to the informal processes that originated from below and were not initially tied to any singular artefact. Jay Winter has observed that after the initial creative phase in constructing a commemorative form, the second crucial stage occurs when a monument becomes embedded in an official calendar of remembrances and institutionalised as part of civic routine.[26] The Armistice Day commemorations of 11 November 1919 marked the first conscious attempt to impose a 'uniformity' of memory.[27] But these commemorations still took place in an uncertain context and mood.[28] Only a few months earlier, *The Times* had excused a 'pardonably light-hearted crowd'[29] during the July Peace

Day celebrations. A similar mood was registered by Virginia Woolf who, in her diaries, debunked them as nothing but a 'servants festival … got up to pacify the people'.[30] It was not until the following year, when the permanent monument was unveiled, that a fully synchronised public spectacle took place. This re-enactment transformed what in 1919 was still experienced as an uncertain beginning – an uncertainty compounded by ongoing war battles – into an inaugural moment, a foundation in the literal sense of the word, which is always retrospectively constructed.

Foundation, of course, has architectural connotations. When Lutyens designed the permanent structure, he added an entasis to each surface. This was a technique derived from the ancient Greeks of adding a slight curvature to the columns of structures, generating an optical illusion that made the lines appear straighter.[31] This ensured that in the final monument there was not a single straight line or flat plane.[32] Instead, as Allan Greenberg has observed, at each stage and at each setback, the 'eye is drawn latterly' and upward by this constant slight curvature which gives the monument a 'dynamic, vertical spiral movement'.[33] Entasis thus not only orders the space around the Cenotaph in a more sculptural manner; it also draws the eye upwards, towards the empty tomb at the top, and further, beyond it, as if to offer a visual means to transcend death without explicitly endorsing any one religious doctrine of transcendence.[34]

The extensive use of entasis not only gave the Cenotaph the strength of foundations, but also a classical form that made it appear as if one civilisation (now lost) was communicating with another. This formal dynamism encouraged a bodily, physiological interaction that enabled the void at its centre to be experienced subjectively, as the projection of an inner mood or even personal feeling. Nearly twenty years earlier, the art historian Alois Riegl had identified the atmospheres that seem to emanate from certain monuments as part of their timeless 'age value'.[35] Ruins, in particular, according to Riegl, were exemplary instances of monuments that appear to arrive in the present as if transplanted directly from the past, worn away by time but otherwise unaltered by human intervention. We see a similar effect in the Cenotaph, whose formal qualities made it appear as wholly complete, alive, something more akin to a found object, than an intentional structure commissioned by a particular government for a particular effect. In fact, Lutyens' other monuments were explicitly perceived by contemporaries as so many proleptic ruins. Commenting on the Stone of Remembrance, Winston Churchill exhorted parliament to consider its minimalism and abstraction as the highest form of authority, one that would last 'thousands of years' and long after 'it might be, our politics and systems have passed away'.[36]

By November 1920, the Cenotaph's consecration as a 'people's monument' was complete. More than one million people came to pay their respects to the newly unveiled monument in under two weeks. Even those unable to make the journey reportedly drew their curtains closed at the very moment when the Cenotaph was unveiled.[37] The press observed that although the Tomb of the Unknown Soldier had been sanctified in the same ceremony, it was the Cenotaph that retained the most public attention. Unimpeded by the opening and closing times of Westminster Abbey, people were able to pay their respects to the Cenotaph quite literally at any time of the day or night. People came from all over the country to participate in a ceremony that lasted for days, consisted of no more than a simple gesture – the laying of a wreath – and yet refused to be contained within the barriers of urban space. The flow was such that traffic had to be halted for longer than had been planned. Even when traffic resumed after four days, the ceremony continued. If anything, the thin, unbroken, shuffling line of mostly silent people, wedged in between the flow of cars on Whitehall, was hailed as an image more moving than any official, or officially sanctioned, symbolic form.[38]

Given this context, it is entirely plausible that many people experienced the Cenotaph less as an official monument but more as a frame, what the anthropologist Victor Turner has called a set of performances or actions that create a 'bordered space and a privileged time' in which a given community can 'cut out a piece of itself for inspection and retrospection'.[39] It is striking in this respect to note how intimate, even physical, the initial contact with the Cenotaph and its various replicas had been. People were reproached for treating the Cenotaph as if it were a personal grave and leaving inappropriate mementos. Although the base of the Cenotaph was 'never without its covering of flowers', tributes would suddenly increase at certain times of the year that corresponded to the established rituals of the calendar year, including especially those associated with leisure and a break from work: Christmas, Bank and other statutory holidays.[40] The Cenotaph, in other words, was associated with a ritual time of suspension from everyday life, whose meaning had not yet been consolidated in a specific political message.

This same time of suspension also created a liminal space of a different kind, one that enabled a sceptical, even negative attitude towards official culture. Positioned in front of Whitehall, the Cenotaph stopped people and focused their attention on the threshold of state power. These physical acts of stopping, standing still and paying attention had much in common with other actions that also sought to break, interrupt or otherwise stop time. It did not take long for strike action, protest and rallies – obstructive activities that take the form of assembling, and standing still – to coalesce around the monument.

Today it has become nearly impossible to extricate the Cenotaph from the increasingly abstract cult of remembrance that has accrued around it, notably on the Armistice Day commemorations of every year. But I want to suggest that the Cenotaph played a very different, if largely latent, role in its first few years, not just as an unproblematic cipher of empire and nation, but also as a bulwark against civil war and a Bolshevik revolution that, in 1919, directly threatened the West. This ability of the monument to attract disruptive behaviours has been well documented. In 1920 and 1921, protests and what *The Times* called 'revolutionary and seditious speeches against the Crown and Commonwealth' accompanied the Armistice Day commemorations.[41] In 1921, the annual rite was swollen by some 5,000 unemployed men and multiple cart- and lorry-loads of women and children from the East London neighbourhood of Poplar. Carrying such banners as 'Work or Maintenance', they tried to lay wreathes bearing inscriptions such as 'To the Dead Victims of Capitalism from the Living Victims of Capitalism', 'To the dead not forgotten, from the living forgotten', and one man wore pawn-tickets in place of his war decorations.[42] In 1922 the first Commission of Works reported receiving complaints about 'political interferences in certain memorial notices'.[43] On 6 November of that year, uniformed Italian *fascisti* marched to the Cenotaph, the first of a series of alternating gestures whereby both fascists and communists of various nationalities competed to lay wreathes at the Cenotaph, a practice that peaked during the Spanish Civil War. In a similar vein, during the late 1920s and 1930s, the Armistice Day commemorations were confronted with countervailing 'peace' rallies that warned of the imminent threat of a new war, thereby challenging the myth of the First World War as the final war. By referring to the Cenotaph as a 'Peace' monument, these rallies also reactivated one of the original functions of all monuments: to serve as a warning for future generations.

Robert Bushaway observes that the increasingly abstract impersonal cult of remembrance that sedimented in the years 1919–25 can be read as a chronology of official reaction to political events, both at home and abroad.[44] The Cenotaph, after all, coalesced into a national monument during a time of great crisis in Britain. The Representation of the People Act of 1918 embarked Britain on an unprecedented extension of parliamentary democracy. Yet, the waves of strikes in 1918 and 1919 – by police, miners, railwayman, dockers, teachers – indicated that the government's hold on civil authority was tenuous. The 1919 general strike in Glasgow Clydeside in particular had been a moment of national emergency, with troops mobilised and public buildings occupied.[45] The threat of unrest was further compounded by the slow pace of demobilisation, which led to revolts in the army and navy. By some accounts, almost 10,000 men refused to serve in Folkestone in January 1919, followed by 20,000 soldiers who refused orders at Calais, with numerous mutinies in the navy.[46]

In November 1918, a similar mutiny in Kiel by some 40,000 sailors, soldiers and workers had triggered the abdication of the Kaiser and the start of the German Revolution, striking fear among the political elites across Western Europe that the socialist revolution had arrived. Bavaria had become a republic in November 1918 and Hungary a Soviet republic in March 1919. In 1919, Berlin and Vienna both witnessed failed uprisings, while the Russian army came close to taking Warsaw in August. Closer to home, a series of self-proclaimed Irish soviets marked the start of the Irish War of Independence and the eventual granting of dominion status to the Irish Free State.

The unrest was felt both at home and abroad. Walter Kendall notes that when armed soldiers demonstrated on Horse Guards Parade in February 1919, the War Office sent out a 'confidential question to the commanding officers of all units to ascertain whether or not it was thought troops would remain loyal in case of a revolution in England'.[47] It has been argued that whether a revolution succeeds or fails often hinges on who controls the army. And yet, as a confidential Home Office Report from 1920 concluded: 'It must be remembered that in the event of rioting, for the first time in history the rioters will be better trained than the troops.'[48] Winston Churchill, as the newly appointed secretary for war instructed military forces throughout the UK to prepare to 'act in aid of the Civil Power in the event of a national strike of a revolutionary character'.[49] From this perspective, a Cenotaph that focalised and controlled mass gatherings under the watchful eye of Whitehall proved a useful image of cohesion and loyalty. So too was the use of the Cenotaph as a saluting base for various military contingents, including the ex-servicemen of the newly formed British Legion, who, in the presence of the Cenotaph, were repeatedly exhorted to remember their duty by representatives of the monarchy and government.[50] By insisting on the sacrality of the dead, this cult of remembrance sought to represent the immense human disaster of the war as a historical chapter that was finished and closed, not as an ongoing event whose ramifications radiated across all levels of society. This fear of a general strike and distrust of the loyalty of ex-servicemen, many of whom returned home to poverty and unemployment, should not be underestimated.[51] Prime Minister Lloyd George would later recall, in a conspicuous use of the double negative, that although he had many anxious moments during the war, he was 'not at all sure that the anxiety was not more acute and intense immediately after the war'.[52]

Cenotaph as figure of stasis

If we take this context of international revolution and potential civil war into account, the Cenotaph appears in a new light, as a figure of stasis that both attracted and repelled civilian strife. As we have already seen in Chapter 1, the term 'stasis' has political as well as aesthetic connotations. Ordinarily, *stasis* is associated with connotations of stillness or repose, a period of inactivity or equilibrium. For instance, the Cenotaph's neoclassical form, harmoniousness and symmetry can be considered an exemplary instance of aesthetic repose.[53] But *stasis* is also the ancient Greek expression for civil war, used to 'describe a group of citizens taking a political stance, thus becoming a party or faction and by extension applied to political activity leading to civil war and foreign intervention'.[54] As the classicist Nicole Loraux reminds us, *stasis* is synonymous with *kinēsis*, movement or agitation. Deriving from the Greek verb *histēmi*, which signifies a standing up or stopping, *stasis* expresses the moment when time and the normal progress of family and civilian life stands still, as it does when a group of citizens rises up to stand against another group.[55] In ancient Greece, *stasis* variously referred to rebellion; political catastrophe; or the moment of stoppage that takes place whenever the chorus interrupts the play in a tragedy. These connotations are retained today in medical terminology, where stasis refers to the halting or stopping of a flow, for example of blood. What connects these diverse uses of the term is the reference to a suspension of time. In an interesting formulation, Loraux relates this ancient understanding of civil war to the act of erecting a *stele* or statue in the middle of the commons, dividing it into symmetrical and opposing forces.[56] She also notes its connection to the term 'dissensus' (from the Latin verb *sedere*, to sit), which literally means to sit apart, arguing that similar connotations are evident in the Latin term *seditio*, the origin of the English term sedition, which can also refer to the act of founding (as in to erect a statue or altar), much like a statue erected among the citizens can function as a foundational moment as well as something more akin to a 'fixed explosive'.[57]

Following Loraux, I want to suggest that the Cenotaph attracted so much attention during the interwar years because it conjoined two behaviours normally taken as mutually exclusive: the aspect of verticality, repose and standing still, which is characteristic of public monuments in their functional aspect, and the opposing tendency towards agitation and resistance, captured by such actions as holding your ground. On the one hand, the Cenotaph was experienced as a powerful focal point that assembled people together, its verticality, neoclassical simplicity and visual repose serving to cast any movement or agitation outside it – outside civilisation so to speak. For a key function of the Cenotaph was to promote the message that the Great War remained a 'civilized war', a war fought between sovereign powers and with specific combatants, and not a generalised or 'civil war'.[58] On the other hand, the Cenotaph was also construed, at least by some, as a hostile object. Sitting awkwardly on the threshold of power, like an uninvited guest might sit at one's doorstep, it provided an occasion for people to place themselves apart (like the one man who stood without taking off his hat during the moment of silence in a sea of onlookers during the commemorations of 1920[59]). In this sense the Cenotaph also created what Giorgio Agamben, following Loraux, calls a 'zone of indifference' in which distinctions between friend and foe, war and peace, life and death, domestic and foreign are no longer clear.[60]

By stopping, interrupting or otherwise suspending time, the Cenotaph triggered new types of collective behaviour that reacted to the monument as an animating presence. These public behaviours demonstrated what had been acknowledged as early as 1916, namely that the staggering numbers of war dead had rendered all past attitudes to monumental culture obsolete. In this context, it is worth noting that the Cenotaph's early life as a *model* – that is, not as a sited monument but as an incomplete, transitory object that could be adapted, altered and deployed in various public spaces – overlapped with the avant-garde and progressivist art movements that had emerged in this same period and which too sought new plans for a 'participatory' art, frequently focused on architecture.

To remain briefly with the British context, it is useful to recall that a Civic Commission of Arts had been convened in January 1916 to deal precisely with the challenge of designing memorials to the war dead.[61] Widely reported in the press, this sudden attention to – and need for – a public language of art under-scored just how urgent the question of representation had become. It was as if war, and the imminent expansion of democratic suffrage, had liberated the aesthetic possibilities of both objects and individuals. There were calls to end patronage culture and abolish museums and art galleries.[62] Artists and crafts-men were exhorted to overcome the traditional divisions between the arts and bring art closer to life, whether through a 'union of art and architecture' or through greater 'cooperation between artists and public'.[63] The commission even envisioned an experimental memorial art of a reduced scale, for a strictly domestic setting. Needless to say, and despite some vigorous campaigning, no avant-garde artist was invited to take part in the Memorial War Graves Commission. The same held for most of the state-commissioned memorial projects across Europe, with the notable exception of Russia. Instead, the government appointed three architects to the commission, including Lutyens, and one poet, Rudyard Kipling. By indicating its preference for an architect's blueprint, the state made clear that monuments to the war dead were not to be confused with these calls for a new civic or participatory living art.

This raises important questions about how performance relates to the language of art in moments of social upheaval and political unrest. Penelope Curtis observes that when the idea for a cenotaph was first mooted in 1919, the structure was defined in functional terms, as an object for an action, namely the 'laying of wreaths' so 'that future generations shall know what has taken place now'. When the same question was posed in 1967, the Office of Works no longer defined the Cenotaph in functional terms but instead clas-sified it as a public sculpture, according to the Public Statues Act 1854.[64] The passage of the Cenotaph into the category of official art, it seems, happened only once it had ceased to make immediate demands on perception. This supports Paul Veyne's thesis that public monuments function most effectively when they are ignored, exerting at best a 'weak presence' on the edges of our perceptual field.[65] As Veyne ironically notes, this would bring them in line with how we usually behave around art objects. For these too struggle for our attention, the vast majority of people finding it difficult to focus on any given work for more than a few moments, even in a museum or art gallery where the works are hung at eye level.

Building upon this observation, we can say that the Cenotaph came closest to embodying a public language of performance when it was experienced as the object of numerous, diverse actions, none of them expressing a single or unique telos. These performance behaviours, moreover, bring us closest to what a language of art might convey prior to its 'monumentalisation' in galleries and museums. For it is the nature of art to produce intended as well as unintended meanings, in contrast to propaganda, which always has a specific communication in mind. It is ironic, therefore, that the Cenotaph was officially recognised as a 'public statue' only when it had more or less exhausted its power to create new meanings. In other words, when it became what Brisley calls an 'icon' 'an empty shell of its former substance' a 'civilian carcass in Portland stone'.[66]

To return once more to the *Cenotaph Project*, we can say that by liberating the Whitehall Cenotaph from a national, imperial context, the *Project* asks viewers to engage with its origins as a provisional architect's model whose iterative potential had captured the public imagination. A model, after all, expresses a new order that is still in its 'design phase'. As Norbert Lynton has observed, 'wars and the immediate aftermath of wars are times for fantasy, architectural or otherwise [...] paper architecture thrives under these conditions, and also in periods of open social dissent'.[67] That many of these designs were never built, due to prevailing hardships and political instability, makes them not less but more powerful as *models* capable of articulating multiple, alternative futures, not all of which come to pass.

In the *Cenotaph Project*, Balcioglu and Brisley correlate Lutyens' model to other monuments, famous either for being left unfinished or for being torn down. Among these is *The Monument to the Third International* by the Russian Bolshevik Vladimir Tatlin, a structure directly contemporary with Lutyens' Cenotaph (figure 4.4). Designed in response to Lenin's decree for a new monumental propaganda to be erected to replace the old monuments of Tsarist Russia in the quickest possible time, Tatlin designed a gigantic, perpetually moving tower (figure 4.5). This iconic structure was to be made up of three different shapes, each functioning as a place of assembly, administration and communication. The top cube, rotating once a year, was to be used for legislative purposes; a pyramid, rotating once a month, would house administrative offices, and a cylinder rotating once a day would contain information services, including radio, telephone and telegraphic equipment. In Tatlin's design, a continual revolution (in the cyclical sense) would entirely bypass the traditional channels of art and politics, in favour of new modes of political action and communication.

As a monument seeking to capture a perpetual revolution, Tatlin's Tower would appear to have nothing to do with Lutyens' paean to restoration and repose. It did, however, share one aspect with its British counterpart: the lack of any visible foundations. Like Lutyens' Cenotaph, this was a monument designed without a specific location in mind. It is tempting to speculate that, in a revolutionary situation, there is no ground or foundation for choosing one particular site or 'institution' over another (apparently Tatlin even toyed with the idea of a gigantic monument straddling the river Neva). Of course, the key aspect of Tatlin's Tower is that it was never built. Unlike Lutyens' Cenotaph, this was a monument that remained a model, existing solely in the form of two drawings and an approximately five-metre-high model, built of laths, tin, paper and glue, whose purpose and function was elaborated in art-critical essays by Nikolai Punin.[68] The model was exhibited in Tatlin's studio and subsequently in an official exhibition that took place from December 1920 to January 1921. A simplified version travelled to Paris in 1925, for the International Exposition of Modern Decorative and Industrial Arts. A rougher, even more simplified model – this time 'elliptical to fit in the back of a lorry' – was displayed during Leningrad's 1925 May Day Parade.[69] In the reverse procedure of Lutyens' Cenotaph, as time progressed, Tatlin's Tower became more rudimentary, abstract, provisional and discursive: as if the revolution had created a situation of stasis that had left the model in permanent suspension, unable to bridge the gap between art and life.

A similar suspension of time and turn towards the model is also evident in those monuments that are dismantled or destroyed in periods of social unrest or revolution. *The Cenotaph Project* cites the Vendôme Column, destroyed by the Communards during the 1871 uprising of the Commune (figure 4.6). This column had courted controversy from its origins. Designed by Napoleon to commemorate his victories in 1803, its crown was to be topped by a statue of Charlemagne but eventually came to be occupied by a statue of Napoleon himself as Emperor in Roman Dress. When Napoleon was defeated in 1814, the statue was pulled down, apparently with considerable 'difficulties'. Unable to pull it down, one royalist allegedly contented himself with 'slapping it continuously on the cheeks' before, eventually, a 'noose' accomplished the task.[70] During the July Monarchy, a statue of Napoleon returned to reoccupy the column, this time created by the sculptor Charles Emile Marie Seurre depicting him as a 'Little Corporal'. However, this too was replaced under the Second Empire, this time by a replica of Napoleon's original statue. As for the Communards, according to one contemporary, what was most objectionable was the column's height, as if this colossal aspect itself stood as 'a permanent insult to the vanquished by the victors'.[71] The dismantled column, by contrast, appeared curiously lightweight and illusionistic; 'as if it was stage décor … fragile, empty, miserable!', according to one eye-witness.[72] This underscores once more how social and collective behaviours can change not just the cultural or symbolic meaning of a given object but also how it is materially perceived.

As the *Cenotaph Project* reminds us, in the same period that the Cenotaph coalesced to become the UK's national monument, other symbols of monarchy and empire were being actively dismantled, notably in Ireland. Consider for instance the dismantling of a statue of Queen Victoria, in Dublin, demanded in 1933 and accomplished in 1948, or of the one in University College, Cork, where the statue was removed and ritually buried beneath a lawn in 1935, only to be exhumed in 1995. Or the fact that although a national monument for the Irish war dead was called for by the viceroy in 1919, it was not until 1929 that a plan for a memorial garden, also designed by Sir Edwin Lutyens, was approved. Completed in 1939, this garden was formally inaugurated only in 1994, when the Irish experience of the First World War was integrated with that of Britain and a firmly post-revolutionary context for European history was officially established.

For Brisley and Balcioglu, what relates these otherwise historically distinct episodes and monuments is a shared suspension of time. Monuments serve as sites of collective action and reaction whenever they occupy a space of power or authority otherwise left empty or in flux. The artists' preferred term for this experience is 'interregnum'. They reference Gramsci's use of the term to describe the same interwar period in Italy. 'The old is dying and the new cannot be born,' he wrote, 'in this interregnum appears a variety of morbid symptoms.'[73] In this much-cited description, Gramsci detached the term 'interregnum' from its habitual association with the death of one king and the investiture of another. Instead, he used it to describe a more general, ongoing crisis in which the ruling class, and its main ideologies, still dominated but without leadership or much innate authority, while the popular masses had become detached from the traditional ideologies they used to believe in. Interestingly, Gramsci resorted to the visual metaphor of the *incomplete sketch* to describe how, in the absence of any genuinely revolutionary change, any 'lines of construction will as yet be "broad lines", sketches, which might (and should) be changed at all times so as to be consistent with the new structure as it is formed'.[74]

In a more recent gloss on Gramsci's interregnum, the sociologist Zygmunt Bauman has used a related visual vocabulary, describing it as the moment when the 'extant legal frame of social order loses its grip' but a 'new frame … responsible for making the old frame useless is still at the design stage'.[75]

To say that something is still at its design phase is to suggest that the pattern, composition or blueprint that frames the content is still missing or that its overall purpose is provisional or still unclear. In such a period, any expression of a new order remains self-referential – a provisional and ever-changing model – while extant images of power continue to circulate, 'mummified' visions that are out of joint, anachronistic or perhaps even subject to decay.

For the remainder of this chapter, I want to consider in more detail what this model architecture can reveal about individual and collective performance behaviours in times of revolution when, as Brisley observes, 'everything is broken, everything is opened, everything becomes feasible'.[76] To do so I will return to the period of the French Revolution, arguably the first time a state government tried to create a truly public monument and a moment when the cenotaph itself was privileged as a revolutionary aesthetic form. Along the way, I will continue my method of extending and expanding on the artists' own references to the histories and imaginaries of revolution to address the more general questions that we have been tracking throughout this book. Can the language of art be used to express a more public, or shared, relation to the historical past? Or does art ultimately end up always inscribing this public or shared history in some kind of monumental form? To rephrase this question in more overtly political terms: can the eruption of

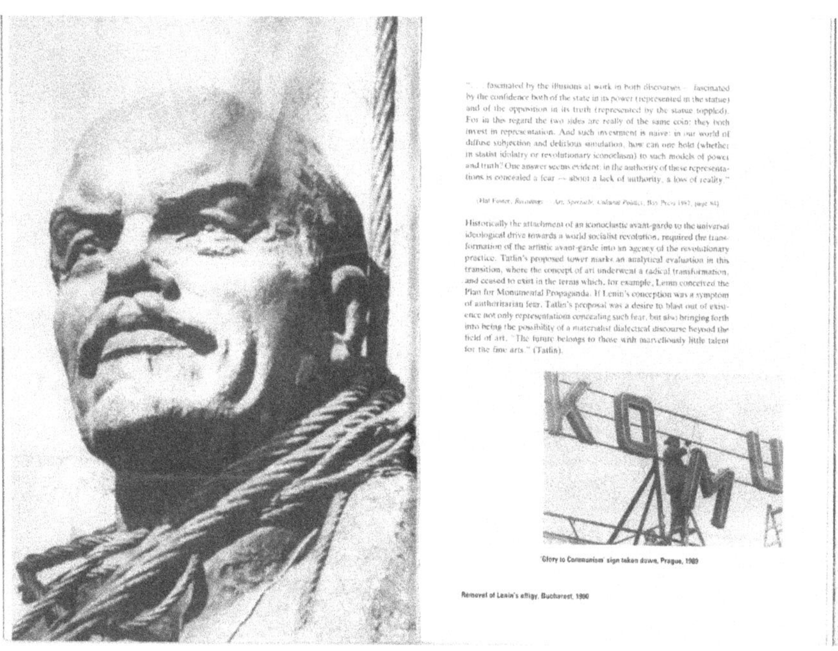

Stuart Brisley and Maya Balcioglu, *The Cenotaph Project*, 1987–91   **4.4**

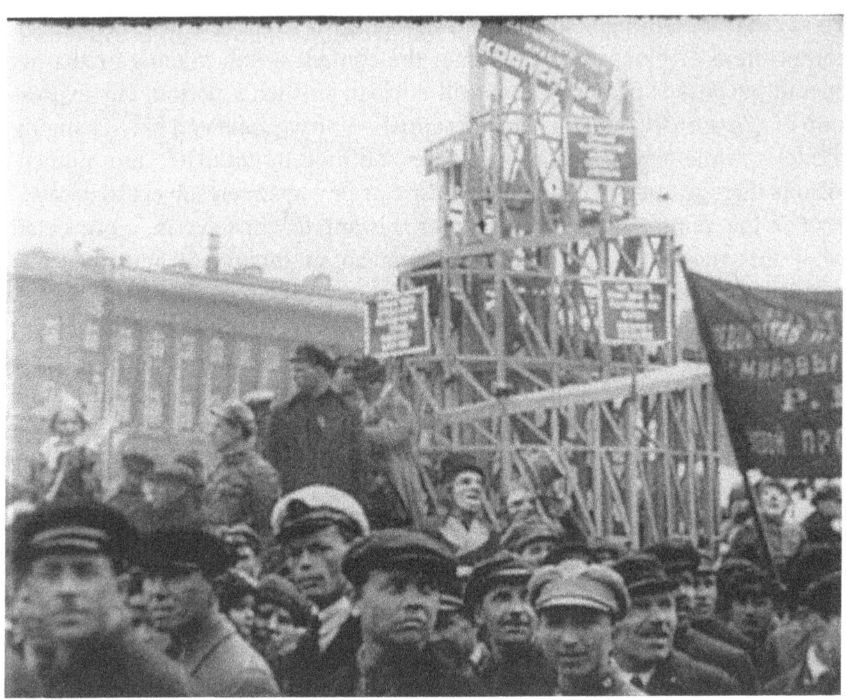

4.5 Parade with a model of Vladimir Tatlin's *Monument to the Third International* (1919–20) in the streets on the May Day celebration in 1925

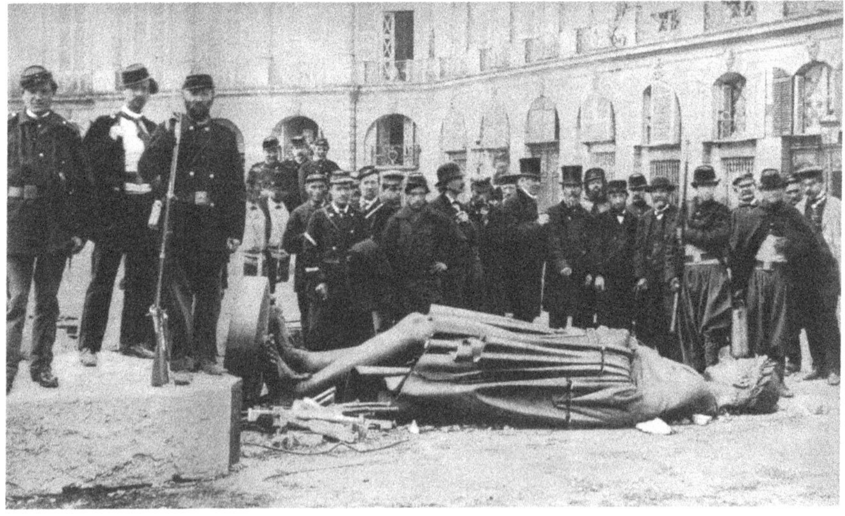

4.6 Vendôme Column, after it was pulled down on 16 May 1871

popular sovereignty be expressed openly, as the coming together of people to found a new order whose final form and outcome is unknown? Or will sovereignty always be expressed through ersatz forms of majesty and authority, what Bataille has described as the masses 'huddled in silence' at the base of monuments?[77]

The French Revolution and the empty space of performance

Until the French Revolution, there was no conception of a collective or shared monument. Within a hierarchical, estates-based society, monuments commemorated either individual persons or famous deeds. All political representation was tied to the individual body, ultimately represented by the body of the king. Just as all representation was tied to individual or corporate bodies, so all art was made in the service of either religion, wealth or power. There was no such thing as an autonomous, much less 'public', language of art.

The conflicts over sovereignty that followed the Enlightenment, however, generated new lines of demarcation between the individual and social body. In France, these intensified after 1793, when the execution of the king terminated once and for all any self-evident connection between an individual 'representative' body (that of the king) and the body politic. As Pérouse de Monclos observes, before the Revolution, the term 'monument' was restricted to its commemorative function; after the Revolution, it was extended to refer to any grand public structure, including buildings.[78] For instance, when Quatremère de Quincy, the leading architectural theorist of the day, elaborated on this new understanding of the term 'monument', he claimed that only buildings which directly expressed the people's needs encapsulated the full 'meaning, luxury and magnificence' of the word.[79] This emphasis marked a move away from a commemorative understanding of the monument as a type of statue – based on the human body and physical likeness to the deceased – and towards an abstract architectural order.

Even before the Revolution, cemeteries had become the privileged site for experimenting with this new architectural order. In 1788 the hygienicist and doctor Félix Vicq d'Azy had admonished the rich and powerful for constructing mausoleums that perpetuated a hierarchical vision of humanity even in the afterlife. Instead of mausoleums for the rich and a common graveyard for the poor, he suggested public gardens. Landscaped with cenotaphs, mausoleums and epitaphs, these gardens were to be located outside the precinct of both city and church. Thomas Lacquer observes that over this period, references to the actual dead body were increasingly replaced by 'memories' of the deceased.[80] Cemeteries increasingly resembled memorial gardens rather than church graveyards. Care of the dead was no longer seen as something that belonged exclusively to a Christian community and the Church.

With the Revolution, and especially once church property had been expropriated, these architectural visions of equality in death briefly became a political reality. In October Year II (1793), Chaumette and Fouché put forward the motion that all cemeteries be moved outside of Paris.[81] This motion also ordered crosses and statues to be removed from graveyards, commemorative markers to be identical, and all cemetery gates to bear the one inscription: 'Death is an eternal sleep'.[82] The decree of Prairial Year XII (1804) forced all cemeteries outside of Paris, banned private mausoleums or tombstones and ordered that all graves be the same size. To be sure, these new strictures were unevenly implemented, not to mention short lived. By 1806, a price scale was reintroduced as well as division according to social class. Nevertheless, in their efforts to overturn burial practices that were over one thousand years old, the revolutionaries developed a new attitude towards death that fundamentally reworked the dividing line between individual and communal identity.[83] These debates about what to do with the dead body, which persisted throughout the 1790s, raised a host of new questions. What part of the body was public and what part remained private? Should physical remains be cremated, buried in common graves or individual rows? Should there be individual tombstones or uniform stone monuments? This suddenly uncertain status of the dead body provoked an intense polemic as revolutionaries sought to clarify the new lines of inclusion and exclusion that had been generated by the revolutionary experience itself. In 1796, Roederer even suggested paired cemeteries, one for deserving citizens, the other for executed criminals.[84]

There is no space to go into all the details of this complex debate, except to note that this fundamental rupture in nearly one thousand years of caring for the dead stimulated the urgent need for a new architectural order. Even more significant for our discussion of cenotaphs is that it generated a *model* architectural order centred on the absent body, the empty tomb and hollow spaces. In the years immediately preceding the French Revolution, pyramids, classical temples, ancient burial mounds and cenotaphs abounded in the public imagination as architects and urban planners turned to the oldest and simplest of forms to recover an allegedly original function of architecture as a social art. As Emil Kauffman has argued, architects such as Étienne-Louis Boullée and Claude Nicholas Ledoux treated antiquity not as a historical precedent but as a source for *models* that approximated natural forms. In their exploration of stereometric (readily measurable) volumes such as cubes, spheres and pyramids, these architects treated architecture as a first or primary art, what Kauffman calls an 'archicraft' through which they could 'express their longing before they dare[d] reform their social institution'.[85]

For the purposes of this chapter, it is interesting to observe just how central visions of empty tombs and hollow spaces were to these utopian imaginings.

As Boullée observed, funerary monuments are those with the longest duration, designed to 'withstand the ravages of time'.[86] They reach back to the most ancient, elementary forms of civilisation and also forward into the future, to perpetuate a living memory. Among funerary buildings, the cenotaph was simultaneously positioned as the most ancient and the most contemporary. Precisely because cenotaphs were constructed in the absence of human remains, they did not have to be designed in accordance with pre-existing rites of burial, tied to particular bodies and specific places. Moreover, in their freedom from the past, cenotaphs also encapsulated a new understanding of sovereignty as freedom from all authority. Of all the utopian forms of the eighteenth century, the cenotaph expresses most completely the awareness that an autonomous society is one that creates its own institutions in full knowledge that there is no higher authority or deeper foundation to justify any one choice.

Boullée's *Newton Cenotaph* (1784) is a case in point (figure 4.7). Like with Lutyens' Cenotaph, it is a symbolic structure built around an empty space. Circular in form, it consists of a vast, hollow sphere whose vault is pierced by light shafts, enabling daylight to create the pattern of the night sky on the darkened ceiling. The sarcophagus to Newton lies on the lower pole as the 'only material object that the onlooker sees'.[87] Boullée considered the sphere as the simplest form that 'offers the greatest possible surface to the eye', thereby lending it 'majesty'.[88] Self-sufficient, the sphere represents a world unto itself, a world in repose. Yet it also draws the eye upwards so that the 'more we look the larger it appears'. The curvature suggests not only majesty

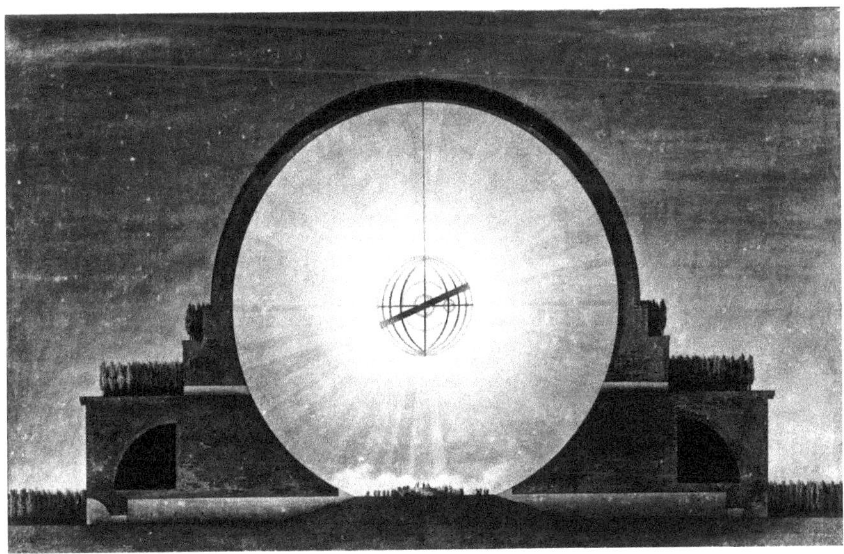

Étienne-Louis Boullée, *Newton Cenotaph*, day effect cut   **4.7**

but also distance and authority because it ensures that the onlooker can never approach what they are seeing.

In his *Newton Cenotaph*, Boullée captured all the elements that later became the revolutionary style. It is a symbolic structure built around an empty space. It captures a new understanding of eternal life based not on Christian images but on material presence (here light and shadow). It is a living memory constructed around a shared public reference (here Newton the great hero of scientific reason). Finally, and perhaps most significantly, it incorporates the *subjective experience* aroused by the monument into the monument's aesthetic language. A similar idea is found in Boullée's *Cenotaph in the Egyptian Genre* (1785), which takes the form of a truncated pyramid. The pyramid was used extensively in Boullée's plan for a cemetery, which stands out for its use of negative space. This model cemetery was designed according to his two principles of 'buried architecture', which emphasised 'low, sagging proportions buried in the earth',[89] and an architecture of shadows, in which 'light-absorbing materials, stripped of all details' are used to create 'a play of shadows, outlined by deeper shadow'.[90]

Richard Etlin has suggested that these empty spaces express what is most revolutionary about such monuments, which is the search 'for the basic and primal', achieved by 'making a temple-like enclosure, by opening a hole, a cavity in the ground, or by gathering a dense mass of stone around a restricted area'.[91] These monuments present empty space as something dynamic rather than static. Whether levitating like a sphere, or with the gravitational force of a pyramid, Boullée's plans capture movement at rest. They capture architecture not in the conventional sense as a fixed form but as the energy and process of creation. Specifically, they are concerned with what happens when the perception of form becomes part of the form itself. It is not without interest to observe that Boullée had wanted to be a painter before becoming an architect.[92] He viewed architecture as a means to go beyond the limits of painting, because it used nature and not artifice to simulate the effects produced by bodily perception itself.

Boullée's architecture can be qualified as revolutionary, then, not just because it anticipates modern architecture in its emphasis on geometric forms and standardised units. Nor simply because of the homology he posed between artistic and political revolution, recognised at the time.[93] It is also revolutionary in positing architecture as a kind of performance or action. In this it can be said to belong to a non-representational art activity of the most radical kind, capable of responding, at least theoretically, to a new experience of time and duration in which hierarchical structures are constantly overturned in the effort to return to the most original, basic forms.

Finally, it is revolutionary insofar as it remained a provisional model. Boullée's funerary monuments, like the designs of his contemporary Ledoux, were mostly executed in the 1780s, a period of great turmoil. But although both these architects designed their monuments in the absence of any knowledge of the French Revolution as a specific historical event, they nevertheless captured a prevailing sense of an open future, still in its design phase. In their drawings and plans, past traditions and forms have become obsolete, and new ones remain to be implemented.

Once the Revolution itself erupted, a different expression of emptiness emerged, however. When, in 1791, Armand-Guy Kersaint delivered a report on behalf of the revolutionary *commission des monuments*, he pointed to the problem of the Revolution's empty spaces. Paris was full of buildings from the *ancien régime* that 'immortalised the memory of servitude',[94] he lamented. By contrast, the Revolution was marked not by presence but by absence, whether because of the monuments it had razed to the ground, or because the newly instituted public festivals had left no trace. Even the site of the former Bastille was marked only by a plaque, 'here lay the Bastille'.[95] As for the Champ de Mars, the site of the great Festival of the Federation, when the French nation and king had declared their loyalty to the new constitution, it was 'abandoned'.[96] Kersaint conceded that for his contemporaries the vacant Bastille might well be more evocative than any 'superb portico'; future generations, however, would see only empty space. As he poignantly observed, the very emptiness of the Champ de Mars evoked the even more ominous message that the Revolution 'will be as fragile and transitory as I am'.[97]

In place of this empty space, Kersaint proposed monuments that would serve as so many sanctuaries of the law. These were to be modelled after the ancient Prytaneion, a civic structure that had served as a kind of state hearth, with its perpetual fire and 'quasi-archive' of important political and historical documents.[98] Revolutionary France, Kersaint argued, needed to erect similar Temples of Law all over the country, including at the Champ de Mars, which would serve as the model for all the others. Inscribed with the Declaration of the Rights of Man and Citizen but mostly kept empty, the Temple would be open to the public only one day a year: for the celebration of 14 July. But 14 July was an ambiguous date. Officially, it celebrated the anniversary of 1790 – when the nation was regenerated – but unofficially recalled the 1789 storming of the Bastille, when a crowd of demonstrators attacked the notorious state prison, thereby marking the entry of a wholly new concept of 'popular sovereignty' into politics. In other words, 14 July demarcated a missing Year I, just like the other declarations of revolutionary time discussed in Chapter 1. In their winning design, the architects Molinos and Legrand insisted that simplicity and uniformity would serve to distinguish these temples from all other public buildings. Just as importantly, these same formal qualities would allow them to be reproduced all over the country. We see here once more how an abstract form, massed around an empty space, compensated for what was still, in practical terms, a fragile constitution and a governing body in its 'design' phase.

In the event, Kersaint regretted that such public monuments were unable to be erected at the place where they were most needed: the crowded spaces of crossroads and public thoroughfares where 'the greatest number of citizens gathered and who needed to be reminded to respect the law'.[99] For their part, Molinos and Legrand insisted that an architecture based on uniformity and abstraction must prohibit any disrespect towards the monument, including 'all publication and posters that do not pertain to the law' and, therefore, create 'impolitical admixtures'.[100] Here we have arguably the most explicit use of an abstract monument as a placeholder in what is otherwise strongly experienced as a state of exception. The abstract monument, bereft of any specific commemorative references, was used to prop up a fledging regime, with a tenuous hold on civil authority, against other competing, and arguably more 'participatory' ways of occupying space. To rephrase this in terms of the performance behaviours that we have been tracking throughout this chapter, we can say that the empty monument was designed to oppose all those perishable performances that aimed to reoccupy the empty spaces of civic infrastructure. In the context of the French Revolution, these performances ranged from public demonstration to a proliferating print and pamphlet culture that circulated through wall posters, placards, songs, caricatures or other popular art forms, to, in 1791, increasingly effective uses of local assembly by the radical Jacobins and sans-culottes.

We seem to be far removed from our discussion of the Whitehall Cenotaph. Nevertheless, this comparison of attitudes towards monuments in two very different historical contexts reveals an important affinity. Like with the 1919 Cenotaph, the abstract form was used in revolutionary France throughout the 1780s and 1790s to occupy a space in which political power appeared to vacillate or even be temporally suspended. In both cases, visionary architects designed monuments which staged, demarcated or otherwise brought to public attention an empty space, eschewing specific historical, artistic or religious references. In both contexts too, the authorities of the day concurred that these formal qualities alone – vertical height and the sense of amassed density around a void rather than any specific message – were best placed to communicate a vision of social stability and consensus. Cenotaphs became privileged monuments because they marked not the presence but the absence of the dead body: missing in the case of the First World War monument, and 'absent' in the revolutionary monument because its status and meaning was highly disputed. Finally, in both cases, abstract form served as a bulwark against other forms of communication which came from below or outside its structure.

Irrespective of the different historical contexts of Lutyens' Cenotaph on the one hand and the unrealised monuments of various revolutionary epochs on the other, this comparison reveals how any monument needs to be thought alongside its model. For the model expresses not just the hopes but also the fears of the future, whose uncertainties and limitations the structure seeks to overcome. In the case of post-war Britain, this fear remained largely implicit, reverberating in almost subterranean ways through the many opposing behaviours the Cenotaph provoked. In the case of the French Revolution, the fear was explicit. The surfeit of model monuments that rushed to fill the breach opened up by revolutionary rupture responded not just to a frighteningly open and uncontrollable future but also to the fear that recent events might be all too easily forgotten or overcome in turn. This sense of unease continued long after the Revolution was over. Bataille observes that the Place de la Concorde, the site first designed to host an equestrian statue of Louis XV before it became the place where Louis XVI was executed, remained a wasteland for many years, serving as the site of various temporary festivals or fairs but no permanent monument.[101]

By way of conclusion, we can say more generally that a trans-historical comparison of monuments has shown just how closely their form expresses – and compensates for – a period of social and political instability. Whether this interregnum is experienced implicitly, as a potential 'civil war' or as an outright revolution, it can be reconstructed through the monuments it destroys or the models it projects. It seems thus fitting to conclude with Michelet's famous lament in which he bemoaned the failure of the French Revolution to produce any lasting monument:

> The Champ de Mars! This is the only monument that the Revolution has left. The Empire has its Column and engrosses almost entirely the arch of Triumph; Royalty has its Louvre, its Hospital of Invalids; the feudal Church of the twelfth century is still enthroned in Notre Dame; nay, the very Romans have their imperial Ruins, the Thermae of the Caesars! And the Revolution has, for its monument – empty space.[102]

Michelet readily acknowledges that the Revolution – as a living process – has no need for an 'external monument'. Nevertheless, he regrets its absence. The Champ de Mars once teemed with people, action and events. It was a site where the Revolution's greatest expectations and harshest disillusions were experienced in equal measure. Now it lay barren, an 'arid plain' of 'parched grass'. But just because it was empty did not mean that it was without meaning. The Revolution's failure to erect a monument, Michelet reflects, was symptomatic of its ongoing power of disruption. It could not achieve a final form because it continued to divide generations and to *struggle* to retain its place in the historical memory. Indeed, to see this emptiness as the site of a *missing* or *future* monument was to misunderstand its power. If the Revolution ultimately lacked a monument, it is because its true expression was found elsewhere, in the memories it left behind or within the empty spaces it had created within an established architectural order.

We return once more to the main question of this book: whether and how the evanescent nature of performance art can also reveal something about the nature and experience of revolutionary time. As the *Cenotaph Project* demonstrates, performance art can be used forensically to uncover something about the historical situation of this interregnum because it too expresses itself through the gaps or empty space of the established order, recoverable through the models it projects, or the traces or memories it leaves behind. It thus can be used to reveal, if only indirectly and by analogy, the performative nature of monuments as structures constructed against the fear of the void, the empty space left behind by all periods of cataclysmic social change.

This brings me to my final point. If I have been able to use the *Cenotaph Project* to speculate on a trans-historical link between different historical monuments, it is because the *Project* itself taps into a far longer history of social and ritual performances, organised around the fear of death and burial.[103] The monument, after all, has long been hailed as an archaic object that bears the imprint of some of the earliest performance behaviours in human history, in which the body was used to leave a trace. Michel Serres, for instance, has suggested that the first statue was a mummified corpse, and that the first representation of the human body originated as a tumulary stone, stele or cippus signifying the person buried at its site.[104] These first foundations, however, became authoritative only by means of a second foundation, when death was objectified in the form of a primitive statue. Standing over and against the subjects that created them, statues were taller, more vertical and more permanent than any living body. Serres argues that by pushing, expulsing or otherwise burying evidence of the mortal body further underground, statues also instantiated an image of authority in which the dead object took the place of the perishable body – be it a tomb, statue, god, icon or another kind of permanent object.[105]

I bring this up not because I want to suggest that the monuments discussed in this chapter belong to this (admittedly imagined and projected) prehistorical moment. The point is, rather, that all monuments retain traces of the human body, and its mortal experiences, that lie somewhere at its base, even and perhaps especially when these are missing. In times of cataclysmic change, these first foundations – that of the first human collectivity – appear to revolt against the permanent images that try to displace them. Georges Bataille has suggested that the seeds of revolution can be located here: in a collective and visceral reaction against the monument's vertical height by those situated at the bottom of the social hierarchy. For great monuments, Bataille argues, are 'erected like dikes, opposing the logic of majesty and authority against all disturbing elements'.[106]

Of course it goes without saying that today's architectural order is characterised less by tall monuments than by institutional spaces. The following chapter pursues Bataille's notion of revolution as an ongoing resistance against the architectural order, by shifting the focus towards the institutions of performance art. For the *Cenotaph Project* was also Brisley's last public project. His subsequent performances would be undertaken in his capacity as a private individual, who creates and controls his own institutions.

Notes

1 Stuart Brisley and Maya Balcioglu, *The Cenotaph Project 1987–1991* (Derry, Londonderry: Orchard Gallery, 1991), unpaginated. See www.stuartbrisley. com/pages/28/80s/Works/The_Cenotaph_Project/page:37 (accessed 7 February 2014).

2 Figures cited in Robert Bushaway, 'Name upon Name: The Great War and Remembrance', in Roy Porter (ed.), *Myths of the English* (Cambridge: Polity Press, 1993), pp. 136–167, p. 137.

3 Allan Greenberg, 'Lutyens's Cenotaph', *Journal of the Society of Architectural Historians*, 48:1 (1989), 5–23, p. 5, doi.org/10.2307/990403.

4 Brisley, National Life Stories, C466/43/13 F5285B, p. 267.

5 Sergiusz Michalski, *Public Monuments: Art in Political Bondage 1870–1997* (London: Reaktion Books Ltd., 1998), p. 79.

6 'The Art of the Cenotaph', *The Times* (11 November 1919). The Times Digital Archive.

7 Brisley, National Life Stories, C466/43/13/ F5285A, p. 264.

8 Horst Bredekamp, *Image Acts: A Systematic Approach to Visual Agency*, trans. Elizabeth Clegg (Berlin: De Gruyter, 2017), pp. 247–252, p. 252.

9 For the *Cenotaph Project* within the British art context of the 1980s/1990s, see Gabriel Gee, 'From Stone to Flesh: The Deconstruction and Reconstruction of the British Monument', in Catherine Lanone et al. (eds), *Monument et Modernité: dans l'art et la littérature britaniques et américains* (Paris: Press Sorbonne Nouvelle, 2015), pp. 289–301. http://books.openedition.org/psn/7355 (accessed 1 June 2022).

10 Reinhart Koselleck, 'War Memorials: Identity of the Survivors', in *The Practice of Conceptual History: Timing History, Spacing Concepts*, trans. T. Presner, K. Behnke and J. Welge (Stanford, CA: Stanford University Press, 2002), pp. 285–326, pp. 322–323.

11 Koselleck, 'War Memorials', p. 322.

12 Brisley and Balcioglu, *The Cenotaph Project*.

13 Penelope Curtis, 'The Cenotaph, Whitehall', in Stuart Brisley and Maya Balcioglu, *The Cenotaph Project 1987–1991* (Derry, Londonderry: Orchard Gallery, 1991).

14 War Cabinet meeting 4 July 1919. For an account of this debate see Eric Homberger, 'The Story of the Cenotaph', *Times Literary Supplement*, 12 November 1976; Lord Curzon's words cited by Alex King in: Alex King, *Memorials of the Great War in Britain: The Symbolism and Politics of Remembrance* (Oxford: Berg, 1998), pp. 143–144. See also Thomas Laqueur, *The Work of the Dead* (Princeton, NJ: Princeton University Press, 2015), pp. 482–483.

15 This included nearly one million White troops from the dominions and the 140,000 Indian recruits who had fought alongside British soldiers on the Western Front. A further 700,000 Indian troops also served in the Middle East, emphasising the need for a secular monument. See Norman Bonney, 'The Cenotaph: A Consensual and Contested Monument of Remembrance', www.secular ism.org.uk/uploads/cenotaph-a-consensual-and-contested-monument-of-remembrance.pdf (accessed 13 August 2018).

16 Neil Hanson, *The Unknown Soldier* (London: Doubleday, 2005), p. 342.

17 'At The Cenotaph', *The Times* (21 July 1919), p. 15.

18 'Cenotaph, Whitehall: Erection of Permanent Cenotaph' (The National Archives' Catalogue, 1932 1919), work 20/139, The National Archives, Kew.

19 As reported in *The Times* (31 July 1919), p. 12.

20 'The Glorious Dead', *The Times* (18 December 1919), p. 13.

21 'The Art of the Cenotaph', *The Times* (11 November 1919), p. 11.

22 Cited by Greenberg, 'Lutyens's Cenotaph', p. 10.

23 'A temporary cenotaph on the common was adorned by wreaths, and a second cenotaph was carried on a van in one of the processions.' 'Drum-head Memorial Service', *The Times* (8 September 1919), p. 7.

24 'In response to numerous requests the Trustees of the Imperial War museum have decided to open certain of the galleries … on Armistice Day at 10:00 am. Following the custom practised when the Museum was at the Crystal Palace, visitors are permitted to deposit wreaths and flowers on the original Cenotaph …'. 'Imperial War Museum', *The Times* (6 November 1924).

25 Alex King notes that 'in spite of its formal originality, it readily fitted the convention established by war shrines. It was seen from the very first as a shrine. Lord Curzon had referred to the Cenotaph in a Cabinet Meeting as a "temporary shrine", and members of the public showed that they saw it in the same way placing flowers at it both before and after the military parade on 19 July.' King, *Memorials of the Great War in Britain*, p. 146.

26 Jay Winter, *Sites of Memory, Sites of Mourning: The Great War in European Cultural History* (Cambridge: Cambridge University Press, 1998), p. 30. See also the discussion on the cenotaph as a lieu de mémoire in Paul Gough and Sally Morgan, 'A Faux Cenotaph: Guerilla Interventions and the Contestation of Rhetorical Public Space', *Journal of War & Culture Studies*, 6:2 (2013), 99–100.

27 'The King's invitation to his Peoples … was accompanied by a short note from the Home Secretary, containing a few suggestions for ensuring as much uniformity of practice as possible.' 'The Glorious Dead', *The Times* (11 November 1919). A two-minute silence was introduced across the Empire, along with the obligatory parade past the temporary Cenotaph.

28 Bushaway suggests this uncertain mood persisted until 1925. 'Name upon Name', p. 153.
29 'At The Cenotaph', *The Times* (21 July 1919).
30 See Virginia Woolf, *The Diary of Virginia Woolf: Volume I: 1915–1919* (London: The Hogarth Press, 1977), on Diary Entry 19 July 1919, p. 292. This citation was part of the wall text for the Cambridge, Kettle's Yard installation of the Cenotaph Project, May–July 1987.
31 To compensate for the optical illusion of concavity in columns with truly straight lines. For an alternate hypothesis that entasis was added for engineering reasons, the slightly bulging columns providing greater stability, see Peter Thompson, Georgia Papadoulou and Eleni Vassiliou, 'The Origins of Entasis: Illusion, Aesthetics or Engineering?', *Spatial Vision*, 20:6 (2007), 531–543.
32 Entasis expressed Lutyens's theosophical convictions. If the Cenotaph were extended further above the ground, the vertical surface of the columns would meet at 1,000 feet. Similarly, if the monument were extended underground, its horizontal surfaces would appear as arcs of a circle whose centre was 900 feet below the surface. This aspect has been much discussed; see Greenberg, 'Lutyens's Cenotaph', p. 10. See also Andrew Crompton, 'The Secret of the Cenotaph', *AA Files*, 34 (1997), 64–67, p. 66.
33 Greenberg, 'Lutyens's Cenotaph', p. 14.
34 Maya Balcioglu notes that this plinth-less structure is reminiscent of Eastern shrines, which Lutyens may have encountered while designing India's imperial city in New Delhi. Conversation with author, 15 June 2017, London.
35 Alois Riegl, 'The Modern Cult of Monuments: Its Character and Its Origin', trans. W. Kurt Forster and Diane Ghirardo, *Oppositions*, 25, (1982), 20–51, p. 30.
36 'Narrow Divorce Division', *The Times* (5 May 1920), p. 16. The War Stone, too, avoids the 'tyranny of the enforced cross'. Tim Skelton and Gerard Gliddon, *Lutyens and the Great War* (London: Francis Lincoln, 2008), p. 34.
37 Catherine Moriarty, 'The Material Culture of Great War Remembrance', *Journal of Contemporary History*, 34:4 (1999), 653–62, p. 661.
38 'For four days Whitehall had been a sacred backwater. Yesterday it was again thrown open to traffic. On either side vehicles of every kind went up and down, but in the middle there was still a narrow strip of road sacred to the mourners. They formed into queues quite regardless of the turmoil around them, and slowly went past the monument. It is difficult to determine which scene was the more impressive. Last week Whitehall was officially set apart for London's tribute to the dead. Yesterday the official mourning had finished, but the tribute of the people steadily went on.' 'Our 1,000,000 Pilgrims', *The Times* (16 November 1920).
39 Victor Turner, *The Anthropology of Performance* (New York: Performance Art Journal Publications, 1987), p. 140.
40 'Christmas Wreaths at the Cenotaph', *The Times* (23 December 1919), p. 7.
41 'News in Brief', *The Times* (26 November 1920). p. 14.
42 'Armistice Day, 1920', *The Times* (12 November 1920). p. 5.
43 'House of Commons', *The Times* (27 July 1922).

44 Bushaway, 'Name upon Name', p. 137.

45 Keith Jeffrey, *The British Army and the Crisis of Empire* (Manchester: Manchester University Press, 1984), p. 24.

46 See Jeffrey, *The British Army and the Crisis of Empire*, pp. 15 and 24; Walter Kendall, *The Revolutionary Movement in Britain 1900–21: The Origins of British Communism* (London: Weidenfeld & Nicolson, 1969), pp. 189–190.

47 Kendall, *The Revolutionary Movement in Britain*, p. 190.

48 Cited by Jeffrey, *The British Army and the Crisis of Empire*, p. 28.

49 Cited by Keith Jeffrey, 'The British Army and Internal Security 1919–1939', *The Historical Journal*, 24:2 (1981): 377–397, p. 377.

50 This includes the reintroduction of Church rituals around an originally secular monument. See Bonney, 'The Cenotaph', pp. 21–22.

51 See Jeffrey, *The British Army and the Crisis of Empire*, p. 28.

52 'Politicians' Part in the War', *The Times* (10 February 1925).

53 The *Oxford English Dictionary* (OED), for example, cites the 'sense of grand stasis, of timeless repose' to describe the frescoes of Piero Della Francesca. 3rd edn, online (accessed 2 November 2022).

54 M. C. Howatson (ed.), *Oxford Companion to Classical Literature*, 3rd edn, online (accessed 2 November 2022).

55 Loraux, *The Divided City*, pp. 64–65, 104.

56 Ibid., p. 106.

57 Loraux links sedition to the Latin verb *sedere* (to sit), but acknowledges the disputed etymology of *seditio* on p. 286.

58 For a good discussion of this distinction, for the period leading up to the Great War see Mufti, *Civilizing War*, p. 28.

59 'Over the long array of heads, as far as the eye could reach, only one man's head remained covered; and the prevailing gravity can be measured by the fact that no protest or remonstrance was addressed to this singular being.' 'Armistice Day', *The Times* (12 November 1920).

60 Giorgio Agamben, *Homo Sacer: Sovereign Power and Bare Life*, trans. Daniel Heller-Roazen (Stanford, CA: Stanford University Press, 1998), p. 122.

61 See Michael Heffernan 'For ever England: The Western Front and the Politics of Remembrance in Britain', *Ecumene*, 2:3 (1995), 293–323, p. 299.

62 See William Rothenstein, 'The War and the Arts', *Manchester Guardian* (26 January 1916) and the impassioned article 'Architects, Sculptors and Monuments', *Manchester Guardian* (19 August 1916).

63 Rothenstein, 'The War and the Arts'.

64 Curtis, 'The Cenotaph, Whitehall'.

65 Paul Veyne and Louis Marin, *Propagande expression roi, image idole oracle: lisibilité et visibilité des images du pouvoir* (Paris: Arkhê Editions, 2011), p. 38. First published in: Paul Veyne, 'Propagande expression roi, image idole oracle', *L'Homme*, 114 (1990), 7–26; see also Dario Gamboni, *The Destruction of Art: Iconoclasm and Vandalism since the French Revolution* (London: Reaktion Books, 1997), p. 21.

66 Brisley, National Life Stories, C466/43.13 F5285 A, p. 265.

67 Norbert Lynton, *Tatlin's Tower: Monument to Revolution* (New Haven, CT: Yale University Press, 2009), p. 72.

68 Nikolai Punin, 'Tatlin's Tower', trans. John Bowlt, in Stephen Bann (ed.), *The Tradition of Constructivism* (New York, NY: Viking Press, 1974), pp. 14–17; also, Nikolai Punin, 'Pamyatnik III Internatsionala, 1920', trans. Kestutis Paul Zygas, *Oppositions*, 10 (1977), 72–74.

69 For this description see Lynton, *Tatlin's Tower*, pp. 94–102.

70 Alexander Mikaberidze, *Russian Eyewitness Accounts of the Campaign of 1814* (London: Frontline Books, 2013), p. 272.

71 Catulle Mendes, *Les 73 Journées de la Commune: du 18 mars au 29 mai 1871* (Paris: Lachaud, 1897) as cited by Kristin Ross, *The Emergence of Social Space: Rimbaud and the Paris Commune* (Minneapolis, MN: University of Minnesota Press, 1988), p. 8. Also cited by the artists in the *The Cenotaph Project*.

72 Communard Louis Barron, cited by Ross, *The Emergence of Social Space*, p. 7.

73 Antonio Gramsci, *Selections from the Prison Notebooks of Antonio Gramsci*, trans. and ed. Geoffrey Nowell and Quintin Hoare (London: Lawrence and Wishart, 1971), p. 276.

74 Ibid., p. 264

75 Zygmunt Bauman, *44 Letters from the Liquid Modern World* (Cambridge: Polity, 2010), p. 120.

76 Stuart Brisley et al., *Drawing Room Confessions*, p. 45.

77 See Georges Bataille, 'Architecture', *Documents*, 2 (1929), p. 117; extensively discussed in Denis Hollier, *Against Architecture: The Writings of Georges Bataille*, trans. Betsy Wing (Cambridge MA: The MIT Press, [1989] 1992), pp. 46–56. As Hollier notes, 'This smothering of social life under a stone monument is a constant theme of Bataille's earliest articles', p. 47.

78 Jean-Marie Pérouse de Montclos, *Étienne-Louis Boullée (1728–1799): Theoretician of Revolutionary Architecture* (London: Thames and Hudson, 1974), p. 27.

79 'Le mot de monument, l'idée qu'il exprime, et le luxe ou la magnificence qui s'attache à cette idée, conviennent surtout à ces grands établissemens d'utilité publique qui entrent en première ligne dans les besoins des peoples, et auxquels une sorte d'instinct de convenance a toujours voulu que l'art imprimât un caractère extérieur qui marquât leur importance et avertit le spectateur de leur destination.' See Antoine-Chrysostome Quatremère de Quincy, *Dictionnaire historique d'architecture comprenant dans son plan les notions historiques, descriptives, archéologiques, biographiques, théoriques, didactiques et pratiques de cet art*. Tome Second (Paris: Librairie D'Adrien le Clere Et Cie, 1832), p. 124.

80 Laqueur, *The Work of the Dead*, pp. 279–280.

81 On the ambition and limitations of this reform see Erin-Marie Legacey, *Making Space for the Dead: Catacombs, Cemeteries and the Reimagining of Paris, 1780–1830* (Ithaca, NY: Cornell University Press, 2019), pp. 36–43.

82 Chaumette was also involved in establishing a new atheistic religion. Churches across France were turned into Temples of Reason, symbols of Christianity were covered up and replaced by new rituals deemed appropriate for a Cult of Reason.

83 Dominique Poulot, *Une Histoire du patrimoine en Occident (XVIIe–XXIe siècle): Du monument aux valeurs* (Paris: Presses universitaires de France, 2006), p. 23.

84 Pierre-Louis Roederer, *Des Institutions funéraires convenables à une République qui permet tous les cultes, & n'en adopte aucun: mémoire lu par Roederer, dans la séance publique de l'Institut national des sciences & des arts, le 15 messidor, l'an 4* (Paris: Desenne, Lib., Palais Egalite, 1796) p. 11; also in Thomas Doderet, *Catéchisme de toutes les religions en abrégé: dédié au Cercle constitutionnel de la commune de Langres* (Chaumont: chez le citoyen Cousot, 1798), p. 24; also in Pierre Dolivier, *Essai sur les funérailles* (Versailles: chez Jacob, Libraire-Imprimeur de École Centrale de Seine et Oise, 1801), p. 66. See also Legacey, *Making Space for the Dead*, pp. 56–60.

85 Emil Kaufmann, *Three Revolutionary Architects: Boullée, Ledoux, and Lequeu* (Philadelphia, PA: American Philosophical Society, 1952). p. 545.

86 Helen Rosenau, *Boullée and Visionary Architecture, Including Boullée's 'Architecture, Essay on Art'* (London: Academy Editions/Harmony Books, 1976). p. 105.

87 Ibid., p. 107.

88 Ibid., p. 86.

89 Ibid., p. 90.

90 Ibid., p. 106.

91 Richard Etlin, *Symbolic Space: French Enlightenment Architecture and Its Legacy* (Chicago, IL: University of Chicago Press, 1995), p. 172.

92 Rosenau observes that Boullée envied writers and painters for their freedom from patronage: *Boullée and Visionary Architecture*, pp. 7–8.

93 As Jean Marie Pérouse de Monclos notes, 'the parallel between this art revolution and the political revolution was recognized as early as 1788 by the theorists of the academic reaction', *Étienne-Louis Boullée (1728–1799): Theoretician of Revolutionary Architecture* (Thames & Hudson, 1974), p. 113.

94 'élevés par-tout pour éterniser le souvenir de sa servitude'. Armand-Guy Kersaint, *Discours sur les monuments publics: prononcé au Conseil du Département de Paris, le 15 décembre 1791* (Paris: De l'Imprimerie de P. Didot L'Aine, 1792), p. 5.

95 'ici fut la Bastille'. Ibid., p. 5.

96 'abandonnée.' Ibid., p. 28.

97 'sera fragile et passager comme moi'. Ibid., p. 28.

98 'There was no generic architectural form to this civic structure.' See Stephen G. Miller, *The Prytaneion: Its Function and Architectural Form* (Berkeley, CA: University of California Press, 1978), p. 27.

99 'se réunissoit cependent le plus grand nombre de citoyens, auxquel il importe de rappeler le respect dû aux lois', in Kersaint, *Discours sur les Monuments Publics*, p. 21.

100 'toute publication ou affiches étrangères aux loi qui, par une mélange impolitique, nuiroient au respect qui leur est dû', in Kersaint, *Discours sur les Monuments Publics*, pp. 61–62.

101 See Hollier, *Against Architecture*, pp. xxi–xxiii.

102 Preface from Jules Michelet, *History of the French Revolution*, trans. Charles Cocks, ed. Gordon Wright (Chicago, IL: University of Chicago Press: 1967), p. 2.
103 As Robert Harrison observes, the tomb 'is the place where our sense of mortality (the fact that we fundamentally exist in time) and our sense of place (that the world we enter is a built world) coincide'. Robert Pogue Harrison, *The Dominion of the Dead* (Chicago, IL: University of Chicago Press, 2004), pp. 18–19.
104 Michel Serres, *Statues: The Second Book of Foundations*, trans. Randolph Burks (London: Bloomsbury Publishing Plc, 2014), pp. 23, 31.
105 As Serres observes, when it comes to authority, 'a man can inhabit that place but an object can as well'. *The Second Book of Foundations*, p. 103.
106 Bataille, 'Architecture', p. 117. Cited in Hollier, *Against Architecture*, p. 47.

5 Time after history: collections, archives, museums

> The more classification there is, the less evolution there is, the more classes there are, the less history there is, the more coded sciences there are, the less invention and knowledge there are, the more administrating there is, the less movement there is.[1]

As we have seen in previous chapters, a performative relation to the past requires maintaining a kind of lived or tensed time. To maintain this sense of 'liveness', a performance must resist becoming a fixed data point in the past, whether as part of a collection or as an event locked onto a chronological timeline. As all depositories require administration, any attempt to 'collect' performance art signals a move away from a communicative memory embodied by people, towards a cultural memory managed by intermediaries and, in the last instance, institutions. Yet performance increasingly takes place in art galleries and museums: places of collecting *par excellence*.

This has implications both for the holdings of the institutions in question and for the nature and reception of performance art. In terms of the former, the recent push by many museums to expand their collections of live art has collapsed the long-established distinction between a museum's 'collections' and its 'archives'. On the traditional understanding, a museum collects objects while its archives hold the documents and other supplementary material surrounding the work or the artist featuring in the museum's collections. But in the case of live art there are no objects to collect, only traces of past performances. Archives instead have become the chief place where the material objects associated with live art are assembled and collected, a process which has also considerably extended the meaning of an 'archive'.[2] This raises a host of difficult, and much discussed, questions about where to locate such art: is it found in the idea behind the work or its material substrate, including the archive, or the entire body of work associated with the artist?[3] What happens when, as in the case of the *Peterlee Project*, an archive contains works contributed by others?

This increasingly 'archival' treatment of performance art not only alters the nature of what is collected; it also brings performance into the orbit of a kind of power that is analogous to that of the state. Like sovereign states, museums maintain their own archives. Like sovereign states too, they operate according to their own historical laws, writing their history on the basis of what they manage to accumulate and preserve. Finally, like many sovereign states, at least in the liberal West, museums present themselves as democratic institutions that are publicly accountable. This gives rise to inevitable contradictions. On the one hand, museums are public institutions that play an increasingly prominent role in mediating a public understanding of history. In this future-oriented capacity, they rearrange their collections and displays to appeal to present users and future beneficiaries. On the other hand, it is well known that some of the world's greatest collections originated in colonisation, forced sales, war booty and so forth. Yet, as Peter Friedl observes, despite this ambiguous provenance of its collections, the museum's centrality as a public good is rarely, if ever, questioned. On the contrary, the museum's power to frame and reframe context runs largely unchecked. Friedl notes that the museum's privileged status as a public good, combined with the increasing tendency of museums to reflect the interests of a new global elite, makes it exceedingly difficult to 'find out exactly who history belongs to'.[4]

Given this complex evolution of the contemporary museum, what remains then of the revolutionary potential of performance art? What happens to performance when museums exert their sovereign power to frame and reframe historical context? Can works assert a right to exist beyond that ordained by the museum collection and, if so, how? In what follows, I will explore these questions through the *Georgiana Collection* (1981–86) and the *Museum of Ordure* (from 2004), two of Brisley's long-durational works that deal explicitly with the nature of collecting, accumulating and preserving. Both collections present themselves as institutions. Both consist solely of detritus or waste, human or otherwise. Both are long lasting, involving time spans lasting several years. The *Museum of Ordure*, in particular, has a very long time span, encompassing all of Brisley's mature and late works and, at the time of writing, still ongoing. Both collections, moreover, operate by expanding or stretching the moment when the decision is first made over which part of the past is to be preserved or discarded. In this sense, both collections explore the problem of how to make a cut in time, which, as we have already seen, is also the problem and challenge of all revolutions. What happens then in the aftermath of revolution, when the past has been declared dead yet continues to survive, either as detritus to be discarded or as remains to be collected and preserved?

Waste; the time of the aftermath

So far in this book, we have been discussing how performances can be reconstructed through their remains – whether these be considered 'traces' or 'survivals', like those discussed in Chapter 2, the shared memories of the practical past considered in Chapter 3 or the empty spaces that are created within and around monuments analysed in Chapter 4. But rubbish and ordure are rather special kinds of remains. Left behind after an object's useful life is over, waste occupies what we might call a time after history, a time of the aftermath, which is characterised by formlessness and universal dissolution. Dirt, in particular, is the material with the longest duration. It is what remains behind when all symbols, identities, uses and meanings have dissolved. As the anthropologist Mary Douglas explains: 'the attitude to rejected bits and pieces goes through two stages. First, they are recognisably out of place, a threat to good order, and so are regarded as objectionable and vigorously brushed away. [...] This is the stage at which they are dangerous: their half-identity still clings to them. But a long process of pulverizing, dissolving and rotting awaits any physical things that have been recognised as dirt. In the end, all identity is gone.'[5] Demarcating the dividing line between order and disorder, dirt stands at the limit of what can be represented or symbolised. Yet, although dirt may lack value in itself, it is subject to actions, even if only the basic action of being immediately swept away, placed out of sight.

This chapter argues that performance art, like rubbish and waste, occupies a similar time after history. Once actions cease to be part of an embodied or communicable memory, they become remnants or traces. In their aggregate, these traces might yield a description of the past, but on their own they offer little insight into what took place. In this sense, they are more akin to hapaxes, neither generalisable nor repeatable.[6] But, no matter how silent, inert or unchangeable, these traces are nonetheless subject to further action, even if only the natural processes of decay and destruction. They may even circulate in an economy of other waste products. In this latter sense, they are also collectible.

A *collection* of past performances thus can be said to occupy a kind of negative space, akin to what the anthropologist Michael Thompson has called a zone of transience.[7] In his book *Rubbish Theory* (1979), Thompson argues that rubbish provides the key to understanding how old value-systems die and new ones emerge, precisely on account of its inertness and resistance to change. He gives the example of bodily by-products. Excrement, urine or nail-clippings are normally discarded as having no value. But even these waste products gain value when they change categories. Throughout history, excrement has been used as fertiliser; urine as disinfectant. The same holds for objects of cultural value. Nowhere is this more apparent than when yesterday's rubbish becomes today's collector's item. As Thompson explains, these transformations are made possible because rubbish functions as a covert category. Waste escapes existing systems of values because it passes unnoticed. As such, it exists in a suspended state of almost endless duration.

What, then, does it take for waste to leave this state of suspension and re-enter time-bound categories of value? The short answer is time extension. Thompson considers it axiomatic that all change of value involves a change in social hierarchy. In a society in which culture is associated with permanence, durable objects are situated at the apex of a hierarchy of value. Durability, in other words, expresses a power relation in which 'those people near the top have the power to make things durable and to make things transient so they can ensure that their own objects are always durable and those of others transient'.[8] Moreover, it is precisely because rubbish occupies 'a timeless and valueless limbo'[9] that it serves as a permanent resource for the creation of new values and new hierarchies. For while things may 'drift into obscurity, they leap into prominence'.[10] The passage from rubbish to valued item, then, is not gradual but takes place as a cut in time, when an unnoticed or invisible object suddenly gains visibility through an act of reframing.

This capacity of rubbish to be an agent of change – potentially even revolutionary change – is something explored by both the *Georgiana Collection* and the *Museum of Ordure*. Both focus on the effects of time extension and both seek to recover the actions by which value is created and hierarchies are overturned. In contrast, however, to those items of rubbish that can be recycled or that retain some semblance of their previous form, Brisley's collections consist of objects that have come to the end of even this kind of afterlife. What would it mean to perform the act of time extension on objects otherwise destined for oblivion, be it through human neglect or natural processes of decay? Can even this more or less indistinguishable matter be reframed as an item of value and therefore gain what Thompson calls 'real, actual life-spans' as collectible objects?

In approaching the limit-case of the possible collection, both the *Georgiana Collection* and the *Museum of Ordure* illuminate the close contact between the forces of destruction and those of preservation that attend all collections. This is because rubbish and high-value collectible objects also share another aspect in common: both consist of objects taken out of economic production and circulation. In the case of rubbish, this state of suspension is expressed as a lack of history, a kind of falling out of the historical record. An equal if opposite state of suspension characterises the collectible item, whose permanent or 'eternal' value is also seen to exist outside of the normal course of historical or natural time. In this jointly shared state of suspension, an item classified as rubbish can become collectible and, vice versa, a formerly collectible item can be discarded as today's rubbish. Reflecting on the close ontological identity between rubbish and archivable objects, Aleida Assman notes that they are 'linked not merely by figurative analogy but also by a common boundary, which can be transgressed in both directions'.[11] As Assman explains:

> Outside the archive, *waste* accumulates. This is made up of all the remnants of civilization that have not been collected and yet form a collection that can be defined as the converse image of the archive. Waste as a 'negative store', does not stand only for disposal, destruction and oblivion; it also stands for latent memory which takes its place between functional and storage memory and lives on from one generation to the next in a no-man's land between presence and absence. The border between archive and refuse is a very flexible one.[12]

But whereas archives preserve the collections of already existing institutions, the *Georgiana Collection* and the *Museum of Ordure* focus not on things in themselves but on the boundary between things, where pre-existing distinctions and procedures no longer hold. This makes them rather different from the many archival arts projects that have emerged since the 1980s and 1990s. According to Hal Foster, who popularised the term, the archival arts movement refers to the growing number of artists who have either used archives in their own works or have presented their works as archives or collections of some kind.[13] Influenced by the postmodern distrust of historical narrative, these works seek to interrogate the records of history, the source material of historical understanding.[14] In these works, artists frequently adopt what Okwui Onwezor has characterised as the posture of the *archon*, which is also the Greek term for ruler, the one holding the power to enable or discredit contexts.[15] The subject of the *Georgiana Collection* and the *Museum of Ordure*, however, is not historical time but what happens when historical time breaks apart, when all values, measures, categories or reasons for existing have either disappeared or are momentarily suspended.

In contrast thus to Brisley's other performances, which attempted to create a cut in time frontally – as a direct action – these two collections approach the same problem from the 'back end' so to speak: by exploring the aftermath that follows any prolonged period of destruction. According to Boris Groys, such a 'post-revolutionary perspective' is typical of much modern and contemporary art:

> art sees contemporaneity not merely from the revolutionary, but rather, the postrevolutionary perspective. One can say: modern and contemporary art sees modernity and contemporaneity as the French revolutionaries saw the design of the Old Regime – as already obsolete, reducible to pure form, already a corpse.[16]

Thus, even in cases when a modern or contemporary artist is not a 'revolutionary' in the political sense, their works embody what Groys calls the revolutionary tendency to 'look at the historical period in which we live from the perspective of its end'.[17] I want to suggest that a similar attitude characterises Brisley's two collections. Although not dealing with revolutionary events per se, both collections operationalise all the variables associated with a time after history. Given Brisley's own pessimism about the possibility of ever achieving a revolutionary rupture in the current social and political climate, this time after history can at best be recovered indirectly, through a kind of *metanoia* or reversal of perspective that too sees the present from the perspective of its end.

But there is yet another way in which these two institutions can be said to re-enact a revolutionary situation, namely by exploring what links collections of things to collectivities of people. As Michael Newman observes, this link is evident in the etymology of the term 'collection', whose Latin roots signify both collections of objects and the gathering together of people.[18] According to the *OED*, in medieval and late Latin, collecting referred to the act of meeting, assembling, gathering together, all extensions of the earlier meaning of collecting 'as representing'. This idea of individuals coming together as one is also captured in later expressions such as a 'collective life' or a 'collective mind' or even 'collectivization', all connotations which imply a certain degree of self-organisation. Brisley's self-instituting collections express a similar search for a collective or assembly that exists outside of prevailing structures, by opposing those museological practices that seek to expand the prestige of already existing institutions. The question thus arises whether a collection can be self-organising or whether its value always comes from outside, in the form of an externally imposed order.

The *Georgiana Collection*

This question lies at the heart of the *Georgiana Collection*, the idea for which first emerged in the early 1980s after the self-professed failures of the *Peterlee Project*. As we recall from Chapter 3, the *Peterlee Project* was conceived as an experiment in public assembly. By collecting memorabilia, the town's inhabitants were invited to jointly construct a collective resource that could also serve as the basis for future political engagement, outside of prevailing institutional structures. But Brisley's inability to sustain collecting as a public process meant that this bid to harness 'people power' had failed and, with it, Brisley's own attempts to become a public artist. Of course, by the early 1980s, the role of the public artist had become untenable for other reasons as well. The retraction of the welfare state meant there was less support for public art centres. Meanwhile the expansion of the global market in contemporary art had made clear that the language of performance was, in fact, congruent with that of dominant culture and could no longer activate the dissident cultures its early practitioners had imagined. This meant that a new relation to 'making public' was needed, one that would replace revolutionary avant-gardism, which, for Brisley, was by this time thoroughly reactionary.

The increasing realisation that direct action was just as manipulable as other kinds of art led Brisley to adopt an overtly passive stance, one that expended little energy or effort. Brisley continued to address public subjects, but from the perspective of a private individual; in his own words, from a 'rearguard rather than avant-garde' position.[19] This did not mean his work became less political, however. If anything, the work of the 1980s and 1990s is more overtly political than his earlier physical interventions, grappling as it does with the long aftermath of the so-called revolutionary decade of the 1960s.

This conscious embrace of a private position led Brisley to the idea of creating his own institution, according to a model whose parameters and public manifestations he could control. The *Georgiana Collection* (1979–86) consisted in the first instance of objects, images and sound recordings acquired over several years from an unused lot that abutted Brisley's home on Georgiana Street, in Camden, London, where the clients of a nearby hostel for the homeless also congregated. As a site-specific, long-durational performance, it aimed to give visibility to three interrelated spaces: an inner-city road, an abandoned site and the informal and transient social groupings that formed around it. Through passive collecting of wasted objects, chiefly via photos and sound recordings, Brisley hoped to make visible the excluded, largely homeless, community that lived among this rubbish and sometimes still made use of it (figures 5.1 and 5.2). For this was a community which too lived outside the 'organised system' and for whom the difference between being inside or outside mattered very little. We are of course familiar with the surrealists who used found objects directly and displayed them with no, or minimal, alteration in or as a work of art. And there is a long line of twenty- and twenty-first-century artists who have worked with rubbish: for instance, Schwitters, Chamberlain, Arman, Spoerri, Beuys, Mühl, Kabakov.[20] But whereas for some of these artists the provocation was to bring rubbish *into* the art world and the art gallery, the *Georgiana Collection* points *outside* the art world and the gallery. Indeed, the *Collection* was simultaneously intended as a provocation and a proposition: what would it take for a collection that merely consisted of the 'floating matter of all cities' to be recognised as a work of art?

Central to this provocation was the idea of revelation over time. The very broad time span of seven years enabled a kind of passive discovery. Images and sounds were recorded but not set up or staged by the artist, who instead adopted the persona of a collector and curator of the collection. A collector is not an artist. A collector does not transform this flotsam into a symbol of something else. He does, however, add value to what he collects.

Once captured by, say, a static photo or sound recording, this flotsam that would otherwise decay and disappear naturally becomes more durable. By effectuating a cut in time, the collector interrupts the inevitable loss of form and identity. He produces a further cut in time by placing this image or object in his collection. Objects that have no value thereby gain value by appearing to belong to a series or set. They can be exhibited or even bought and sold and enter other people's collection as some of the photographs eventually did.

By according to waste products the kind of attention normally reserved for high-status items, the *Collection* demonstrates the axiological value of all collections, including the porous boundary between archives and refuse alluded to by Assmann in the remarks above. For to collect or archive anything is to make a decision between who or what is given permanent value as part of a series or, in the case of rubbish, no value at all.[21] Yet the challenge of the *Georgiana Collection* is not merely to collect rubbish but to maintain a contextual relation between the objects of its collection and the urban space whence they came. How does one keep alive a life context – in this case the relation between rubbish and the loose community of people who live and work within and around it – given the power of any collection to reframe its objects? The challenge, in other words, is to demonstrate how a marginal community, situated outside the economic processes of production and consumption, might also gain visibility, be 'represented' while remaining free from an external, or imposed, order.

Leaching Out at the Intersection at the Institute of Contemporary Arts (ICA) in 1981 was the first major exhibition of the *Georgiana Collection*, the idea for which was conceived while Brisley watched a cardboard suitcase disintegrate over an eighteen-month period (figure 5.3).[22] Every day for one month, Brisley took a bag of rubbish found at the waste site into the art gallery and sorted its items into what he called 'intuitive heaps' on thirty trestle tables.[23] Clothing, which constituted the major part of the rubbish, was hung on lines strung across the gallery. Once the sorting of the rubbish was complete, each table was then hoisted up and left suspended from the ceiling, spilling any left-over contents on the floor. According to Brisley, when the table was in the air it became 'a sign of order and control';[24] meanwhile the rubbish on the floor assumed the natural order in which it fell. Amassing and sorting did not just replicate the gestures of a collector. As actions they redirected attention to items that otherwise would be measurable by weight and volume alone. Crucially, Brisley's actions also involved touch, which extended even to objects soiled with human faeces, urine or blood. This broke the taboo that we should never see – and especially never touch – the membrane separating culture from its waste products. The stench increased as the days progressed, further eroding the boundaries between culture and natural effluvia. It necessitated the use of a fan, which imparted movement to the hanging clothes. By the end of the installation, the floating clothes, suspended tables and the amassed heap attained what Brisley described as something like a 'coherent image'.[25]

Visitors to the gallery were thus asked to affirm an aesthetic unity that was produced not through art labour but by basic human actions: collecting, sorting, amassing, touching. Taken together, these actions sought to recreate a group 'portrait' not of people per se, but of a 'mode of living as found in those rubbish bags in that particular place'.[26] This intensive effort to point outwards, beyond the institutional frame of the art gallery, was further reinforced by the two maps that greeted the visitors. One map indicated Georgiana Street, the provenance of the collection; the other the position of the ICA, situated between Whitehall and Buckingham palace, the respective seats of the British government and monarchy. Brisley drew a circle around both, figuratively bringing the waste site into the geographical frame of national institutions, including the institution of art. Could waste be seen for what it was as well as something more durable? Could Georgiana Street also be reframed as a subject or a referent of an art activity? In other words, the collection required public affirmation to complete the metamorphosis of its objects. By insisting that only the public could complete the *metanoia* – and therefore also an implied redistribution of agency away from institutions – Brisley affirmed once more his position that it is not up to the artist to decide what is or is not art. Rather, art activity takes place if the public can recognise it as belonging to the language of art.

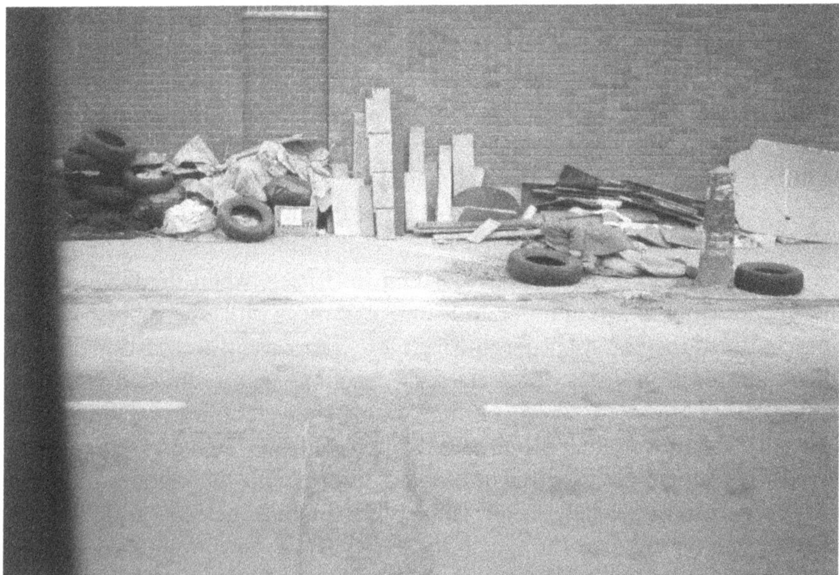

5.1   *Georgiana Collection*, 1979–86

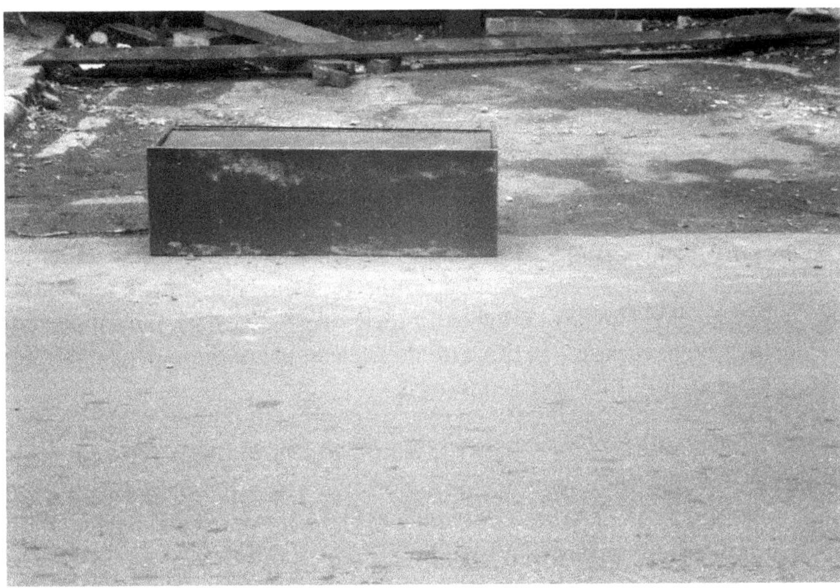

Georgiana Collection, 1979–86   **5.2**

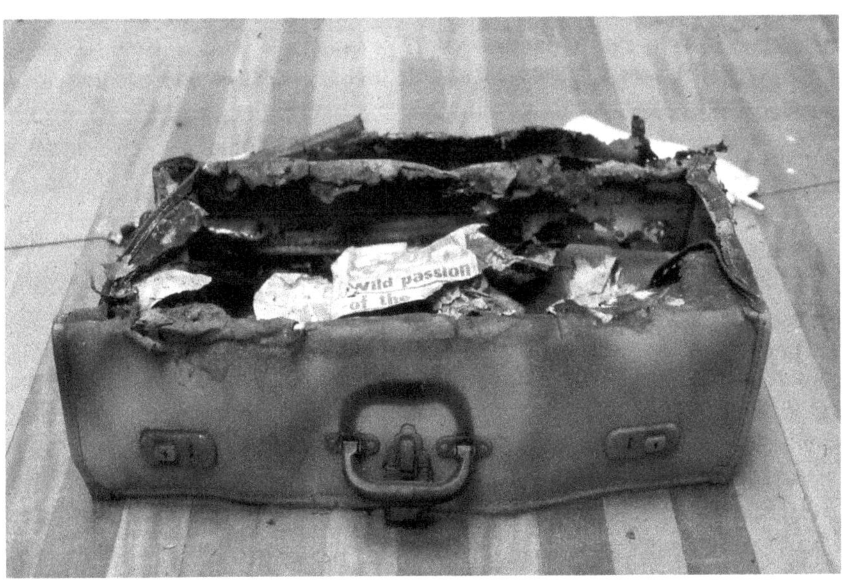

Leaching Out at the Intersection, ICA, London, 1981   **5.3**

Any institution is by definition long lasting. The *Georgiana Collection* appeared in a number of other installations and exhibitions, all of which staged a similar 'transaction' between the institution and the 'situation' or 'life context' in which its collection first emerged.[27] A particularly eloquent installation is *1=66,666*, a temporary structure first exhibited in 1983.[28] It consisted of a cage with wires hanging inside. At the end of each wire hung an old plastic glove, filled with plaster. A note indicated that each glove represented 66,666 unemployed people, the total of which Brisley had calculated was roughly four million in 1983.[29] Cut off from action and belonging to no hands, the gloves dangled like dead weights. In their suspended state, they appeared to touch a negative space – in this case the life context of the expendable, and unrepresented, four million unemployed.

Museum of Ordure; Public Shit

But it is only with the *Museum of Ordure* that Brisley developed a truly ideal institution – an almost virtual museum with communication as its core function. Museum critique, of course, is not new. Already in the nineteenth century, the imaginary museum, such as those founded by Nodier or Valéry, sought to frame an unlikely set of objects as a museum. Twentieth-century heirs of this tradition include such well-known artists as Marcel Broedthaers, Joseph Beuys and Hans Haacke.[30] But whereas museums, whether real or imaginary, are ordinarily associated with the permanent values they seek to bring to public attention, ordure lacks differentiation. In its stench, it is also noxious. Like the corpse with its putrid smells, ordure is associated with cultural taboo. A museum of ordure, thus, acts as a double invitation. Human excrement links the physically repulsive to the morally offensive; while a *museum* of ordure forces its visitors to consider what happens when excrement, what is normally repressed and out of sight, returns to the fields of cultural value, including especially the spaces of the modern museum (figure 5.4).

Human faeces in particular is digested matter that has passed through the entire human body before it is excreted. At the same time, and unlike dirt, ordure can be reused and recycled, whether as fertiliser or in other kinds of products. This point is driven home by the French historian Dominique Laporte in his short book, *History of Shit*, an acknowledged influence on the *Museum of Ordure*. As Laporte observes, in ancient Rome, women smeared human faeces on their hair and face to preserve a youthful complexion;[31] while in eighteenth-century Europe, aristocratic ladies used 'stercorary fluid' as cosmetics.[32] Urine has been used to whiten the teeth, cure dandruff, disinfect draperies.[33] It is telling that the world's earliest and still most desirable perfumes are made from musk, a secretion from a gland situated near the testes or cloaca in animals such as deer, civet and crocodile.[34] Human waste thus connects each person's physical body to the political, economic and social processes by which waste – human or animal – is managed and disposed. This makes ordure a political subject as well as a radical subject, especially if radical is understood in the sense of going to the root of the matter.

But the *Museum of Ordure* also essentially concerns the passage of time – what remains behind once any action is complete. In fact, ordure has featured in a number of Brisley's performances. In *180 Hours Work for Two People* (1978), Brisley occupied two floors of the Acme Gallery and adopted two personas (figure 5.5). Person A was a mostly silent, civic individual while Person B was a vocal bureaucrat who lived above Person A. Every day B carefully preserved his faeces and urine, which he hung through a hole in the ceiling. On the fourth day of the action, A left, but B kept on talking, 'as if needing A in a way that A didn't need B'.[35] In this action, the bag of faeces was imagined to designate the 'bureaucracy, power, shit, hanging over the heads of those underneath'.[36] Or how, as Brisley expressed it in a more recent performance, 'if they tell you to eat shit, you become shit'.[37] In *180 Hours*, the bag of faeces was both part of the performance and evidence of time passed. Once the action finished, it entered the process of natural decay until it too was discarded, both part of the performance but also what remained outside it after the performance was over. Brisley recalls that *180 Hours* was attended by a young woman from a mental institution who arrived on the final day, only to discover that the performance had ended earlier than scheduled. In her disappointment, she experienced a kind of breakdown. Clearly, the performance had communicated with her in some way. Although this person's reaction was entirely fortuitous, it too has influenced the meaning of the work, at least for the artist. Like the bag of faeces, it testifies to the emotions that may pile up over the course of any extended action, as well as the human costs of a prolonged commitment to an action that unspools in uncontrollable ways.

A rather different confrontation with ordure took place at Documenta 6, Kassel, Germany in 1977 when Brisley undertook *Survival in Alien Circumstances*. For this performance, Brisley had decided to dig a hole with a colleague, Christoph Gericke, and live in it over the length of time it took to complete the action (figure 5.6). As the title suggests, the aim was to survive in an alien environment, analogous to the working conditions of the miners whose lives had preoccupied Brisley that same year in Peterlee. The action had been scheduled to take place in front of the Fridericianum museum, located on one side of the handsome, eighteenth-century Friedrichsplatz, one of Kassel's main squares. But when Brisley arrived he was told this location had been given to the American landscape artist Walter De Maria for his *Vertical Earth Kilometer*. This highly controversial installation involved drilling a one-kilometre hole into the earth into which a one-kilometre brass rod was inserted, resulting in a sculpture that existed entirely underground, with only the end of the narrow rod visible at the surface. This discrepancy between De Maria's extraordinarily ambitious action and barely visible outcome had sparked significant protest at the time – against both the exorbitant cost, borne by corporate sponsorship, and the lengthy disruption to public life that boring the hole entailed.

Forced to move to a less prominent location, Brisley's action was a notable contrast to the high-profile De Maria installation. His action also involved digging a hole, but using only human labour and a few rudimentary tools. Brisley and Gericke also built a wooden structure on stilts in which Brisley lived for the seventeen days the dig lasted. In a further unintended contrast, the action was terminated when it reached a natural end, in this case when the artists hit the water table and were unable to dig further. But what emerged over the course of the action completely changed its meaning.[38] As they dug past the sandy soil, and then past the floor of a building that took a day and a half to break through with pickaxes, they came across rubble that contained bits of bone. A doctor who was present verified that these were human remains. Kassel had been a railway junction during the war and was extensively bombed. The rubble that had been used to create the park after the war was made up of indiscriminate bits of brick, concrete and, as was now apparent, human remains. Gericke spoke German and so was able to communicate with onlookers, some of whom said the hole reminded them of a mass grave. This sudden – and shocking – reappearance of human remains into the space of an art fair completely changed the meaning of the action. A digging downwards became a digging up. What was once inhumed, buried into the earth, became exhumed, with all the associated connotations of unearthing and bringing to light. Moreover, what was exhumed was detritus, bits of human bones unconnected to individual humans. The action brought formlessnesss itself to the surface – the human waste of war that had been left unregistered and practically forgotten until it was rediscovered through the act of digging.

Although very different from one another, *180 Hours Work for Two People* and *Survival in Alien Circumstances* both reveal how a latent or unexpected context can be made present when a given action is stretched or extended in time. The detritus that piled up over the course of either performance marked the passage of time *and* influenced the meaning of the action, whose significance changed as it unfolded, even though, after the action was complete, these left-overs, on their own, carried little or no meaning. Finally, in both performances we witness Brisley's refusal to engage in a cultural politics of 'tidying up', whether by hiding his own waste products or by imposing his own sense of an ending to the action. Instead these waste products were left exposed as remnant of time's passage that resists sublimation as an aesthetic or cultural activity.[39]

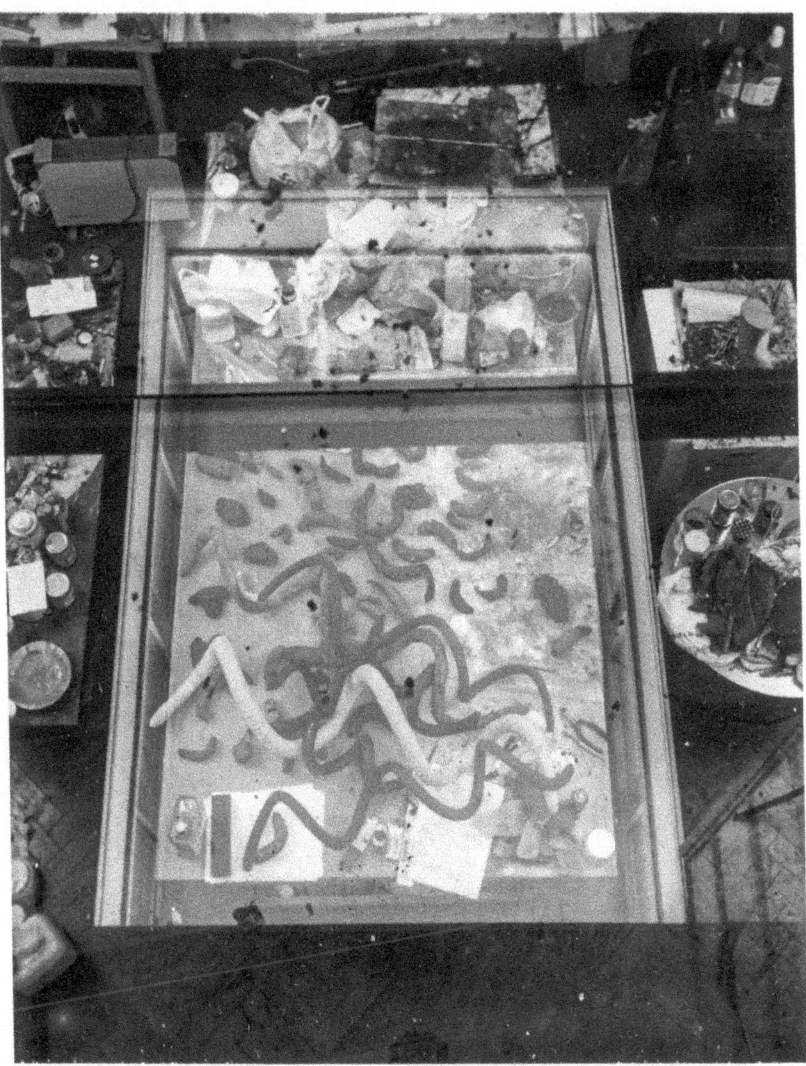

Museum of Ordure, 2000   **5.4**

This procedure of divulging the by-products of lived or mortal time lies at the heart of the *Museum of Ordure,* whose mission is to 'examine the cultural value of ordure, shit and rubbish' and the 'waste of human resources through various ownership, production and management regimes'. Like all museums, it has a website (in fact it exists primarily as a website).[40] It also has a curator and a rotating collection that is loaned on occasion for temporary

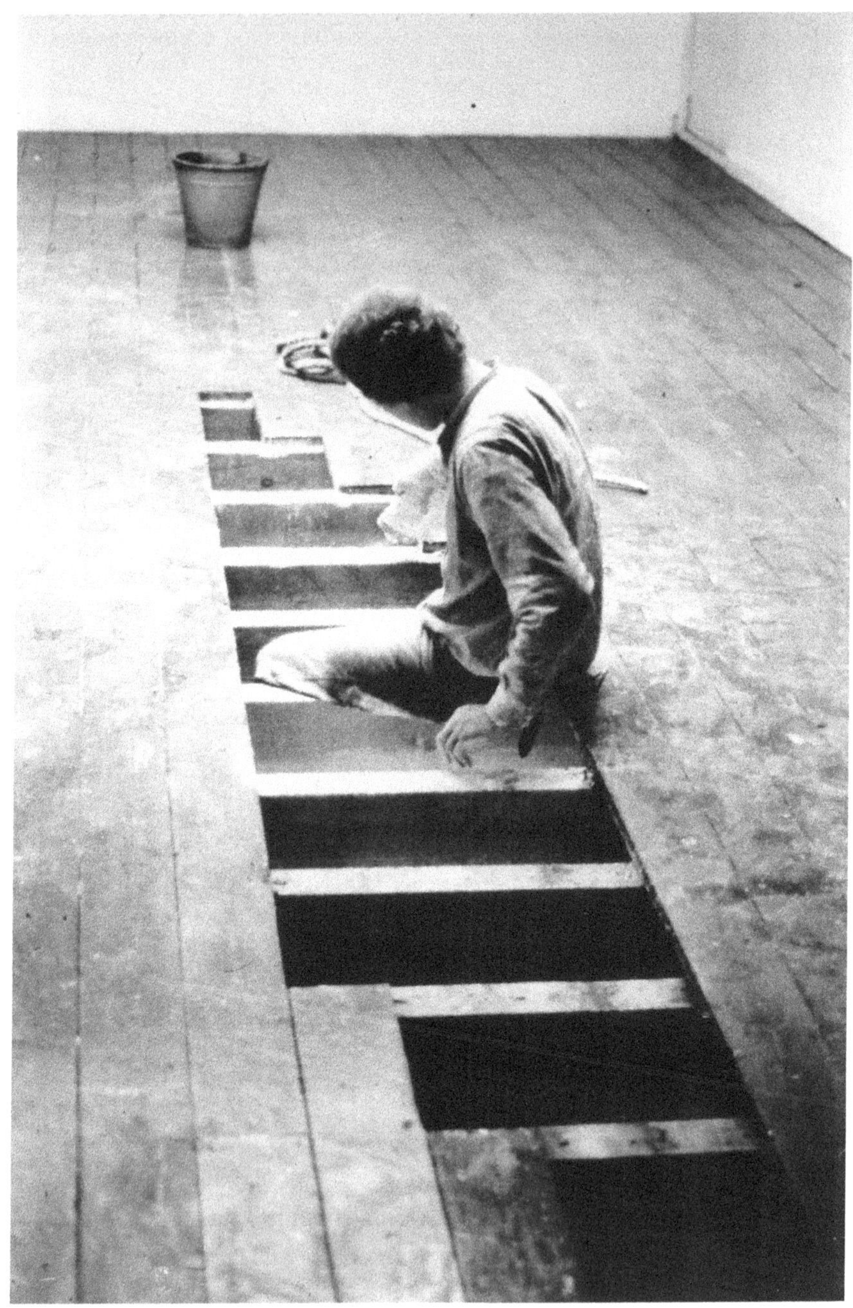

5·5   *180 Hours Work for Two People*, London, 1978

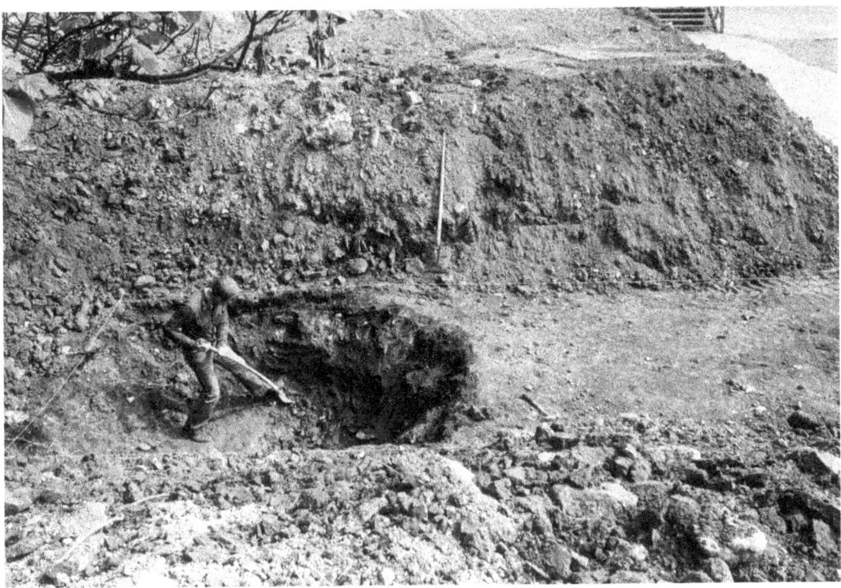

Survival in Alien Circumstances, Documenta, Kassel, 1977   **5.6**

exhibitions. Consisting exclusively of found objects, the museum acknowledges Duchamp's urinal as well as Piero Manzoni's *Merda d'artista* (1961) as important precursors. But its preservation policy is what truly sets it apart:

> Everything that is represented in the Museum of Ordure is subject to the vagaries of an uncontrolled internal process which slowly deforms and disables all information held in the museum. This is comparable to the decaying processes which affect all artifacts in museums, regardless of all attempts at preservation: the retouching, repainting, cleaning, etc, which are incorporated risks to the purity of artifacts when first acquired by museums. Even 'successful' renovations are subject to periodic changes resulting from shifts in conservation policies. Eventually (and in accordance with the fallibility of memory) artifacts are institutionally, progressively, determinedly and inadvertently altered by acts of conservation (sometimes unintentional acts of institutional vandalism) until they cease to be recognisable as the objects first acquired. Of course in both cases – in the virtual environment and in the material world – the processes of generation, decay, and entropy are paramount. Museums are by this definition charged with achieving the impossible.[41]

This, then, is the key innovation of the *Museum of Ordure*: it exists in real time. Even Manzoni's cans, in this sense, do not qualify as ordure, properly speaking. Not just because they would need to be opened for their contents to be verified, thereby destroying their status as high-art objects, but also because this threat remains hypothetical so long as Manzoni's cans circulate as permanent, unchanging images in the art world. In contrast, the *Museum of Ordure* takes place in real time. It suggests that decay, preservation, vandalism and entropy are inseparable from the creation of artistic value and meaning. It thus makes explicit what remains implicit in Manzoni's cans: what would it mean to open the can of shit and thereby cross the boundary separating art from life?

This question takes us beyond the world of art into the highly contested domain of what counts as 'public ordure'. Here again Dominique Laporte's *History of Shit* serves as a guide. Like the aforementioned *Rubbish Theory*, Laporte's brief text was first published in the late 1970s, around the same time that Brisley began to reflect on the public functions of collections.[42] In it, Laporte sketches out the ways in which human waste has always been intimately related to sovereign power. According to Laporte, the birth of modern power originated alongside a certain aesthetics of the public sphere, itself linked to the management of human waste. Laporte demonstrates this by analysing two royal edicts proclaimed in France in 1539. The first edict demanded the purification of the French language, which at the time was not standardised and still riddled with Latin terminology. The second, which appeared a few months later, enjoined the inhabitants of Paris and its surroundings to take charge of their own refuse, typically left to pile up outside their doors. Refuse, offal, putrefactions and other kinds of 'unspeakable waste' were no longer allowed on the streets. Human discharge was instead to take place indoors, in cesspools and earth closets constructed for that purpose. Laporte argues that these two edicts are of a piece, both demonstrating how purity requires submission to the law, for the sovereign decides who is clean and who remains dirty.

Although these laws were never successfully enforced, Laporte connects them to two subsequent developments, relevant also for understanding today's museum culture. First, the emergence of a new public language of purity in which, over the course of the next two centuries, the domestication of waste came to express 'an ideology linking propriety to property'.[43] Second, a new understanding of the human body as something separated from its odours. 'Smell', Laporte writes, 'resists symbolization. It obstinately clings to the index, where the materiality of its referent cannot be suppressed.'[44] The public language of hygiene, by contrast, is expressed through a visual regime in which 'the triumph of the sign, of the exchangeable is a direct accomplice of the elimination of smells'.[45] This public language of hygiene, Laporte argues, is also the language of capitalism. Playing on the connotations of the French term *privé*, which means both water-closet and the private or domestic sphere, Laporte writes that:

In opposition to the virginal public, le privé is cast as the place of commerce, of notorious dirtying business of primitive accumulation – but it is also cast as the dejected space of domesticity. The place where one 'does one's business' is also the place where waste accumulates.[46]

This public language of purity not only conditions the privatisation of waste; it also suppresses everything filthy about the primitive accumulation of money.

Laporte's analysis is relevant for understanding the *Museum of Ordure* in two ways. First, because this public language of hygiene, based on the primacy of vision, is also the language of museum culture, especially as it emerged after the eighteenth century. Second, Laporte underlines how this public language of hygiene is also a language of power. In the aforementioned sixteenth-century edicts, the sovereign expresses his power by deciding who or what is cleaned or remains dirty. In a similar manoeuvre, modern states express their power by introducing new distinctions between what is private and what remains public. In both cases, the state is understood to be pure and inviolable. And in both cases, it is by means of accumulation and collection that ordure (whether money or shit) is privatised so that the public sphere can appear purified (cleansed). A museum that claims to make public a collection of ordure thus functions as a double negation. It negates the discourse of the state 'in which it is a contradiction in terms to speak of public shit'[47] as well as further blocks the passage into symbolisation, that is to say, towards those processes of communication that turn all waste products into something rich, beautiful or attractive. It negates, in other words, those processes of communication that concede power and agency to institutions, be they public or private.

The *Museum of Ordure* makes explicit reference to this language of hygiene on its website, when it recounts how its curator (Brisley in his persona as R. Y. Sirb) once undertook a (fictional) performance at the Deutsches-Hygiene Museum in Dresden, Germany.[48] This museum stands out for being a purely communicative museum from its very inception. It was founded in 1912 as a medical museum that aimed to provide information about public health and the human body. It gained notoriety in the 1930s when it was used as a platform to propagate the Nazi policy of eugenics. With German reunification, this museum has returned to its original foundations as a purely conceptual museum. But even this almost entirely communicative museum cannot avoid the trace elements of human effluvia, if only in its bathrooms. There, Brisley/Sirb claims, he once encountered neo-Nazi graffiti. No matter how pristine, public space is always invaded somewhere with base matter – whether linguistic or material.

More generally, Laporte's analysis illuminates Brisley's long-standing efforts to make public the ordure that conditions the image and exercise of sovereign power. This is evident in a series of paintings and installations from the 1990s which besmirch or otherwise violate media-produced images of British royalty.[49] For instance, *Study for Semenal Sequences* (1995–96) takes its subject from a newspaper photo of Princess Diana in her car, taken a couple of years before her death in a car crash while fleeing the paparazzi. The painting is 'realistic' insofar as it is based on a publicly circulated image meant to radiate a certain understanding, or manipulation, of sovereign power. Brisley's portrait, however, subtly alters the composition of this found object, representing the Princess as if seen through semen-splattered windows. Natural effluvia intrudes on a mass-circulated image, creating a distance between the viewer and what is viewed. This distance is reinforced by the subject's downcast eyes, which evade the public gaze. The title performs an additional act of reframing, underscoring the private desires that circulate alongside the public representation of power, potentially even imploding it. The painting is dated not conventionally, according to when it was completed, but according to the duration over which it was undertaken, another element of Brisley's 'realism'.

A contrasting reflection on public ordure is evident in Brisley's portrait of Mairéad Farrell, the Irish Republican Army (IRA) activist shot dead by the British army in Gibraltar in 1988 (figure 5.7). Brisley's portrait is based on a xeroxed photo of Farrell in Armagh prison, taken illegally while she was on the dirty protest. It was intended in part as a counterpoint to Richard Hamilton's more overtly heroic painting *The Citizen*, which also featured a republican detainee in a British prison. These so-called dirty protests were undertaken by Farrell and other IRA prisoners over a period of five years in Northern Irish prisons, after the British decision to treat paramilitary fighters as ordinary prisoners (as opposed to designated prisoners of war, a category in keeping with their own self-understanding). Prisoners refused to shower or empty out their chamber-pots. They smeared the walls of their cells with excrement and, in the women's prison, with menstrual blood. In a system in which the British state expressed its sovereign power by reclassifying political action as a private crime, Irish paramilitaries chose to deliberately occupy a permanent state of dirt, obscenity or lawlessness.

Brisley's portrait enlarges the figure in the original photo so that Farrell and not the bed or prison cell becomes the main subject. The figure is dark, androgynous. The face is striated by even darker streaks, reproducing the effect of an image seen through prison bars. Or maybe these were just the streaks left behind by the photocopier. Whatever their source, these streaks recall the dirty protest and the political use of ordure. But they also appear, *en filigrane*, as a veil, separating the viewer from what is viewed. These almost delicate streaks restore an element of privacy to its subject, possibly even a sense of personal freedom. The portrait thus makes public a forbidden image (and a dirty war waged out of the public eye), while at the same time shielding its subject from a public gaze that projects its own desires.

Comparing just these two portraits, it is evident that both women occupy equal, if opposing, states of exception. The one is used in the media as a cipher for the royal body; the other is a criminal or fugitive, subject to the sovereign ban. Both portraits reference natural effluvia to demarcate a shifting boundary between private and public representation. And both capture a suspended time, in which normal systems of governance or behaviour no longer seem to apply. By manipulating the frame through which these states of exception are represented, both images attempt to shift the boundary separating purity from ordure.

In striving to capture the moment of contact between the private and public domains, these portraits invite a reflection on the exercise of sovereign power. According to the traditional understanding, the sovereign is the one individual able to occupy both positions of the rule and its exception; purity and ordure. This duality is captured in older representations of sovereignty, intimately tied to the king's body and its functions. As Laporte observes,

> there is a good reason to believe that an analysis of power should take seriously both the sight of sovereign holding court on his pierced chair, and the splendor of the throne as a theatre of resplendent love that splatters its subjects as they bow and kneel in pursuit of a royal turd (This ceremony, incidentally, can be understood as a lingering residue of the ancient ritual of papal coronation in which the elected pontiff was made to sit on a pierced, porphyry throne.)[50]

In this early Church ritual, the newly elected pope was made to sit first on a bedunged chair or toilet (called *sedes stercorata* from the word *stercus* meaning dung, mud, filth or excrement), to remind him that he 'rises out of clay and dung'.[51] It is only once passing through this 'toilet' that he was permitted to sit between two pierced 'porphyry chairs' and given the papal keys to govern. The implication is that an imperial throne made of indestructible marble actually receives its 'founding power' from something else – a shared human condition that is cast aside, repressed or forgotten.

Brisley's paintings and installations from the 1990s suggest that the sanitised and institutionalised language of public culture is created out of similar acts of repression. For ordure is not just something to be cast aside; it also reminds us of our common mortality, denied by all states of exception. This point was forcefully brought home in *State of Denmark*, Brisley's 2014 retrospective at Modern Art Oxford co-curated by the *Museum of Ordure*. The retrospective included such paintings as *Royal Ordure*, an entirely abstract painting, with painted matter as the substance or subject of the work (figure 5.8). Only the title suggests that the thick, black smears might reference something outside the world of art. In fact, the painting originated in Brisley's studio as he attempted to find ways to physically engage with a distant,

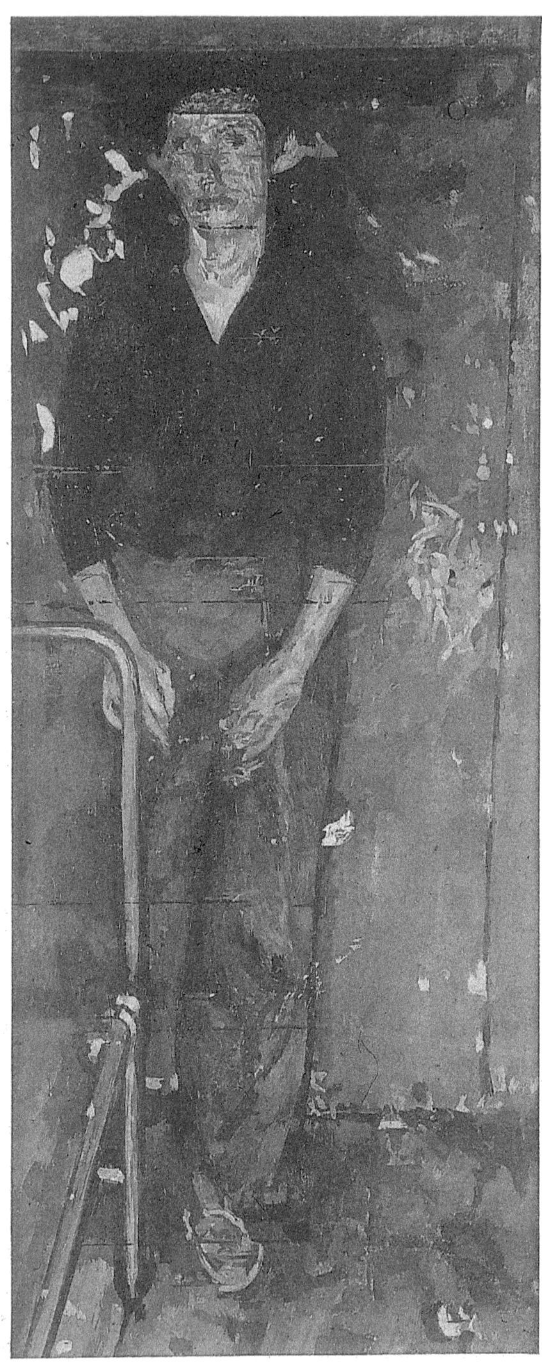

5.7 Stuart Brisley, *Dirty Protest Armagh,* 1993–96

untouchable monarchy. This led him to the idea of placing a canvas 'on its knees', as it were, with only the thin edge facing the artist as he repeatedly lobbed a messy ball of sand, acrylic medium and bits of newspaper at it.[52] As Brisley recounts, 'throwing something at the monarchy is so difficult that I made an analogy of the process. It is called Royal Ordure because it is made up of stuff that looks like shit. If the material substance managed to hit the painting, it would skid along to a certain extent.'[53] Tellingly, *Royal Ordure* was placed in the same room as *Chair*, an installation consisting of an ordinary chair smeared with the same, sticky material (see figure 5.9). In the context of

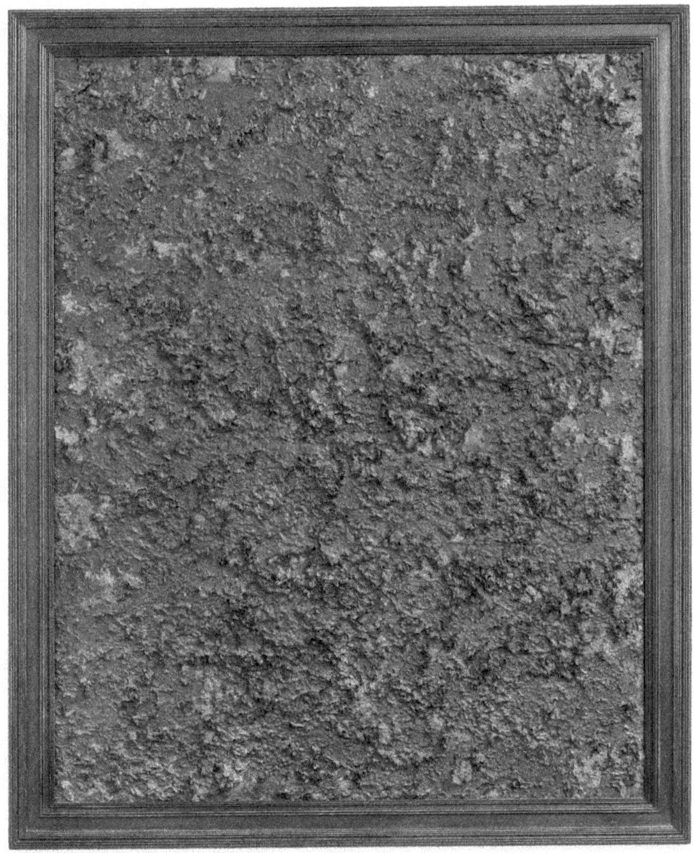

Stuart Brisley, *Royal Ordure*, 1996   **5.8**

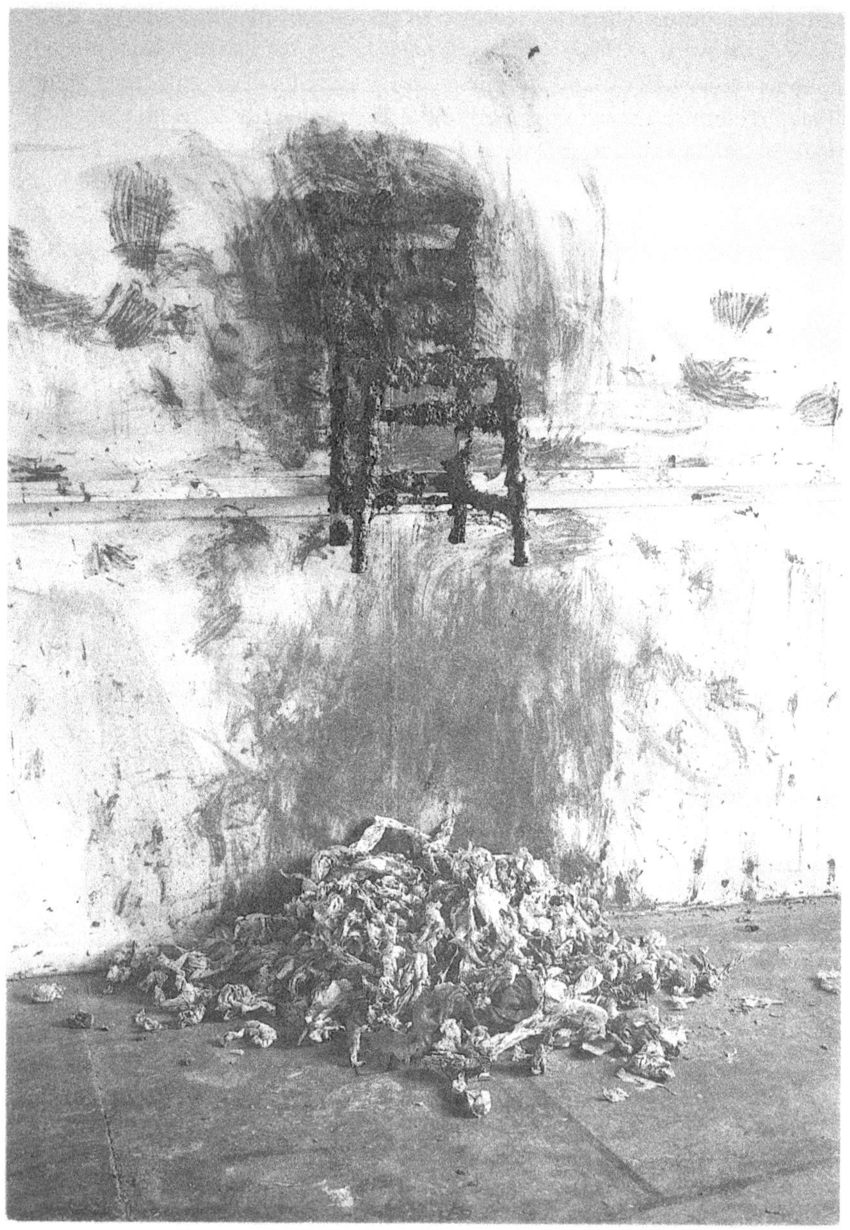

5.9 Stuart Brisley, *Chair*, 1996

this exhibition, it appeared, on the one hand, as simply an empty chair. On the other hand, the reference to Shakespeare's *Hamlet* in the exhibition's title, and the fact that the entire space was arranged under an oversized crown, hanging high up, invited viewers to consider this otherwise singular chair as a kind of ersatz throne, or even an empty seat of power.[54] The implication is that public culture too is made in the image of sovereign power. But in a modern political system in which sovereign power is expressed primarily as an absence, ordure has entirely negative connotations. It occupies a permanent state of dirt, obscenity and lawlessness – a permanent state of exception.

Seen in this light, the *Museum of Ordure* extends an abiding concern of all of Brisley's mature and late works, namely how to make present, analyse and understand any period of interregnum. For the interregnum too can be defined as a situation in which the attempt to make a cut in time has been extended over an intolerable duration, resulting in unforeseen and involuntary outcomes. By the same token, the challenge of many, if not all, of Brisley's durational works is how to keep this cut in time open for as long as possible in order to consider what happens when the exception becomes the rule. What happens when an anticipated royal succession fails to take place, like in *Hamlet*? Or when government fails to function, like in the case of a hung parliament in Britain in 2010? Or when royal succession is blocked, which happens whenever there is a regicide or a revolution?

It is important to note, however, that Brisley never answers these questions directly. In both the *Georgiana Collection* and the *Museum of Ordure*, we witness instead a constantly shifting boundary between private and public ordure, the transient and the durable, or what Michael Thompson calls the 'sliding scale that relates private and public, informality and formality, expediency and principle'.[55] In a contemporary context in which public culture remains synonymous with hygiene, one way to escape the sovereign power is by publicising what is essentially 'private shit'. For this reason, the *Museum of Ordure* also serves a more personal function as a private act of resistance against the distorting aspects of public culture. Importantly, by focusing not on collectible items per se, but on the boundaries between things, the *Museum of Ordure*, like the *Georgiana Collection*, provides an alternative framework for situating Brisley's own performances. This includes the crucial question of what is to be done with the by-products of Brisley's past performances, which too are increasingly subject to collection and preservation by various contemporary museums.

The museum as memoir; or private shit

To answer this last question, we need to consider *Museum of Ordure* not just as a collection of objects, but also how it functions as a subject with its own genesis, narrated in a satirical text by Brisley entitled *Beyond Reason: Ordure* (2004). This fictional story of the *Museum*'s foundations suggests that museums gain value not only through their collections but also through narrative frameworks, which come equipped with their own conventions and expectations of how time and history operate. Satire, in particular, is a genre strongly associated with human excreta and disgust. One need only recall Rabelais' perorations on human effluvia or the close connection between satire and the grotesque or exaggerated body.

Beyond Reason is also an occasional text, written by Brisley to mark the temporary installation of the *Museum of Ordure*'s collection at the Freud Museum in London in 2002–3. The text, as well as the installation as whole, references Freud's desire for a museum of excrement, which appeared to him in the form of a dream. It is worth dwelling a moment on Freud's extraordinary dream in which he recalled urinating on a gift from one of his patients, a chair of fine material. In his dream it appeared as an open-air toilet, 'its back edge thickly covered with small heaps of faeces of all sizes and degrees of freshness', which his urine washed away.[56] But instead of feeling revulsion, Freud claims to have experienced only overwhelming pleasure, akin to that of a Rabelaisian superman urinating on the city of Paris or a Hercules clearing the Augean stables. In his post-dream analysis, Freud traced the manifest content of the dream (faeces and urine) to his sense of personal failure at his lectures the evening before, what he describes as 'all this grubbing about in human dirt'.[57] In the dream, however, these feelings of failure and self-disgust presented themselves as pleasure and wish-fulfilment. Now a Hercules adored by his patients whose problems he washes away, Freud claimed that 'even the museum of human excrement could be given an interpretation to rejoice my heart'.[58] Ordure, Freud implies, only makes itself visible as a kind of forced entry into consciousness, an entry that also moves the boundary between pleasure and disgust.[59]

The *Museum of Ordure* asks a similar question. Is there a way to force an entry into those 'unpleasant' aspects of culture that are obliterated or that remain unseen within the altogether hygienic language of the public museum? In his satire, Brisley refracts his answer through the voices of his three main characters: the anonymous Collector, the Curator (Rosse Yael Sirb) and the Artist (John East). All three reflect roles that Brisley himself has played, whether in his capacity as a collector of rubbish; as an artist who has worked with rubbish and natural effluvia; or as the curator Rosse Yael Sirb, who, as we have already noted, has been Brisley's alter ego in various performances and installations from the late 1970s to the present.

Let's begin with the *anonymous collector*. He owns a waste-disposal business over the course of which he has developed an interest in identifying a collection of human stools that are either interesting or aesthetically pleasing.

Although aware that the objects of his collections are by no means artworks, he has employed a curator as well as an artist in the attempt to have his collection as a whole be recognised as art. If he succeeds, he will have achieved the ultimate investment. Buying nothing, selling nothing, he will have turned an object of no or even negative value into an absolute commodity, a commodity of the highest value against which nothing can be exchanged and which therefore can belong only in a museum. From the collector's point of view, the curator's task is to cut this collection off from its sordid origins in human waste (and waste-disposal business) by giving it a new context, a new past in which the human stool can be perceived as aesthetically pleasing and morally virtuous. The 'beautiful stool', after all, is the product of a healthy body. It sits well within a culture that prizes health and well-being.

The *curator Sirb* agrees to be employed because, from his perspective, this collection already has the features of an art collection. It consists of stools chosen that are 'carefully selected, preserved and presented' in accordance with the principles of aesthetic excellence. Like great works of art, 'stools in the collection represent frozen moments in the passage of time, rupturing continuity'.[60] The challenge for the curator, then, is to transform this informal grouping into an art collection by relying entirely on the immaterial bases of art labour, which happen to be those of advanced capitalist economies: namely communication, networks and personal relations.[61] The collection will become art once it is talked about as art; in other words, through a series of speech acts that publicly perform the language of art.

For this reframing to be truly accomplished, however, an artist is needed; or at least, someone who can give the collection 'life', that is to say, ongoing value as a collection that can expand, and acquire new works. The English *artist John East* is employed on the understanding that no matter how new or different his works may be, their basic function is to strengthen the museum's existing collection of ordure. John East has used excreta in previous works and this has attracted the curator's attention. However, John East also has his own philosophy. He neither shares the Duchampian position of using ordure as art, nor does he support the position of those artists who seek in ordure potential artworks or objects that can be reconfigured as artworks. Rather, it is formlessness itself that fascinates East, the 'sprawl of dirt' that needs to be put into a 'form', however provisional and inadequate. The curator and artist thus form a contingent relationship (or a relationship of convenience) based on their mutual rejection of any redemptive value for art. They also hope to subversively use the collection for their own ends. The curator's challenge is to make use of the collection to manifest the 'contradictions inherent in the puritanism that seems to underscore capitalism'. The artist aims to see whether artworks themselves can 'act like ordure in the cultural field', expanding art activity beyond the merely aesthetic.

It goes without saying that both the curator and the artist share aspects of Brisley's own personality and self-understanding. Like Brisley, both the fictional artist and curator are drawn to the malignant presence of the Berlin Wall and the cultural politics of East and West in the Cold War period. Like Brisley, the curator Sirb began collecting detritus at the base of the Berlin Wall, a dead zone in which 'the division between the two ideologies produced a no-space of lethal toxicity'. Like Brisley too, the artist John East was a conscript in the British army in West Germany after the war. He too he is fascinated by the Berlin Wall as a dead zone, that is to say, an unregulated space free from the conventions binding productive life in both East and West.

It is in such a dead zone where the artist Brisley/East may have met the curator Brisley/Sirb for the first time. According to the fictional text, Sirb was part of the Mixed Services Organisation, an organisation made up of stateless and displaced persons from Eastern Europe after the war who worked for the British government. This fictional biography thus directly references the prisoners of war, concentration camp inmates and forced labourers left behind in western sectors of Germany after the Soviet retreat, some of whom Brisley may have encountered or heard about during his own military service in post-war Germany and whose experiences informed Brisley's own explorations of the prison, the wall, the camp and labour as sites for performance art. The curator's name too, partly based on an anagram of Brisley's own name, but also evoking vaguely Hebrew and Slavic origins, underlines Brisley's affinity with displaced persons and all those citizens who have lost their rights, whether they are treated as human waste to be discarded or as an economic resource to be exploited, including by victorious nations after the war. Some, like Sirb, chose never to return to their country of origin, permanently occupying, as it were, this space of exception.

This obsession with the Wall and what lies beyond it crops up throughout the text. At one point John East travels from West Berlin to Warsaw, where he has been invited to undertake a performance, only to find himself stymied by disappearing travel documents and obstructionist tactics used by both British and Polish governments. In the fictional text, the British ambassador arrives to view East's performance and leaves early to go and vomit in the toilet, apparently revolted by what he sees. Tipped off by a mysterious Polish woman, John East learns that the British Foreign Office has been watching him, possibly even colluding with the Polish authorities to deny him travel authorisation.

This darkly comic fictional scene echoes Brisley's own travails with the British Foreign Office in Poland, conflated here with several performances which featured vomiting, including *Celebration of Due Process* and the film *Arbeit Macht Frei* discussed in Chapter 1. As we already saw in Chapter 2, Brisley had been one of the few English artists who actively sought to engage with artists across the Iron Curtain. This began in 1972, when Brisley made a trip from West Berlin to Warsaw to make contact with the Polish artist Józef Szajna, a Nazi concentration camp survivor and leading figure in the movement to combine theatre and the plastic arts, whose work Brisley had seen in Edinburgh in 1972. In 1975 Szajna invited Brisley to undertake a performance at the Galeria Studio (then known as the Teatr Studio) in Warsaw, resulting in *Moments of Decision/Indecision*, an action that referenced Brisley's attempt to look East and beyond the Wall (figure 5.10). Naked and with a shaved head, he spent six days trying to climb a vertical wall that was covered in black and white paint. Each day, Brisley attempted to climb the 'wall, from an ideological non-position, as it were',[62] and each day he failed as he became blinded and covered by the slippery paint. Brisley recalls that Szajna introduced him to the British ambassador and his wife before the performance and that the couple left shortly after the performance began.[63] Like his fictional alter ego, Brisley was dimly aware that he was being tracked during his stay in Poland, and not just by the Polish. He was eventually alerted by the Polish authorities that the British embassy disapproved of his presence.

In fact, the British ambassador at the time of Brisley's visit was Norman Reddaway, who held the post from 1974 to 1978. Although not publicly known at the time, Reddaway had been involved during the 1960s in black propaganda against the Indonesian government, orchestrating a disinformation campaign that some have claimed incited the massacre of Indonesia's communists.[64] Upon his arrival in Warsaw, Reddaway continued his anti-communist efforts by seeking to block the visits of British communists and other 'sharp-edged people' to Poland at the time, an activity that created friction with the head of the British Council, whose job was to promote Polish–British academic and cultural exchange.[65] Reddaway also keenly promoted the art of his wife, Jean Reddaway, as an example of British art painted to the 'highest standard' and a means to further align the 'sentimental Poles' with their natural allies in the West.[66] Reddaway's political interventionism, not to mention personal tastes and interests, reveal how a public culture of art was instrumentalised during the Cold War period. Although Brisley is not mentioned by name in any of the correspondence that I have seen, Reddaway's efforts to block visits to Poland by prominent but politically undesirable British citizens, coupled with the strong possibility that he did in fact witness Brisley's performance, give a good indication of how Brisley's art may have been viewed by influential representatives of the state in the 1970s and early 1980s, a far cry from his current status as an artist whose works feature in public and private collections around the world.

The inclusion of these and other incidents drawn from Brisley's own life in this fictional narrative suggests that the *Museum of Ordure* is about much more than a collection of stools. For it also essentially asks the question

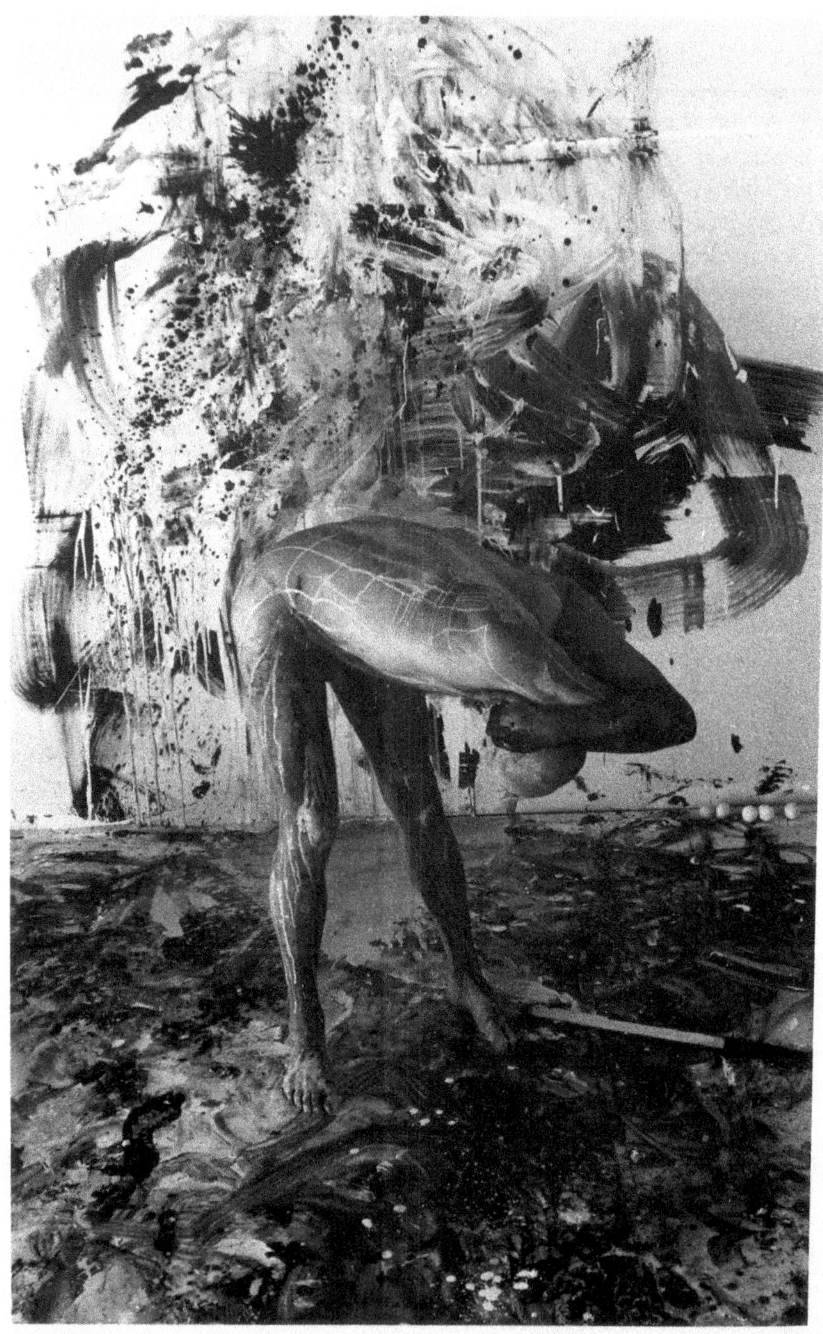

5.10   *Moments of Decision/Indecision*, Galeria Studio, Palac Kultury i Nauki, Warsaw, 1975

whether memory itself is a kind of 'detritus, excreta of experience, which can only be reconstituted as fiction'. The problem of time, after all, is that it deforms or dislocates all processes. Just as artefacts in a museum can be retouched to the point where they cease to be recognisable, so too the immaterial traces of past experiences undergo a similar process of unspooling. As Sirb acerbically notes: 'Shit floats. Some of it. Heavy shit as memory requires other means of recuperation.'

Seen in this light, a collection of ordure is a way to make visible the passage of time itself, including the time in which Brisley's past performances can also be 'recollected'. This is replicated in the structure of *Beyond Reason*. Unpaginated, consisting only of numbered sections, the text reworks episodes of Brisley's past into so many loosely 'differentiated heaps' of remembered events and feelings.[67] These include Brisley's early experiences as a conscript in the British army stationed in West Germany and his subsequent fascination with, and travels to, Eastern Europe. This suggests that, in addition to being a satire, this book is also a *kunstlerroman*. It accounts for Brisley's own evolution as an artist and his changing relation to the question of what art activity might be, especially in relation to institutional power.

Performance art has traditionally prided itself on an unmediated relation to the human body. Yet this fictional artist's memoir foregrounds not the presence of the body but also its absence. What is offered to the reader instead is a fictionalised narrative voiced through several artistic personae, each of whom remediate the traces of Brisley's past in different ways. By insisting on the elusive nature of personal memory, Brisley clearly seeks to escape the myth of the artist, whose life-story is used to historically locate, and therefore contain, the meaning of their works of art. Instead he presents us with the criss-crossing tales of multiple agents, including institutional ones, that determine, as well as curtail, what counts as art in the first place.

The *Museum of Ordure*, and other long-durational works of Brisley's late career, seem far removed from the original 'revolutionary' ambitions of his early performances. I want to insist, however, on the continuity between these late works and Brisley's earlier attempts to make a cut in time. In particular, Brisley's extensive engagement with the time of the aftermath asks the viewer to consider not just what takes place whenever an attempt at revolutionary rupture is undertaken, but also what happens to the waste products that remain behind, whether these be an empty throne, a vacated seat of power or, more discreetly, a language of hygiene that circulates even in the sovereign's absence.

In the last part of this chapter, I want to widen the discussion to consider what the privileged moment of the French Revolution can reveal about Brisley's practices of working with waste products as well as his own attempts to enact a revolutionary situation from the perspective of its aftermath, when the attempt at making a total rupture with the past is acknowledged to have failed. For a revolutionary rupture does not just destroy the 'old past'. It also creates new pasts and new institutions in its wake which rework the boundary between waste products and collectible objects. It is well known, for instance, that the Revolution gave birth to the Louvre, the world's first public state museum, as well as the French national archive, the first of its kind, and a national library. Since the 1990s, a number of important studies have made clear the extent to which these institutions emerged out of what Edouard Pommier has called the 'Revolution's double language of destruction and preservation'.[68] But, as Brisley's own collections make clear, this dynamic is inseparable from the less salubrious actions of burning, breaking, digging, amassing, sorting, all actions through which the distinction between what is transient and what is permanent is first made. In such moments revolutionary action confronts the experience of reaction, when an awareness arises of how time's passage distorts all intentions, including revolutionary ones. What happens when institutions arrogate for themselves the sovereign power to decide what remains and what is destroyed of the past? In other words, what happens when a revolution's failure to enact a complete break with the past is put in the service of other ends, including institutional ones?

The cut in time: revolution and/as ordure

It was Bataille who first linked the 'origin of the modern museum to the development of the guillotine'.[69] Although acknowledging that the Louvre was not the first museum in Europe to make its collection public, Bataille argues nevertheless that it was the world's first truly public museum, opening its doors 'for the people' in August 1793 to celebrate the first anniversary of Year I of the Republic. More significantly, the impetus for its creation was the colossal piling up of wealth generated by the Revolution's attempt to destroy the past. In these heaps, objects that had previously been markers of prestige, power or wealth appeared as if 'liberated from material concerns'. Art became an object of contemplation and, according to Bataille, the doctrine of art for art's sake was born.[70]

This liberation of art went hand in hand with a new attitude to the experience of time and duration. Before the Revolution, social time had been marked by the numerous festivals and weekly Sabbaths of a crowded church calendar. After the Revolution, Bataille claims that the laity began to spend their Sundays not at church but at the museum, where they acquired a new, publicly shared experience of both time and space. Yet, even as crowds flocked to the museum to appreciate 'art for art's sake', Bataille argues that they encountered a 'colossal mirror' in which they saw only each other.

Artworks that had previously been contained by museums now became the container for a new collective activity, the spectacle of society itself.

But before the past can be preserved as such, objects must pass through an intermediate phase – Michael Thompson's zone of transience, which, as we have already seen, can be likened to the time of the aftermath. Here Bataille's reference to the 'guillotine' assumes a new significance, for plans for the revolutionary Louvre accelerated in the tumultuous period between the overthrow of the monarch on 10 August 1792 and the king's execution on 21 January 1793, an interregnum period when the king was symbolically dead yet physically still alive. This was a period of great fear, not only that the past was still alive, physically embodied in people like the king, his relatives and descendants, but also that it could come back to haunt the present, in the form of a counter-revolution that would reverse the Revolution's hard-won gains. Expressing this fear of a potentially reversible revolution, the French deputy Cambon hit upon the idea of preserving the royal monuments as artistic ones, arguing, on 21 August 1792, that the best way to prevent the return of the past was to turn it into art.[71] Cambon was strongly supported by another deputy, Dusaulx, who argued that a museum would prevent a counter-revolution because it would retain monuments of the past as 'images of horror'.[72] The implications could not be clearer: art collections would complete the act of regicide by destroying the authority of the royal monument, preserving only aestheticised images of the past as pleasing or terrifying.

But the most important moment comes a month later, when the Assembly designated the Louvre as a temporary depot for all the remains associated with the royal past.[73] The Louvre, after all, was a royal palace. Breaching this 'inviolable sanctum' had afforded one of the great 'pleasures' of revolution.[74] By transforming it into a depot or storage, the revolutionary administration transgressed this hallowed place once more. Anything judged useless for posterity was to be melted down to its base material – lead, copper, bronze – and reused. Anything worth saving was to be decided by the newly established *commission temporaire des arts*, which included artists in its ranks. Pommier observes that at this point a political problem of rupture (how to stop counter-revolution, or the return of this supposedly 'dead past') transmuted into a problem of culture. Comprised of specialists, the commission knew better how to destroy the past than 'uneducated citizens'.[75] The Revolution's aftermath, in other words, introduced a new function for art, alongside a new functionary: the conservator or curator, who would henceforth administer the heap on behalf of the people. As Pommier observes, this commission also took pains to separate the work of conservation from the interests of the art market, a significant first step in the elaboration of a public culture of art.[76]

For the purposes of my argument, it suffices to note that if the Louvre conserved objects from the past, it did so in the name of ongoing rupture rather than historical continuity with the past. As Dominique Poulot has suggested, collecting was a way to continue revolutionary vandalism by other means.[77] The term 'vandalism' is a revolutionary neologism, claimed by Abbé Grégoire, who said he had 'invented the term to kill the thing'.[78] In a series of speeches to the National Convention in 1794, he urged revolutionaries to put an end to the great scenes of iconoclastic destruction that aimed to destroy the objects and images associated with the *ancien régime* and preserve them instead as museum pieces. Grégoire argued that whereas destruction affirmed the ongoing power of a still living past, conservation ensured a sharp separation between past and present. It was a means of 'inspiring genius' while 'perpetually pillorying' the tyrants of the past.[79]

But there is perhaps no greater expression of this ambiguous zone of transience than the decision to mark the anniversary of the Revolution's Year I not just with the opening of the new Louvre but also with the digging up of the royal tombs at Saint-Denis, where royal families had been buried in continual succession since the tenth century. It was the Jacobin Bertrand Barère who first linked the problem of celebrating a missing Year I with that of the Revolution's remains in his speech of 1 August 1793.[80] The king may be dead, Barère conceded, but Marie Antoinette and her children were still alive, and with them the possibility of counter-revolution. So long as any 'remains' of the past existed, the Revolution's premise of rupture, announced a year prior, remained incomplete. To ensure that the past was truly dead, therefore, Barère urged the deputies to mark the anniversary of the Revolution's Year I by putting Marie Antoinette on trial, confiscating all remaining émigré property for the public good *and* destroying the royal tombs – a digging up of the past in one final effort to bury it altogether.[81]

The French psychoanalyst Paul-Laurent Assoun has characterised the destruction of the royal tombs as a collective, post-mortem regicide, a second regicide that sought to go beyond the physical act of execution to kill the symbolic body of all kings.[82] To exhume any dead body touches a cultural taboo. This is not just because it violates a corpse but also because it goes against the ancient human injunction to bury the dead. By violating the royal tombs, revolutionaries undertook a double transgression that repeated and extended the original act of regicide. In the first instance, the mummified corpses of the royal bodies were exhumed and made to reveal what is ordinarily concealed: their base material existence as putrefying and decaying human matter. Secondarily, the corpses were stripped of any remaining symbolic accoutrements, which now became museum pieces.

That the opening of the revolutionary Louvre coincided with the digging up of the tombs of Saint-Denis is significant for several reasons. In the first place, it showcases the physical actions – digging, breaking, collecting – by which a still living past is turned into a 'dead', historical past. In the second place, it enacts a new authority, in which an original crime against the past (and the authority of the past) is reconstituted in the name of a future heritage and a public good. Finally, it demonstrates the actions by which a new collectivity is formed. Assoun characterises this prolonged exposure to the 'undefined slurry' of human decay as a kind of 'hapax', a one-of-a-kind event without historical precedent and that was never repeated.[83] In its deliberate yet excessive quality, this act approaches a limit-case of social performance, a 'border-line event', in which the public life of the imagination is also revealed.[84]

But for this revelation to take place, the royal body had to be seen for what it was: base matter or political ordure. This extended confrontation with human decay took place not over days, but over weeks. In total 170 bodies were exhumed, presenting in various states of decay.[85] Although the vast majority of the monarchical families were dug up in the autumn of Year II, the process continued sporadically over several months and years. Tellingly, on 18 January 1794, on the first anniversary of Louis XVI's execution, there was another exhumation. Contemporary reports provide a fascinating insight into how this encounter might have taken place.[86] Some bodies were in a state of 'liquid putrefaction'; others were reduced to formless 'dust'; still others continued to putrefy once exposed to the air. Henri IV's mummified body leaked a preserving liquid whose odour was unbearable, but also sported a 'well-preserved moustache', allegedly promptly cut off by a soldier as a talisman.[87] Louis XIV had skin 'as black as ink', while Alphonse de Poitiers, who died in 1271, was nothing but ashes, although his hair too was well-preserved.[88] As the workers dug further back into the past, extraordinary images of majesty emerged, all destined for their final graveyard in the museum. The skeleton of King Philippe-le-Bel was recovered with a golden ring and a gilded copper sceptre topped with extraordinary metalwork in the shape of leaves and a bird.[89] Everything became identical in this pestilential atmosphere and only the items with the longest duration – the future museum pieces – stood out from general formlessness.[90]

It is significant that the committee that oversaw the destruction of the royal tombs was comprised of a trio of artists: a sculptor, an engraver and a poet/antiquarian.[91] Alexandre Lenoir was also present to register and collect valuable objects for what was to become the second great revolutionary museum in Paris: this was the Musée des Monuments français, which opened in 1795. Even more than the Louvre, this museum, was a 'pure product of Revolution'.[92] Its collection consisted mainly of French sculpture and tomb monuments, objects of little aesthetic value or considered too closely aligned with the royalist past. The idea for the museum can be traced back to 1791, when Lenoir had been put in charge of the depot established at the former convent of the Petits-Augustins. Essentially a clearing house for the government, this is where objects were piled up as they waited to be assessed regarding their future use.[93] Lenoir had originally intended his collection to be part of the new Louvre. When this project failed to materialise, he decided to create a separate institution made up of remnants deemed worthy of 'historical interest' and therefore conservation. Out of this storage room, Lenoir managed to design an entirely novel kind of museum 'collection', arguably expressing for the first time the sovereign power of the museum itself to revise the past based on the history of its own collections.[94]

It is tempting to call the Musée des Monuments the first successful Museum of Ordure. Originating as a storage depot designed to contain the dead past created by revolutionary rupture, it was transformed into a museum through acts of institutionalisation that since have become part and parcel of modern museum practice. This stretches from the authoritatively presented catalogue, written by Lenoir, to the reorganisation of space into 'period rooms', to the chronological exposition. Even the proposed itinerary through the museum space reframed what were essentially waste products of the Revolution as an initiation into a public language of enlightenment and national regeneration. Visitors were invited to first gaze upon the remnants of the medieval past, housed in a darkened room with no natural light, before encountering subsequent historical epochs under progressively better light, until the eighteenth century, whose objects were arranged in a room flooded by light. This chronological exposition expressed the museum's sovereignty – its ability to rearrange history according to its own collections and its own conceptions, here presented as enlightenment progress. It also served to eradicate all memory of the museum's prior existence as a heap, a storage depot, a clearing housing: a murky zone of transience where the contradictory desires to obliterate and preserve the past still commingled.

Andrew McClellan notes that over time Lenoir 'came to identify with his collection', with a 'fierce possessiveness common to collectors and museum curators'.[95] Lenoir's mania for collecting sometimes made little difference between actual bodily remains and monuments. One of Lenoir's prized possessions was the mummified remains of the seventeenth-century military general Turenne, whose body was reburied in the gardens of Lenoir's museum, before being exhumed again under the orders of Napoleon in 1800 and reburied one final time in the Dome of the Invalides.[96] The terms in which Lenoir propositioned the revolutionary government for possession of this mummy are telling: due to his 'artistic capabilities [qualité d'artiste]' he was able to perceive a shape and identity 'across the undefined mass [à travers cette masse informe]'.[97] But this appeared a step too far for some revolutionaries. Roland, the minister of interior overseeing the commission, initially refused this request, observing that mummification was a technique that flattered the pride of kings; it was unfit for republicans, who should be remembered solely for their virtuous deeds.[98]

Historical ruptures and the heap

Today these extravagant events have become the stuff of history, even legend. Little remains of the pestilential atmosphere of the royal tombs in the spacious – and altogether hygienic – layout of the contemporary museum. And yet today's museums share with their revolutionary ancestors a similar insistence on their sovereign power to reframe their collections according to their own internal sense of history, one that enhances the value of their collections while at the same time adjusting itself to suit the values of the assumed present and future beneficiaries of their collection.

To be sure, there are important differences between the revolutionary period and today. During the Revolution, the past piled up with extraordinary speed, giving rise to the feeling that time itself was accelerating. This could not be further removed from the contemporary situation, in which the past piles up in the absence of any expectation of rupture, much less that of revolution. Nevertheless, I want to suggest that what links the contemporary museum to its revolutionary predecessor may well be this experience of the colossal heap, the way piles of undifferentiated objects can emit a kind of malevolent presence that disrupts all efforts at rational organisation. In a striking image, Brisley has even likened contemporary art to 'an enormous sort of dung heap'; 'what gets put on top is more recent … and there's a hell of a lot of steaming that is coming up from underneath'.[99] Contemporary art institutions, of course, are not revolutionary. Yet they too express a similar fear of debris. As Dominique Poulot observes, this fear is double sided.[100] First, there is the fear that the collection may lose value because it cannot differentiate itself from what remains outside it (namely, debris, waste, everything that is not art). Second and conversely, institutions fear that what is left out of the collection may indeed have a value which, if excluded, would negatively impact on the value of the collection.

To return to Brisley's own performances, we have seen over the course of this chapter how Brisley has sought to escape the sovereign power of the museum, structured around fear of the debris, which is also the fear of what remains outside the institution. We have also seen how Brisley's frameworks have become, over time, elaborate narrative devices, with a cast of characters expressing different facets of the artist's life and works. If Brisley's self-instituting collections, then, can be considered 'revolutionary', it is precisely in their attempt to keep open the relation between any collection and what remains outside it, be it the heaps, debris, waste or, conversely, the ceaseless processes associated with life itself, including especially the shifting sands of memory and forgetting.

This increasingly discursive nature of Brisley's late practice extends also to the kind of art writing that I have been elaborating over the course of this book. For it is by expanding on the analogies between Brisley's own institutions and the kinds of institutions created in actual moments of revolution that we can gauge how far they differ. In this respect, the tale of the revolutionary museum is also a cautionary one, revealing how new institutions and hierarchies arise whenever a revolution tries to complete itself, or even when it turns against itself, forgetting its democratic impulses. To call Brisley a revolutionary artist, then, does not mean equating his attempts at rupture with revolution understood as a singular event in time, much less an action capable, however momentarily, of overturning state or institutional power. On the contrary, for Brisley, performance – like revolution – is an ongoing process, by turns confrontational and evasive, that ceaselessly overturns all hierarchies and frameworks, including those made possible by his own art.

To illustrate this last point, I would like to conclude this chapter with a brief consideration of how one of Brisley's performances has been received as part of a museum collection, and what this reveals about the relationship between the museum and performance today. On 5 March 1968, Brisley undertook a direct action at the Tate Gallery, occasioned by the visiting French artist César, who was scheduled to demonstrate his 'expansionist art' to invited 'friends of the Tate'.[101] This involved pouring polyurethane liquid onto the floor, which expanded into giant foam drops that hardened into plastic resin over the course of approximately two minutes. Objecting to what he perceived as the use of art as spectacle, Brisley, along with fellow artist Peter Sedgley, posed as BBC reporters. They took large sections of the foam sculptures outside, impaled them on the railings and then asked a friend and audience member to light a match.[102] It quickly transpired that César had used a banned flammable substance, contravening gallery regulations, as Brisley had indeed suspected. The match triggered a thirty- to forty-foot high blaze, the fire brigade was called, and burn marks were visible for many months after.

At the time, this intervention was considered a criminal act: the police, the fire brigade and other critical services were called in and the damage was extensive. The action also prompted a discussion among the trustees of the Tate as to how César came to use a forbidden substance. Sir Robert Sainsbury's report admits that although the 'party itself had been a success, the 'bonfire … on the pavement in front of the Tate' meant that 'the evening was less satisfactory aesthetically'.[103] This same report assures the trustees that 'every precaution' had been undertaken 'to ensure that the materials to be used by César were non-combustible', insisting that even if César had used different materials, 'these were not highly inflammable'. This was a significant understatement, as Brisley's intervention had demonstrated to extraordinary effect. If the Tate were found to have permitted such a dangerous substance, it would have affected its insurance policy – difficult to justify for an institution reliant on public funding.

Flash-forward to the present, and Brisley's action is now part of the Tate rather than an action originally taken against the art gallery and its management. In 2015 it was written up as a prominent case study of live art on the Tate's website, even briefly occupying pride of place as the first performance piece on the gallery's timeline.[104] In the process, the original context of the action has been changed. Brisley's action is both neutralised (it is no longer presented as criminal) as well as amplified (it is now the work of an established artist and his collaborator). An act *against* the gallery has become something that, since it took place at the Tate, is now also part of *its* history and *its* collection. Given a title, it lies at the origin of a new timeline that demonstrates 'that performance has been in the museum for a long time', 'at least as long' as 'Tate has been collecting objects and documents related to these kinds of works'.[105] According to Tate's own narrative, *Unscheduled Action* exemplifies how the Museum itself has changed, expanding its notions of what art might be, as live art becomes a 'major acquisition and display priority for Tate and other galleries'.

Unsurprisingly, the modern museum, like its revolutionary predecessor, rewrites history according to its own historical laws, its own Year Is. It also shares a revolutionary tendency to redefine any past in the image of a future public: that is to say, the hypothetical visitors or beneficiaries of their collections. Yet, as the reception of Brisley's *Unscheduled Action* also makes clear, what gets preserved in the process is not a record of conflict but, rather, the Museum's own power to revise the past. It is precisely on this last point that Brisley's self-institutions prove most stimulating. For they too engage a revolutionary understanding of art as a means to address and bring into being a public. Unlike the sovereign museum, however, they fail to close the gap between the solicited and actual public. In so doing they make visible the cost of success, or what happens when the revolutionary claim to make a cut in time is put into the service of other ends.

Notes

1 Michel Serres, *Genesis*, trans. Geneviève James and James Nielson (Ann Arbor, MI: Michigan University Press, 1995), p. 94.

2 This point has been much discussed in the recent literature. On the expansion of the term more generally see Marlene Manoff, who observes that 'conflation and inflation' characterise contemporary 'archival discourse' (p. 21): in Marlene Manoff, 'Theories of the Archive from across the Disciplines', *Libraries and the Academy*, 4:1 (2004), 9–25. For performance specifically, see Gunhild Borgreen and Rune Gade (eds), *Performing Archives/Archives of Performance*

(Copenhagen: Museum Tusculanum Press, 2013); Sarah Jones, Daisy Abbott and Seamus Ross, 'Redefining the Performing Arts Archive', *Archival Science*, 8:3 (2009), 165–171. For the archive in relation to the modernist imagination see Sven Spieker, *The Big Archive: Art from Bureaucracy* (Cambridge, MA: MIT Press, 2008).

3 For an in-depth discussion see Alex Potts, 'The Artwork, the Archive, and the Living Moment', in Michael Ann Holly and Marquard Smith (eds), *What Is Research in the Visual Arts? Obsession, Archive, Encounter* (New Haven, CT: Yale University Press, 2008), pp. 119–137.

4 Peter Friedl, 'The Impossible Museum', *E-Flux Journal*, 23 (2011), www.e-flux. com/journal/23/67778/the-impossible-museum/ (accessed 20 July 2017).

5 Mary Douglas, *Purity and Danger: An Analysis of Concepts of Pollution and Taboo* (London: Routledge, 2002), p. 161.

6 Hapax is a term drawn from linguistics that refers to a word that only ever appears once or in one text only. Carlo Ginzburg, following François Furet, has used hapax to refer to those original documents that never become part of an archive or a series. Because they exist as singularities, these traces of the past cannot be used either to make historical generalisations about the past or as an example that proves the rule. See Carlo Ginzburg, *Threads and Traces: True False Fictive*, trans. Anne C. Tedeschi and John Tedeschi (Berkeley, CA: University of California Press, 2012), p. 202.

7 Michael Thompson, *Rubbish Theory: The Creation and Destruction of Value* (Oxford: Oxford University Press, 1979), p. 8.

8 Ibid., p. 9. Also pp. 45–46 and 52.

9 Ibid., p. 10.

10 Ibid., p. 26.

11 Aleida Assmann, 'Beyond the Archive', in Brian Neville and Johanne Villeneuve (eds), *Waste-Site Stories: The Recycling of Memory* (Albany, NY: State University of New York Press, 2002), pp. 71–82, p. 71.

12 Aleida Assmann, *Cultural Memory and Western Civilization*, pp. 13–14.

13 Foster, 'An Archival Impulse'. As Foster notes, archival art is 'distinct from art focused on the museum', p. 5.

14 See, notably, the writings anthologised in Charles Merewether (ed.), *The Archive* (London: Whitechapel Venture Ltd., 2006).

15 Enwezor, *Archive Fever*, p. 4.

16 Groys, 'On Art Activism', p. 14.

17 Ibid., p. 10.

18 See Newman, *Stuart Brisley*, p. 5. In addition to the *OED*, see also Elizabeth Kirkpatrick and Catherine Schwarz (eds), *Chambers 20th Century Dictionary* (Edinburgh: Chambers, 1987).

19 Brisley, National Life Stories, C466/43/13 F5285A, p. 262.

20 See Susanne Hauser, 'Waste into Heritage: Remarks on Materials in the Arts, on Memories and the Museum', in Brian Neville and Johanne Villeneuve (eds), *Waste-Site Stories: The Recycling of Memory* (Albany, NY: State University of New York Press, 2002), pp. 39–54, in particular pp. 41–46.

21 As Brien Brothman has observed with regard to archival collections, 'regardless of whether or not a set of archival documents is ever consulted, once having been judged to have permanent value, the document's right to a place in the archives and society is irrevocable'. See Brien Brothman, 'Orders of Value: Probing the Theoretical Terms of Archival Practice', *Archivaria*, 32 (1991), 78–100, at 81.

22 www.stuartbrisley.com/pages/28/80s/Works/Leaching_Out_at_the_Intersection/page:4 (accessed 30 September 2022).

23 Brisley, conversation with the author, 20 August 2020, Lydd-on-Sea.

24 Ibid.

25 Brisley, National Life Stories, C466/43/12 F5284A, p. 237.

26 Ibid., p. 235.

27 For this description, and the terms 'transaction' and 'situation', see Michael Archer, 'Neither One Thing nor the Other', in *Stuart Brisley: Georgiana Collection* (Glasgow: Third Eye Centre, 1986), pp. 5–26, at pp. 5–6.

28 At the Lewis Johnston Gallery. See Ken Hollings, 'Stuart Brisley', *Performance Magazine: The Review of Live Art*, 24 (1983), 27.

29 Brisley notes that the official government figures were three million, but this did not include those that did not declare themselves unemployed or had ceased looking for work. See: Brisley, National Life Stories, C466/43/12 F5284A, p. 240.

30 As Andreas Huyssen observes, 'a number of auteurist exhibitions in the 1980s were presented as museums: Harald Szeemann's Museum of Obsessions, Claudio Lange's Museum for the Utopias of Survival; Daniel Spoerri and Elisabeth Plessen's Musée sentimental de Prusse'. Huyssen, *Twilight Memories*, p. 20.

31 Dominique Laporte, *History of Shit*, trans. N. Benabid and R. El-Khoury (Cambridge, MA: The MIT Press, 1993), p. 102.

32 Ibid., p. 106.

33 Ibid., p. 98.

34 Ibid., p. 104.

35 As described by Mitchell Algus, 2011, www.stuartbrisley.com/pages/27/70s/Works/180_Hours_Work_for_Two_People/page:32 (accessed 3 July 2020).

36 Brisley, conversation with author, 6 December 2017.

37 Stuart Brisley, 'Interregnum: 11:30–16:30' (17 February 2018). Turf Gallery, Croydon, London. Personally recorded by the author.

38 See Brisley, National Life Stories, C466/43/11 F5283A, pp. 211–216.

39 Andrew Wilson observes: 'These are works that can be situated in terms of the abject – not as an image of dirt, but in terms of a complex understanding of how the body defines its limits and boundaries in relation to a dirt that is outside or alien to a body – and what happens when those limits and boundaries are crossed.' Andrew Wilson, 'Touching, Crossing and Passing Through', in *Stuart Brisley; Crossings* (Southampton: John Hansard Gallery, 2008), 17–21, p. 18.

40 It began in 2001 as an online art project (UK Museum of Ordure) initiated by Brisley, Geoffrey Cox and Adrian Ward. It has subsequently been relaunched as a global museum: www.ordure.org.

41 www.ordure.org/collection/preservation/ (accessed 27 December 2019).

42 It was intended as a prolegomena to a much longer work, cut short by the author's untimely death.

43 Laporte, *History of Shit*, p. 30.

44 Ibid., p. 86.

45 Ibid., p. 83.

46 Ibid., p. 46.

47 Ibid., p. 66.

48 In fact, a reference to Brisley's performance *Talking Hygiene*, 5th International Performance Festival Kunsthaus, Dresden 2000, in which he accidentally tipped over a jar full of cockroaches that he found in the museum.

49 Brisley has described this method as being the 'paparazzi of the paparazzi'. Conversation, 25 June 2022, Lydd-on-Sea.

50 Laporte, *History of Shit*, p. 13.

51 For this description of the papal ritual see: Agostino Paravacini-Bagliani, *The Pope's Body*, trans. David S. Peterson (Chicago, IL: University of Chicago Press, 2000), pp. 44–49. The porphyry chairs were made of a red marble.

52 Calling to mind the series of paintings by Murakami Saburo, associated with the Gutai group, also created by throwing an ink-soaked ball.

53 Telephone conversation, 30 June 2022.

54 An association also discussed by Newman, *Stuart Brisley*, p. 30.

55 Thompson, *Rubbish Theory*, p. 93.

56 Sigmund Freud, 'The Interpretation of Dreams', in *The Complete Psychological Works of Sigmund Freud*, vol. V (1900–1) (London: Hogarth Press and the Institute of Psycho-analysis, 1953), pp. 468–469.

57 Ibid., p. 470.

58 Ibid., p. 469.

59 '[N]othing in our dream-thoughts which is distressing can force an entry into a dream unless it at the same time lends a disguise to the fulfilment of a wish.' Ibid., p. 471.

60 Stuart Brisley, *Beyond Reason: Ordure* (London: Book Works, 2003).

61 On this point see: Geoffrey Cox, 'The Object of Corruption', in Julie Bacon (ed.), *The Suicide of Objects* (Belfast: Catalyst Arts, 2004).

62 This formulation is from a personal communication dated 3 August 2017.

63 Conversation with Brisley, December 2018, London.

64 See Paul Lashmar, Nicholas Gilby and James Oliver, 'Slaughter in Indonesia: Britain's Secret Propaganda War', *The Guardian*, 17 October 2021.

65 Letters were exchanged between Reddaway and the Foreign and Commonwealth Office (FCO), some of which went over the head of the British Council. The secret teleletter to Mr Ian Sutherland, FCO from Reddaway, dated 15 November 1976, states: 'I am, however, a little anxious about one or two of those sent out here from Britain at public expense or with public support. I wonder whether careful enough scrutiny is made of the political complexion of those sent […] My main please is that, if these sharp-edged people are sent here and handled under British Council auspices, the British Council representative and the Embassy

should be given adequate background. The Council representative is not aware of this letter.' FCO File reference 291/4.

66   Annual Information Policy Report Warsaw, 27 May 1976 from Reddaway to N. J. Barrington Esq.: 'The Poles are a sentimental people and are grateful for us for our wartime activities […] My wife's exhibitions of paintings owe much of their success to the gratification which the Poles feel at seeing their own country painted by a British artist of Royal Academy standard.' FCO 34/342.

67   Conversation with Brisley, 3 August 2017, London.

68   Pommier, *L'Art de la liberté*, p. 108; also: Dominique Poulot, *Une Histoire du patrimoine en Occident*, pp. 70–72, 84–85; Gamboni, *The Destruction of Art*, pp. 31–36.

69   Georges Bataille, 'Museum: Writings on Laughter, Sacrifice, Nietzsche, Un-Knowing', trans. Annette Michelson, *October*, 36:102 (1986), 24–25.

70   As Groys observes, we owe to the French revolutionaries the 'most trenchant formulation that everything which relates to power is not art; that art's true value lies in its autonomy and liberation from power and hierarchy.' See Groys, 'On Art Activism', *E-Flux Journal*, 56 (June 2014), *www.e-flux.com/journal/56/60343/on-art-activism/* (accessed 30 June 2014).

71   On 21 August 1792, Joseph Cambon declared: 'Le peuple ne veut plus de royauté; rendons-en le retour impossible; mais respectons pour les arts les monuments consacrés à cette royauté. Réunissons-les dans un seul endroit pour en former le Muséum.' In J. Mavidal and E. Laurent (eds) *Archives Parlementaires de 1787 à 1860*; Première série (1787 à 1799) Tome XLVIII du 11 août 1792 au 25 août 1792, p. 624. Discussed in Pommier, *L'Art de la liberté*, p. 104.

72   'Gardons-les comme un simulacre d'horreur'. Jean Dusaulx, in Mavidal and Laurent, *Archives Parlementaires de 1787 à 186*, Tome XLVIII, p. 624.

73   On 16 September 1792. See Pommier, *L'Art de la liberté*, p. 52.

74   Andrew McClellan, *Inventing the Louvre: Art, Politics, and the Origins of the Modern Museum in Eighteenth Century Paris* (Berkeley, CA: University of California Press, 1999), p. 98.

75   Pommier, *L'Art de la liberté*, p. 107.

76   Ibid., p. 114.

77   Poulot, *Une Histoire du patrimoine en Occident*, pp. 72, 84.

78   Henri Jean-Baptiste Grégoire, *Mémoires*, ed. Hyppolite Carnot (Paris: Ambroise Dupont, 1837), p. 346.

79   'peut simultanément alimenter le génie et reenforcer la haine des tyrans, en les condamnant par cette conservation même, à une espèce de pilori perpétuel'. *Rapport sur les destructions opérées par le Vandalisme, et sur les moyens de le réprimer. Par Grégoire, séance du 14 Fructidor, l'an second de la République une et indivisible, suivi du Décret de la Convention nationale* (Paris: de l'Impr. Nationale, 1794), p. 11.

80   Bertrand Barère, *Rapport fait au nom du comité de salut public, le premier aout 1793, l'an II de la rèpublique française* (Paris: de l'Impr. Nationale, 1793). Also in *Archives Parlementaires*, 70, pp. 90–112.

81   'Pour célébrer le journée du 10 août qui a abbatu le trône, il fallait, dans le jour anniversaire, détruire les mauselées fastueux qui sont à Saint-Denis. Dans la

monarchie, les tombeaux mêmes avaient appris à flatter les rois.' Barère, *Rapport*, p. 28. Also in: *Archives Parlementaires*, Tome 70, p. 103.

82 Paul-Laurent Assoun, *Tuer le mort: Le désir révolutionnaire* (Paris: Presses Universitaires de France, 2015), p. 13.

83 Ibid., p. 21.

84 Ibid., p. 67.

85 Ibid., p. 54; for an account see also Legacey, *Making Space for the Dead*, pp. 33–36.

86 Notably, the *Journal historique fait par le citoyen Druon, ci-devant bénédictin de la ci-devant abbaye de Saint-Denis, lors des extractions des cercueils de plomb des Rois, Reines, Princes et Princesses, abbés et autres personnes qui avaient leurs sépultures dans l'église de Saint-Denis*, Archives nationales, AE1/15/12 A. See also Alexandre Lenoir, *Journal historique de l'extraction des cercueils de plomb des rois, reines, princes, princesses, abbés et autres personnes qui avaient leurs sépultures dans l'église de l'abbaye royale de Saint-Denis en France du 12 octobre 1793 au 12 novembre 1793 et un supplément de quelques lignes pour la journée du 18 janvier 1794*, Archives nationales, AE/1/15/12 B, available at http://www2.culture.gouv.fr/ Wave/image/archim/Pages/03185.htm (accessed 15 September 2022), republished by Lenoir as *Notes historiques sur les exhumations faites en 1793, dans l'abbaye de saint-denis in Description historique et chronologique des monumens de sculpture, réunis au musée des monuments français par Alexandre Lenoir* (Paris: An X de la République), pp. 338–356. See also Georges D'Heilly, *Extraction des cercueils royaux à Saint-Denis en 1793: relation authentique* (Paris: Jouaoust et Roquette, 1866), which reworks the eye-witness account by Dom Germain Poirrier.

87 See Lenoir, *Notes historiques*, pp. 341–342; Heilly, *Extraction des cercueils royaux*, p. 12.

88 Lenoir, *Notes historiques*, pp. 342, 350; Heilly, *Extraction des cercueils royaux*, p. 28.

89 Lenoir, *Notes historiques*, p. 251; Heilly, *Extraction des cercueils royaux*, p. 30.

90 Lenoir describes 'une vapeure noire et épaisse, d'une odeur infecte' causing diarrhoea and fevers, *Notes historiques*, p. 244.

91 Assoun, *Tuer la mort*, pp. 44–45.

92 McClellan, *Inventing the Louvre*, p. 155, also pp. 155–197; Alexandra Stara, *The Museum of French Monuments 1795–1816: 'Killing art to make history'* (Farnham: Ashgate, 2013).

93 McClellan, *Inventing the Louvre*, p. 158.

94 'Lenoir was constant in his proposal for a unified public display of these monuments, founded upon the idea of a chronological sequence as a medium for communicating a loftier narrative.' Stara, *The Museum of French Monuments*, p. 19.

95 Ibid., p. 159.

96 As Poulot observes, 'Turenne a parcouru en quelques sorte l'arc complète des types et des valeurs de conservation.' Poulot, *Une Historie du patrimoine en Occident (XVIIIe–XXIe siècle)*, p. 85.

97 M. Louis Tuetey, *Procès-verbaux de la commission temporaire des arts*, tome première, 1er Septembre 1793–30 frimaire an III' (Paris: Imprimerie Nationale, 1912), p. 8.

98 Roland, 18 Frimaire Year II (8 December 1793), Archives Nationales F17 1257. Quoted by Tuetey, *Procès-verbaux*, p. 26.

99 Brisley, National Life Stories, C466/43/12 F5284B, p. 246.

100 See Poulot, *Une Historie du patrimoine en Occident*, p. 185.

101 Pierre Restany, 'Modern Magic at the Tate', *Studio International*, June (1968).

102 Dr Marion Spencer, who was an invited guest. Conversation with the artist 8 December 2016.

103 Minutes of a meeting of the Trustees of the Tate Gallery held on Thursday, 21 March 1968, p. 3.

104 Since taken down; see 'Timeline', *Performance at Tate: Into the Space of Art*, Tate Research Publication (2016) available at https://www.tate.org.uk/docu ments/1183/performanceattatetimeline_text_only.pdf (accessed 2 July 2017); for the case-study see 'Stuart Brisley Born 1933 with Peter Sedgely Born 1930: Unscheduled Action 1968' Tate Gallery, 1968, https://www.tate.org.uk/research/ publications/performance-at-tate/perspectives/stuart-brisley (accessed 5 January 2018).

105 Jonah Westerman, 'Performance at Tate: Into the Space of Art: Project Overview' Tate Gallery, 2016, https://www.tate.org.uk/research/publications/performance- at-tate/project-overview (accessed 2 July 2017).

6 Portrait of the artist *en abîme*

As this book has demonstrated, performance is situated at the limits of both art and history. It is situated at the limit of art because it can be anything (political, social, aesthetic) depending on how it is framed and received. By the same token, the status of a live action as a hapax, a unique event that never repeats, makes it difficult, if not impossible, to historicise. As the preceding chapters have shown, architectural models, film footage, photographs, collections, memoirs, paintings, witness statements, sedimented habits and ritual structures, all function as circumstantial evidence for a lost past. As forms with a logic of their own, they cannot be treated simply as historical traces, much less as a documentary record that can be used to lock an event into its original context. Nor can they be assimilated to a cultural memory that privileges permanence over transience, remaking the past in its own image. Perhaps, then, performance art is better described as a singular event that, so long as it is continually mediated in new forms, participates in a kind of repetition without origins.

Repetition features strongly across the ensemble of Brisley's actions. It is used to draw attention to a historical referent that lies outside the frame of art as in the *Cenotaph Project*, which references the Whitehall Cenotaph; *Arbeit Macht Frei*, whose title repeats the Nazi slogan; *Talking Hygiene*, which names an existing museum; *Before the Mast*, which unfolds over the actual time span of a revolutionary hour. Repetition also occurs when new works take up structures or materials explored in previous works. For instance, the film *Arbeit Macht Frei* takes up the plastic sheet and water used in *And for today … nothing*, making it integral to the structure of a new work, in a new medium; *Drawn* (2016) refers to the myth of Procrustes but also *Procrustean Bed*, a subtitle of a 1973 performance; the *Museum of Ordure* expands a process of collecting detritus that began with the *Georgiana Collection*, itself a reaction to the failures of the *Peterlee Project*. Finally, repetition occurs whenever quotations, titles or fragments of other people's works are nested within new works. The way, for instance, a quote from Clarice Lispector, William Blake or Shakespeare is used to reframe a performance or installation by instigating other associations across time and space.

These nested references to previous works and performances – whether by Brisley or by others – open a space for viewers to consider the relation between what repeats and what is novel in any given performance, creating a perspective on the past that is simultaneously close up and distant; embodied and self-reflexive. Brisley has addressed the nature of this type of repetition in *Writing on the Wall Is*, a seventy-two-hour action that took place at Raven Row in London in 2017, when artists who had worked in Gallery House in 1972–73 were invited to 'rethink their original contribution in this space'.[1] Brisley's rethinking took the form of an entirely new performance. Rather than 're-enact' one of his iconic 'Life Situation' performances from that year, Brisley aimed instead to create a continuous action, possibly even a 'non-performance' in which he did nothing for the three days and three nights of the installation. Enclosed behind a ceiling-high particle-board wall, the octogenarian artist endured both the permanent phosphorescent light and the endless stream of visitors who came throughout the day and, on one occasion, far into the night. The artist was visible to the public through several small holes in the wall, placed at varying heights; he could also be seen via a door that was kept open, with the artist cordoned off from the public, unless he needed privacy or sleep (figure 6.1). This confined, yet voyeuristic, installation recalled *ZL656395C*, one of Brisley's iconic Gallery House performances discussed in Chapter 1, and whose documentation was displayed in an adjoining room in glass display cases, typical of museums.[2] The high wall with peepholes offered one way of seeing the artist, its narrow focalisation – as if through a camera hole – inviting the viewer to see the artist as an object. This structure subtly referenced *Artist as Whore*, another action undertaken at Gallery House that same year, which interrogated the objectification of the artist in a commercial market (figure 6.2). In that performance, Brisley spent several hours a day over a period of one week passively lying on a sloping oversized bed covered with paint and fluid, including urine, while wearing lipstick and kohl to emphasise the simultaneously 'dirty and seductive' nature of the artist/whore.[3] Additionally, for those familiar with Brisley's work, the high Wall may have reminded them of Brisley's long-term preoccupations with walls of all kinds, expressed, for instance, in his attempt to climb a wall in *Moments of Decision/Indecision* (1975), discussed in Chapter 5; his repeated references to the Berlin Wall, in text and image; or indeed his extensive explorations of states of confinement, such as those experienced by prisoners, miners, concentration camp survivors and others forced to *survive in alien circumstances*.

The title *Writing on the Wall Is* cited the oft-repeated idiomatic expression indicating what is blindingly obvious. But by inverting the grammatical position of the verb 'to be' the title also suspended this commonplace observation, as if leaving it to others to complete. A stumbling block was thus created in a hackneyed expression, opening a verbal breach between what is blindingly obvious and therefore unseen, or what is not obvious and for this reason also passes unseen. The incomplete phrase invited viewers to complete its meaning. It also brought attention to the artist's stated aim, which was to do as little as possible for as long as possible, as if to test

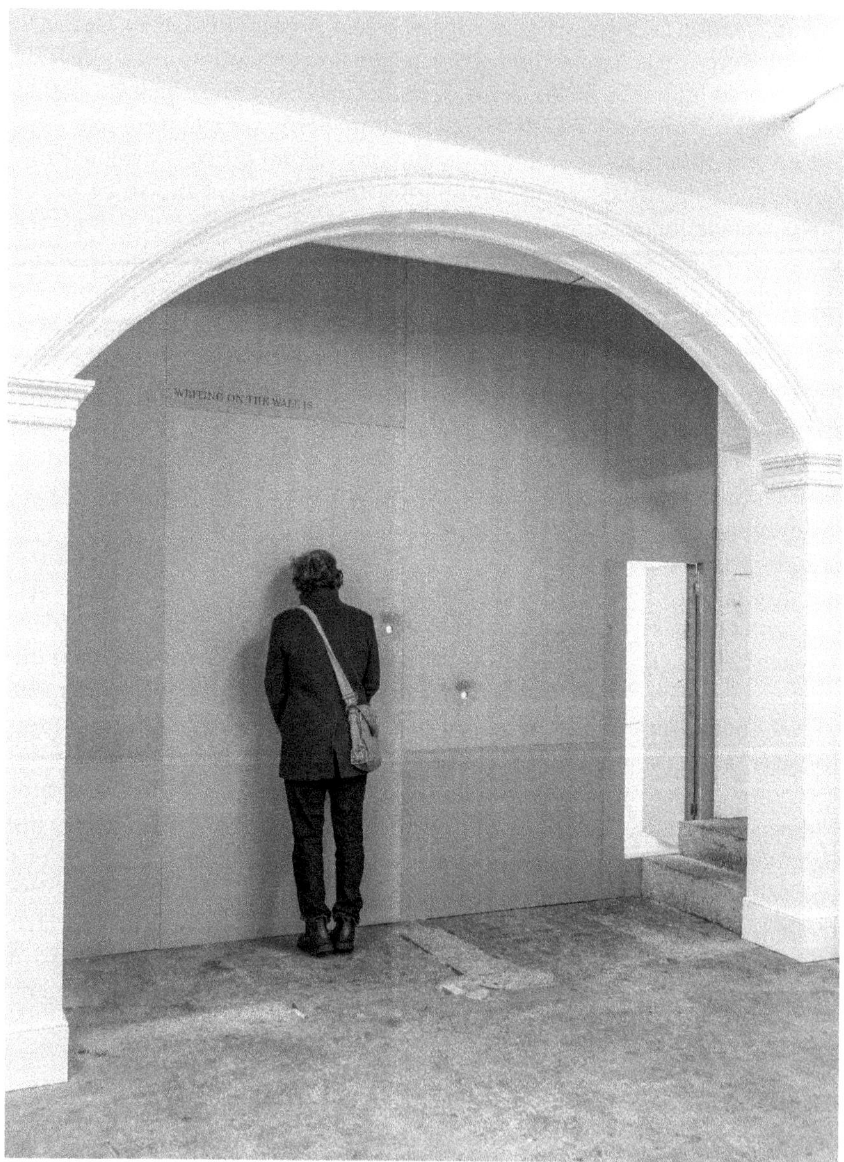

6.1   *Writing on the Wall Is*, Raven Row, London, 2017

whether the passage of time alone could make visible what is already there but lies unacknowledged.

This performance was accompanied by another installation that took place upstairs, entitled *From the Freezer … Thaw* by Maya Balcioglu, Brisley's frequent collaborator. This installation consisted solely of 'writings on the wall'. It took place in a room that was otherwise left empty except for a

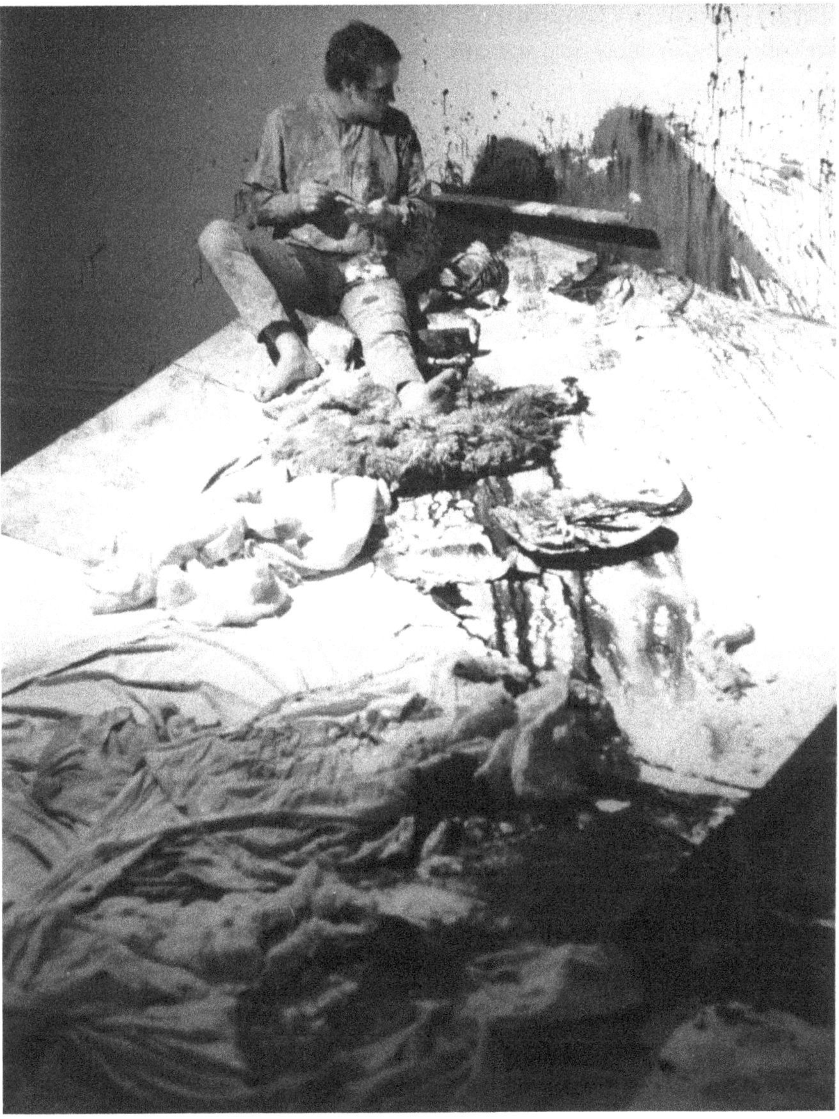

Artist as Whore, Gallery House, London, 1972   **6.2**

large mirror on one wall. To enter, you had to go past plastic panels like the ones found in the entrance to freezer rooms in butchers' shops. On the wall opposite the mirror hung the titles of two other performance undertaken by Brisley at Gallery House in 1972–73: the aforementioned *Artist as Whore* and *And for today … nothing*, discussed in Chapter 1. What the viewer thus saw reflected in the mirror was their own self-image alongside the titles of long-ago performances. More discreetly, Balcioglu's installation made use of the upstairs/downstairs class structure alluded to in Brisley's other well-known performances, notably *10 Days* and *180 Hours Work for Two People*, both at Acme Gallery, London. Here this same upstairs/downstairs division was used to highlight the difference between performances in which the artist was present and those from which he was absent. Downstairs, Brisley was physically present, undertaking an entirely new work that partially refer-enced *ZLC656395C*, a previous work, while also alluding to *Artist as Whore*. Downstairs too were the historical documents associated with *ZLC656395C*. Upstairs, all that remained from these previous performances at Gallery House were the titles, reflected in the mirrors that hung in the otherwise empty room, whose freezer panels brought to mind associations with frozen meat, possibly even the offal that featured in *And for today … nothing*. The implication was that past performances lived on only in the form of frag-ments, citations and the viewer's own *self-reflections*. Any efforts to revisit the past, then, posed the question of what to do with this past. As Balcioglu's exhibition notes observe, once the past is taken out of the freezer and thawed, 'we must either cook it or junk it'.[4]

The philosopher Paisley Livingston has used the term 'nested artwork' to refer to this phenomenon of duplicating components of previous works in new works. As Livingston observes, when a previous work reappears in a new work it can put into play the 'suspenseful and surprising qualities of a structure of a work'.[5] At first glance, one might think that this play of repetition is ahistorical and can tell us nothing about the historical specific-ity of the original work, much less about how it might have been originally experienced. Livingston, however, suggests otherwise, arguing that, as these suspenseful qualities of a work are context-specific, they impose a 'significant constraint' on 'what is appropriately imaginable with regard to that work'.[6] Due to these constraints, nested art communicates the historically concrete aspects of a work across time via the indexical qualities of ostension rather narrative description.[7] To ostend (an obsolete term today) means to exhibit, to manifest, to define something by the act of pointing to it. Much like how we point to things when we do not know their name or do not have the language to describe them, it is a way of conveying meaning in the absence of other contextual information. Unlike historicism, which locks a given work in an original context, nested art operates in a manner akin to direct citations in a literary work or essay. Just as an example operates by dint of repetition (it appears as an example when it can serve as a model for others), the embedding of a title, term, saying or even structure in another work always involves a re-enactment of some kind. This re-enactment, in turn, reveals which element of an artistic structure is capable of breaking through the present, whether in the uptake of a mood, manner or form.

Livingston's examples are drawn from literature, painting and music: all forms of art that exist in time as stable objects or, in the case of scored music, have a built-in repetitive structure. But performance art, as we have continuously observed throughout this book, is a hapax, a unique event, that struggles to retain a place either in recorded history or as a cultural memory mediated by institutions. For Brisley and Balcioglu, the partial embedding of previous works in new works thus has a specific function, namely to prolong the experience of the performance or at least to use it to open up a space for continual reflection. Their preferred term for this process of self-reflection is *mise en abîme*, a concept with a long art-historical and literary lineage. Michael Newman has observed that the concept of *mise en abîme* can be applied across the ensemble of Brisley's works.[8] Through a kind of ceaseless citation, past performances are embedded not only in new performances and installations but also through film, photography, painting and soundworks in ways that also permit a reflection on the difference between past and present.[9] While this self-reflection expresses Brisley's own perceptions of his past performances, it also includes an element of historical reflection as well. In particular, it allows the viewer to consider what remains of the political radicalism of the 1960s, the original context in which Brisley's performance practice first emerged.

At this point I must ask for the reader's indulgence one last time. Although I initially wrote this chapter as a conclusion to a book on Brisley's performance art, it quickly became apparent that the inconclusive nature of his performances warrants a different type of 'concluding remark', one that considers his own efforts to keep past performances alive and belonging to the future in some way. By way of conclusion, therefore, I would like to elaborate upon Brisley's complex use of *mise en abîme*, and how it relates to his life-long efforts to cross the boundary separating art and life.

In the most general terms, *mise en abîme* has been defined as a reflexive strategy where the content of the medium is the medium itself (eg. plays within plays, films within films). Although mostly studied as an artistic, narrative or symbolic device, *mise en abîme*, as I will show, can also be used forensically to reveal that part of the past that remains present even when everything else about it is dead and gone. Historical time is often imagined as a 'container' that holds events. *Mise en abîme*, in contrast, enables past events to block or interrupt the historicising process, exposing the multiple layers of duration that underlie any representation. Through repetition and change of scale, past events can be seen to interrupt, and upend, chronological sequence in a way that calls into question the inevitability of all narratives, especially establishment ones. Importantly, by disrupting the boundary between what is inside and outside, *mise en abîme* draws attention to what is illusionistic about the use of all frames.

A reflection on *mise en abîme* is thus a fitting conclusion for a book on an artist who has attempted throughout his long career to widen the framework for the understanding of performance art. Brisley has always insisted that his own life and career as an artist should never be considered the subject of his actions because his performances, in a crucial sense, belong to the future. They are continually changing, depending on how they are received, whether by other people, in different contexts or by his own self-reflection. By nesting references to past performances in new installations and performances, Brisley refuses to stand still. This continuous movement short-circuits any attempt to establish a static or permanent link between the artist and his works. More significantly, Brisley's extensive use of *mise en abîme* deflects attention away from himself as sole creator of meaning by asking the viewer to reflect on what changes or stays stable in our relation to the past. For a past that persists also implies a past that can resist, even act back in some way on those chronological narratives that attempt to constrain and contain it.

This question of retroaction is, of course, also crucial for any study of revolution. Given the current climate, in which there appears to be no future capable of reactivating the historical record of past struggles, there is an increasing tendency to treat the revolution as part of a dead past, that is to say, as something contained, or framed, by historical time and not as something that ruptures with it. By contrast, Brisley's use of *mise en abîme* invites us to pose afresh the guiding questions of this book. Is there a way to re-experience the attempt to enact a revolutionary rupture with the past as an event with as yet undetermined outcomes, which is to say, an event that still has the capacity to act back on us? Conversely, if revolutionary intentions remain, for the most part, unfulfilled, what, if anything, can performance art reveal about the traces of these erstwhile intentions, the debris left behind in the absence of collective transformation?

Mise en abîme

Mise en abîme was first identified by the French writer André Gide. A slippery concept even in Gide's own writings, it has been extensively discussed ever since, mostly by literary critics and philosophers, without a consensus being reached on its core properties. As Moshe Ron pithily observed, 'one man's *mise en abîme* is another man's mush'.[10] Despite these disagreements – or perhaps because of them – *mise en abîme* remains a provocative figure across several fields and disciplines.

Gide's own rather exploratory definition first appeared in a journal entry of 1893:

> I wanted to suggest […] the influence of the book upon the one who is writing it, and during that very writing. […]
>
> No action upon an object without retroaction of that object upon the subject. I wanted to indicate that reciprocity, not in one's relation with others, but with oneself. The subject that acts is oneself; the object that retroacts is a literary subject arising in the imagination. […] In a work of art I rather like to find transposed, on the scale of the characters, the very subject of that work. […] Thus, in certain paintings of Memling or Quentin Metzys a small convex and dark mirror reflects the interior of the room in which the scene of the painting is taking place. Likewise in Velázquez's painting of the Meninas (but somewhat differently). Finally, in literature, in the play scene in Hamlet, and elsewhere in many other plays. In Wilhelm Meister, the scenes of the puppets or the celebration at the castle. In the Fall of the House of Usher, the story that is read to Roderick, etc. None of these examples is altogether exact. What would be more so, and would explain much better what I strove for in my Cahiers, in my Narcisse, and in the Tentative, is a comparison with the device of heraldry that consists in setting in the eschutcheon a smaller one 'en abyme', at the heartpoint. That retroaction of the subject on itself has always tempted me. It is the very model of the psychological novel. An angry man tells a story; there is the subject of a book. A man telling a story is not enough, it must be an angry man and there must be a constant connection between his anger and the story he tells.[11]

The variety of examples that Gide cites makes clear that he is less interested in defining what *mise en abîme is*, than in what it *could be*. Drawing indiscriminately on both art and literature, Gide suggests that *mise en abîme* does not easily fit our usual conceptual distinctions between 'showing' and 'telling'. To my mind, the fact that *mise en abîme* can function as both a visual and a narrative device is highly relevant for understanding the performances of Brisley's late career, which have increasingly incorporated a retrospective 'telling' in addition to the 'showing' that is the usual domain of the visual arts. More broadly, because it cuts across visual and narrative forms, *mise en abîme* undermines any 'documentary' attitude that we might be tempted to take towards past performances. As any historian will tell you, primary sources 'show' us traces of a past which then need to be put together by the historian in order to 'tell' a story. By plotting relations of sequence, the historian identifies who or what is the subject of the historical narrative they wish to recount.

Gide, however, suggests that when it comes to understanding the process of artistic creation, simultaneity and not sequence is revelatory. Only a simultaneous interaction between two narrative or visual levels can maintain the 'constant connection' (Gide's term) between the conditions of production of any given work and the manner in which it unfolds.

Most crucial for the purpose of my argument, however, is Gide's strong focus on the experience of retroaction. *Mise en abîme* happens when a given work acts back to allow the artist or author to reflect on the process of creation itself. Here it is not clear whether Gide is describing a self-reflexive or an interrupting strategy. Does *mise en abîme* draw attention to the formal parameters of, say, a painting or a narrative (for example, the way a story-within-a-story might reveal something about how an author understands narrative form)? Or is it better understood as a device that enables the content of a given painting or narrative to break through the conventions of form, the way, for instance, the angry man's anger becomes *present* in the story he tells, contaminating it in some way? Mieke Bal prefers the term 'interruption' and observes that all fictional *mise en abîme* is 'anachronic by definition' because it 'destroys expectations enforced by chronological sequence'.[12] Yet, as Bal notes, Gide is ambiguous about who or what is the subject of *mise en abîme*, whether the creator or his creation.[13] Even if this ambiguity was unintended, it nonetheless reveals something about the non-binary logic of *mise en abîme*, notably the way it resists any clear-cut distinction between who or what is the subject of any aesthetic creation.

As we have seen over the course of this book, this question of who or what is the subject of a performance has been central to Brisley's life-long efforts to create a public form of art. It is thus fitting that *State of Denmark* (2014), an important retrospective of Brisley's work briefly discussed in Chapter 4, references Shakespeare's *Hamlet*, whose play-within-a play is one of Gide's imperfect examples of a *mise en abîme*. The title itself – a partial citation that many English-speakers will almost unconsciously complete – repeats the famous remark made by Marcellus to Horatio in Act I, when Hamlet meets the ghost of his father: 'Something is rotten in the state of Denmark'. It is significant that the first suspicions of illegitimate rule are voiced not by Hamlet, the presumptive heir to the throne, but by a commoner using a commonplace expression that refers to the way a fish begins to rot from its head. These embedded and shared cultural references frame Brisley's exhibition, which confronts the ghost-like images of British monarchy – presiding over a rotting state – with his own life-long attempts to create a republican, 'living' form of art.

Upon entering the main gallery, the visitor first encountered a large installation made of interlocked metal chairs without seats or backs. The chairs were arranged in a perfect circle on the ground, subtly referencing the free-standing sculpture that Brisley built with factory workers at the Hille Factory in 1970, his first placement in industry. The circle has long been considered the ideal republican form, with every point equidistant from any other point. In this installation, however, the interlocked chairs were placed horizontally: as if a once buoyant circle, or perhaps even an attempt to create a truly public 'sphere', had been grounded. This image of deflated equality contrasted sharply with the next installation: a large, wedge-shaped triangular structure, with an entrance on one side but no exit. One outer wall of this structure was labelled 'monarchical'. Painted royal blue, it faced the defeated chairs. This same royal blue colour covered another large panel that hung askance on one of the gallery walls. The other side of this triangular structure was labelled 'republican' and was constructed out of moveable panels with empty gaps between them. To get inside the structure the visitor passed beneath an oversized steel crown hanging from the ceiling of the gallery. Once inside, you could see hung on the internal side of the 'monarchical' panel a small drawing of the infant Prince George, based on a newspaper image. The future heir to the throne was placed as if gazing outside of his enclosure through the gaps in the republican panel directly opposite, which also resembled prison bars.

This concentration of monarchical and republican references acted to create a field of tension that was as much visual as conceptual. Monarchical references were expressed vertically while republican references occupied space at or below eye level. Barely visible beneath Prince George's enclosure and shoved into gaps in the plywood close to the floor were piles of old clothes, suggesting the detritus upon which monarchical rule is based and a further reference to Brisley's long-standing attention to waste, dirt and ordure, the subject of the *Georgiana Collection* as well as the *Museum of Ordure*, which co-curated the installation. The other walls of the room were given over to expressions of a republican time. On one wall hung a series of black and white photos depicting scenes of destruction and chaos from *Before the Mast*. As we saw in Chapter 1, this was an action in which Brisley attempted and ultimately failed to enact a revolutionary day one. On the wall opposite were hung white notice-boards inviting visitors to record their thoughts, a discreet reference to the Hille Fellowship and Brisley's (also failed) attempt to use notice-boards to instigate a more lateral means of communication, so that workers on the factory floor could communicate with each other without the intercession of management.

Meanwhile the infant heir – a future Hamlet? – looked out towards the next room, which displayed documentation on the *Peterlee Project*, Brisley's pioneering public art project that now exists only as an archive, dispersed among several institutions. The final room of the exhibition contained a lone chair and several large-scale paintings. As we discussed in Chapter 5, this installation, titled *Chair*, was splattered with the same dark, sticky matter as the painting called *Royal Ordure* that hung nearby. The painting's title recast the solitary, empty chair as an ersatz throne, possibly even a shit-smeared, but empty, seat of power. On the wall opposite *Royal Ordure* hung three large-scale paintings, entitled *The Missing Text, Interregnum*. As we also saw in Chapter 1, these paintings were derived from photographs taken by Maya Balcioglu during Brisley's 2010 performance at Peer Gallery in which Brisley – in his persona as R. Y. Sirb, curator of a *Museum of Ordure* – occupied an abandoned shop over a period of ten Republican days, moving around the detritus of failed businesses, while the coalition government in Britain was being formed. In this exhibition, these references to, and images of, increasing disorder were held in check by the suspended oversized crown that presided over the entire installation as its most vertical point. Its presence underscored what was also missing in all these nested references to prior works: the absence of those factory workers no longer employed in British industries that made the Hille Fellowship possible; the loss of a living working-class culture that provided the impetus and concept of the *Peterlee Project*; and last, but hardly least, the sovereign body which appeared to be missing from the oversized crown.

This suspended crown loomed over the entire exhibition. It drew attention to a space not yet occupied by the child prince, who was present in absentia, drawn from media images that represented the future heir to the throne as both child and prince. It also hung over Brisley's works. Under this voided crown, the photos, paintings and installations, all citing or using material from past performances that attempted to reach a revolutionary day one of sorts, appeared as *models* arrested in their design phase, blocked by a future that was never realised. The implication was that in the presence of the crown – and the implied absence of a different, republican future – Brisley's performances had also taken place in a suspended time, constrained to continually remodel traces of a still-born future. But while remodelling is in many ways deficient with respect to an original concept behind a work, it also adds something new to it. Every time a prior work is taken up in a new work, it adds new perspectives on this past. It is worth reiterating in this respect that *State of Denmark* was co-curated by David Thorp and Brisley in the persona of R. Y. Sirb, the curator of a Museum of Ordure. As we saw in Chapter 5, this doubling creates a distance between Brisley the artist, the nominal creator of a work, and Brisley the curator, the one who establishes the frame, the boundary that distinguishes art from what lies outside it. When placed 'en abîme', this narrative doubling opens a vital temporal displacement that, as I will now show, enables the viewer to participate in a kind of analogical reasoning that too can shift the boundary between what lies inside and outside Brisley's performances.

Time extension: analogy and *mise en abîme*

Ever since Gide invented the term, much ink has been spilt trying to understand how visual and narrative *mise en abîme* relate. This discussion need not detain us except to note that Lucien Dällenbach was the first to ask a question that also pertains to Brisley's own practices. How does one connect a visual *mise en abîme*, such as the use of the two-dimensional mirror in paintings, to temporal forms of *mise en abîme*, such as those occurring in narrative fiction? In his pioneering study, Dällenbach suggested that narrative *mise en abîme* – of the type that occurs when the narrator of the story becomes a character in his own story – involves a temporal dislocation that sets up an 'analogy between the situation of the narrator and that of the character'.[14] The narrator stands to his text in the same relation that a fictional character stands to his fictional text. What ties the two together is the recognition of a *shared situation*. A narrator *changes* once he sees himself from the perspective of his persona or fictional character who, crucially, engages in a similar or related sort of activity. This act of recognition maintains what Gide describes as the 'constant connection' between an original context in which something is produced and the work itself.

Now one of the complaints about *mise en abîme* as a device is precisely that it dissolves into analogy.[15] Taking the form of A is to B what C is to D, analogy is often considered a weak form of reasoning, especially when it comes to establishing spurious connections between past and present. I bring this up because, as we have already seen, Brisley often has recourse to analogies in trying to understand what performance art does. I, too, over the course of this book, have made extensive use of analogy. Indeed this book can be partly described as trying to show how analogy can be used constructively, to understand the points of contact between revolutions that happen in the real world (historical revolutions) and attempts to create a revolutionary cut in time in performance art.

But Brisley's extensive doubling and redoubling of his own performances, in visual as well as narrative forms, shows just how thoroughgoing this temporal displacement can be. This capacity of analogy to be more than a simple argument by comparison has been observed by Roselyne Koren.[16] Arguments by comparison, she claims, begin from a reality that has already been tagged, coded or marked out, that is to say, a world that is measured and controlled.[17] A popular example of such an argument is when people claim that the 'global financial crisis of 2008 was *like* the financial crisis during the Weimar republic'. Often, such comparisons tend to reinforce conventional, highly reductive, understandings of both historical periods. They consolidate what we think we already know (using commonplace references that have become truisms) rather than pointing us towards what we do not know.

Analogies, by contrast, go beyond such simple comparisons because they seek to change our understanding of both terms under discussion. In so doing, they stage a confrontation between two distinct heterogeneous situations without necessarily drawing any conclusions. Analogy, understood in this sense, as Koren notes, has a foundational value. It enables us to depart from reality *as it is* to imagine or model what the future *could be*, based on what we know from the past.

This same understanding of analogy as a modelling device pertains to Brisley's own uses of analogy as a means to engage the viewer. It goes without saying that Brisley's analogies are merely suggestive. They are left to others to accept, expand, modify or reject. Nevertheless, his frequent use of the term to explain his own intentions interpolates the viewer in a certain way. What is arguably most original about Brisley's performances is the way they incorporate their own reception, conceived as an ongoing collaborative process of expansion that can be undertaken both by physically present witnesses and by historically distant commentators. The artist provides us with an analogy. We complete the analogy in ways that uncover the latent elements of the work in question, including elements that the artist himself may not have noticed or known about. This completion not only brings the 'outside' into the work; it also puts what is 'inside' the work in contact with what lies outside it, in ways that can open new perspectives on reality as it is lived and experienced outside the world of art. In this sense too, the frequent association of analogy with a kind of popular or degraded history is not without pertinence. Analogy is often dismissed as a device used by those who do not know much history. But when it comes to something as elusive as performance art, most, if not all, people who were not direct witnesses approach this 'history' from a similar position of ignorance. We approach the traces of past performances much like non-experts approach the past, as a potential resource for making a personal connection, which presupposes, at least hypothetically, that a sense of history can be publicly constructed and shared.

Does this mean that anything goes? That I, as a witness or commentator, am free to complete the analogy in any way I choose, no matter how persuasive or far-fetched it might be? In a very general sense, yes, performance (and maybe all art) is open to any kind of interpretation and there is nothing the artist can do about it. However, if we take seriously this understanding of *mise en abîme* as a time-based process created by Brisley himself, then unfolding the analogy requires being attentive to the way the artist's own historical modelling works. For *mise en abîme* refers ultimately to a 'world made, and not *found*.'[18] It offers a key to a constructed past. This constructed past, moreover, remains concrete, tied to particular references that are transformed when placed in relation to one another. When repeated inside a new work, a prior work becomes a model for understanding the subsequent work.

By the same token, the subsequent work provides a new context or frame for understanding the prior work. It too becomes a model in this way.

It is the nature of performance to enable a prior work to be experienced simultaneously as part of a new work. But repetition is also something that takes place serially across time. In a related set of remarks, Giorgio Agamben has suggested that, in its concreteness, analogy overlaps with the ancient Greek understanding of 'paradigm', which, he notes, is 'simply an example, a single case that by its iterability acquires the capacity to model'.[19] It derives from the verb *paradeiknynai*, 'to exhibit, represent', 'show side by side'.[20] Agamben argues that a paradigm makes visible a given situation by showing side by side two examples.[21] But, as is the case with any serial relation, these examples do not remain inert but are transformed by their confrontation. The first (the paradigm, the model) becomes the context or frame for the second (which is then understood to be part of a set).

Keeping these related, if distinct, concepts of nested art, *mise en abîme*, analogy and model, in mind, let us turn now to Brisley's 2014 performance *Breath* that accompanied the *State of Denmark* installation. On Brisley's website, he references Gide's definition of *mise en abîme* in relation to this performance. In these same remarks he draws attention to the two iconic uses of *mise en abîme* also mentioned by Gide: the picture within the mirror depicted in *Las Meninas* by Diego Velázquez and the play-within-the-play staged in Shakespeare's *Hamlet*. Both examples famously use *mise en abîme* to reflect on the nature of sovereign power and what it might mean to escape or resist it. In both cases too, *mise en abîme* is used to reverse the question of who or what is sovereign and who or what is the subject of the work. In keeping with the usual method of this book, I will briefly expand on each one of these references to see how they shed light on the performance itself, which I also happened to witness.

Las Meninas and *Hamlet*

Since the early modern period, it has been the role of art not just to illuminate the symbolic images of power but also misappropriate them. In *Las Meninas*, Velázquez pictured himself at work painting a portrait of his sovereign and patron: King Philip IV and his consort Mariana. The sovereign himself is not represented within the painting. Instead, his presence can be only dimly perceived in the mirror hanging on the wall in the background of the painting. What the painting foregrounds instead is the artist at work, alongside the other people there for the king's amusement as he sits for this portrait: the child infanta, the dwarves and even the dog, all caught in a kind of restless movement. But the person who appears most alive and vital is Velázquez himself, who looks directly at the sovereign, who occupies the same position as the implied viewer of the painting. In an extraordinary feint, then, the painting also addresses the viewing subject, who occupies the same position outside the frame of the painting as the monarch and his consort. In real life, this would not be possible. No one can occupy the sovereign's place at the same time as the sovereign. However, thanks to the strategic use of a second mirror that lies outside the painting, Velázquez can see what the monarch himself sees: namely himself, the artist, in the act of painting the sovereign's portrait.

In a by now classic interpretation of the painting, Michel Foucault elaborates on the importance of this *mise en abîme* for understanding how art itself can be used to reveal what is normally excluded from representation whenever a new culture comes into historical being.[22] Foucault argues that Velázquez' self-portrait is about much more than the artist because it points to what lies outside its frame and makes its representation possible. In this case, this includes both the excluded sovereign, whose gaze organises the entire painting, and the implied viewer, the 'sovereign individual' who is invited to experience the monarch's boredom or delight, his pleasures and displeasures. By drawing attention to what is missing from the representation, Velázquez' painting makes visible what is normally invisible, namely that all art production is also social production, in this case directly answerable to the sovereign gaze, which is also the gaze of the early modern subject.

This question about what it means for an artist to occupy – and displace – the sovereign power runs across the ensemble of Brisley's works. It is evident not only in Brisley's fixation with images of monarchy, but also in his efforts to reveal what is normally excluded from spaces of representation: the unemployed, the political prisoners, the displaced and dispossessed, all those objects and people that occupy analogous 'states of exception'. But whereas Velázquez' self-portrait takes the form of a painting that relies on a double mirror – a reflection of a reflection – Brisley's performances focus on the physical presence of the artist's body as it occupies similar states of exception. In so doing they ask us to ponder a second, related question: how can *mise en abîme* be used to reveal the power of time itself to unravel and destroy images of sovereign power?

This is where the reference to *Hamlet* becomes illuminating, especially when we unpack its own relation to *mise en abîme*. Carl Schmitt has famously argued that the play-within-the-play in *Hamlet* is the moment when events that are normally irreversible suddenly appear endowed with the power to momentarily suspend, and even stop, the flow of time.[23] Schmitt insists that Shakespeare uses this *mise en abîme* not simply as a fictional device, but to express a 'hard core of historical reality' unable to be openly acknowledged in his own time, namely a public anxiety about succession.[24] I want to expand on this interpretation because a similar understanding of *mise en abîme* is relevant to Brisley's own practice, including his references to *Hamlet* and the English experience of an 'interregnum'. It is worth going into some detail, as narrative *mise en abîme* is not commonly discussed in relation to the visual arts, even though re-enactment has become a regular practice in contemporary and performance art.

Key to Schmitt's argument is his assumption that Hamlet is not simply a fictional character but a composite character based partly on the real historical personage of James I, whose mother, Mary Stuart, married the presumed murderer of James' father, just like Hamlet's mother in the play.[25] As Schmitt observes, *Hamlet* was written between 1603 and 1605, just after the coronation of James I. As his mother had been forced to abdicate her right to the throne in favour of her son, this period could still be characterised as an interregnum both politically – as the state of exception between the death of one king and the ascension of another – and in the tragic sense of an ambiguous period when the unburied dead still haunt the living. Significantly, Schmitt claims to have recovered this context not so much via the historical evidence, but through the play's most fictional aspect: the revenge drama that Hamlet summons his mother and her new husband to watch.

We tend to think of plays within plays or stories within stories as 'less real' than the bigger work in which they are nested. Schmitt, however, argues that the repetition and change of scale enabled by the play-within-the-play is not more fictional than *Hamlet* but more real, because it captures the latent context, the unspoken truth around which the play operates. This would have been immediately recognised by the audience because they shared a 'public understanding' that 'the play in the third act of Hamlet is no peep behind the backcloth, but on the contrary, it is the true play itself, replayed in front of the backcloth. It assumes a core of reality, of an extremely powerful present and actuality.'[26] This 'irreversible reality' cannot be expressed directly but takes the form of repetition, a displacement of a taboo. Indeed, for Schmitt only that which is capable of being repeated reflects the true historical content of otherwise ephemeral, and irreversible, historical events.

Schmitt relies heavily on a concept of a shared public space which, he claims, 'sets a permanent limit to the dramatist's freedom of convention'.[27] One could object that this inference of a shared public understanding is unwarranted and therefore a kind of historical fiction. Yet, as is so often the case, claims about what is more 'real' and what is more 'fictive' feed off each other. In *Hamlet*, the play-within-the-play is physically witnessed by both the fictional characters and the real-life audience. Invited to re-enact the position of the fictional audience in the play, Elizabethan-age spectators would have been able to physically experience, unfolding in real time, what could never be directly expressed by words: namely the blush and flight of the king, and the tears of the queen, when faced with the recreation of their actions.

Absent bodies – like the ghost of Hamlet's father – would have been made physically present through other bodies whose reactions and feelings were publicly shared.

Schmitt's reading of *Hamlet* emphasises the importance of the body as a site of public recognition, capable of expressing a latent or haunted past as *presence*. A related emphasis is central to Brisley's performance practice. This is especially obvious in those performances which seek to extend the attempt to make a cut in time over a long duration, resulting in unforeseen and involuntary outcomes. In his work of the 1960s and 1970s, physically demanding actions were extended over periods of several hours, days or weeks, in the attempt to create a cut in time that enabled this exceptional situation to reveal something about the general rules of governance, the recursive structures that underpin all human behaviour. Once such feats of endurance were no longer possible –because of both physical limitations and, more importantly, the failure of a truly public form of art – Brisley focused on a more nuanced understanding of the body as an intermittent presence. Like the ghost of Hamlet's father, this body appears as most present and real in those representations where it is also absent.

Breath

This simultaneous presence and absence of the artist's body as a shared, if not quite public, body is the subject of *Breath*, a performance that stands out for its multiple uses of *mise en abîme* (figure 6.3). Like with *Las Meninas*, the performance presented itself as a kind of self-portrait. Enclosed in the invitation to the private view was *4.35pm 25.12.77/Self-Portrait*, a photo etching of Brisley's skull from 1979, based on an X-ray taken after a car accident (figure 6.4). This *memento mori* depicted a man who, in 1979, was still in his prime and contrasted sharply with the octogenarian artist undertaking the 2014 performance, foreshadowing how self-portraiture – and the intersecting time frames of life and death that it implied – would constitute the subject of the action.

Breath took place in the Royal Academy Schools Life Room, an institution founded in 1768 by a monarch who eventually came to oppose the French Revolution. Brisley entered the room crawling on all fours, his hair wet, face smeared in paint. Throughout the performance, Brisley manipulated various found objects that are normally used as props for life-drawing lessons, notably the *ecorché* horse and the human skeleton. He also wheeled around a large mirror. Sometimes he made marks upon this mirror using his own body and its paint to leave a trace. At other times it was used to multiply the perspectives in the room or even to mirror the viewers' own images back to them. As the performance unfolded, a film based on the performance *Before the Mast*

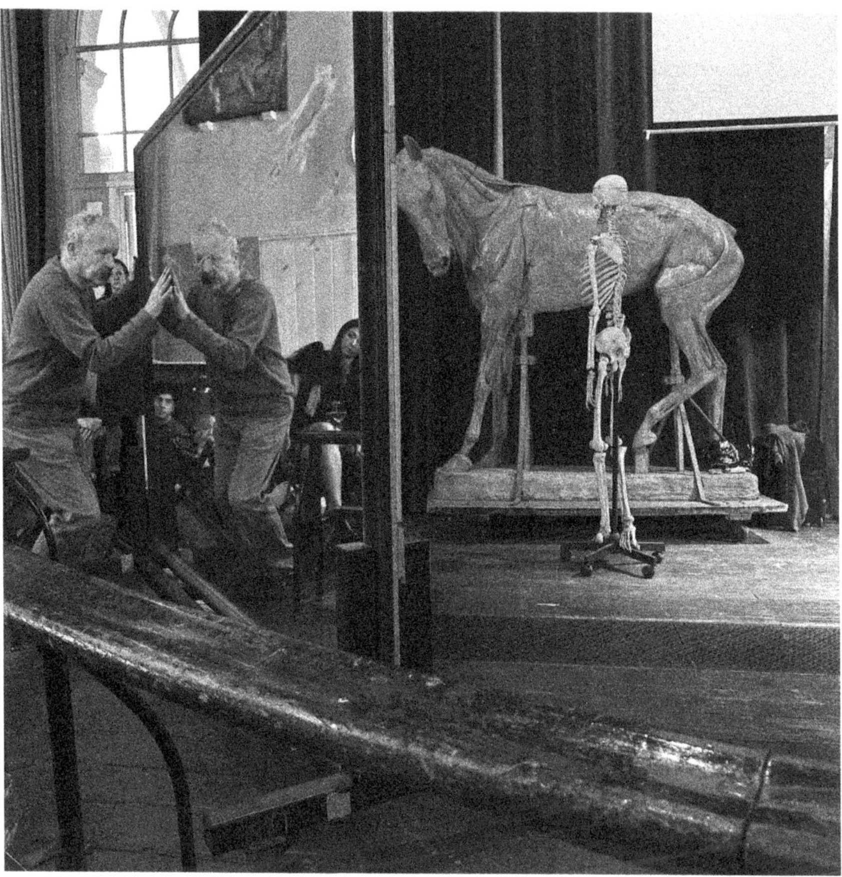

Breath, Royal Academy Life Room, London, 2014   **6.3**

(2013) was also projected into the room. We thus saw the artist duplicated, both in the mirror and in the film, in a kind of continuous *mise en abîme* that prevented any straightforward identification of the artist with a singular space or time. A royal space – which is also the place of elite art education – was thus amplified through a series of projections, all of which aimed to re-enact a Republican time equally experienced by everyone. Yet the film is also shorter and more eventful than the original performance, which, as we saw in Chapter 1, was distended over ten days, and came to reveal the increasingly static, toxic or uncertain qualities of a rupture that remains incomplete. What the audience experienced within *Breath*, therefore, was a new work in a different medium, moreover, one that presented a highly charged and altogether different perspective on the revolutionary situation. What held the two performances together was the repetition of the title, which, as we recall

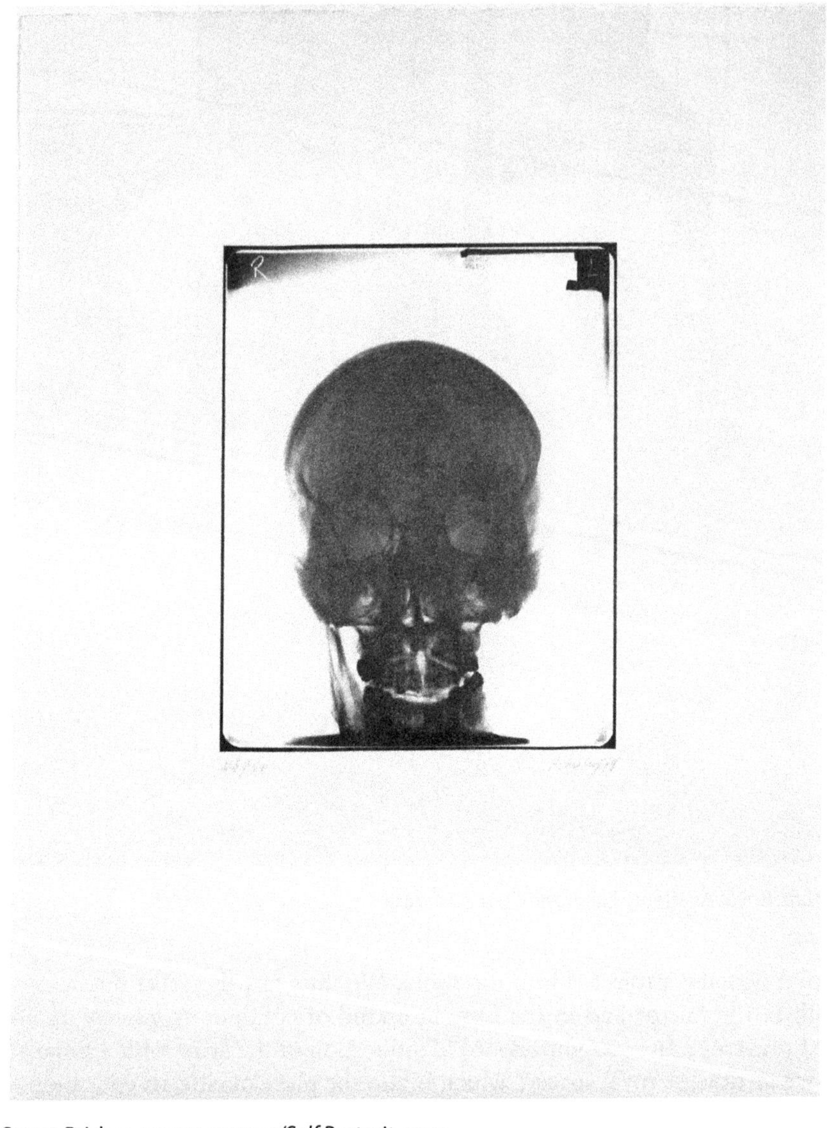

6.4   Stuart Brisley, *4.35pm 25.12.77/Self Portrait*, 1979

from Chapter 1, was itself a kind of nested citation, referring to that part of the ship where the lowest-ranked sailors sleep, those who are most prone to mutiny and revolt. For some members of the public, it may also recall *Two Years before the Mast*, a travel memoir published in 1840 by Richard Dana about his own youthful experiences travelling 'before the mast', formative for his subsequent activism against slavery and on behalf of land reform. In the performance *Breath*, these nested references to resistance, mutiny, revolt and revolution all served to enact 'multiple departures within a departure'.[28] They suggested the persistence of a latent context or even a counter-history of incomplete revolution that runs alongside the sovereign space of the Life Room, where the permanent value of art is continually asserted over and against the transient, living model.

As the performance unfolded, the mirror played an increasingly central role, used both to reflect the artist and to mirror back to the public its own living image. At certain moments in the action, the viewing public saw themselves seeing the action unfold before them, a *mise en abîme* that also operated a *metonoia*, or reversal of perspective. Viewers were offered a glimpse of a collective gaze, a kind of utopia in which the person seeing and the person seen become one and the same. In these moments, the living public reoccupied, as it were, the position of the sovereign gaze, the monarch for whom all art is made, who breathes 'life' into the dead objects (the skeleton, the paints, the *écorché* horse) that make up the Life Room. In Brisley's action, however, this tantalising image of a collective gaze was also withdrawn. We ultimately saw ourselves reflected *as spectators* and not actors, physically seated in an indoor amphitheatre, gazing at a focal point, just like at a theatrical stage. As the artist physically wheeled the mirror around, reflecting only a few people at a time, he drew attention to himself as a mediating figure, someone who was both the subject and object of the action. This underscored just how historically removed any live action was from naïve evocations of a completely participatory art – so influential for the revolutionary tradition and so alien to a contemporary society thoroughly mediated by the image.

The use of a mirror thus testifies both to the presence of the artist's body and its absence. In fact, mirrors have played an important role in Brisley's artistic practice, as he has explored the limitations of drawing and painting. To give just one example, in the mid-1960s, while undertaking 'Visual Research' with his students at Hornsey College of Art, Brisley and his students attempted to capture the likeness of a person rolling between two mirrors, an ultimately impossible task, given that the distinction between the subject and object of the painting was continually blurred.[29] Brisley's early experiments with the double mirror – which is also a kind of moving, perpetual *mise en abîme* – demonstrates how the time factor changes both the object reflected and the object of reflection. What the second mirror reflects is not strictly speaking the first mirror, but a mirror that reflects the second mirror. An external image, thus, has become internal.[30]

Over the course of *Breath*, these two aspects of *mise en abîme* – as a literal mirroring and as a temporal mirroring remediated by dislocation and retrospection – converged to solicit a reflection on the limits of the human body itself and its ability to make a trace. Because the mortal body is never fixed but always changing, it is most 'like itself' at the point where it is most unlike itself, subject to both form and dissolution. This attempt to capture a likeness of the human body at the edge or limit of social recognition has been a leitmotif of Brisley's performance practice. It was expressed in extreme form in *And for today ... nothing* in which the artist juxtaposed his submerged, barely breathing body to rotting flesh. It was also thematised by the abject imprisoned body of *ZL656395C*; the cellophane-covered almost faceless man continually vomiting in *Arbeit Macht Frei*; or indeed in *Beneath Dignity*, in which Brisley presented himself as a Vitruvian man, using his arms and legs to draw an outline of his body within a series of highly confined circles that also attempted to reproduce the cramped physical conditions of the miner. In each of these actions the artist's body was pushed to the limits of form where it tips over into formlessness.

In *Breath*, the artist presents himself as an old man, an aging figure for whom this experience of formlessness has become subjective and personal. Getting down on all fours, still using the body to make a trace, Brisley's performance encouraged the onlooker to reflect on the relation of this and other performances to posterity. The use of the human body to make a trace is, after all, the most primal of acts. As we saw in Chapter 4, the human body also lies at the base of the earliest monuments. Michel Serres has speculated that corpses and mummies were the first statues; while the stele or cippus used to mark the burial mound were the first sculptures.[31] As vertical forms of authority, however, these primitive statues and sculptures also erected the human body as an immobile object over and against a more collective understanding of humanity as expressed through rituals and other forms of behaviour in which the active human body is both subject and object of an action. From this broader, more anthropological perspective, the regressive gestures of *Breath* can be interpreted as enacting a timeless revolt against physical verticality, the outward signs of social hierarchy. What we were offered was a portrait of the artist as an old man, reduced to all fours but still making and communicating his ongoing struggles against authority; which is also a perpetual struggle against the forces of permanence, in the name of art's perpetual capacity to begin anew.

This discussion of the body and its trace may appear far removed from the sophisticated and highly self-conscious use of *mise en abîme* that characterises much of Brisley's later works. Yet the anecdote about the double mirror and the impossibility of drawing the likeness of a person rolling between the two mirrors goes beyond that of art. For it has to do with identifying the gap, the breach in time in which the distinction between subject and object is first made. Formulated in this way, the language of art is also that of power. It is about marking the distinction between a creative or constituent power (the act of creating, founding, assembling in the search of a form) and a constituting power (which draws its legitimacy from already established forms).

Upon leaving, spectators were given a copy of the *Manifesto of Equals*, probably written by the same Sylvain Maréchal whose anti-monarchical and atheistic almanac of 1788 was the prototype of the revolutionary calendar that, as we saw in Chapter 1, has structured several of Brisley's long-durational performances from the 1970s to the 2010s. This manuscript was never published and was presented as evidence of treason in the trial of Gracchus Babeuf and other members of the 'Conspiracy of Equals' in 1796, in what was the first revolution against a revolutionary state. In it Maréchal expressed the dangerous idea that true equality is not a formal or legal notion, but requires a real change in material conditions, including potentially even the destruction of all the arts and culture, to start anew.[32] Without real equality, the manifesto declares, the arts produce nothing but invidious distinctions in which the leisure time of an extreme minority is bought with the sweat of the majority.[33]

By reviving this historical confrontation between monarchical and republican time within the otherwise consecrated space of art, Brisley asked his viewers to engage once more with the question of popular sovereignty. Will expressions of popular sovereignty merely serve as a disruptive energy? Or can they enact a founding power in their own right? Brisley's late works suggest that, for the moment at least, this question can be answered only in the negative. The failure to create a positive situation in Peterlee and elsewhere suggests a vision of performance art that enacts something closer to what Foucault has called a 'heterotopia'. It is an action that creates a real place in society; however, because this place also exists outside the boundaries of time and space as ordinarily perceived, it acts as a 'counter-site', expressive of strategies of evasion and survival in the absence of an actual utopia.[34]

From this perspective, Brisley's repeated invocation of the revolutionary calendar throughout his long career functions as more than a red thread connecting the themes of republicanism, egalitarianism and atheism in his long-durational performances. For it exemplifies the temptation and paradox of all revolutionary beginnings, which is the desire to make a cut in time while remaining situated in time and history. Working only with time and duration as its material, the revolutionary calendar hoped to make a rupture in time so radical that it could only be permanent. Thanks to the calendar's recursive, social time, a fragile, ephemeral, potentially reversible, declaration of a new Year I would become the basis of a new social foundation, a permanent revolution (in the cyclical sense). The boundary between the revolutionary model and life would finally be crossed. Yet, as we all know, the calendar also failed in this attempt. Unable to create a new collective memory, the calendar functioned at best as a missing frame: a projection of a future that never came to pass. To recall Michelet, it is the fate of most revolutions to struggle to be stabilised. Raising no monuments, the revolutionary impulse is made visible in retrospect through the gaps it creates within an architectural order, so many memories of a future that has not come to pass but may still arrive.

One can say something similar about Brisley's performance practice. It emerged in the 1960s as a search for models that could yield a new and different future. Yet, even if these models ultimately failed to cross the threshold separating art from life, they redrew the boundaries of what art – and the language of art – might mean. In the end, there may be no way to transform art into life without the continual intervention of a mediating figure. If this is the case, then revolution, like performance, is an event that lives on only in a perpetual remediation of its traces, which is to say through multiple, and often conflicting, retrospectives. If anything, performance is analogous to revolution on precisely this point, because it too must struggle for a place in historical memory. Recovering the logic of this historical memory has been one of the main challenges of this book. Like revolutions, performances continually exceed their original contexts. Like revolutions too, they are best conceptualised from the perspective of their outcomes, the posterity to which they give rise. This posterity, as I have tried to show, is as much discursive as aesthetic. Events that disappear and leave behind no object or monument can be recollected only so long as they are written and talked about; but with the caveat that they are written and talked about as *events* and not monuments, that is to say, as events open to multiple futures because they contain within them more than one past.

This brings me finally to my own role and motivation in writing this book. While perusing the Tate archive on Stuart Brisley I came across a newspaper clipping that contained an essay published in 1979 by the Hungarian art critic Lázló Beke, in which he provocatively defined the role of the critic as the person 'who tries his hand *in further creating the works of art* he tackles'.[35] Beke observed that, given the tendency of contemporary artists to supply their own critical vocabularies, the only role left for the critic was to expand the work of art by taking 'non-artistic phenomena as the starting point of creative interpretation'. 'In the long run', Beke goes on to note, 'the differences between artistic and non-artistic phenomena are indeed to be eliminated; that is, we must look at things as if they were works of art.[36]. I would like to offer this book as an attempt at such an interpretative expansion. Using the historical record of revolution, I have tried to expand the range of references that could be associated with Brisley's performances. By the same token, I have tried to show how Brisley's performances can be used to reframe our ordinary understanding of revolution as a historical event, revealing those elements of the revolutionary past that remain capable of repetition and re-enactment of some kind. Through conversations with the artist, undertaken from 2013 to 2023, as well as my own impressions of his late performances, I have attempted to write a history of performance art that goes beyond art history.

This double-pronged perspective captures the revolutionary intention of Brisley's performances, which, like everything else, can be constructed only retrospectively, as the expression of a commitment to a certain vision of time and history that must be actively modelled to be revealed. It also captures a goal of this book, which argues for a history of revolution considered not from the viewpoint of historical events and dates, but as forged out of collective behaviours whose faint traces we can recapture through Brisley's own repeated attempts to make a cut in time. My hope was to offer neither a 'dialogue with the dead' nor simply a 'monologue with the living'[37] but, rather, to enable the various pasts – whether those of Brisley's performances or the more distant pasts of revolution – to be re-experienced in the here and now as a permanent overturning of past contexts.

Notes

1 Stuart Brisley, Marc Camille Chaimowicz and Gustav Metzger were the London-based artists who contributed to 3 *Life Situations*, the inaugural exhibit of Gallery House, organised by Sigi Krauss and Rosetta Brooks. See Antony Hudak, Alex Sainsbury, Elizabeth Stanton (eds), 'This Way Out of England: Gallery House in Retrospect', *Newsheet* 1, 9–12 February 2017.

2 Stuart Brisley, 'ZL656395C' (Gallery House, London, 1972), www.stuartbrisley.com (accessed 4 February 2017).

3 For this description see www.stuartbrisley.com/pages/27/70s/Works/Artist_as_Whore/page:11 (accessed 4 February 2017).

4 Maya Balcioglu, 'From the Freezer … Thaw' (installation, Raven Row, London, 2017). www.stuartbrisley.com/pages/36/10s/Works/from_the_freezer____thaw/page:34 (accessed 12 February 2017).

5 Paisley Livingston, 'Nested Art', *The Journal of Aesthetics and Art Criticism*, 61:3 (2003), 233–245, p. 238.

6 Ibid., p. 237.

7 Livingston quotes Jane Heal: 'Indexical Predicates and Their Use', *Mind*, 106:424 (1997), 619–640.

8 Newman, *Stuart Brisley*, p. 32.

9 Livingston, on the other hand, disputes this frequent linkage of nesting art with *mise en abîme*, arguing for a more restricted understanding than I am following here, in which 'a work of art has been *mise en abîme* in another work of art just in case it is at least partially nested there and the two works bear the same title or subtitle' ('Nested Art', p. 240).

10 Moshe Ron, 'The Restricted Abyss: Nine Problems in the Theory of Mise En Abymé', *Poetics Today*, 8:2 (1987), 417–428, p. 437.

11 André Gide, *Journals: 1889–1913: Volume 1 of Journals*, trans. Justin O'Brien (Chicago, IL: University of Illinois Press, 2000), pp. 29–30.

12 Mieke Bal, 'Mise en abyme et iconocité', *Littérature*, 29 (1978), pp. 116–128, p. 120.

13 Bal, 'Mise en abyme et iconocité', p. 119.

14 Lucien Dällenbach, *Le Récit spéculaire: essai sur la mise en abyme* (Paris: Seuil, 1977), p. 30.

15 Brian McHale, 'Cognition en Abyme: Models, Manuals, Maps', *Partial Answers: Journal of Literature and the History of Ideas*, 4:2 (2006), 175–189, p. 176. Also see Ron, 'The Restricted Abyss', p. 426.

16 Roselyne Koren, 'Exemple Historique, Comparison, Analogie, Metaphor: Sont-ils Interchangeables?', *Argumentation & Analyse Du Discours*, 16 (2016), https://doi.org/DOI:10.4000/aad.2123 (accessed 17 May 2017).

17 As Koren explains: 'Ces arguments contribuent à la fondation d'un savoir ou à sa reconfiguration, alors qu'un raisonnement par comparaison est ancré dans un réel déjà balisé et donc dans un savoir avéré permettant non pas de fonder, mais de mesurer l'importance d'un air de famille avec un rigueur quasi-logique.'

18 For this proximity to the model see also McHale, 'Cognition en Abyme', p. 181.

19 Giorgio Agamben, *The Signature of All Things: On Method*, trans. Luca Di Santio and Kevin Attell (New York, NY: Zone Books, 2009), p. 11.

20 The ancient Greek word *paradeigmata* can be found in Greek texts such as Plato's 'Timaeus' and 'Parmenides', where *paradeigmata* is repeatedly used referring to 'models'.

21 Agamben, *The Signature of All Things*, pp. 23–24.

22 Foucault elaborates how this double mirror can be used to reveal everything that 'lies outside the frame' of visibility but nonetheless organises the space of social production. Michel Foucault, *The Order of Things* (London: Routledge, 2002), pp. 3–18.

23 Carl Schmitt, *Hamlet or Hecuba: The Irruption of Time in the Play*, trans. Simona Draghici (Corvallis, OR: Plutarch Press, 1985).

24 Ibid., p. 38.

25 Schmitt also sees in the character of Hamlet, Robert Devereux, the Earl of Essex, a patron of Shakespeare's troupe. This one-time confidante of Queen Elizabeth was executed for treason a few years before the queen's death.

26 Ibid., p. 38.

27 Ibid., p. 31.

28 Livingston's term; see 'Nested Art', p. 243.

29 '[W]e were required to use a model so one of the things I did was to have two mirrors put on opposite sides and the model would roll slowly towards one mirror and back making it impossible [to draw]; It's like a way of trying to come to terms with an impossible reality, how to deal with that in a visual sense.' Brisley, National Life Stories, C466/43/07 F5279A, p. 140.

30 As the philosopher Iddo Dickmann has observed, in its mirroring capacity, *mise en abîme* includes an element of temporal dislocation that 'always reconstitutes the (accumulative) chain of circuits to which it was added'. Iddo Dickmann, 'Using Mise en Abyme to Differentiate Deleuze and Derrida', *Journal of the British Society for Phenomenology*, 48:1 (2017), 63–80, p. 78. I thank Michael Newman for this reference.

31 Michel Serres, *Statues: The Second Book of Foundations*, trans. Randolph Burks (London: Bloomsbury Academic, 2015), pp. 91–92, 188–189. Also in Michel Serres, *L'hermaphrodite: Sarrasine Sculpteur* (Paris: Flammarion, 1987), pp. 21–23.

32 Sylvain Maréchal, 'Manifeste des Egaux' (1796) in Philippe Buonarroti, *Conspiration pour l'Égalité dite de Babeuf*, ed. Jean-Marc Schiappa, Jean-Numa Decange, Alain Maillard and Stéphanie Roza (Paris: Éditions la ville brûle, 2014), pp. 313–317, p. 314.

33 Ibid., p. 315. I discuss this Manifesto in Perovic, *The Calendar in Revolutionary France*, pp. 193–197.

34 Foucault discusses this concept of heterotopia in several places. See the radio lecture *Les Hétérotopies*, France-Culture, 7 December 1966; 'Des Espaces Autres' (March 1967 lecture), translated as Michel Foucault and Jay Miskowiec, 'Of Other Spaces', *Diacritics*, 16:1 (1986), 22–27. https://doi.org/10.2307/464648 (accessed 2 August 2017.

35 László Beke, 'Towards a Voluntaristic Criticism', *Art Monthly*, 3:26 (1979), 2–5, p. 3.

36 Ibid., p. 5.

37 I borrow this felicitous turn of phrase from Mark Hewitson in Emmanuel Akyeampong, Caroline Arni, Pamela Kyle Crossley, Mark Hewitson, and William H. Sewell, 'AHR Conversation: Explaining Historical Change; or, The Lost History of Causes', *The American Historical Review*, 120:4 (2015), 1368–1423, p. 1416, https://doi.org/10.1093/ahr/120.4.1369 (accessed 6 November 2017).

Select bibliography

Adorno, Theodor W., *Prisms*, trans. Samuel and Shierry Weber (Cambridge, MA: MIT Press, 1981), pp. 17–34.

Agamben, Giorgio, *Homo Sacer: Sovereign Power and Bare Life*, trans. Daniel Heller-Roazen (Stanford, CA: Stanford University Press, 1998).

——, *Stasis: Civil War as a Political Paradigm*, trans. Nicholas Heron (Stanford, CA: Stanford University Press, 2015).

——, *The Signature of All Things: On Method*, trans. Luca Di Santio and Kevin Attell (New York, NY: Zone Books, 2009).

Agnew, Vanessa and Jonathan Lamb (eds), *Extreme and Sentimental History*, Special Issue, *Criticism*, 46:3 (2004).

Ahlskog, Jonas, 'Michael Oakeshott and Hayden White on the Practical and the Historical Past', in *Rethinking History: The Journal of Theory and Practice* 203 (2016), 375–394. https://doi.org/DOI:10.1080 (accessed 2 August 2021).

Allan, John, 'Lubetkin and Peterlee', in Thomas Deckker (ed.), *Modern City Revisited* (London: Taylor & Francis, 2000), pp. 103–124.

Althusser, Louis, Étienne Balibar, Roger Establet, Jacques Rancière and Pierre Macherey, *Reading Capital*, trans. Brewster Ben and David Fernbach (Paris/London: Maspero François, New Left Books, 1965).

Archer, Michael, 'Neither One Thing nor the Other', in *Stuart Brisley: Georgiana Collection* (Glasgow: Third Eye Centre, 1986), pp. 5–26.

'Architects, Sculptors and Monuments', *Manchester Guardian*, 19 August 1916.

Armitage, David and Jo Guldi, *The History Manifesto* (Cambridge: Cambridge University Press, 2014).

Artist Placement Group and Stuart Brisley. Tate Archive. TGA 20042.

Assmann, Aleida, 'Beyond the Archive', in Brian Neville and Johanne Villeneuve (eds), *Waste-Site Stories: The Recycling of Memory* (Albany, NY: State University of New York Press, 2002), pp. 71–82.

——, *Cultural Memory and Western Civilization: Functions, Media, Archives* (Cambridge, NY: Cambridge University Press, 2011).

Assmann, Jan, 'Collective Memory and Cultural Identity', trans. John Czaplicka. *New German Critique*, 65 (1995), 125–133.

Assoun, Paul-Laurent, *Tuer le mort: Le désir révolutionnaire* (Paris: Presses Universitaires de France, 2015).

Augé, Marc, *The Future*, trans. John Howe (London: Verso Books, 2015).

Auslander, Philip, *Liveness: Performance in a Mediatized Culture* (London: Routledge, 1999).

——, *Reactivations: Essays on Performance and Its Documentation* (Ann Arbor, MI: University of Michigan Press, 2018).

——, 'The Performativity of Performance Documentation', *PAJ: A Journal of Performance and Art*, 28:3 (2006), 1–10.

Badiou, Alain, *Being and Event*, trans. Oliver Feltham (London: Continuum, 2005).

——, *Handbook of Inaesthetics*, trans. Alberto Toscano (Stanford, CA: Stanford University Press, 2004).

——, Steve Corcoran and Bruno Bosteels, 'Logic of the Site', *Diacritics*, 33:3/4 (2003), 141–150.

Bagcioglu, Neylan, 'Delegating (Community) Action: Stuart Brisley's Peterlee Project', *Stedelijk Studies*, 3 (2016), 1–14.

Bal, Mieke, 'Mise en abyme et iconocité', *Littérature*, 29 (1978), 116–128.

Barber, Stephen, *Performance Projections: Film and the Body in Action* (London: Reaktion Books, 2014).

Barère de Vieuzac, Bertrand, *Rapport fait au nom du comité de salut public, le premier aout 1973, l'an II de la règublique française* (Paris: de l'Impr. Nationale, 1973).

Bataille, Georges, 'Architecture', *Documents* 2 (Paris: 1929), p. 117.

——, 'Museum: Writings on Laughter, Sacrifice, Nietzsche, Un-Knowing', trans. Annette Michelson, *October*, 36:102 (1986), 24–25. https://doi.org/DOI:10.2307/778543 (accessed 4 January 2017).

——, *Oeuvres complètes de Georges Bataille I, Premiers écrits (1922–1940)* (Paris: Gallimard, 1970).

Bauman, Zygmunt, *44 Letters From the Liquid Modern World* (Cambridge: Polity Press, 2010).

Beke, László, 'Towards a Voluntaristic Criticism', *Art Monthly*, 3:26 (1979), 2–5.

Best, Janice, 'Une Statue Monumentale de La République', *Nineteenth-Century French Studies*, 34:3/4 (2006), 303–322.

Bishop, Claire, *Artificial Hells: Participatory Art and the Politics of Spectatorship* (London: Verso, 2012).

Bleeker, Maaike, Adrian Kear and Heike Roms (eds), *Thinking Through Theatre and Performance* (New York, NY: Bloomsbury, 2019).

Blocker, Jane, *Becoming Past: History in Contemporary Art* (Minneapolis, MN: University of Minnesota Press, 2015).

Boltanski, Luc and Eve Chiapello, *The New Spirit of Capitalism*, trans. Gregory Elliott (London: Verso Books, 2007).

Bonney, Norman, 'The Cenotaph: A consensual and contested monument of remembrance'. www.secularism.org.uk/uploads/cenotaph-a-consensual-and-contested-monument-of-remembrance.pdf (accessed 13 August 2018).

Borgreen, Gunhild and Rune Gade (eds), *Performing Archives/Archives of Performance* (Copenhagen: Museum Tusculanum Press, 2013).

Boullée, Étienne-Louis, 'Architecture, Essay on Art', in Helen Rosenau (ed.), *Boullée and Visionary Architecture: Including Boullée's Architecture, Essay on Art* (London: Academy Editions, 1976), pp. 82–116.

Braudel, Fernand, 'History and the Social Sciences: The Long Duration', *American Behavioral Scientist*, 3:6 (1960), 3–13. https://doi.org/DOI:10.1177 (accessed 17 April 2014).

Bredekamp, Horst, *Image Acts: A Systematic Approach to Visual Agency*, trans. Elizabeth Clegg (Berlin: De Gruyter, 2017).

Brennan, Tim, 'Of Commune and Community', in Stuart Brisley, *The Peterlee Project 1976–1977* (Aarhus: Antipyrine with the Museum of Ordure, 2014), pp. 131–136.

Brisley, Stuart, *12 Days* (London: domobaal/Mummery +Schnelle, 2013).

——, 'Anti Performance Art' (1975), in *Inglese Arte Oggi Milano, Palazzo Reale, Febbraio-Maggio 1976*, 2 vols. (Milano: Electa, 1976), pp. 416–417.

——, *Beyond Reason: Ordure* (London: Book Works, 2003).

——, *Hille Fellowship Poly Wheel* (London: domobaal/Mummery +Schnelle, 2013).

——, *Homage to the Commune* (London: domobaal/Mummery +Schnelle, 2013).

——, National Life Stories: Artists' Lives. Interview by Melanie Roberts (1996), The British Library.

——, *Next Door (the missing text)* (London: domobaal/Mummery +Schnelle, 2013).

——, 'No, It Is Not On', *Studio International*, 1972.

——, 'Stuart Brisley: Arbeit Macht Frei in Conversation with Catherine Wood', curator, Tate Audio, 7 October 2011, www.tate.org.uk/search?type=media&q=Stuart+Brisley (accessed 10 January 2015).

——, *Stuart Brisley, The Peterlee Project 1976–1977* (Aarhus: Antipyrine with the Museum of Ordure, 2014).

——, Tate Archive. TGA 201114.

——, 'The Photographer and the Performer', in Alice Maude-Roxby (ed.), *Live Art on Camera: Performance and Photography* (Southampton, UK: John Hansard Gallery, 2007), pp. 83–88.

——, website: www.stuartbrisley.com.

——, and Gilane Tawadros, *The Stuart Brisley Interviews: The Art of Performance and Its After-Lives* (London: DACS/Book Works, 2020).

——, and Maya Balcioglu, *The Cenotaph Project 1987–1991* (Derry, Londonderry: Orchard Gallery, 1991).

——, Jem Finer, Maya Balcioglu and Francesca Hughes, in V. Honoré and M. Ribadaneira (eds), *Drawing Room Confessions: Stuart Brisley* (London: Mousse Publishing, 2017).

——, Sanja Perovic and Tony White, *Before the Mast: Into Day One of the Revolutionary Period: A Conversation* (London: domobaal/Mummery +Schnelle, 2013).

——, Sanja Perovic and Tony White, Unpublished conversation (2013).

Brothman, Brien, 'Orders of Value: Probing the Theoretical Terms of Archival Practice', *Archivaria*, 32 (1991), https://archivaria.ca/index.php/archivaria/article/view/11761 (accessed 26 October 2016).

Bryzgel, Amy, *Performance art in Eastern Europe since 1960* (Manchester: Manchester University Press, 2017).

Bushaway, Robert, 'Name upon Name: The Great War and Remembrance', in Roy Porter (ed.), *Myths of the English* (Cambridge, UK: Polity Press, 1993), pp. 136–167.

Canning, Charlotte, and Thomas Postlewait (eds), *Representing the Past: Essays in Performance Historiography* (Iowa City, IA: University of Iowa Press, 2010).

Castoriadis, Cornelius, 'Time and Creation', in John B. Bender and David E. Wellbery (eds), *Chronotypes: The Construction of Time* (Stanford, CA: Stanford University Press), pp. 38–64.

'Cenotaph, Whitehall: Erection of Permanent Cenotaph'. The National Archives' Catalogue, 1932 1919. Work 20/139. The National Archives, Kew.

Chilvers, Ian and John Glaves-Smith, *Dictionary of Modern and Contemporary Art* (Oxford: Oxford University Press, 2009).

Clark, Timothy James, 'Painting in the Year Two', *Representations*, 47 (Summer 1994), 13–63.

Clarke, C. W., 'Farewell Squalor', 1946. Tate Gallery Archive. TGA 201114/4/19.

Cornish, Helen, 'Not All Singing and Dancing: Padstow, Folk Festivals and Belonging', *Journal of Anthropology*, 814 (2016), 631–647. https://doi.org/DOI:10.1080/001418 44.2014.989871 (accessed 2 May 2022).

Cox, Geoffrey, 'The Object of Corruption', in Julie Bacon (ed.), *The Suicide of Objects* (Belfast: Catalyst Arts, 2004).

Crinson, Marc, 'The Incidental Collection: Stuart Brisley's Peterlee Project', *Mute* 1:28 (2004), www.metamute.org/editorial/articles/incidental-collection-stuart-brisleys-peterlee-project (accessed 3 April 2018).

Crompton, Andrew, 'The Secret of the Cenotaph', *AA Files*, 34 (1997), 64–67.

Curtis, Penelope, 'The Cenotaph, Whitehall', in Stuart Brisley and Maya Balcioglu, *The Cenotaph Project (1987–1991)* (Derry, Londonderry: Orchard Gallery, 1991).

Cutler, Ian, *Cynicism from Diogenes to Dilbert* (London: McFarland & Co, 2005).

Dällenbach, Lucien, *Le Récit spéculaire : essai sur la mise en abyme* (Paris: Seuil, 1977).

De Groot, Jerome, *Consuming History: Historians and Heritage in Contemporary Popular Culture* (Abingdon: Routledge, 2008).

Derrida, Jacques, *Specters of Marx: The State of the Debt, the Work of Mourning, and the New International*, trans. Peggy Kamuf (Abingdon, UK: Routledge, 1994).

D'Heilly, Georges, *Extraction des cercueils royaux à Saint-Denis en 1793: relation authentique* (Paris: Jouaoust et Roquette, 1866).

Dickmann, Iddo, 'Using Mise En Abyme to Differentiate Deleuze and Derrida', *Journal of the British Society for Phenomenology*, 48:1 (2017), 63–80. DOI: 10.1080/00071773.2016.1217664 (accessed 2 November 2017).

Didi-Huberman, Georges, trans. Shane B. Lillis, *Images in Spite of All: Four Photographs from Auschwitz* (Chicago, IL: University of Chicago Press, 2012).

——, trans. Lia Swope Mitchell, *Survival of the Fireflies* (Minnesota, MN: University of Minnesota Press, 2018).

——, trans. Harvey Mendelsohn, *The Surviving Image: Phantoms of Time and Time of Phantoms: Aby Warburg's History of Art* (State College, PA: Penn State University, 2016).

Dimock, Wai Chee, 'A Theory of Resonance', *PMLA*, 112:5 (1997), 1060–1071. https://doi.org/10.2307/463483 (accessed 18 December 2015).

Doderet, Thomas, *Catéchisme de toutes les religions en abrégé, dédie au cercle constitu-tionnel de la commune de Langres* (Chaumont: chez le citoyen Cousot, 1798).

Dolivier, Pierre, *Essai sur les funérailles* (Versailles: Chez Jacob, Libraire-Imprimeur de École Centrale de Seine et Oise, 1801).

Douglas, Mary, *Purity and Danger: An Analysis of the Concepts of Pollution and Taboo* (London: Routledge, 1966).

Elster, Jon (ed.), *Karl Max: A Reader* (New York: Cambridge University Press, 1986).

Enstice, Wayne, 'Performance Art's Coming of Age', in Gregory Battcock and Robert Nicklas (eds) *The Art of Performance: A Critical Anthology* (New York: E. P. Dutton, 1984), pp. 80–87.

Enwezor, Okwui, *Archive Fever: Uses of the Document in Contemporary Photography* (Göttingen: Steidl, 2008).

Ericson, Staffan, 'The Lecture Room (1962) – On Dark Rooms, Antennas, and the Synchronization of Education'. Presented at the Centre for Advanced Studies (CAS), Oslo, 2018. www.diva-portal.org/smash/get/diva2:1307041/FULLTEXT01.pdf (accessed 3 September 2020).

Etlin, Richard, *Symbolic Space: French Enlightenment Architecture and Its Legacy* (Chicago, IL: University of Chicago Press, 1995).

Felski, Rita, 'Context Stinks', *New Literary History*, 42:4 (2011), 573–91. https://doi.org/10.1353/nlh.2011.0045 (accessed 18 December 2015).

Fischer-Lichte, Erika, *The Transformative Power of Performance*, trans. Saskya Iris Jain (London and New York: Routledge; Taylor & Francis Group, 2008).

Flynn, Brendan, 'Stuart Brisley as a Performance Artist', Master's thesis. Tate Archive, 1974. TGA 201114/3/5/10.

Foreign and Commonwealth Office, FCO File reference 291/4; FCO 34/342.

Forster, Kurt W. and David Britt, 'Aby Warburg: His Study of Ritual and Art on Two Continents', *October*, 77 (1996), 5–24. https://doi.org/10.2307/778958 (accessed 28 June 2022).

Foster, Hal, 'An Archival Impulse', *October*, 110 (2004), 3–22. DOI: 10.1162/0162287042379847.

Foucault, Michel, *The Order of Things* (London: Routledge, 2002).

——, and Jay Miskowiec, 'Of Other Spaces', *Diacritics*, 16:1 (1986), 22–27. https://doi.org/10.2307/464648 (accessed 2 August 2017).

Freud, Sigmund, 'The Interpretation of Dreams', in *The Complete Psychological Works of Sigmund Freud*, vol V (1900–1) (London: Hogarth Press and the Institute of Psycho-analysis, 1953).

Friedl, Peter, 'The Impossible Museum', *E-Flux Journal*, 23 (2011), www.e-flux.com/journal/23/67778/the-impossible-museum/ (accessed 20 July 2017).

Furet, François, *Interpreting the French Revolution*, trans. Elborg Forster (Cambridge: Cambridge University Press, 1981).

——, *The Passing of an Illusion: The Idea of Communism in the Twentieth Century*, trans. Deborah Furet (Chicago, IL: University of Chicago Press, 2000).

Gamboni, Dario, *The Destruction of Art: Iconoclasm and Vandalism since the French Revolution.* (London: Reaktion Books, 1997).

Gee, Gabriel, 'From Stone to Flesh: The Deconstruction and Reconstruction of the British Monument', in Catherine Lanone et al. (eds), *Monument et Modernité: dans l'art et la littérature britaniques et américains* (Paris: Press Sorbonne Nouvelle, 2015), pp. 289–301. http://books.openedition.org/psn/7355> (accessed 1 June 2022).

Giannachi, Gabriella, and Jonah Westerman (eds), *Histories of Performance Documentation: Museum, Artistic, and Scholarly Practices* (Abingdon: Routledge, 2017).

Giannachi, Gabriella, Nick Kaye and Michael Shanks (eds), *Archaeologies of Presence: Art, Performance and the Persistence of Being* (Abingdon: Routledge, 2012).

Gide, André, *Journals of André Gide, Volume I: 1889–1913*, trans. Justin O'Brien (Chicago, IL: University of Illinois Press, 2000).

Ginzburg, Carlo, *Threads and Traces: True False Fictive*, trans. Anne C. Tedeschi and John Tedeschi (Berkeley, CA: University of California Press, 2012).

Gorsen, Peter, 'The Return of Existentialism in Performance Art', in Gregory Battcock and Robert Nicklas (eds), *The Art of Performance: A Critical Anthology* (New York: E. P. Dutton, 1984), pp. 76–79.

Gough, Paul and Sally J. Morgan, 'A Faux Cenotaph: Guerilla Interventions and the Contestation of Rhetorical Public Space', *Journal of War and Culture Studies*, 6:1 (2013), 92–108. DOI:10.1179/1752627212Z.000000007.

Gramsci, Antonio, *Selections from the Prison Notebooks of Antonio Gramsci*, trans. and ed. Quintin Hoare and Geoffrey Nowell-Smith (London: Lawrence and Wishart, 1971).

Greenberg, Allan, 'Lutyens's Cenotaph', *Journal of the Society of Architectural Historians*, 48:1 (1989), 5–23. DOI:10.2307/990403.

Grégoire, Henri Jean-Baptiste, *Mémoires*, ed. Hippolyte Carnot (Paris: Ambroise Dupont, 1837).

——, *Rapport sur les destructions opérées par le Vandalisme, et sur les moyens de le réprimer. Par Grégoire, séance du 14 Fructidor, l'an second de la République une et indivisible, suivi du Décret de la Convention nationale* (Paris: de l'Impr. Nationale, 1794).

Groys, Boris, *Art Power* (Cambridge, MA: Massachusetts Institute of Technology Press, 2008).

——, 'On Art Activism', *E-Flux Journal*, 56 (June 2014), www.e-flux.com/journal/56/60343/on-art-activism/ (accessed 30 June 2014).

Guilhamou, Jacques, *La Mort de Marat, 1973* (Brussels: Éditions Complexe, 1989).

Guldi, Jo and David Armitage, *The History Manifesto* (Cambridge: Cambridge University Press, 2014).

Gumbrecht, Hans Ulrich, *After 1945: Latency as Origin of the Present* (Stanford, CA: Stanford University Press, 2013).

——, *Atmosphere, Mood, Stimmung*, trans. Erik Butler (Stanford, CA: Stanford University Press, 2012).

——, 'How (If at All) Can We Encounter What Remains Latent in Texts?', *Partial Answers: Journal of Literature and the History of Ideas*, 7:1 (2009), 87–96.

——, *In 1926: Living at the Edge of Time* (Cambridge, MA: Harvard University Press, 1997).

——, *Our Broad Present: Time and Contemporary Culture* (New York: Columbia University Press, 2014).

Habermas, Jürgen, *The Structural Transformation of the Public Sphere: An Inquiry into a Category of Bourgeois Society*, trans. Thomas Burger and Frederick Lawrence (Cambridge, MA: Massachusetts Institute of Technology Press, 1962).

Halbwachs, Maurice, *On Collective Memory*, trans. Lewis A. Coser (Chicago, IL: University of Chicago Press, 1992).

Harrison, Robert Pogue, *The Dominion of the Dead* (Chicago, IL: University of Chicago Press, 2004).

Hartog, François, *Regimes of Historicity: Presentism and Experiences of Time*, trans. Saskia Brown (New York: Columbia University Press, 2015).

Hauser, Susanne, 'Waste into Heritage: Remarks on Materials in the Arts, on Memories and the Museum', in Brian Neville and Johanne Villeneuve (eds), *Waste-Site Stories: The Recycling of Memory* (Albany, NY: State University of New York Press, 2002), pp. 39–54.

Heal, Jane, 'Indexical Predicates and Their Uses', *Mind*, 106:424 (1997), 619–640.

Hershman, Lynn and Michael Shanks, 'Here and Now', in *Archaeologies of Presence: Art, Performance and the Persistence of Being* (Abingdon, UK: Routledge, 2012), pp. 225–234.

Hewitson, Mark, in Emmanuel Akyeampong, Caroline Arni, Pamela Kyle Crossley, Mark Hewitson, and William H. Sewell, 'AHR Conversation: Explaining Historical Change; or, The Lost History of Causes', *The American Historical Review*, 120:4, (2015), 1368–1423, https://doi.org/10.1093/ahr/120.4.1369 (accessed 6 November 2017).

Hollier, Denis, *Against Architecture: The Writings of Georges Bataille*, trans. Betsy Wing (Cambridge, MA: The Massachusetts Institute of Technology Press, [1989] 1992).

Hollings, Ken, 'Stuart Brisley', *Performance Magazine: The Review of Live Art*, 24 (June/July 1983), 27.

Hudak, Antony, Alex Sainsbury and Elizabeth Stanton (eds), 'This Way Out of England: Gallery House in Retrospect', *Newsheet* 1, 9–12 February 2017.

Hunt, Ronald, 'Introduction', in *Transform the World! Poetry Must Be Made by All!* Modern Museet Stockholm, 15 November–21 December 1969, exhibition catalogue.

Huyssen, Andreas, *Twilight Memories: Making Time in a Culture of Amnesia* (Abingdon: Routledge, 1994).

Jay, Martin, 'Historical Explanation and the Event: Reflections on the Limits of Contextualization', *New Literary History*, 42:4 (2011), 557–571.

Jeffery, Keith, 'The British Army and Internal Security 1919–1939', *The Historical Journal*, 24:2 (1981), 377–397. DOI: 10.1017/S0018246X00005525.

——, *The British Army and the Crisis of Empire* (Manchester: Manchester University Press, 1984).

Jones, Amelia, *Body Art/Performing the Subject* (Minneapolis, MN: University of Minnesota Press, 1998).

——, '"Presence" in Absentia: Experiencing Performance as Documentation', *Art Journal*, 56:4 (1997), 11–18. https://doi.org/10.1080/00043249.1997.10791844 (accessed 15 March 2021).

——, and Adrian Heathfield (eds), *Perform, Repeat, Record: Live Art in History* (Bristol, UK: Intellect Ltd, 2012).

Jones, Sarah, Daisy Abbott and Seamus Ross, 'Redefining the Performing Arts Archive', *Archival Science*, 8:3 (2009), 165–171.

Jordheim, Helge, 'Against Periodization: On Koselleck's Theory of Multiple Temporalities', *History and Theory: Studies in the Philosophy of History*, 51:2 (2012), 151–171. https://doi.org/10.1111/j.1468–2303.2012.00619.x (accessed 2 August 2014).

Journal historique fait par le citoyen Druon, ci-devant bénédictin de la ci-devant abbaye de Saint-Denis, lors des extractions des cercueils de plomb des Rois, Reines, Princes et Princesses, abbés et autres personnes qui avaient leurs sépultures dans l'église de Saint-Denis, Archives Nationales, AE1/15/12 A.

Kalela, Jorma, *Making History: The Historian and the Uses of the Past* (New York, NY: Springer, 2011).

Kalyvas, Andreas, 'Constituent Power', in J. M. Bernstein (ed.), *Political Concepts* (New York, NY: Fordham University Press, 2018), pp. 87–117.

Kaprow, Allan, 'The Legacy of Jackson Pollock (1958)', in Jeff Kelley (ed.), *Essays on the Blurring of Art and Life* (Berkeley: University of California Press, 2003), pp. 1–9.

Kaufmann, Emil, *Three Revolutionary Architects: Boullee, Ledoux, and Lequeu* (Philadelphia, PA: American Philosophical Society, 1952).

Kaye, Nick, *Art into Theatre: Performance Interviews and Documents* (London: Harwood Academic Publishers, 1996).

——, *Multi-Media: Video – Installation – Performance* (Abingdon: Routledge, 2007).

Kedward, Roderick, *Occupied France: Collaboration and Resistance 1940–1944* (Oxford: Wiley-Blackwell, 1991).

——, 'Resiting French Resistance', *Transactions of the Royal Historical Society*, 9 (1999), 271–282. https://doi.org/DOI:10.2307/3679404 (accessed 20 May 2022).

Kemp-Welch, Klara, *Networking the Bloc: Experimental Art in Eastern Europe 1965–1981* (Cambridge, MA: Massachusetts Institute of Technology Press, 2019).

Kendall, Walter, *The Revolutionary Movement in Britain 1900–21: The Origins of British Communism* (Manchester: Manchester University Press, 1969).

Kersaint, Armand-Guy, *Discours sur les monuments publics: prononcé au Conseil du Département de Paris, le 15 décembre 1791* (Paris: De l'Imprimerie de P. Didot L'Aîné, 1792).

King, Alex, *Memorials of the Great War in Britain: The Symbolism and Politics of Remembrance* (Oxford: Berg, 1998).

Kirkpatrick, Elizabeth McLaren and Catherine M. Schwarz (eds), *Chambers 20th Century Dictionary* (Edinburgh: Chambers, 1987).

Koren, Roselyne, 'Exemple Historique, Comparison, Analogie, Métaphore: Sont-ils Interchangeables?', *Argumentation & Analyse du Discours*, 16 (2016). https://doi.org/DOI:10.4000/aad.2123 (accessed 17 May 2017).

Koselleck, Reinhart, 'Histories in the Plural and the Theory of History: An Interview with Carsten Dutt', in *Sediments of Time: On Possible Histories*, trans. Sean Franzel and Stefan-Ludwig Hoffman (Stanford, CA: Stanford University Press, 2018), pp. 250–254.

——, 'War Memorials: Identity of the Survivors', trans. Todd Presner, Kerstin Behnke and Jobst Welge, *The Practice of Conceptual History: Timing History, Spacing Concepts* (Stanford, CA: Stanford University Press, 2002), pp. 285–326.

La Barre, Weston, *The Ghost Dance: The Origins of Religion* (New York, NY: Doubleday, 1970).

Laporte, Dominique, *History of Shit*, trans. Nadia Benabid and Rodolphe El-Khoury (Cambridge, MA: The MIT Press, 1993).

Laqueur, Thomas, *The Work of the Dead: A Cultural History of Mortal Remains* (Princeton, NJ: Princeton University Press, 2015).

Legacey, Erin-Marie, *Making Space for the Dead: Catacombs, Cemeteries and the Reimagining of Paris, 1780–1830* (Ithaca, NY: Cornell University Press, 2019).

Lenoir, Alexandre, *Journal historique de l'extraction des cercueils de plomb des rois, reines, princes, princesses, abbés et autres personnes qui avaient leurs sépultures dans l'église de l'abbaye royale de Saint-Denis en France du 12 octobre 1793 au 12 novembre 1793 et un supplément de quelques lignes pour la journée du 18 janvier 1794*, Archives nationales AE/1/15/12 B.

——, 'Notes historiques sur les exhumations faites en 1793, dans l'abbaye de saint-denis', in *Description historique et chronologique des monumens de sculpture, réunis au musée des monuments français par Alexandre Lenoir* (Paris: An X de la République), pp. 338–356.

Livingston, Paisley, 'Nested Art', *The Journal of Aesthetics and Art Criticism*, 61:3 (2003), 233–245.

Loraux, Nicole, *The Divided City: On Memory and Forgetting in Ancient Athens*, trans. Corinne Pache and Jeff Fort (New York, NY: Zone Books, 2002).

Lorenz, Chris and Berber Bevernage (eds), *Breaking Up Time: Negotiating the Borders Between Present, Past and Future* (Göttingen: Vandenhoeck & Ruprecht, 2013).

Lorenz, Chris and Marek Tamm, 'Who Knows Where the Time Goes?' *Rethinking History: The Journal of Theory and Practice*, 18:4 (2014), 499–521. https://doi.org/10.1080/13642529.2014.893664 (accessed 5 January 2016).

Lynton, Norbert, *Tatlin's Tower: Monument to Revolution* (New Haven, CT: Yale University Press, 2009).

Manoff, Marlene, 'Theories of the Archive from across the Disciplines', *Libraries and the Academy*, 4:1 (2004), 9–25.

Maréchal, Sylvain, 'Manifeste des Egaux' (1796) in Philippe Buonarroti, *Conspiration pour l'Égalité dite de Babeuf*, ed. Jean-Marc Schiappa, Jean-Numa Decange, Alain Maillard and Stéphanie Roza (Paris: Éditions la ville brûle, 2014), pp. 313–317.

Mavidal, Jérôme and Émile Laurent (eds), *Archives Parlementaires de 1787 à 1860: Recueil complet des débats législatifs et politiques des chambres françaises imprimé par ordre du Sénat et de la Chambre des deputes sous la direction de J. Mavidal et E. Laurent*, series 1, 1787–99, vols 48 and 70 (Paris: Dupont, 1896).

McClellan, Andrew, *Inventing the Louvre: Art, Politics, and the Origins of the Modern Museum in Eighteenth-Century Paris* (Berkeley, CA: University of California Press, 1999).

——, 'Musée Du Louvre, Paris: Palace of the People, Art for All', in Carole S. Paul (ed.), *The First Modern Museums of Art. The Birth of an Institution in 18th- and Early-19th Century Europe* (Los Angeles, US: Getty Trust Publications, 2012), pp. 213–237.

McHale, Brian, 'Cognition en Abyme: Models, Manuals, Maps', *Partial Answers: Journal of Literature and the History of Ideas*, 4:2 (2006), 175–189.

McLuhan, Marshall, *The Gutenberg Galaxy* (Toronto: University of Toronto Press, 1962).

——, *Understanding Media: The Extensions of Man* (New York: McGraw-Hill, 1964).

Merewether, Charles (ed.), *The Archive* (London: Whitechapel Venture Ltd., 2006).

Metzger, Gustav, 'A Critical Look at Artist Placement Group', *Studio International*, 182:940 (January 1972), 4–5.

——, and Andrew Wilson, *Damaged Nature, Auto Destructive Art* (London: Coracle Press, 1996).

Michalski, Sergiusz, *Public Monuments: Art in Political Bondage 1870–1997* (London: Reaktion Books Ltd., 1998).

Michaud, Philippe, *Aby Warburg and the Image in Motion*, trans. Sophie Hawkes (New York: Zone Books, 2004).

Michelet, Jules, *History of the French Revolution*, trans. Charles Cocks, ed. Gordon Wright (Chicago, IL: University of Chicago Press, 1967).

Mikaberidze, Alexander (ed. and trans.), *Russian Eyewitness Accounts of the Campaign of 1814* (London: Frontline Books, 2013).

Miller, Stephen Gaylord, *The Prytaneion: Its Function and Architectural Form* (Berkeley, CA: University of California Press, 1978).

Moriarty, Catherine, 'The Material Culture of Great War Remembrance', *Journal of Contemporary History*, 34:4 (1999), 653–662.

Mufti, Nasser, *Civilizing War: Imperial Politics and the Poetics of National Rupture* (Evanston, IL: Northwestern University Press, 2017).

——, 'Seeing Stasis', www.stuartbrisley.com/media/1124779795887a78bafc1b0.584606 66.pdf (accessed 12 July 2017).

Munslow, Alun, 'On "Presence" and Conversing with the Past: Do Historians Communicate with the Past?', *Rethinking History: The Journal of Theory and Practice*, 18:4 (2014), 569–74. https://doi.org/10.1080/13642529.2014.893667 (accessed 7 December 2015).

Nagel, Alexander and Christopher S. Wood, *Anachronic Renaissance* (New York, NY: Zone Books, 2010).

Negt, Oscar and Alexander Kluge, *Public Sphere and Experience: Toward an Analysis of the Bourgeois and Proletarian Public Sphere*, foreword by Miriam Hansen, trans. Peter Labanyi, Jamie Owen Daniel and Assenka Oksiloff (London: Verso Books, [1993] 2016).

Newall, Venetia, 'Throwing the Hood at Haxey: A Lincolnshire Twelfth-Night Custom', *Folk Life*, 18:1 (1980), 7–23. https://doi.org/Doi:10.1179/043087780798254701 (accessed 2 June 2022).

Newman, Michael, *Stuart Brisley: Performing the Political Body and Eating Shit* (Belfast: MAC Belfast, 2015).

Oakeshott, Michael, *On History and Other Essays* (Oxford: Blackwell, 1983).

Oeser, Hans-Christian, 'Ice as a Metaphor for Political Stagnation: Some Cultural Parallels between Germany after 1815 and West Germany after 1972', *The Maynooth Review/Revieú Mhá Nuad*, 11 (1984), 60–75.

Paravacini-Bagliani, Agostino, *The Pope's Body*, trans. David S. Peterson (Chicago, IL: University of Chicago Press, 2000).

Parratt, Catriona M., 'Of Place and Men and Women: Gender and Topophilia in the "Haxey Hood"', *Journal of Sport History*, 27:2 (2000), 229–245.

Péguy, Charles, *Clio: Dialogue de l'histoire et de l'âme paaïenne* (Paris: [1909–12], 1931).

Pérouse de Montclos, Jean-Marie, *Étienne-Louis Boullée (1728–1799): Theoretician of Revolutionary Architecture* (London: Thames and Hudson, 1974).

Perovic, Sanja, *The Calendar in Revolutionary France: Perceptions of Time in Literature, Culture, Politics* (Cambridge: Cambridge University Press, 2012).

——, 'Dead History, Live Art: Encountering the Past with Stuart Brisley', Rethinking History, *The Journal of Theory and Practice*, 21:2 (2017), 274–295, DOI: 10.1080/13642529.2016.1275288.

——, 'No Future or Still in Year One? Revisionist versus Lyricist Approaches to the French Revolution', *Poetics Today*, 37:2 (2016), 249–268.

Phelan, Peggy, *Unmarked: The Politics of Performance* (Abingdon: Routledge, 1993).

Phillips, Mark Salber, *On Historical Distance* (New Haven, CT: Yale University Press, 2013).

Pihlainen, Kalle, 'There's Just No Talking with the Past', *Rethinking History: The Journal of Theory and Practice*, 18:4 (2014), 575–582.

Pommier, Édouard, *L'Art de la liberté: Doctrines et débats de la Révolution française* (Paris: Gallimard, 1991).

Popular Memory Group, CCCS, 'What Do We Mean by Popular Memory?', trans. Faculty of Commerce and Social Sciences. Vol. 67. Stencilled Occasional Paper. University of Birmingham, January 1982, pp. 1–20.

Potts, Alex, 'The Artwork, the Archive, and the Living Moment', in Michael Ann Holly and Marquard Smith (eds), *What Is Research in the Visual Arts? Obsession, Archive, Encounter* (New Haven, CT: Yale University Press, 2008), pp. 119–137.

Poulot, Dominique, *Une Historie du patrimoine en Occident (XVIIIe–XXIe siècle)* (Paris: Presses universitaires de France, 2006).

Prochasson, Christophe, *François Furet: Les chemins de la mélancholie* (Paris: Stock, 2013).

Punin, Nikolai, 'Pamyatnik III Internatsionala, 1920', trans. Kestutis Paul Zygas, *Oppositions*, 10 (1977), 72–74.

——, 'Tatlin's Tower', trans. John Bowlt, in Stephen Bann (ed.), *The Tradition of Constructivism* (New York, NY: Viking Press, 1974), pp. 14–17.

Quatremère de Quincy, Antoine-Chrysostome, *Dictionnaire historique d'architecture comprenant dans son plan les notions historiques, descriptives, archéologiques, biographiques, théoriques, didactiques et pratiques de cet art*. Tome Second (Paris: Librairie D'Adrien le Clere et Cie, 1832).

Raunig, Gerald, *Art and Revolution: Transversal Activism in the Long Twentieth Century*, trans. Aileen Derieg (Cambridge, MA: Massachusetts Institute of Technology Press, 2007).

Reason, Matthew, *Documentation, Disappearance and the Representation of Live Performance* (London: Palgrave Macmillan, 2006).

Restany, Pierre, 'Modern Magic at the Tate', *Studio International*, June (1968), 332–33.

Ricoeur, Paul, *Memory, History, Forgetting*, trans. Kathleen Blamey and David Pellauer (Chicago, IL: University of Chicago Press, 2006).

Riegl, Alois, 'The Modern Cult of Monuments: Its Character and Its Origin', trans. W. Kurt Forster and Diane Ghirardo, *Oppositions*, 25 (1982), 20–51.

Roberts, John, 'Between: Stuart Brisley and Iain Robertson Friends, Enemies and Rivals', *The Performance Magazine*, 5 (1980), 20–21.

Roederer, Pierre-Louis, *Des institutions funéraires convenables à une République qui permet tous les cultes, & n'en adopte aucun: mémoire lu par Roederer, dans la séance publique de l'Institut national des sciences & ses arts, le 15 messidor, l'an 4* (Paris: Desenne, Lib., Palais Égalité, 1796).

Roms, Heike, 'Eventful Evidence: Historicizing Performance Art', in Barbara Büscher and Franz Anton Cramer (eds), *Fluid Access: Archiving Performance-Based Art* (Hildesheim: Georg Olms Verlag, 2017), pp. 93–101. Available online www.perfomap.de/map2/geschichte/romsengl/eventful-evidence (accessed 13 July 2021).

——, and Rebecca Edwards, 'Oral History as Site-Specific Practice: Locating the History of Performance Art in Wales', in Shelley Trower (ed.), *Place, Writing, and Voice in Oral History*, Palgrave Studies in Oral History (New York: Palgrave Macmillan, 2011), pp. 171–192.

Ron, Moshe, 'The Restricted Abyss: Nine Problems in the Theory of Mise En Abymé', *Poetics Today*, 8:2 (1987), 417–428. https://doi.org/doi.org/10.2307/1773044 (accessed 18 October 2017).

Rosenau, Helen, *Boullée and Visionary Architecture, Including Boullée's 'Architecture, Essay on Art'* (London: Academy Editions/Harmony Books, 1976).

Ross, Kristin, *The Emergence of Social Space: Rimbaud and the Paris Commune* (Minneapolis, MN: University of Minnesota Press, 1988).

Rothenstein, William, 'The War and the Arts', *Manchester Guardian*, 29 January 1916.

Rousseau, Jean-Jacques, *Lettre à d'Alembert sur les spectacles* (Paris: Flammarion, 1993).

Samuel, Raphael, 'History Workshop Journal', *History Workshop*, 1 (1976), 1–3.

Schmidt, James, 'Poetry After Auschwitz – What Adorno Didn't Say', *Persistent Enlightenment*, 2013, https://persistentenlightenment.com/2013/05/21/poetry-after-auschwitz-what-adorno-didnt-say/ (accessed 2 October 2018).

Schmitt, Carl, *Hamlet or Hecuba: The Irruption of Time in the Play*, trans. Simona Draghici (Corvallis, OR: Plutarch Press, 1985).

Schneider, Rebecca, *Performing Remains: Art and War in Times of Theatrical Reenactment* (Abingdon: Routledge, 2011).

Serres, Michel, *Genesis*, trans. Geneviève James and James Nielson (Ann Arbor, MI: Michigan University Press, 1995).

——, *L'hermaphrodite: Sarrasine Sculpteur* (Paris: Flammarion Père Castor, 1987).

——, *Statues: The Second Book of Foundations*, trans. Randolph Burks (London: Bloomsbury Publishing, 2014).

Shalson, Lara, *Performing Endurance Art and Politics since 1960* (Cambridge: Cambridge University Press, 2018).

Skelton, Tim and Gerard Gliddon, *Lutyens and the Great War* (London: Francis Lincoln, 2008).

Sloterdijk, Peter, *Critique of Cynical Reason*, trans. Michael Eldred (Minneapolis, MN: University of Minnesota Press, 1988).

Soussloff, Catherine M., 'Art History's Dilemma: Theories for Time in Contemporary Performance/Media Exhibitions', *Performance Research, A Journal of the Performing Art*, 19:3 (2014), 93–100. https://doi.org/10.1080/13528165.2014.935189 (accessed 17 December 2014).

Spencer, Catherine, *Beyond the Happening: Performance Art and the Politics of Communication* (Manchester: Manchester University Press, 2020).

Spieker, Sven, *The Big Archive: Art from Bureaucracy* (Cambridge, MA: MIT Press, 2008).

Spooner, B. C., 'The Padstow Obby Oss', *Folklore*, 69:1 (2012), 34–38. https://doi.org/DOI:10.1080/0015587X.1958.97 (accessed 2 June 2022).

Stara, Alexandra, *The Museum of French Monuments 1795–1816: 'Killing art to make history'* (Farnham: Ashgate, 2013).

Szajna, Józef, *Replique*, 1972. Demarco digital archive collection.

Tanaka, Stefan, *History without Chronology* (Amherst: Lever Press, 2019).

Taylor, Paul, 'Being and Doing', *Monthly Film Bulletin*, 52:612 (1985), 16–17.

The Times, 'Armistice Day', 12 November 1921.

——, 'Art in Memorials', 29 January 1916.

——, 'At The Cenotaph', 21 July 1919.

——, 'Christmas Wreaths at the Cenotaph', 23 December 1919.

——, 'House of Commons', 27 July 1922.

——, 'Narrow Divorce Division', 5 May 1920.

——, 'News in Brief', 26 November 1920.

——, 'Our 1,000,000 Pilgrims', 16 November 1920.

——, 'Politician's Part in the War', 10 February 1925.

——, 'The Art of the Cenotaph', 11 November 1919.

——, 'The Glorious Dead', 18 December 1919.

——, 'The Perfect Citizen', 29 December 1919.

Thompson, Michael, *Rubbish Theory: The Creation and Destruction of Value* (Oxford: Oxford University Press, 1979).

Thompson, Peter, Georgia Papadoulou and Eleni Vassiliou, 'The Origins of Entasis: Illusion, Aesthetics or Engineering?', *Spatial Vision*, 20:6 (2007), 531–543, doi: 10.1163/156856807782758359.

Tickner, Lisa, *Hornsey 1968: The Art School Revolution* (London: Frances Lincoln, 2008).

Tisdall, Caroline, 'Caroline Tisdall Describes How the People of Peterlee, a 30-Year-Old "New Town" Are Creating Their Own Archive', *Guardian*, 10 June 1977.

Traverso, Enzo, *Left-Wing Melancholia: Marxism, History, and Memory* (New York, NY: Columbia University Press, 2016).

Tuetey, M. Louis, 'Procès-verbaux la commission temporaire des arts. Tome première, 1er Septembre 1793–30 frimaire an III' (Paris: Imprimerie Nationale, 1912).

Turner, Victor, *The Anthropology of Performance* (New York, NY: Performance Art Journal Publications, 1987).

Valie Export, 'Expanded Cinema, Expanded Reality', in A. L. Rees et al. (eds), *Expanded Cinema: Art, Performance, Film* (London: Tate Publishing, 2011), pp. 288–298.

Veyne, Paul, 'Propagande expression roi, image idole oracle', *L'Homme*, 114 (1990), 7–26.

——, and Louis Marin, *Propagande expression roi, image idole oracle: lisibilité et visibilité des images du pouvoir* (Paris: Arkhê Editions, 2011).

Warburg, Aby, *The Renewal of Pagan Antiquity*, trans. David Britt (Los Angeles, CA: Getty Publications, 1999).

Westerman, Jonah, 'Performance at Tate: Into the Space of Art: Project Overview'. Tate Gallery, 2016. https://www.tate.org.uk/research/publications/performance-at-tate/project-overview (accessed 2 July 2017).

——, 'Stuart Brisley Born 1933 with Peter Sedgley Born 1930: Unscheduled Action 1968'. Tate Gallery, 1968. www.tate.org.uk/research/publications/performance-at-tate/perspectives/stuart-brisley (accessed 5 January 2018).

——, 'Timeline', *Performance at Tate: Into the Space of Art*, Tate Research Publication (2016), available at https://www.tate.org.uk/documents/1183/performanceattate timeline_text_only.pdf (accessed 2 July 2017).

White, Hayden, 'The Future of Utopia in History', *Historein*, 7:12 (2007), 12–19. https://doi.org/10.12681/historein.48 (accessed 15 June 2021).

——, *The Practical Past* (Chicago, IL: Northwestern University Press, 2014).

Williams, Raymond, *Communications* (London: Penguin Books, 1962).

——, *The Existing Alternatives in Communication. Socialism in Sixties* (London: Fabian Society, 1962).

Wilson, Andrew, 'Gustav Metzger's Auto-Destructive/Auto-Creative Art: An Art of Manifesto, 1959–1969', *Third Text*, 22:2 (2008), 177–194. https://doi.org/10.1080/09528820802012844 (accessed 1 June 2022).

——, 'Touching, Crossing and Passing Through', in *Stuart Brisley; Crossings* (Southampton: John Hansard Gallery, 2008), 17–21.

Winter, Jay, *Sites of Memory, Sites of Mourning: The Great War in European Cultural History* (Cambridge: Cambridge University Press, 1998). doi:10.1017/CBO9781107050631.

Woolf, Virginia, *The Diary of Virginia Woolf: Volume I: 1915–1919*, ed. Anne Olivier Bell (London: The Hogarth Press, 1977).

Index

Note: page numbers in *italic* refer to illustrations; 'n' after a page reference indicates the number of a note on that page

EU authorised representative for GPSR:
Easy Access System Europe, Mustamäe tee 50,
10621 Tallinn, Estonia
gpsr.requests@easproject.com

www.ingramcontent.com/pod-product-compliance
Ingram Content Group UK Ltd.
Pitfield, Milton Keynes, MK11 3LW, UK
UKHW022227070425
457221UK00008B/368